New Progress in MATHEMATICS

Series Consultants

Adrienne Aiken
Mathematics Consultant
Galveston-Houston Diocese
Houston, Texas

Dyanne B. Dandridge
Instruction Coordinator
Chicago Public Schools
Chicago, Illinois

Pat Echols
Instructional Officer
Klein School District
Spring, Texas

Claire M. Fanning
Teacher of Gifted Children
Ridley School District
Folsom, Pennsylvania

Sr. Helen Lucille Habig
Assistant Superintendent
Archdiocese of Cincinnati,
Cincinnati, Ohio

Rowland Hughes
Professor of Mathematics
Education
Fordham University
New York, New York

Sr. Ellenore Mary Jordan
Mathematics Coordinator
Archdiocese of Hartford
Hartford, Connecticut

Jeanne Joseph
Teacher
Robbinsdale School District
Minneapolis, Minnesota

Mary E. Lester
Director of Mathematics
Dallas Independent School
District
Dallas, Texas

Teresa Meyer
Teacher
Diocese of Louisville
Louisville, Kentucky

Jane L. Stone
Computer Consultant
Houston, Texas

Sr. Margaret Zimmermann
Associate Superintendent
Diocese of Orange
Orange, California

Rose Anita McDonnell

Geraldine M. Quinn
Mary Virginia Quinn
Dolores Therese Kurley
Anne Veronica Burrows

with
Elinor R. Ford

SADLIER · OXFORD

Table of Contents

Home Office: 11 Park Place, New York, NY 10007
ISBN: 0-87105-364-0
123456789/98765

Edward Williams, *Executive Editor*
Kao & Kao Associates, *Art Direction and Photo Editing*
Julius Bronstein, *Creative Group, Inc.*
Bob Gleason, *Cover*

Illustrators
Debra Smith D'Agostino, Debbie Dieneman,
S. Michelle Wiggins, Guy Brison, Linda Miyamoto,
Diane J. Ali, David Wander

8 GEOMETRY 211

9 FRACTIONS 231

10 DIVISION: TWO-DIGIT DIVISORS 263

Photo Credits
Mary Ellen Donnelly-Ridder, *Director of Photo Research*

The photographs reproduced on the pages listed are from the following sources:
Comstock: Jack Elness 1; Tom Grill 23; Michael Stuckey, 113, 317.
D.P.I.: Bettina Cirone 217; Paul Simcock 171.
F.P.G.: Schiavone 237; M. Wolf 249.
Index Stone International: Rita Davis 143; John D. Luke 53; Charles Shaffner 289.
Image Bank: Bill Carter 87.
Omni: John Lei 271; Ken Karp 333.

PROBLEM-SOLVING STEPS

To solve a problem, read the problem very carefully to find out:

- What facts are given

- What facts are hidden

- What facts are missing

- The exact question or questions that are being asked

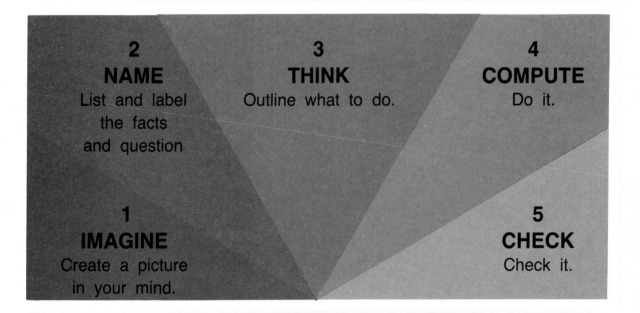

The five problem-solving steps are:

1 **IMAGINE**—Create a picture in your mind.

2 **NAME**—List and label the facts and questions.

3 **THINK**—Outline what to do.

4 **COMPUTE**—Do it!

5 **CHECK**—Check it!

IMAGINE

Create a picture in your mind.

Read the problem. Create a picture in your mind, making believe you are there in the problem. This will help you think about:

- what the problem is asking
- what facts you will need to answer the questions
- how you will solve the problem

After reading the problem, draw and label a picture of what you imagine the problem is all about.

NAME

List and label.

Facts: List and label all the facts you can find in the problem. Look for "hidden facts." These are words that hide more information.

> Jim rides his bicycle 4 miles a day. How far does he ride in a week?

>> FACT: 4 miles a day
>> HIDDEN FACT: 7 days = 1 week
>> The word "week" hid this fact.

Questions: Write the question or questions that the problem is asking.

THINK

Choose and outline a plan.

Think about how to solve the problem by:

- Looking at the picture you drew.

- Remembering what you did when you solved similar problems. (Pages 8 to 10 and every unit in this book show you how to solve different kinds of problems.)

- Choosing a plan for solving the problem, such as
  - Use simpler numbers.
  - Draw a picture.
  - Make a table.
  - Guess and check.

COMPUTE

Do it!

Do the computations.

CHECK

Check it!

Check your computations.

Ask yourself: Does my answer make sense?

7

Problem Solving: Guess and Test

Problem: There are many ways to make $1.00 from nickels and dimes. Can you do this using only 15 coins?

Combinations of 15
0 + 15
1 + 14
2 + 13
3 + 12
4 + 11
5 + 10
6 + 9
7 + 8

1 IMAGINE

Imagine different combinations of nickels and dimes.

2 NAME

Facts: $1.00 total
15 coins
Use only nickels and dimes

Question: Which combination of 15 coins has a value of $1.00?

3 THINK

Look at your combinations of 15. Think of one addend as a number of nickels, and the other as a number of dimes.

Guess which combinations of 15 coins have a value of $1.00.

Start with 7 dimes and 8 nickels.
Make a table to keep track of your guesses.

4 COMPUTE

	Value of Dimes	Value of Nickels	Total Value
Guess 1	7 × $.10 = $.70	8 × $.05 = $.40	$.70 + $.40 = $1.10 too large
Guess 2	6 × $.10 = $.60	9 × $.05 = $.45	$.60 + $.45 = $1.05 too large
Guess 3	5 × $.10 = $.50	10 × $.05 = $.50	$.50 + $.50 = $1.00 just right!

5 CHECK

Guess 3 is correct because:
5 dimes + 10 nickels = 15 coins.
The value of 5 dimes and 10 nickels is $1.00.

8

Problem Solving: Hidden Facts

Problem: Bill's Blueberry Booth made 136 sundaes. How many quarts of ice cream were used for the pint sized sundaes?

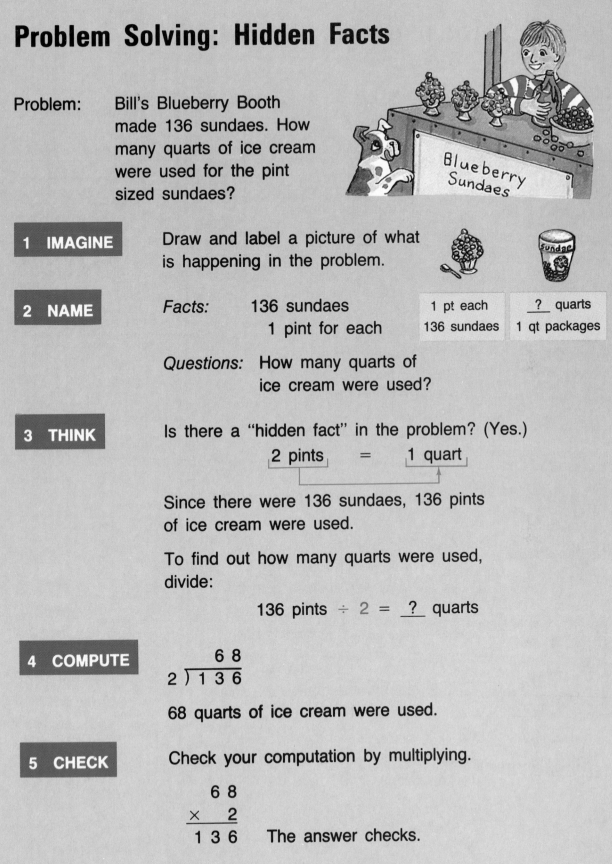

1 IMAGINE

Draw and label a picture of what is happening in the problem.

2 NAME

Facts: 136 sundaes
1 pint for each

1 pt each	? quarts
136 sundaes	1 qt packages

Questions: How many quarts of ice cream were used?

3 THINK

Is there a "hidden fact" in the problem? (Yes.)

2 pints = 1 quart

Since there were 136 sundaes, 136 pints of ice cream were used.

To find out how many quarts were used, divide:

136 pints ÷ 2 = ? quarts

4 COMPUTE

$$2\overline{)136} = 68$$

68 quarts of ice cream were used.

5 CHECK

Check your computation by multiplying.

```
    6 8
  ×   2
  1 3 6
```
The answer checks.

9

Problem Solving: Reading a Table

Problem: May left for school one cold winter day. The air temperature was 20 degrees Fahrenheit (20°F). A wind blew at 25 miles per hour (mph). How cold did it feel to May?

Wind Chill Table					
MPH ↓	Temperature (°Fahrenheit)				
	35	30	25	20	15
5	33	27	21	19	12
10	33	27	21	19	− 3
15	16	9	2	5	−11
20	12	4	− 3	−10	−17
25	8	1	− 7	−15	−22
30	6	− 2	−10	−18	−25
35	4	− 4	−12	−20	−27

1 IMAGINE

You go to the library to look for an answer to May's question. You look up the *Wind Chill Table.*

2 NAME

Facts: 20°F temperature
25   mph wind speed

Question: How cold did it feel to May?

3 THINK

The table shows a large amount of data or information. Choose only the data needed to solve the problem.

4 COMPUTE

Read down (↓) to 25 mph and across (→) to 20°F, to find −15 °F.

The 25 mph wind makes 20°F feel like −15°F or minus 15°F.

5 CHECK

Read across (→) to 20°F and down (↓) to 25 mph to find the same answer −15°F.

Numbers and Numeration

1

In this unit you will:

- Understand place value through millions
- Read and write standard numerals to millions
- Compare and order numbers to millions
- Round numbers
- Use Roman numerals
- Solve problems by reading a table

Do you remember?

Number is a quantity.

This is a picture of six balls.

Numeral is a symbol for a number.

6 is the numeral representing the balls.

Hundreds

3 hundreds   4 tens 5 ones

The value of each **digit** depends on its **place** in the numeral.

345 is the standard numeral for this number.

This is a place-value chart for the numerals 3, 34, and 345.

Read: three hundred forty-five

HUNDREDS	TENS	ONES
		3
	3	4
3	4	5

STANDARD FORM

EXPANDED FORM

345   =   300 + 40 + 5

The digit 3 means 3 ones.

The digit 3 means 3 tens.
The digit 4 means 4 ones.

The digit 3 means 3 hundreds.
The digit 4 means 4 tens.
The digit 5 means 5 ones.

In what place is the underlined digit? What is its value?

1. <u>4</u>82

2. 36<u>9</u>

3. 1<u>4</u>1

4. 9<u>6</u>3

5. 1<u>7</u>4

6. 21<u>8</u>

7. 5<u>2</u>2

8. <u>6</u>97

For each standard numeral name the place of the digit 3. Then write the number in words.

9. 342

10. 132

11. 387

12. 983

13. 113

14. 321

15. 883

16. 374

Complete the place-value chart.

	HUNDREDS	TENS	ONES
17. 876	?	7	?
18. 198	?	?	8
19. 945	9	?	?
20. 87	?	?	?
21. 301	?	?	?

Write the standard numeral.

22. five hundred eighteen

23. sixty-three

24. nine hundred seventy-one

25. one hundred one

26. three hundred

27. seven hundred seventeen

Use these standard numerals to answer the questions.

a. 811   **b.** 984   **c.** 479   **d.** 733   **e.** 157

28. Which numeral shows 7 tens? 7 ones? 7 hundreds? 1 ten? 8 tens?

29. In which numerals are the number of tens and ones the same?

CHALLENGE

The tens-frame can be used to show the place value of numbers. 143 is shown on this tens-frame.

Draw a tens-frame showing each of these numbers:

30. 873   **31.** 754

32. 208   **33.** 407

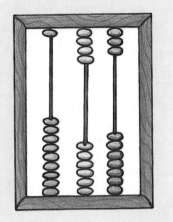

Thousands

Light travels 186,284 miles per second.

A place-value chart makes understanding large numerals easier.

The value of each digit in 186,284 is:

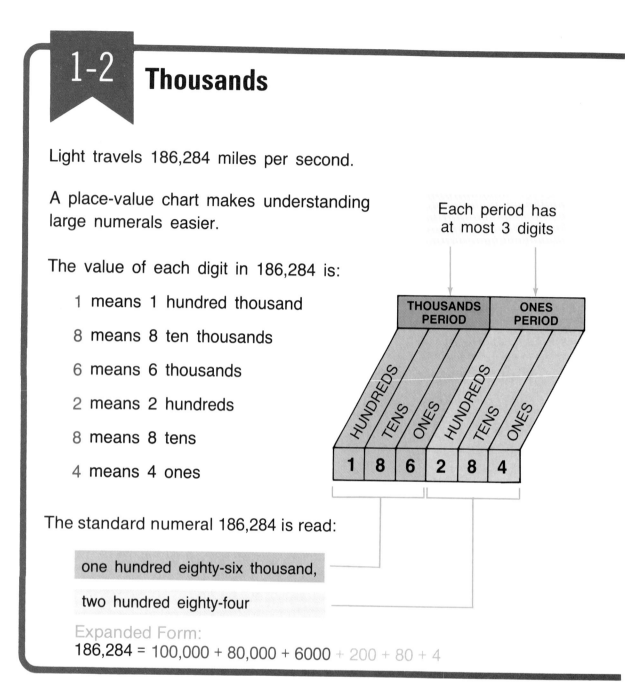

Each period has at most 3 digits

1 means 1 hundred thousand

8 means 8 ten thousands

6 means 6 thousands

2 means 2 hundreds

8 means 8 tens

4 means 4 ones

The standard numeral 186,284 is read:

one hundred eighty-six thousand,

two hundred eighty-four

Expanded Form:
186,284 = 100,000 + 80,000 + 6000 + 200 + 80 + 4

In what place is the underlined digit? What is its value?

1. <u>6</u>541

2. 7<u>8</u>43

3. 39<u>6</u>2

4. <u>2</u>7,142

5. 4<u>6</u>,359

6. <u>9</u>83,567

7. <u>4</u>59,638

8. <u>4</u>6,123

9. 4<u>7</u>,321

10. <u>5</u>9,304

11. 113,<u>2</u>74

12. 974,<u>1</u>32

13. 8<u>8</u>9,110

14. <u>9</u>00,189

15. 7<u>3</u>4,384

16. 6<u>2</u>,483

Read the standard numeral.

17. 814	**18.** 5219	**19.** 7801	**20.** 6001
21. 93,456	**22.** 80,703	**23.** 564,781	**24.** 989,999
25. 606,145	**26.** 15,300	**27.** 802,501	**28.** 100,203

Write the standard numeral.

29. nine hundred four

30. twelve thousand, twelve

31. seven hundred eighty-one

32. six hundred thousand, one

33. sixty-one thousand, twenty-eight

34. fourteen thousand, two hundred

35. eight thousand, four hundred ninety-one

36. fifty-four thousand, nine hundred seventeen

37. three hundred thirteen thousand, five hundred sixty-three

38. one hundred seventy-one thousand, two hundred seventy-eight

39. five hundred eight-two thousand, four hundred ninety-one

Use these standard numerals to answer exercises 40-43.

    a. 870,400   **b.** 511,007   **c.** 410,703

40. Which numeral shows 410 thousands?

41. Which numeral shows 70 thousands?

42. Which numeral has 10 thousands?

43. Which numerals have 0 tens?

Millions

In 1790 the population of the United States was 3,929,214. In 1890, the population was 62,947,714. Finally, in 1980 it was 226,545,805.

To read a standard numeral:

- Start at the left.

- Read the digits in the first period. Then say the name of the period.

- Continue reading the digits in each period. Then name the period.

The standard numeral 226,545,805 is read:

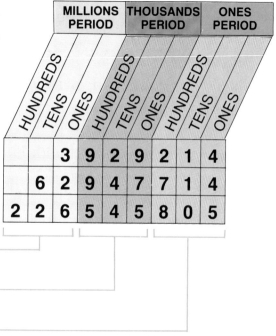

	MILLIONS PERIOD			THOUSANDS PERIOD			ONES PERIOD	
HUNDREDS	TENS	ONES	HUNDREDS	TENS	ONES	HUNDREDS	TENS	ONES
		3	9	2	9	2	1	4
	6	2	9	4	7	7	1	4
2	2	6	5	4	5	8	0	5

two hundred twenty-six million,

five hundred forty-five thousand,

eight hundred five

Name the period of the underlined digits.

1. <u>45</u>,678

2. 59,<u>650</u>

3. <u>26</u>,545

4. <u>456</u>,789

5. 567,<u>890</u>

6. <u>148</u>,337

7. <u>9</u>,456,789

8. 567,<u>890</u>,000

9. <u>617</u>,148,337

Read the standard numeral.

10. 6820

11. 10,525

12. 38,513

13. 761,435

14. 100,000,001

15. 8,402,000

16. 63,748,912

17. 802,909

18. 101,000,101

19. 183,902

20. 9,706,410

21. 3,458,926

Write the standard numeral.

22. three million, four hundred sixty-seven thousand, seven hundred fifty-three

23. sixty-four million, seven hundred thirty-three thousand, eight hundred two

24. five hundred forty-two million, eight hundred ninety-one thousand, six hundred seventy-three

25. eight hundred five million, two hundred seventy-three thousand, six

26. four hundred seventy-nine million, six hundred thousand, three hundred

Complete.

Which correctly shows the place values of 1453804?
(Hint: Insert commas to separate the periods in the numeral.)

27.
	a.	**b.**	**c.**
	100,000	1,000,000	1,000,000
	40,000	400,000	400,000
	5,000	50,000	50,000
	300	3,000	3,000
	80	80	800
	4	4	4

Comparing Whole Numbers

Jenkins won 6241 of the votes for mayor of Ourtown. Caldwell won 6232. Who won more votes?

To find who won more votes, compare the numbers 6241 and 6232.

To compare whole numbers:

- Line up the places in each number.

- Start at the left and compare the digits in the greatest place-value position.

- If these are the same, compare the next digits to the right.

- Keep doing this until you come to digits that are *not* the same.

is less than...

is more than...

Line up the places.

6	2	4	1
6	2	3	2

Jenkins won more votes.

Compare the digits.

6 = 6 and 2 = 2

Compare the tens.

4 > 3

So, 6241 > 6232

Compare. Write <, =, or >.

1. 48 _?_ 84

2. 232 _?_ 323

3. 454 _?_ 454

4. 8463 _?_ 8436

5. 267 _?_ 1267

6. 193 _?_ 139

7. 350 _?_ 360

8. 101 _?_ 110

9. 487 _?_ 478

Which is greater?

10. 906 or 909   **11.** 4532 or 4632   **12.** 8917 or 8971

13. 86 or 68   **14.** 911 or 910   **15.** 6735 or 6753

16. 5459 or 5495   **17.** 606 or 660   **18.** 9870 or 9807

Which is less?

19. 78 or 87   **20.** 54 or 95   **21.** 78 or 87

22. 5550 or 5505   **23.** 9062 or 9061   **24.** 7424 or 7404

Write the smaller number.

25. three hundred thirty or 339   **26.** five hundred five or 555

27. two hundred seventy or 207   **28.** ninety-eight or 908

29. nine thousand one or 901   **30.** one thousand and one or 1010

31. nine thousand three hundred sixty-two or 9061   **32.** seven thousand four hundred twenty-four or 7404

Solve.

33. The Caspian Sea is 3363 ft deep. The Malawi Lake is 2280 ft deep. Which is deeper?

34. Lake Albert is 2030 ft above sea level. Lake Victoria is 3720 ft above sea level. Which lake is higher above sea level?

35. The Cape Cod Canal drawbridge has a span of 544 ft. The Delair, New Jersey, drawbridge has a span of 542 ft. Which bridge has a shorter span?

19

Ordering Numbers

Juan delivers newspapers. The papers are addressed to: 918, 912, 956, 894, and 810 Moore Street. Juan can make his job easier if he arranges the numbers in order.

To order numbers from least to greatest:

- Line up the places in each number.

- Start at the left place and put the digits in order from least to greatest.

- Do this for each place.

Put the **hundreds** digits in order.	Put the **tens** digits in order.	Put the **ones** digits in order.
8 9 4	8 1 0	8 1 0
8 1 0	8 9 4	8 9 4
9 1 8	9 1 8	9 1 2
9 1 2	9 1 2	9 1 8
9 5 6	9 5 6	9 5 6

Juan should arrange his papers in this order: 810, 894, 912, 918, and 956.

Write the numbers in order from least to greatest.

1. 23; 29; 25; 21

2. 426; 505; 431; 424

3. 671; 680; 707; 679

4. 843; 839; 841; 836

Write the numbers in order from least to greatest.

5. 4500; 3200; 7600; 1100; 4400

6. 8333; 7333; 7339; 8339; 8336

7. 3451; 3450; 2567; 3399; 2561

8. 5601; 5456; 5873; 5970; 5297

9. 7759; 7845; 7844; 7751; 7756

10. 9868; 9879; 9860; 9877; 9864

11. 24,316; 34,316; 24,416; 34,416; 24,404

Complete.

12. Write a rule for ordering numbers from greatest to least.
    Use the numbers: 2938; 3417; 2945; 2816; 2940.
    (Hint: Look at the rule in this lesson.)

CHALLENGE

Some students at the Lincoln School made this chart showing the land areas of their ancestors' birthplaces.

Student	Ancestors' Country	Area (mi²)
Gretchen	Germany	137,746
Ino	Japan	142,727
Jean	France	210,039
Maria	Italy	116,304
Patrick	Ireland	27,136
Roberto	Mexico	761,604
Reginald	Kenya	224,960

13. List the land areas of the countries from least to greatest.

1-6 Rounding Numbers

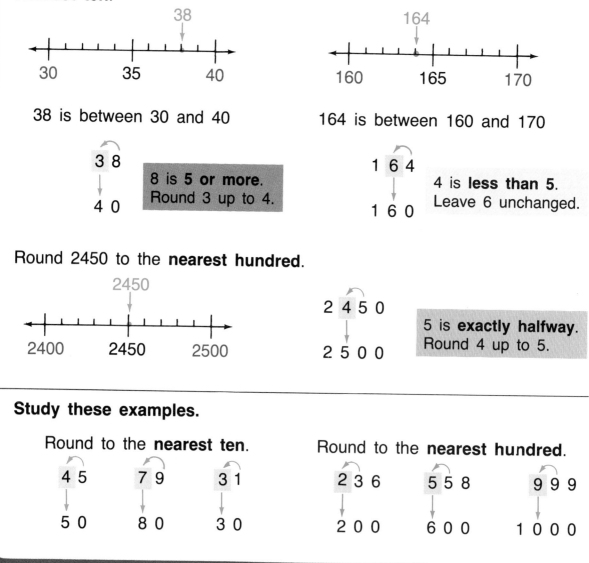

You can find "*about* how many" by rounding numbers.

A number line can help you round numbers.

Round the numbers in blue to the **nearest ten**.

38

```
◄──┼──┼──┼──┼──┼──┼──┼──┼──┼──┼──►
   30        35        40
```

38 is between 30 and 40

3 8
↓
4 0

| 8 is **5 or more**.
| Round 3 up to 4.

164

```
◄──┼──┼──┼──┼──┼──┼──┼──┼──┼──►
  160      165      170
```

164 is between 160 and 170

1 6 4
↓
1 6 0

4 is **less than 5**.
Leave 6 unchanged.

Round 2450 to the **nearest hundred**.

2450

```
◄──┼──┼──┼──┼──┼──┼──┼──┼──┼──►
 2400    2450    2500
```

2 4 5 0
↓
2 5 0 0

5 is **exactly halfway**.
Round 4 up to 5.

Study these examples.

Round to the **nearest ten**.

4 5   7 9   3 1
↓   ↓   ↓
5 0   8 0   3 0

Round to the **nearest hundred**.

2 3 6   5 5 8   9 9 9
↓   ↓   ↓
2 0 0   6 0 0   1 0 0 0

Round to the nearest ten.

1. 27   **2.** 18   **3.** 85   **4.** 43   **5.** 91

6. 76   **7.** 66   **8.** 30   **9.** 55   **10.** 98

11. 52   **12.** 576   **13.** 14   **14.** 283   **15.** 313

Round to the nearest hundred.

16. 215   **17.** 876   **18.** 439   **19.** 554   **20.** 948

21. 187   **22.** 332   **23.** 781   **24.** 965   **25.** 619

26. 1437   **27.** 2759   **28.** 3082   **29.** 1319   **30.** 1799

More Rounding

Round to the **nearest thousand**.   Round to the **nearest dollar**.

3 1 1 0   9 9 9 9 $ 7 3. 4 8 $ 8 6. 5 9

3 0 0 0   1 0, 0 0 0 $ 7 3. 0 0 $ 8 7. 0 0

Round to the nearest thousand.

31. 5428   **32.** 7683   **33.** 1290   **34.** 3456   **35.** 5670

36. 19,182   **37.** 24,573   **38.** 7499   **39.** 16,500   **40.** 33,388

41. 8193   **42.** 27,800   **43.** 44,510   **44.** 29,550   **45.** 30,499

Round to the nearest dollar.

46. $86.23   **47.** $16.49   **48.** $7.73   **49.** $18.50

50. $58.73   **51.** $18.70   **52.** $19.26   **53.** $49.95

Roman Numerals

The Romans used letters to write numerals. The letters I, V, X, L, and C are some Roman numerals.

The Roman numerals from 1 to 10:

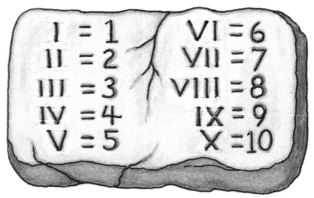

I = 1 VI = 6
II = 2 VII = 7
III = 3 VIII = 8
IV = 4 IX = 9
V = 5 X = 10

A smaller numeral *following* a larger numeral shows *addition*

VI⟶ The I after V means:
5 + 1 = 6

These are the Roman numerals from 10 to 100 in multiples of 10.

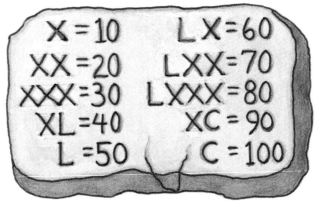

X = 10 LX = 60
XX = 20 LXX = 70
XXX = 30 LXXX = 80
XL = 40 XC = 90
L = 50 C = 100

A smaller numeral *before* a larger numeral shows *subtraction*

XL⟶ The X before L means:
50 − 10 or 40.

When you repeat a numeral, you repeat its value.

III = 1 + 1 + 1, or 3

XX = 10 + 10, or 20

No letter is written more than three times in a row.

Complete.

1. Write the Roman numerals from 1 through 30.

Write the missing Roman numerals.

2. X, XI, XII, _?_ , _?_

3. XXXIII, XXXIV, XXXV, _?_ , _?_

4. L, LI, LII, _?_ , _?_

5. XLI, XLII, XLIII, _?_ , _?_

6. CIX, CX, CXI, _?_ , _?_

7. CXLIV, CXLV, CXLVI, _?_ , _?_

Write each as a standard numeral.

8. XXI

9. XIX

10. XVIII

11. XXIV

12. XL

13. LXIX

14. LXXXVI

15. LXXI

16. XCIV

17. XVI

18. XCIX

19. XLIV

20. CXXX

21. XCV

22. CLXII

23. CXC

24. XXV

25. XLII

26. CCL

27. XCVI

Write each as a Roman numeral.

28. 17

29. 48

30. 72

31. 89

32. 99

33. 94

34. 123

35. 197

36. 200

37. 377

38. 219

39. 339

CHALLENGE

Write each number sentence in Roman numerals.

40. 1 + 3 = 4

41. 18 + 7 = 25

42. 100 − 30 = 70

43. 15 − 3 = 12

44. 300 − 99 = 201

45. 2 + 11 = 13

25

Problem Solving: Making a Table

	Odd Number	Odd Number	Sum
Problem: What is the sum of two odd numbers?	1	3	
1 IMAGINE Make a table of some odd numbers.	1	5	
	1	7	
2 NAME *Facts:* Any 2 odd numbers	1	9	
Question: What is the sum of any 2 odd numbers?	3	5	
	3	7	
3 THINK List the first 5 odd numbers.	3	9	

3 THINK List the first 5 odd numbers.

1, 3, 5, 7, 9

Arrange them in order in the table above.

1 + 3; 1 + 5; 1 + 7; 1 + 9
3 + 5; 3 + 7; 3 + 9
5 + 7; 5 + 9
7 + 9

Find their sums. Place them in the table above.
What do you notice? (All the sums are even.)

4 COMPUTE

1 + 3 = 4   1 + 5 = 6
1 + 7 = 8   1 + 9 = 10
3 + 5 = 8   3 + 7 = 10
3 + 9 = 12   5 + 7 = 12
5 + 9 = 14   7 + 9 = 16

> All the sums are even numbers.

4 CHECK Find the sum of any 2 odd numbers.

31 + 57 = 88

The sum is an even number.

Solve by making a table.

1. How many two-digit numbers can be formed with the digits 1, 2, 3?

First Digit	Second Digit	Two-Digit Number
1	1	11
1	2	12
1	3	13

IMAGINE

Make a table to show the two-digit numbers in an orderly way.

NAME

Facts:　　1, 2, 3

Question: How many two-digit numbers can you make using the digits 1, 2, 3?

THINK

Look at the table.
Start with 1 and combine 1 with 1,
then with 2, and then with 3 to make two-digit numbers. Do the same with 2 and 3.
Count how many numbers you formed.

Then ────────→ **COMPUTE** ──── and ──── → **CHECK**

2. What is the sum of two even numbers?

3. How many even numbers and how many odd numbers are there between 117 and 164?

4. You have pennies, nickels and dimes. How many different ways can you give someone 17¢ change?

5. What is the sum of one even and one odd number?

More Practice

Write the standard numeral.

1. four thousand, forty-two

2. two hundred eighteen

3. seventy two thousand, one hundred four

4. four thousand

In what place is the underlined digit?

5. 5258

6. 73,954

7. 216,879

8. 872

9. 9034

10. 74,182

Write <, =, or >.

11. 875 ? 587

12. 1225 ? 1283

13. 76,450 ? 58,940

14. 465 ? 384

15. 392 ? 431

16. 2006 ? 2060

Round each number:

To the nearest 10: 17. 15 18. 33 19. 26

To the nearest 100: 20. 745 21. 802 22. 296

To the nearest 1000: 23. 1439 24. 4931 25. 3491

Write the standard numerals.

26. CCXXI

27. CVII

28. XCIII

29. LXIV

30. CLX

31. XXXIX

Write in the Roman numerals.

32. 12

33. 8

34. 25

35. 109

36. 350

37. 229

38. 84

39. 167

40. 135

(See *Still More Practice*, p. 357.)

Math Probe

WORDS FOR LARGER NUMBERS

Words like **zillion** and **infinite** are used for very large numbers of things that have *not* been counted. There is a word, first written by a 9-year old boy, that can be used to describe a very large number of things that can be counted. It is GOOGOL.

10000000000000000000000000000000000000000000000000

A GOOGOL is the number 1 followed by a hundred zeros.

Complete.

1. Write a googol.

2. How many commas did you need?

3. How many digits are there in a googol?

4. Name some things that might be counted using a googol.

There is a number even larger than a googol. It is called a **googolplex**.

10000000000000000000000000000000000000000000000000

A GOOGOLPLEX is the number 1 followed by a googol of zeros.

WOW! There must be a zillion stars in the sky!

29

Check Your Mastery

Write the standard numeral.

See pp. 12-17

1. twenty-three thousand, eight hundred seventy-nine

2. one million, two hundred seventeen thousand, one hundred ninety-six

In what place is the underlined digit?

See pp. 12-17

3. 4623   4. 2369   5. 7058   6. 38,423

Compare. Write < or >.

See pp. 18-19

7. 35,221 ? 35,292   8. 118,448 ? 118,848

Arrange in order from least to greatest.

See pp. 20-21

9. 563, 546, 456, 436   10. 1875, 1893, 1921, 1912

Round each number:

See pp. 22-23

to the nearest 10.	11. 76	12. 21	13. 33
to the nearest 100.	14. 296	15. 421	16. 2357
to the nearest 1000.	17. 8179	18. 4902	19. 7592
to the nearest dollar.	20. $14.12	21. $18.57	22. $23.92

Write the standard numeral.

See pp. 24-25

23. XLVII   24. CCCXVI   25. XCIX   26. XXIX

Write the Roman numeral.

See pp. 24-25

27. 83   28. 245   29. 91   30. 101

Addition and Subtraction

2

In this unit you will:

- Review the basic addition and subtraction facts
- Add and subtract mentally using the addition and subtraction properties
- Add two-, three-, and four-digit numbers
- Find missing addends
- Add three or more addends
- Find related facts
- Estimate sums and differences
- Solve problems by choosing the correct operation

Do you remember?

- $9 + 8 = 17$

Addend Sum

- Addition and subtraction are opposites.

$$9 \ + \ 8 \ = \ 17$$
$$17 \ - \ 8 \ = \ 9$$

Minuend

Subtrahend

Difference

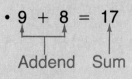

31

2-1 Basic Addition Facts

The turtle has made a stack of 7 blocks. She added 6 more blocks. How many blocks in all has the turtle now stacked?

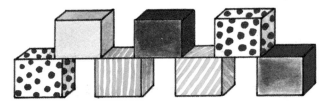

To find how many in all, add: 7 + 6 = __?__

This is a table of basic addition facts.

Addend Columns

Addend Rows

+	0	1	2	3	4	5	6	7	8	9
0	0	1	2	3	4	5	6	7	8	9
1	1	2	3	4	5	6	7	8	9	10
2	2	3	4	5	6	7	8	9	10	11
3	3	4	5	6	7	8	9	10	11	12
4	4	5	6	7	8	9	10	11	12	13
5	5	6	7	8	9	10	11	12	13	14
6	6	7	8	9	10	11	12	13	14	15
7	7	8	9	10	11	12	13	14	15	16
8	8	9	10	11	12	13	14	15	16	17
9	9	10	11	12	13	14	15	16	17	18

The turtle has stacked 13 blocks.

Find these sums in the table:

2 + 2 = 4   5 + 2 = 7   9 + 0 = 9

7 + 8 = 15   8 + 6 = 14   9 + 9 = 18

Add. Use the table to check your answers.

1. 5 ▪▪▪▪▪
   +6 ☐☐☐☐☐☐

2. 8 ▪▪▪▪▪▪▪▪
   +4 ☐☐☐☐

3. 3   4. 6   5. 9   6. 7   7. 6   8. 7   9. 4
   +5   +7   +2   +3   +3   +8   +9

Add mentally. Use the table to check your answers.

10. 5   11. 5   12. 8   13. 8   14. 5   15. 6   16. 7
    +4   +5   +1   +8   +9   +4   +6

17. 8   18. 7   19. 6   20. 4   21. 7   22. 3   23. 5
    +9   +4   +8   +6   +9   +8   +7

24. 9   25. 8   26. 7   27. 9   28. 6   29. 5   30. 7
    +5   +7   +6   +8   +6   +9   +7

Compare. Write <, =, or >.

31. 5 + 5 _?_ 7 + 3   32. 7 + 6 _?_ 6 + 6   33. 4 + 8 _?_ 6 + 5

34. 8 + 8 _?_ 9 + 6   35. 5 + 6 _?_ 6 + 7   36. 9 + 7 _?_ 6 + 8

37. 4 + 8 _?_ 6 + 6   38. 9 + 8 _?_ 7 + 8   39. 7 + 7 _?_ 5 + 9

Solve.

40. 4 people got on the bus at Main Street. 7 more people got on at Broadway. How many people in all got on the bus?

41. There are 9 red crayons and 8 blue crayons. How many crayons in all are there?

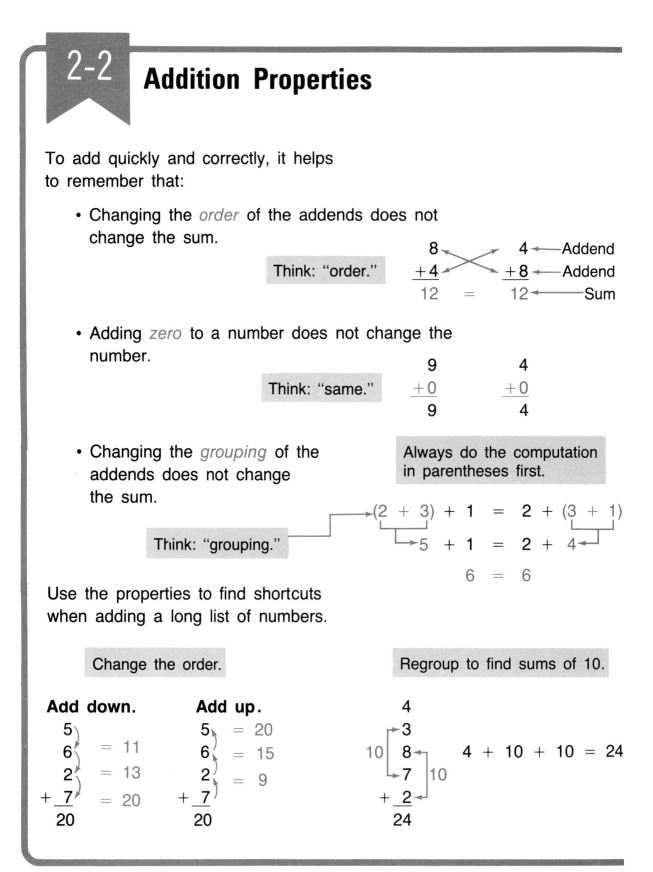

2-2 Addition Properties

To add quickly and correctly, it helps
to remember that:

- Changing the *order* of the addends does not
  change the sum.

  Think: "order."

  $$8 \quad\quad 4 \longleftarrow \text{Addend}$$
  $$+4 \quad\quad +8 \longleftarrow \text{Addend}$$
  $$12 \quad = \quad 12 \longleftarrow \text{Sum}$$

- Adding *zero* to a number does not change the
  number.

  Think: "same."

  $$\begin{array}{cc} 9 & 4 \\ +0 & +0 \\ \hline 9 & 4 \end{array}$$

- Changing the *grouping* of the
  addends does not change
  the sum.

  Think: "grouping."

  **Always do the computation
  in parentheses first.**

  $$(2 + 3) + 1 = 2 + (3 + 1)$$
  $$5 + 1 = 2 + 4$$
  $$6 = 6$$

Use the properties to find shortcuts
when adding a long list of numbers.

Change the order.

Add down.

$$\begin{array}{ll} 5 & \\ 6 & = 11 \\ 2 & = 13 \\ +\ 7 & = 20 \\ \hline 20 \end{array}$$

Add up.

$$\begin{array}{ll} 5 & = 20 \\ 6 & = 15 \\ 2 & = 9 \\ +\ 7 & \\ \hline 20 \end{array}$$

Regroup to find sums of 10.

$$\begin{array}{l} 4 \\ 3 \\ 10 \begin{array}{l} 8 \\ 7 \end{array} 10 \\ +\ 2 \\ \hline 24 \end{array}$$

$$4 + 10 + 10 = 24$$

Add.

1. 3 +0	**2.** 6 +3	**3.** 7 +8	**4.** 8 +7	**5.** 7 +0	**6.** 8 +4	**7.** 0 +5
8. 5 +4	**9.** 0 +6	**10.** 7 +7	**11.** 9 +9	**12.** 5 +8	**13.** 8 +0	**14.** 9 +4

Add quickly. (Use the addition properties to find shortcuts.)

15. 9 0 +3	**16.** 6 8 +4	**17.** 7 0 +5	**18.** 2 8 +0	**19.** 1 3 +9	**20.** 9 7 +0	**21.** 4 3 +6	**22.** 2 7 +8

Find each sum. Add the number in the center to each number around it.

23.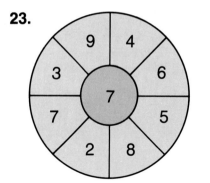

24.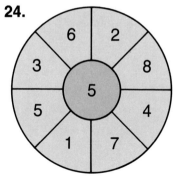

25.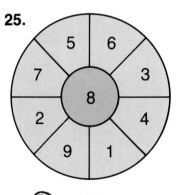

Solve.

26. The Red Sox scored 3 runs in the first inning and 7 runs during the rest of the game. How many runs in all did they score?

27. In two weeks the Dodgers played 5 games that were shown on television and 4 games that were *not* shown. How many games in all did they play?

Adding Two-Digit Numbers

Mr. Walters sold 54 hardball bats and 65 softball bats. How many bats did he sell in all?

To find how many bats he sold in all, add: 54 + 65 = ?

To add two-digit numbers:

- Write the numbers vertically, or in columns, so that the digits in each place line up.

Tens	Ones
5	4
+ 6	5

- Add from right to left, starting with the ones.

    Add ones: 4 + 5 = 9
    Add tens: 5 + 6 = 11

Tens	Ones
5	4
+ 6	5
1 1	9

He sold 119 bats in all.

Study this example: 47 + 72 = __?__

Write in columns.	Add ones.	Add tens.

Tens	Ones
4	7
+ 7	2

Tens	Ones
4	7
+ 7	2
	9

Tens	Ones
4	7
+ 7	2
1 1	9

47 + 72 = 119

Find the sum.

1.	24 +11	2.	38 +21	3.	23 +64	4.	16 +31	5.	32 +51	6.	74 +23	7.	82 +36

Write in columns. Add.

8. 52 + 45   9. 23 + 70   10. 47 + 30

11. 60 + 25   12. 55 + 21   13. 36 + 41

14. 26 + 53   15. 83 + 12   16. 64 + 23

17. 86 + 22   18. 90 + 19   19. 97 + 41

Find the sum.

20.	56 +20	21.	44 +34	22.	62 +47	23.	86 +12	24.	46 +41	25.	64 +63	26.	45 +34
27.	96 +11	28.	87 +50	29.	55 +54	30.	75 +32	31.	87 +60	32.	81 +71	33.	72 +55

Solve.

34. The fourth graders read 37 books in October and 41 books in November. How many books in all were read by the fourth graders?

35. There are 46 storybooks in the closet. 62 more storybooks were received. How many storybooks in all are there?

36. The school spent $64 for regular milk and $53 for chocolate milk. How much did the school spend for milk?

Adding with Three or More Addends

The ice cream shop sold 20 chocolate, 13 strawberry, and 6 vanilla ice cream cones. How many cones did the shop sell in all?

To find the number of cones sold, add: $20 + 13 + 6 = \underline{?}$

To add three or more addends:

- Write the numbers vertically, or in columns, so that the digits in each place line up.

Tens	Ones
2	0
1	3
+	6

- Add from right to left, starting with the ones.

- Regroup where necessary.
    Add ones: $0 + 3 + 6 = 9$
    Add tens: $2 + 1 = 3$

Tens	Ones
2	0
1	3
+	6
3	9

39 cones were sold in all.

Add: $25 + 10 + 32 + 42 = \underline{?}$

Write in columns.		Add ones.		Add tens.	
2	5	2	5	2	5
1	0	1	0	1	0
3	2	3	2	3	2
+ 4	2	+ 4	2	+ 4	2
			9	10	9

$25 + 10 + 32 + 42 = 109$

Find the sum.

1. 42 33 +23	**2.** 40 22 +25	**3.** 15 10 +42	**4.** 32 14 +53	**5.** 23 24 +72	**6.** 31 21 +54
7. 43 21 +30	**8.** 14 34 +30	**9.** 35 22 +50	**10.** 22 40 +45	**11.** 23 34 +62	**12.** 43 12 +60
13. 20 14 32 +23	**14.** 11 26 42 +10	**15.** 20 15 23 +30	**16.** 25 31 42 +10	**17.** 40 11 13 +35	**18.** 41 23 22 +30
19. 53 11 34 +21	**20.** 66 30 42 +11	**21.** 23 44 51 +10	**22.** 15 41 63 +20	**23.** 33 22 43 +11	**24.** 34 24 31 +50

Write in columns. Add.

25. 50 + 15 + 21   **26.** 55 + 21 + 13   **27.** 36 + 41 + 12

28. 61 + 17 + 40   **29.** 52 + 61 + 76   **30.** 20 + 18 + 10

31. 30 + 41 + 10   **32.** 11 + 32 + 64 + 22   **33.** 10 + 41 + 55 + 12

CHALLENGE

Add mentally. (Hint: Find sums of 10, 20, 30, and so on.) Check the answers on your calculator.

34. 17
24
13
+16

7 + 3 = 10
So, 17 + 13 = 30

4 + 6 = 10
So, 24 + 16 = 40

35. 28
44
32
+66

36. 21
33
87
+59

2-5 Adding Three- and Four-Digit Numbers

Add: 162 + 537 = ?

Add ones.	Add tens.	Add hundreds.
1 6 2	1 6 2	1 6 2
+ 5 3 7	+ 5 3 7	+ 5 3 7
9	9 9	6 9 9

Add: 4121 + 7668 = ?

Add ones.	Add tens	Add hundreds.	Add thousands.
4 1 2 1	4 1 2 1	4 1 2 1	4 1 2 1
+ 7 6 6 8	+ 7 6 6 8	+ 7 6 6 8	+ 7 6 6 8
9	8 9	7 8 9	1 1, 7 8 9

Add.

1.	140 +657	**2.**	658 +220	**3.**	128 +820	**4.**	8317 +1222	**5.**	4374 +5015
6.	320 +276	**7.**	166 +403	**8.**	6416 +2103	**9.**	1624 +4254	**10.**	8117 +1782
11.	4521 +7343	**12.**	9054 +3943	**13.**	5310 +4643	**14.**	8457 +3422	**15.**	7789 +4210
16.	424 132 +300	**17.**	120 101 +315	**18.**	1441 4013 +1124	**19.**	2145 4202 +2041	**20.**	1103 4533 +2252

40

Find the sum.

21.	22.	23.	24.	25.
300	201	3214	1014	3102
240	116	1454	2302	1421
156	420	1020	1140	1450
+201	+111	+3201	+1533	+4005

26.	27.	28.	29.	30.
417	333	6007	7116	8655
301	111	4031	1722	210
561	222	8600	2001	2020
+120	+400	+ 351	+ 160	+ 114

Arrange in columns and add.

31. 2341 + 4425

32. 9281 + 18

33. 316 + 200 + 51 + 1002

34. 3321 + 307 + 20 + 4111

35. 103 + 3101 + 321 + 5040

36. 1012 + 24 + 2200 + 312

37. 7010 + 453 + 12 + 8100

38. 4001 + 7230 + 1611 + 5014

Solve.

39. 4021 people saw "Spaceflight II" on Thursday. 3132 people saw it on Friday. How many people in all saw the movie on these two nights?

40. In one scene of the movie there were 13 "Earth people" actors, 220 "space people" actors, and 5500 "extras." How many people were in the scene?

41. The spaceship traveled 4132 mi to one planet and then 2765 mi to a second planet. How many miles in all did the spaceship travel?

2-6 Adding Money

Adding money is almost the same as adding whole numbers.

Lydia wants to buy a warm-up suit for $22.45 and a pair of sneakers for $16.30. Lydia has $42.00. Does she have enough money?

To find if Lydia has enough money, add: $22.45 + $16.30 = ?

Think of

$$\begin{array}{r} \$22.45 \\ +16.30 \end{array}$$

as

$$\begin{array}{r} 2245\cent \\ +1630\cent \\ \hline 3875\cent \end{array}$$

or

$$\begin{array}{r} \$22.45 \\ +16.30 \\ \hline \$38.75 \end{array}$$

3875¢ ⟶ $38.75

Remember to write the dollar sign and decimal point in the sum.

Lydia has enough money.

Study these examples.

$42.31 ⟶ 4231¢
+14.65 ⟶ +1465¢
5696¢ = $56.96

$43.24 ⟶ 4324¢
+86.75 ⟶ +8675¢
12999¢ = $129.99

Write each as cents.

1. $2.99
2. $23.49
3. $10.95
4. $16.47
5. $6.99

6. $11.40
7. $2.69
8. $13.19
9. $112.13
10. $23.00

Write each as dollars and cents.

11. 4329¢
12. 997¢
13. 1095¢
14. 1495¢
15. 2650¢

16. 129¢
17. 1009¢
18. 1889¢
19. 100¢
20. 45010¢

42

Add.

21.	$14.45	22.	$22.30	23.	$82.73	24.	$75.48
	+ 4.52		+16.49		+76.15		+21.20

25.	$402.31	26.	$600.79	27.	$349.62	28.	$750.00
	+795.07		+ 35.20		+ 40.35		+125.55

Compare. Write <, =, or >.

29. $11.49 + $10.30 + $4.20 __?__ $7.12 + $11.61 + $1.10

30. $8.22 + $10.61 + $11.05 __?__ $16.25 + $12.31 + $10.00

31. $32.17 + $101.00 + $26.41 __?__ $112.25 + $23.11 + $24.22

Solve.

32. Greg bought a tennis racket and a can of tennis balls. What was the total price?

33. How much money will Shelley need to buy a baseball glove and a bat?

34. Jay is saving to buy sports socks and sneakers. How much must he save in all?

35. Tanya has $39.00. Does she have enough money to buy a soccer ball and a pair of sneakers?

Missing Addends

There are 14 scout troops in Benson City. Five of them are located on the north side of town. How many are on the south side of town?

To determine the number of scout troops on the south side, find the missing addend: $5 + \underline{?} = 14$

To find a missing addend, subtract the known addend from the sum.

$$5 + \underline{?} = 14$$
$$14 - 5 = \underline{?} \quad \text{or} \quad \begin{array}{r} 5 \\ +? \\ \hline 14 \end{array} \quad \begin{array}{r} 14 \\ -5 \\ \hline 9 \end{array} \quad \begin{array}{r} 5 \\ +9 \\ \hline 14 \end{array}$$
$$14 - 5 = 9$$
$$5 + 9 = 14$$

There are 9 scout troops on the south side of town.

Find the missing addend.

1. $3 + \underline{?} = 4$

2. $7 + \underline{?} = 12$

3. $9 + \underline{?} = 11$

4. $9 + \underline{?} = 16$

5. $8 + \underline{?} = 11$

6. $8 + \underline{?} = 17$

7. $\underline{?} + 8 = 10$

8. $\underline{?} + 6 = 12$

9. $\underline{?} + 6 = 11$

10. $\underline{?} + 9 = 15$

11. $\underline{?} + 4 = 14$

12. $\underline{?} + 7 = 18$

13. $7 + \underline{?} = 13$

14. $\underline{?} + 8 = 15$

15. $9 + \underline{?} = 12$

16. $\underline{?} + 9 = 13$

17. $5 + \underline{?} = 14$

18. $\underline{?} + 8 = 16$

Find the missing addend.

19.	20.	21.	22.	23.	24.	25.
9	8	7	5	6	9	4
+ ?	+ ?	+ ?	+ ?	+ ?	+ ?	+ ?
13	15	14	15	11	14	11

26.	27.	28.	29.	30.	31.	32.
?	?	?	?	?	?	?
+ 3	+4	+ 6	+13	+ 7	+12	+ 9
10	8	14	14	16	15	15

Solve.

33. Matthew became a Cub Scout when he was 8 years old. He is now 14 and is still a scout. How many years has he been a scout?

34. Scouting medals were earned by 15 members of Mrs. Carter's troop. Seven of the scouts are 11 years old, and the rest are 10 years old. How many are 10 years old?

35. Five members of the Carter family belong to the scouts. If Mr. and Mrs. Carter are both scout leaders, how many of their children belong to the scouts?

Mental Math

Find the missing addend.

36. $8 + \underline{?} = 12$

37. $9 + \underline{?} = 12$

38. $10 + \underline{?} = 12$

39. $\underline{?} + 4 = 15$

40. $\underline{?} + 6 = 15$

41. $\underline{?} + 8 = 15$

42. $\underline{?} + 7 = 11$

43. $7 + \underline{?} = 13$

44. $5 + \underline{?} = 14$

Related Facts

Look at the picture. Find addition and subtraction facts.

The related facts for the numbers 4 and 3 are:

Change the order.

$$3 + 4 = 7 \longrightarrow 7 - 4 = 3$$

$$4 + 3 = 7 \longrightarrow 7 - 3 = 4$$

Look at these related facts.

4 and 6 $\longrightarrow$
$$4 + 6 = 10$$
$$6 + 4 = 10$$
$$10 - 6 = 4$$
$$10 - 4 = 6$$

5 and 8 $\longrightarrow$
$$5 + 8 = 13$$
$$8 + 5 = 13$$
$$13 - 8 = 5$$
$$13 - 5 = 8$$

Write the related facts for each pair of numbers.

1. 1, 5
2. 2, 9
3. 8, 2
4. 1, 7
5. 3, 8
6. 7, 2
7. 1, 8
8. 3, 9
9. 9, 5
10. 8, 7
11. 2, 2
12. 4, 4
13. 3, 7
14. 5, 7
15. 3, 1
16. 8, 4
17. 4, 6
18. 6, 6
19. 3, 6
20. 7, 6

Write the related facts for each pair.

21. 4, 6

22. 2, 7

23. 9, 3

24. 5, 8

25. 3, 7

26. 4, 5

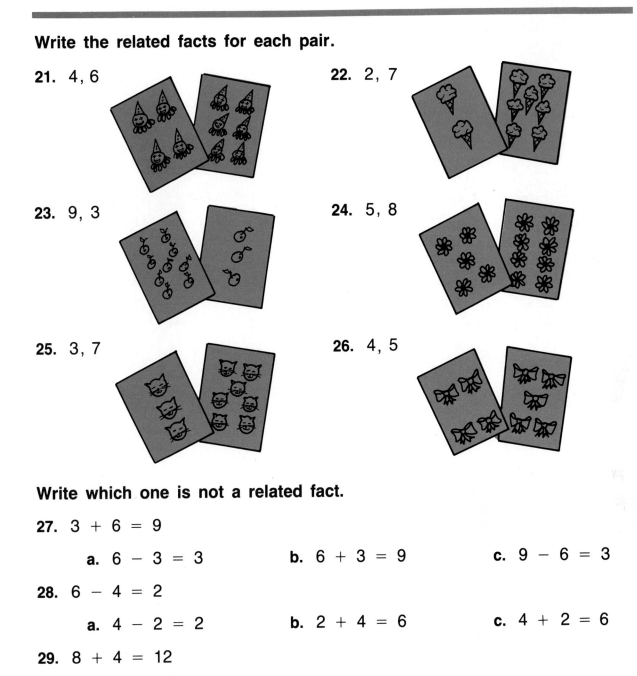

Write which one is not a related fact.

27. 3 + 6 = 9

    a. 6 − 3 = 3   **b.** 6 + 3 = 9   **c.** 9 − 6 = 3

28. 6 − 4 = 2

    a. 4 − 2 = 2   **b.** 2 + 4 = 6   **c.** 4 + 2 = 6

29. 8 + 4 = 12

    a. 4 + 8 = 12   **b.** 12 − 8 = 4   **c.** 8 − 4 = 4

Solve.

30. What is the fewest number of related facts for two addends? Write a pair of addends to prove your answer.

47

Basic Subtraction Facts

Seven bicycles were locked to the bike rack. Four were ridden away. How many bicycles were left in the bike rack?

To find how many were left, subtract: $7 - 4 = $ _?_

Subtraction is the opposite of addition. Use the table of sums in an "opposite" or "backwards" way to find differences.

Addend Columns

Addend Rows

+	0	1	2	3	4	5	6	7	8	9
0	0	1	2	3	4	5	6	7	8	9
1	1	2	3	4	5	6	7	8	9	10
2	2	3	4	5	6	7	8	9	10	11
3	3	4	5	6	7	8	9	10	11	12
4	4	5	6	7	8	9	10	11	12	13
5	5	6	7	8	9	10	11	12	13	14
6	6	7	8	9	10	11	12	13	14	15
7	7	8	9	10	11	12	13	14	15	16
8	8	9	10	11	12	13	14	15	16	17
9	9	10	11	12	13	14	15	16	17	18

To find $7 - 4 = 3$:

Go to the 4 row and move right ($\longrightarrow$) to 7. Now move up from 7 to the name of the column. The name of the column is 3. This is the difference.

3 bicycles were left in the bike rack.

Subtract. Use the table to check your answers.

1. $\begin{array}{r} 11 \\ -10 \\ \hline \end{array}$ △ △ △ △ △ △
    △ △ △ △ △

2. $\begin{array}{r} 14 \\ -\ 5 \\ \hline \end{array}$ □ □ □ ▨ ▨ ▨ ▱
    □ □ □ □ □ □ ▱

3. $\begin{array}{r} 9 \\ -2 \\ \hline \end{array}$

4. $\begin{array}{r} 11 \\ -\ 3 \\ \hline \end{array}$

5. $\begin{array}{r} 15 \\ -\ 7 \\ \hline \end{array}$

6. $\begin{array}{r} 17 \\ -\ 9 \\ \hline \end{array}$

7. $\begin{array}{r} 9 \\ -5 \\ \hline \end{array}$

8. $\begin{array}{r} 14 \\ -\ 8 \\ \hline \end{array}$

9. $\begin{array}{r} 13 \\ -\ 9 \\ \hline \end{array}$

Subtract mentally. Use the table to check your answers.

10. $\begin{array}{r} 6 \\ -2 \\ \hline \end{array}$

11. $\begin{array}{r} 18 \\ -\ 9 \\ \hline \end{array}$

12. $\begin{array}{r} 12 \\ -\ 4 \\ \hline \end{array}$

13. $\begin{array}{r} 8 \\ -4 \\ \hline \end{array}$

14. $\begin{array}{r} 13 \\ -\ 5 \\ \hline \end{array}$

15. $\begin{array}{r} 11 \\ -\ 6 \\ \hline \end{array}$

16. $\begin{array}{r} 14 \\ -\ 9 \\ \hline \end{array}$

17. $\begin{array}{r} 17 \\ -\ 8 \\ \hline \end{array}$

18. $\begin{array}{r} 10 \\ -\ 6 \\ \hline \end{array}$

19. $\begin{array}{r} 9 \\ -6 \\ \hline \end{array}$

20. $\begin{array}{r} 11 \\ -\ 2 \\ \hline \end{array}$

21. $\begin{array}{r} 14 \\ -\ 7 \\ \hline \end{array}$

22. $\begin{array}{r} 16 \\ -\ 9 \\ \hline \end{array}$

23. $\begin{array}{r} 12 \\ -\ 3 \\ \hline \end{array}$

24. $\begin{array}{r} 15 \\ -\ 9 \\ \hline \end{array}$

25. $\begin{array}{r} 11 \\ -\ 4 \\ \hline \end{array}$

26. $\begin{array}{r} 4 \\ -2 \\ \hline \end{array}$

27. $\begin{array}{r} 10 \\ -\ 7 \\ \hline \end{array}$

28. $\begin{array}{r} 9 \\ -3 \\ \hline \end{array}$

29. $\begin{array}{r} 8 \\ -2 \\ \hline \end{array}$

30. $\begin{array}{r} 13 \\ -\ 5 \\ \hline \end{array}$

Compare. Write $<$, $=$, or $>$.

31. $11 - 7 \ \underline{\ ?\ } \ 13 - 9$

32. $14 - 5 \ \underline{\ ?\ } \ 16 - 8$

33. $15 - 7 \ \underline{\ ?\ } \ 17 - 8$

34. $9 - 2 \ \underline{\ ?\ } \ 2 + 4$

35. $14 - 7 \ \underline{\ ?\ } \ 5 + 2$

36. $7 + 4 \ \underline{\ ?\ } \ 14 - 5$

37. $10 - 4 \ \underline{\ ?\ } \ 14 - 8$

38. $12 - 3 \ \underline{\ ?\ } \ 9 + 1$

Solve.

39. Homer Runn missed the first 5 games of the season. His team played 13 games. In how many games did Homer play?

2-10 Subtraction Properties

To subtract quickly and correctly, it helps to remember that:

- When 0 is subtracted from a number the difference is that same number.

$$\begin{array}{r} 6 \\ -0 \\ \hline 6 \end{array} \qquad \begin{array}{r} 8 \\ -0 \\ \hline 8 \end{array}$$

- When a number is subtracted from itself, the difference is 0.

$$\begin{array}{r} 5 \\ -5 \\ \hline 0 \end{array} \qquad \begin{array}{r} 7 \\ -7 \\ \hline 0 \end{array}$$

- Addition is used to check subtraction.

Check

$$\begin{array}{r} 14 \\ -\ 5 \\ \hline 9 \end{array} \qquad \begin{array}{r} 9 \\ +\ 5 \\ \hline 14 \end{array}$$

Subtract.

1.	2.	3.	4.	5.	6.	7.
7	5	6	9	4	1	3
−0	−5	−6	−0	−4	−1	−0

Subtract. Use addition to check your answers.

8.	9.	10.	11.	12.	13.	14.
7	8	6	9	4	7	8
−4	−8	−0	−4	−0	−1	−0

Compare. Write <, =, or >.

15. 7 + 3 _?_ 12 − 2

16. 4 − 0 _?_ 3 + 2

17. 8 + 2 _?_ 13 − 4

18. 11 − 3 _?_ 8 − 0

19. 6 + 5 _?_ 5 − 3

20. 7 + 4 _?_ 13 − 2

21. 4 − 4 _?_ 0 + 1

22. 8 − 4 _?_ 5 − 5

Subtract across and down.

23.
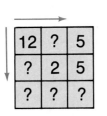

11	6	?
5	0	?
?	?	?

24.

13	5	?
8	0	?
?	?	?

25.

14	13	?
7	6	?
?	?	?

26.

12	?	5
?	2	5
?	?	?

27.

?	6	?
8	?	?
4	1	?

28.

?	8	?
12	?	?
5	3	?

Solve.

29. 17 people work at the local post office. If 5 people sort mail, how many do other jobs?

30. The Fun Toy Company mailed 10 packages in the morning. It mailed 15 packages in all that day. How many packages did it mail in the afternoon?

31. 12 clown dolls are packed in a carton. Jack removed 5 clown dolls. How many clown dolls were left in the carton?

32. Find the difference when $9 is subtracted from $15.

51

2-11 Subtracting Two-Digit Numbers

Subtract: 89 − 52 = _?_

To subtract two-digit numbers:

- Write the numbers vertically, or in columns, so that the digits in each place line up.

Tens	Ones	
8	9	← minuend
− 5	2	← subtrahend
?	?	← difference

- Subtract from right to left, starting with the ones.

- Check by adding the difference and the subtrahend to get the minuend.

Tens	Ones		Check
8	9		37
− 5	2		+ 52
3	7		89

Study this example.

57 − 26 = _?_

Write in columns.	Subtract the ones.	Subtract the tens.	Check by adding.
5 7 − 2 6	5 7 − 2 6 1	5 7 − 2 6 3 1	31 + 26 57

Subtract and check.

1. 53
   − 21

2. 85
   − 23

3. 26
   − 12

4. 74
   − 11

5. 46
   − 25

6. 77
   − 23

7. 69
   − 54

8. 55
   − 24

9. 69
   − 25

10. 38
   − 12

11. 63
   − 22

12. 98
   − 53

52

Find the difference and check.

13.	54	14.	92	15.	57	16.	68	17.	67	18.	69
	− 22		− 21		− 26		− 43		− 20		− 23

19.	68	20.	96	21.	99	22.	83	23.	75	24.	44
	− 34		− 25		− 46		− 63		− 70		− 34

Arrange in columns and subtract.

25. 36 − 25   **26.** 48 − 21   **27.** 82 − 41   **28.** 91 − 61

29. 65 − 24   **30.** 77 − 16   **31.** 78 − 27   **32.** 43 − 33

33. 67 − 35   **34.** 58 − 28   **35.** 34 − 20   **36.** 92 − 90

Mental Math

Compute quickly. (Watch the signs!)

37. 18 − 8 ⟶ + 5 ⟶ − 4 ⟶ + 8 ⟶ − 9 = <u>?</u>

38. 27 − 10 ⟶ − 2 ⟶ + 6 ⟶ − 8 ⟶ + 4 = <u>?</u>

39. 12 + 8 ⟶ − 6 ⟶ + 5 ⟶ − 3 ⟶ + 4 = <u>?</u>

40. 23 − 13 ⟶ + 15 ⟶ − 4 ⟶ + 4 ⟶ − 15 = <u>?</u>

CHALLENGE

41. Make up exercises like 37 through 40. See how quickly your friends can solve them.

2-12 Subtracting Larger Numbers

One jet traveled 957 mph. A second jet traveled 726 mph. How many miles per hour faster was the first jet?

To find how many miles faster, subtract: 957 − 726 = ?

Subtract ones.	Subtract tens.	Subtract hundreds.	Check.
9 5 7 − 7 2 6 1	9 5 7 − 7 2 6 3 1	9 5 7 − 7 2 6 2 3 1	2 3 1 + 7 2 6 9 5 7

The first jet was 231 mph faster.

Study this example.

8679 − 5029 = ?

Check

| 8 6 7 9
− 5 0 2 9
0 | 8 6 7 9
− 5 0 2 9
5 0 | 8 6 7 9
− 5 0 2 9
6 5 0 | 8 6 7 9
− 5 0 2 9
3 6 5 0 | 3 6 5 0
+ 5 0 2 9
8 6 7 9 |

Subtract and check.

1.	279 − 151	2.	657 − 242	3.	879 − 343	4.	984 − 851	5.	765 − 233
6.	899 − 524	7.	678 − 162	8.	536 − 401	9.	793 − 243	10.	886 − 475

54

Subtract and check.

| 11. | 697 −326 | 12. | 585 −241 | 13. | 488 −221 | 14. | 989 −572 | 15. | 895 −231 |

| 16. | 5986 −5082 | 17. | 7925 − 223 | 18. | 9929 −9000 | 19. | 2215 −2010 | 20. | 1968 −1348 |

| 21. | 2124 − 103 | 22. | 1874 −1044 | 23. | 7820 −6700 | 24. | 9044 −5032 | 25. | 7042 −7032 |

Arrange in columns and subtract.

26. 864 − 632   **27.** 756 − 414   **28.** 588 − 476

29. 3526 − 2421   **30.** 5394 − 3301   **31.** 3915 − 2704

32. 2924 − 1801   **33.** 6806 − 4406   **34.** 4644 − 4504

Solve.

35. 6743 alarms were answered in March. 5621 alarms were answered in April. How many more alarms were answered in March?

36. In one year the fire department of Waterville put out 5284 fires. 2072 of these were house fires. How many were *not* house fires?

37. 3271 families took part in a home fire safety program. There are 5894 families in the town. How many families did *not* take part?

38. 1847 students entered the fire safety poster contest. 137 were from the Franklin School. How many were from other schools?

Subtracting Money

Subtracting money is almost the same as subtracting whole numbers.

Neil bought a weight bench which was reduced from $149.99 to $117.49. How much did Neil save?

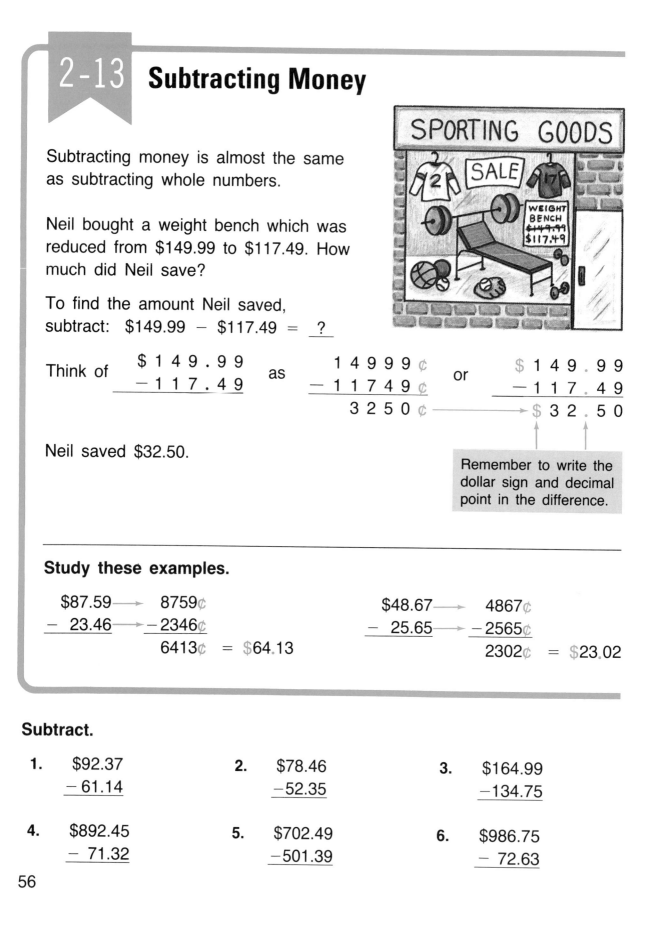

To find the amount Neil saved, subtract: $149.99 − $117.49 = __?__

Think of
$$\begin{array}{r} \$149.99 \\ -117.49 \end{array}$$
as
$$\begin{array}{r} 14999\,\cancel{c} \\ -11749\,\cancel{c} \\ \hline 3250\,\cancel{c} \end{array}$$
or
$$\begin{array}{r} \$149.99 \\ -117.49 \\ \hline \$32.50 \end{array}$$

Neil saved $32.50.

Remember to write the dollar sign and decimal point in the difference.

Study these examples.

$$\begin{array}{r} \$87.59 \longrightarrow 8759\cancel{c} \\ -\ 23.46 \longrightarrow -2346\cancel{c} \\ \hline 6413\cancel{c} = \$64.13 \end{array}$$

$$\begin{array}{r} \$48.67 \longrightarrow 4867\cancel{c} \\ -\ 25.65 \longrightarrow -2565\cancel{c} \\ \hline 2302\cancel{c} = \$23.02 \end{array}$$

Subtract.

1.
$$\begin{array}{r} \$92.37 \\ -\ 61.14 \end{array}$$

2.
$$\begin{array}{r} \$78.46 \\ -52.35 \end{array}$$

3.
$$\begin{array}{r} \$164.99 \\ -134.75 \end{array}$$

4.
$$\begin{array}{r} \$892.45 \\ -\ 71.32 \end{array}$$

5.
$$\begin{array}{r} \$702.49 \\ -501.39 \end{array}$$

6.
$$\begin{array}{r} \$986.75 \\ -\ 72.63 \end{array}$$

Subtract.

7. $8.97 − $4.73

8. $12.60 − $10.00

9. $82.63 − $1.51

10. $47.78 − $21.33

11. $99.99 − $75.49

12. $423.89 − $202.60

13. $79.89 − $23.00

14. $531.40 − $121.30

15. $425.98 − $214.87

16. $600.79 − $200.00

Compare. Write <, =, or >.

17. $29.87 − $11.42 _?_ $35.67 − $21.05

18. $48.98 − $16.78 _?_ $59.99 − $27.79

19. $623.41 − $400.00 _?_ $756.11 − $426.00

20. $823.87 − $13.72 _?_ $956.97 − $145.82

Solve.

21. Joseph bought an exercise mat. What change did he receive from $50.00?

22. Martha has saved $67.90. How much more must she save to buy an exercise bike?

23. Find the difference in price between the weight bench and the exercise bike.

24. Because of a sale, the training bag is reduced $23.50. What is the sale price?

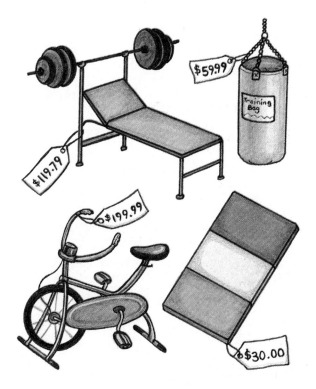

57

Estimating Sums and Differences

Estimate the sum: 58 + 21 = ?

To estimate the sum of two or more numbers:

- Round each number to the greatest place-value position of the *smaller number*.

- Add the rounded numbers.

	Round to tens.	Estimated Sum
5 8	⟶	6 0
+2 1	⟶	+2 0
		8 0

Estimate the difference: 87 − 26 = ?

- Round each number to the greatest place-value position of the *smaller* number.

- Subtract the rounded numbers.

	Round to tens.	Estimated Difference
8 7	⟶	9 0
− 2 6	⟶	− 3 0
		6 0

Estimate the sum.

1.	17 +22	2.	25 +14	3.	53 +66	4.	74 +84	5.	94 +75	6.	24 +30

7.	35 +22	8.	37 +12	9.	53 +34	10.	65 +13	11.	49 +27	12.	78 +18

Estimate the difference.

13.	54 −23	14.	59 −42	15.	38 −16	16.	39 −25	17.	75 −51	18.	49 −27

19.	43 −21	20.	61 −10	21.	56 −22	22.	68 −28	23.	43 −43	24.	81 −47

Using Estimation to Check

Use estimation to check addition or subtraction
to see if your answer is reasonable.

		Estimated Sum			Estimated Difference
3 5 6	⟶	3 6 0	6 7 8	⟶	7 0 0
+ 4 3	⟶	+ 4 0	− 4 5 1	⟶	− 5 0 0
3 9 9		4 0 0	2 2 7		2 0 0

399 is near 400.
The answer is reasonable.

227 is near 200.
The answer is reasonable.

Is the sum or difference reasonable?
Write "yes" or "no." Check by estimation.

25. 34 + 15 = 49   **26.** 61 + 30 = 101   **27.** 56 − 22 = 34

28. 43 − 21 = 22   **29.** 121 + 405 = 626   **30.** 261 + 328 = 589

Use estimation to choose the correct answer.

31. 37 + 12   **a.** 59   **b.** 39   **c.** 49   **d.** 69

32. 76 − 25   **a.** 61   **b.** 51   **c.** 41   **d.** 31

33. 556 − 221   **a.** 445   **b.** 435   **c.** 335   **d.** 245

Problem Solving: Choose the Operation

Problem: 35 of the 48 students in the fourth grade ride the bus to school.
How many do *not* ride the bus?

$$
\times \times \times \times \times \times \times \times \times \\
\times \times \times \times \times \times \times \times \times \times \\
\times \times \times \times \times \times \times \times \times \times \\
\times \times \times \times \times \times \times \times \times \\
\times \times \times \times \times \times \times \times
$$

35 of 48
ride the bus

1 IMAGINE   You are keeping a record of the bus riders. Draw and label a picture.

2 NAME

Facts: 35 bus riders
48 fourth graders

Question: How many do *not* ride to school?

3 THINK   Look at the picture to choose the correct operation to solve the problem.

Do you see:
48 fourth graders − 35 bus riders = ___?___

You need to subtract.

4 COMPUTE

$$
\begin{array}{r}
4\,8 \\
-\ 3\,5 \\
\hline
1\,3
\end{array}
$$

13 fourth graders do *not* ride the bus.

5 CHECK   Check your answer by addition.

$$
\begin{array}{r}
1\,3 \text{ do not ride the bus}\\
+\ 3\,5 \text{ ride the bus}\\
\hline
4\,8 \text{ total number of fourth graders}
\end{array}
$$

The answer checks.

Solve. Choose the correct operation.

1. 4351 people in Clearview watched Halley's Comet. The remaining 8043 people who live in Clearview did *not* watch it. How many people live in Clearview?

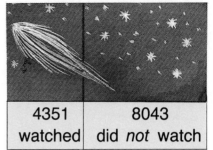

| 4351 watched | 8043 did *not* watch |

IMAGINE

You want to know how many people live in Clearview. Draw and label a picture of the facts.

NAME

Facts: 4351 people watched.
8043 people did *not* watch.

Question: How many people live in Clearview?

THINK

Look at the picture to choose the right operation.

Do you see:
4351 watched + 8043 did not watch
= all the people in Clearview

Then → **COMPUTE** → and → **CHECK**

2. There are 134 truck tires and 255 auto tires on sale. How many tires in all are on sale?

3. How many more auto tires than truck tires are on sale?

4. Saul sold 20 gallons of gas to Mr. Miles, 16 gallons to Ms. Lane, and 24 gallons to Ms. Carr. Who bought more gas, Mr. Miles and Ms. Lane or Ms. Lane and Ms. Carr?

More Practice

Add.

1.	24	2.	81	3.	45	4.	71	5.	48	6.	93
	+32		+18		+21		+11		+41		+42

7.	21	8.	17	9.	83	10.	40	11.	10	12.	21
	13		31		12		17		23		43
	+42		+51		+ 4		+30		+14		+25

Subtract.

13.	73	14.	87	15.	648	16.	577	17.	849
	−42		−35		−327		−432		−517

18.	493	19.	3917	20.	6845	21.	9682	22.	5098
	−132		− 403		− 710		− 632		−5045

Write in columns. Then estimate to check each sum or difference.

23. 124 + 302 = ?   24. 631 + 140 = ?   25. 9438 − 224 = ?

26. 5174 − 4132 = ? 27. 4983 − 2712 = ? 28. 145 + 712 = ?

Solve.

29. The Goldenrod Street School students want to buy 324 pins, and the Triangle Road School students want to buy 355 pins. About how many pins are needed for both schools?

30. Matthew weighed 8 pounds when he was born. He now weighs 75 pounds. How many more pounds does he now weigh?

62

Math Probe

THE ABACUS

The abacus is an old counting device used to compute mathematics problems. It was used many years ago by the Greeks and Romans, and it is used now by some Asians.

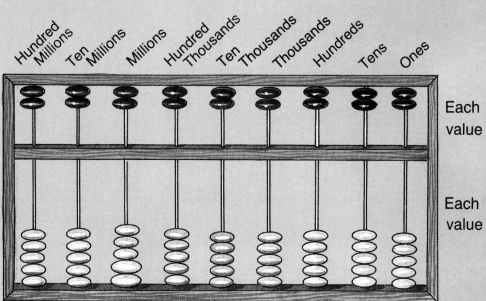

Each bead has a value of 5.

Each bead has a value of 1.

Study these examples:

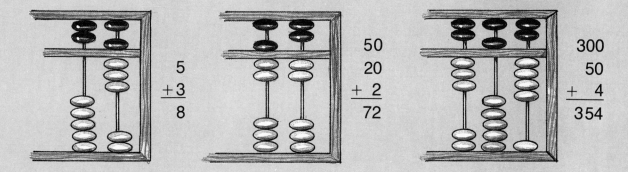

$$\begin{array}{r} 5 \\ +3 \\ \hline 8 \end{array}$$

$$\begin{array}{r} 50 \\ 20 \\ +\ 2 \\ \hline 72 \end{array}$$

$$\begin{array}{r} 300 \\ 50 \\ +\ 4 \\ \hline 354 \end{array}$$

Make your own "abacus." Use buttons, beans, or counters to show the patterns for each number.

1. 83   **2.** 237   **3.** 628   **4.** 371   **5.** 92

Check Your Mastery

Compute.

See pp. 32-57

1. 147
   +652

2. 558
   +221

3. 831
   +455

4. 5329
   +6140

5. 21
   32
   +61

6. 141
   204
   +831

7. 2312
   4021
   + 313

8. 1802
   1013
   5141
   +1011

9. 878
   -564

10. 955
    -354

11. 4616
    -3025

12. 9273
    -1140

13. 8452
    -6231

14. 6768
    -3420

15. 4397
    -2165

16. 5982
    -1102

Write in columns. Compute. Estimate to check.

See pp. 58-59

17. 201 + 34 + 114

18. 2583 − 471

19. 8345 − 1012

20. 216 + 300 + 142

21. 351 + 402 + 22

22. 7654 − 4321

See pp. 36-37,40-41,48-49

Solve.

23. 15 students received scouting medals. 7 are in the fifth grade. How many are not in the fifth grade?

24. Bob scored 13 points in one game and 12 points in the next. How many points in all did he score?

25. 541 orchestra tickets were sold and 458 balcony tickets. How many tickets in all were sold?

3

Multiplication and Division

In this unit you will:

- Recall the multiplication facts
- Study the properties of multiplication
- Find missing factors
- Find number patterns including odd and even numbers
- Recall the division facts
- Study the properties of division
- Review the four operations of addition, subtraction, multiplication, and division
- Solve problems by choosing the correct operation

Do you remember?

The names used in multiplication are:

$$
\begin{array}{r}
3 \longleftarrow \text{Factor} \\
\times 2 \longleftarrow \text{Factor} \\
\hline
6 \longleftarrow \text{Product}
\end{array}
$$

The names used in division are:

$$
\text{Divisor} \longrightarrow 2\overline{)6} \longleftarrow \text{Dividend}
$$
$$
\text{Quotient} \longrightarrow 3
$$

65

Multiplying by 2

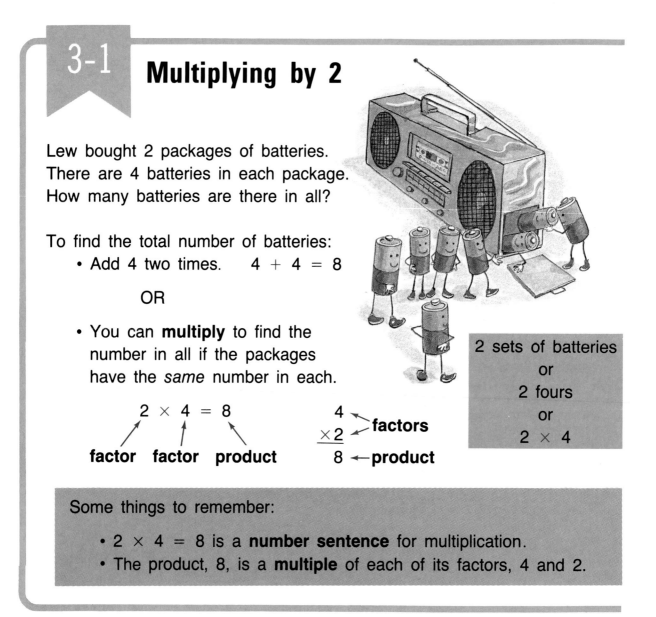

Lew bought 2 packages of batteries.
There are 4 batteries in each package.
How many batteries are there in all?

To find the total number of batteries:
- Add 4 two times. $4 + 4 = 8$

    OR

- You can **multiply** to find the
  number in all if the packages
  have the *same* number in each.

$2 \times 4 = 8$

factor factor product

$$\begin{array}{r} 4 \\ \times 2 \\ \hline 8 \end{array}$$ factors / product

2 sets of batteries
or
2 fours
or
2×4

Some things to remember:

- $2 \times 4 = 8$ is a **number sentence** for multiplication.
- The product, 8, is a **multiple** of each of its factors, 4 and 2.

**Write an addition number sentence and a multiplication
number sentence for each.** (The first one is done.)

1.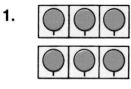

    $3 + 3 = 6$

    $2 \times 3 = 6$

2.

3.

Multiply.

4.

				Multiplying by 2				
1	2	3	4	5	6	7	8	9
×2	×2	×2	×2	×2	×2	×2	×2	×2

Use the products in exercise 4 to answer each question.

5. How much greater is each succeeding product?

6a. The product 8 is a multiple of the factors 2 and 4.
 b. The product 14 is a multiple of the factors 2 and _?_ .
 c. The product 10 is a multiple of the factors _?_ and _?_ .
 d. The product 18 is a multiple of the factors _?_ and _?_ .
 e. The product 12 is a multiple of the factors _?_ and _?_ .

Complete each number sentence.

7. 2 × 7 = _?_ **8.** 2 × 1 = _?_ **9.** 2 × 5 = _?_

10. 2 × 9 = _?_ **11.** 2 × 3 = _?_ **12.** 2 × 8 = _?_

Solve.

13. One factor is 6 and the other is 2. Find the product.

14. One factor is 7. The product is 14. What is the other factor?

15. Make a multiplication fact card.

- Cut out a piece of cardboard 10 inches by 10 inches.
- Divide the card into 100 squares, each 1 inch by 1 inch.
- In the second row, write the results from the "Multiplying by 2" table.
- Label the factor columns and factor rows.
- Save the card. Write in the other multiplication facts as you learn them.

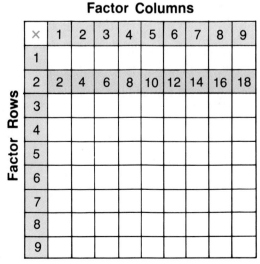

Factor Columns

×	1	2	3	4	5	6	7	8	9
1									
2	2	4	6	8	10	12	14	16	18
3									
4									
5									
6									
7									
8									
9									

Factor Rows

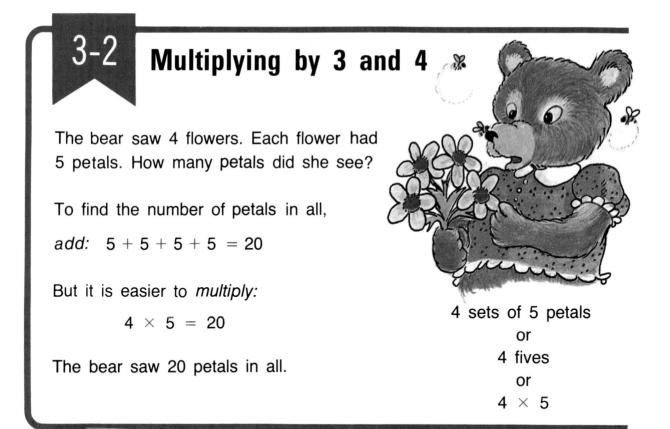

3-2 Multiplying by 3 and 4

The bear saw 4 flowers. Each flower had 5 petals. How many petals did she see?

To find the number of petals in all,

add: $5 + 5 + 5 + 5 = 20$

But it is easier to *multiply:*

$$4 \times 5 = 20$$

The bear saw 20 petals in all.

4 sets of 5 petals
or
4 fives
or
4×5

Complete.

1.
$2 + 2 + 2 = \underline{?}$

3 twos $= \underline{?}$

$3 \times 2 = \underline{?}$

2.
$4 + 4 + 4 = \underline{?}$

3 fours $= \underline{?}$

$3 \times 4 = \underline{?}$

3.
$5 + 5 + 5 + 5 = \underline{?}$

4 fives $= \underline{?}$

$4 \times 5 = \underline{?}$

4.
$6 + 6 + 6 = \underline{?}$

3 sixes $= \underline{?}$

$3 \times 6 = \underline{?}$

5.
$8 + 8 + 8 = \underline{?}$

3 eights $= \underline{?}$

$3 \times 8 = \underline{?}$

6.
$7 + 7 + 7 + 7 = \underline{?}$

4 sevens $= \underline{?}$

$4 \times 7 = \underline{?}$

Multiply. (Write these on your multiplication fact card.)

7.

				Multiplying by 3				
1	2	3	4	5	6	7	8	9
×3	×3	×3	×3	×3	×3	×3	×3	×3

8.

				Multiplying by 4				
1	2	3	4	5	6	7	8	9
×4	×4	×4	×4	×4	×4	×4	×4	×4

Find the product.

9. 3	**10.** 6	**11.** 1	**12.** 5	**13.** 2	**14.** 1	**15.** 2
×3	×4	×3	×4	×4	×4	×3

16. 8	**17.** 4	**18.** 6	**19.** 9	**20.** 5	**21.** 6	**22.** 3
×4	×4	×3	×2	×3	×2	×4

23. 7	**24.** 4	**25.** 7	**26.** 8	**27.** 7	**28.** 9	**29.** 9
×3	×3	×2	×3	×4	×4	×3

Solve.

30. Multiply 4 times 8.

31. What is the product of 9 and 3?

32. The factors are 7 and 3. What is the product?

33. One factor is 4. The product is 24. What is the other factor?

34. Jennifer does 4 exercises in one minute. How many does she do in 3 minutes? in 4 minutes?

35. Stacy reads 5 pages in one minute. How many does she read in 3 minutes? in 4 minutes?

69

Multiplying by 5 and 6

A baker can make 4 loaves of bread in one hour. How many can she make in 5 hours? in 6 hours?

To find the number of loaves of bread in all, multiply:

5 × 4 = 20
20 loaves in 5 hours

6 × 4 = 24
24 loaves in 6 hours

5 sets of 4 loaves
or
5 fours
or
5 × 4

Complete.

1. 6 threes = _?_

6 × 3 = _?_

2. 5 ones = _?_

5 × 1 = _?_

3. 6 sixes = _?_

6 × 6 = _?_

4. 5 fives = _?_

5 × 5 = _?_

5. 5 sevens = _?_

5 × 7 = _?_

6. 6 eights = _?_

6 × 8 = _?_

Multiply. (Write these on your multiplication fact card.)

7.

				Multiplying by 5				
1	2	3	4	5	6	7	8	9
×5	×5	×5	×5	×5	×5	×5	×5	×5

8.

				Multiplying by 6				
1	2	3	4	5	6	7	8	9
×6	×6	×6	×6	×6	×6	×6	×6	×6

Find the product.

9. 3
       ×5

10. 2
        ×6

11. 5
        ×4

12. 2
        ×5

13. 1
        ×6

14. 3
        ×6

15. 1
        ×5

16. 5
        ×6

17. 4
        ×5

18. 6
        ×3

19. 6
        ×5

20. 7
        ×6

21. 4
        ×6

22. 5
        ×5

23. 7
        ×5

24. 8
        ×4

25. 9
        ×5

26. 8
        ×6

27. 8
        ×5

28. 9
        ×3

29. 9
        ×6

Solve.

30. The factors are 7 and 6. What is the product?

31. One factor is 5. The product is 20. What is the other factor?

32. Maria bought 6 records. There are 8 songs on each record. How many songs are there in all?

33. There are 6 shelves in a bookcase. There are 5 books on each shelf. How many books are there in all?

34. 36 is the product. One factor is 9. What is the other factor?

35. One factor is 6. The product is 30. What is the other factor?

71

Multiplying by 7 and 8

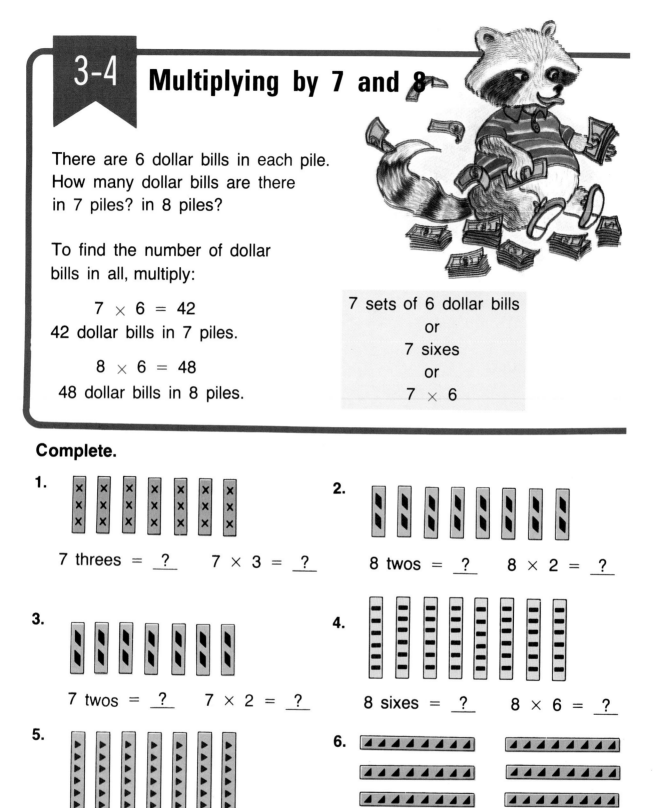

There are 6 dollar bills in each pile.
How many dollar bills are there
in 7 piles? in 8 piles?

To find the number of dollar
bills in all, multiply:

$7 \times 6 = 42$

42 dollar bills in 7 piles.

$8 \times 6 = 48$

48 dollar bills in 8 piles.

7 sets of 6 dollar bills
or
7 sixes
or
7×6

Complete.

1.

7 threes = ___?___ 7×3 = ___?___

2.

8 twos = __?__ 8×2 = __?__

3.

7 twos = __?__ 7×2 = __?__

4.

8 sixes = __?__ 8×6 = __?__

5.

7 sevens = __?__ 7×7 = __?__

6.

8 eights = __?__ 8×8 = __?__

72

Multiply. (Write these on your multiplication fact card.)

7.

Multiplying by 7								
1	2	3	4	5	6	7	8	9
$\times 7$	$\times 7$	$\times 7$	$\times 7$	$\times 7$	$\times 7$	$\times 7$	$\times 7$	$\times 7$

8.

Multiplying by 8								
1	2	3	4	5	6	7	8	9
$\times 8$	$\times 8$	$\times 8$	$\times 8$	$\times 8$	$\times 8$	$\times 8$	$\times 8$	$\times 8$

Find the product.

9. 2 $\times 8$	**10.** 1 $\times 7$	**11.** 3 $\times 8$	**12.** 3 $\times 7$	**13.** 1 $\times 8$	**14.** 4 $\times 6$	**15.** 4 $\times 7$
16. 6 $\times 7$	**17.** 4 $\times 8$	**18.** 5 $\times 7$	**19.** 6 $\times 8$	**20.** 8 $\times 6$	**21.** 2 $\times 7$	**22.** 5 $\times 8$
23. 8 $\times 8$	**24.** 9 $\times 7$	**25.** 7 $\times 8$	**26.** 8 $\times 7$	**27.** 5 $\times 5$	**28.** 9 $\times 8$	**29.** 7 $\times 7$

Solve.

30. Multiply 8 times 7.

31. What is the product of 9 and 7?

32. The factors are 6 and 8. What is the product?

33. One factor is 7. The product is 28. What is the other factor?

34. Paul buys 8 packages of muffins. There are 4 muffins in a package. How many muffins did Paul buy?

35. Carlos ate 7 muffins last week and 8 muffins this week. How many muffins did Carlos eat in all?

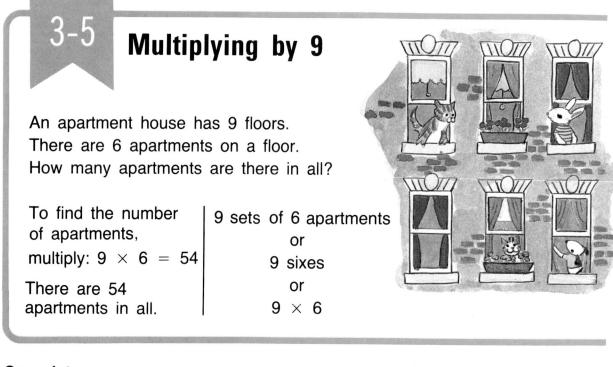

3-5 Multiplying by 9

An apartment house has 9 floors.
There are 6 apartments on a floor.
How many apartments are there in all?

To find the number of apartments, multiply: $9 \times 6 = 54$	9 sets of 6 apartments
	or
	9 sixes
There are 54 apartments in all.	or
	9×6

Complete.

1.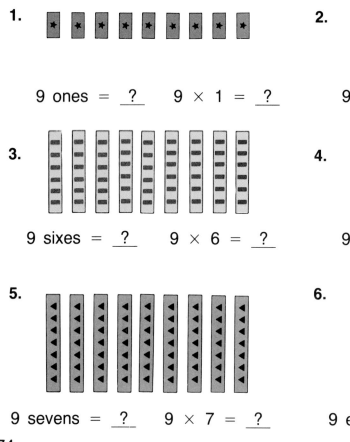

9 ones = __?__ $9 \times 1 = $ __?__

2.

9 threes = __?__ $9 \times 3 = $ __?__

3.

9 sixes = __?__ $9 \times 6 = $ __?__

4.

9 fives = __?__ $9 \times 5 = $ __?__

5.

9 sevens = __?__ $9 \times 7 = $ __?__

6.

9 eights = __?__ $9 \times 8 = $ __?__

74

Multiply. (Write these on your multiplication fact card.)

7.

Multiplying by 9								
1	2	3	4	5	6	7	8	9
×9	×9	×9	×9	×9	×9	×9	×9	×9

Find the product.

8. 3 ×9	**9.** 4 ×8	**10.** 1 ×9	**11.** 5 ×5	**12.** 9 ×2	**13.** 2 ×9	**14.** 9 ×3

15. 9 ×4 **16.** 4 ×9 **17.** 6 ×6 **18.** 2 ×2 **19.** 5 ×9 **20.** 9 ×5 **21.** 2 ×7

22. 6 ×9 **23.** 9 ×6 **24.** 7 ×7 **25.** 7 ×9 **26.** 9 ×7 **27.** 6 ×8 **28.** 5 ×7

29. 8 ×8 **30.** 9 ×9 **31.** 3 ×5 **32.** 7 ×6 **33.** 8 ×9 **34.** 9 ×8 **35.** 7 ×8

Complete each number sentence.

36. 6 × 4 = ___?___   **37.** 7 × 3 = ___?___   **38.** 4 × 8 = ___?___

39. 5 × 6 = ___?___   **40.** 6 × 1 = ___?___   **41.** 2 × 8 = ___?___

42. 3 × 7 = ___?___   **43.** 7 × 4 = ___?___   **44.** 9 × 2 = ___?___

Solve.

45. Multiply 9 times 3.

46. What is the product of 9 and 5?

47. The factors are 6 and 9. What is the product?

48. How many pencils in all are there in 5 packages of 9 pencils?

49. One of two factors is 4. The product is 36. What is the other factor?

50. There are 63 crayons in all. There are 7 colors. How many crayons are there of each color?

Multiplication Properties

Look at the pictures.
They show some properties of multiplication.

3 sets of 2 rings = 6 rings

       3 twos = 6

      $3 \times 2 = 6$

2 sets of 3 rings = 6 rings

       2 threes = 6

      $2 \times 3 = 6$

$$3 \times 2 = 2 \times 3$$

$$\begin{array}{cc} 2 & 3 \\ \times 3 & \times 2 \\ \hline 6 = & 6 \end{array}$$

When the order of the factors is changed, the product does not change.

Order Property

When one factor is 1, the product is the same as the other factor.

One Property

3 sets of 1 ring = 3 rings

      3 ones = 3

      $3 \times 1 = 3$

$$\begin{array}{cc} 1 & 1 \\ \times 3 & \times 2 \\ \hline 3 & 2 \end{array}$$

When one factor is 0, the product is 0.

Zero Property

3 sets of 0 rings = 0 rings

      3 zeros = 0

      $3 \times 0 = 0$

$$\begin{array}{cc} 0 & 0 \\ \times 3 & \times 4 \\ \hline 0 & 0 \end{array}$$

Complete each number sentence.

1. $7 \times 3 = \underline{\ ?\ }$
2. $3 \times 7 = \underline{\ ?\ }$
3. $4 \times 1 = \underline{\ ?\ }$

4. $1 \times 4 = \underline{\ ?\ }$
5. $6 \times 0 = \underline{\ ?\ }$
6. $0 \times 6 = \underline{\ ?\ }$

7. $9 \times 8 = \underline{\ ?\ }$
8. $8 \times 9 = \underline{\ ?\ }$
9. $3 \times \underline{\ ?\ } = 15$

10. $\underline{\ ?\ } \times 3 = 15$
11. $\underline{\ ?\ } \times 1 = 8$
12. $5 \times \underline{\ ?\ } = 0$

13. $2 \times \underline{\ ?\ } = 2$
14. $\underline{\ ?\ } \times 2 = 12$
15. $2 \times \underline{\ ?\ } = 12$

Find the product.

16. 8	17. 7	18. 5	19. 6	20. 9	21. 6	22. 0
$\times 7$	$\times 8$	$\times 0$	$\times 1$	$\times 6$	$\times 9$	$\times 3$

23. 1	24. 5	25. 6	26. 0	27. 9	28. 9	29. 9
$\times 9$	$\times 6$	$\times 5$	$\times 8$	$\times 1$	$\times 0$	$\times 9$

Solve.

30. The factors are 7 and 0. What is the product?

31. The product is 8. One factor is 8. What is the other factor?

32. The product is 0. One factor is 6. What is the other factor?

33. $12 \times 8 = 96$
    $8 \times 12 = \underline{\ ?\ }$

34. $8 \times 1 = 8$. What does 1×8 equal?

35. Write the two multiplication facts using the numbers 5 and 0 as factors.

Do You Remember?

Add or subtract. (Watch for $+$ or $-$.)

36. 4762	37. 5874	38. 58,926	39. $24.35	40. $79.68
$+1037$	-1803	$-\ \ \ 406$	$+\ \ 5.64$	$-\ \ 7.08$

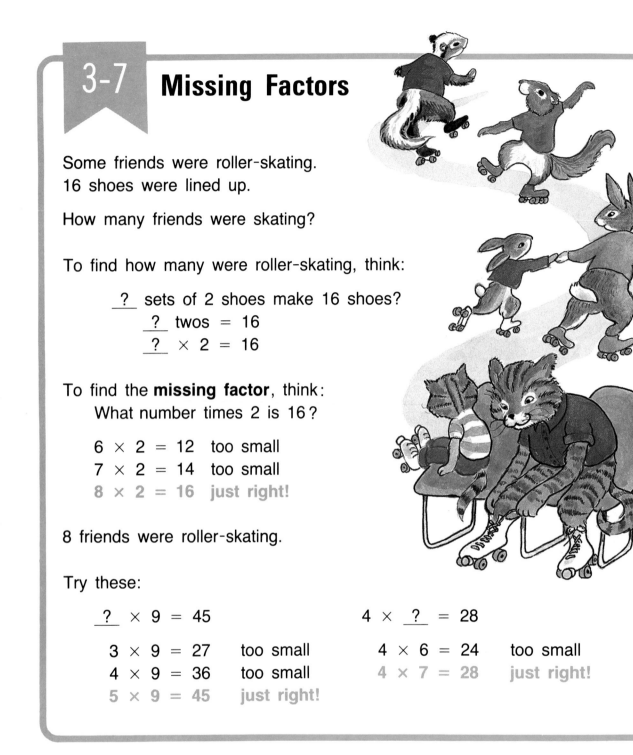

Missing Factors

Some friends were roller-skating.
16 shoes were lined up.

How many friends were skating?

To find how many were roller-skating, think:

    _?_ sets of 2 shoes make 16 shoes?
      _?_ twos = 16
      _?_ × 2 = 16

To find the **missing factor**, think:
What number times 2 is 16?

$6 × 2 = 12$ too small
$7 × 2 = 14$ too small
$8 × 2 = 16$ **just right!**

8 friends were roller-skating.

Try these:

   _?_ × 9 = 45   4 × _?_ = 28

    $3 × 9 = 27$ too small $4 × 6 = 24$ too small
    $4 × 9 = 36$ too small $4 × 7 = 28$ **just right!**
    $5 × 9 = 45$ **just right!**

Find the missing factor.

1. _?_ × 3 = 6   **2.** _?_ × 3 = 15   **3.** _?_ × 3 = 27

4. _?_ × 6 = 24   **5.** _?_ × 7 = 56   **6.** _?_ × 8 = 72

Find the missing factor.

7. $7 \times \underline{\ ?\ } = 21$ **8.** $5 \times \underline{\ ?\ } = 45$ **9.** $8 \times \underline{\ ?\ } = 48$

10. $\underline{\ ?\ } \times 9 = 81$ **11.** $4 \times \underline{\ ?\ } = 32$ **12.** $6 \times \underline{\ ?\ } = 54$

13. $\underline{\ ?\ } \times 5 = 20$ **14.** $6 \times \underline{\ ?\ } = 30$ **15.** $8 \times \underline{\ ?\ } = 40$

16. $9 \times \underline{\ ?\ } = 63$ **17.** $\underline{\ ?\ } \times 8 = 64$ **18.** $\underline{\ ?\ } \times 5 = 35$

19.
$$\begin{array}{r} ? \\ \times 2 \\ \hline 14 \end{array}$$
20.
$$\begin{array}{r} ? \\ \times 4 \\ \hline 16 \end{array}$$
21.
$$\begin{array}{r} ? \\ \times 3 \\ \hline 24 \end{array}$$
22.
$$\begin{array}{r} ? \\ \times 6 \\ \hline 42 \end{array}$$
23.
$$\begin{array}{r} ? \\ \times 9 \\ \hline 63 \end{array}$$
24.
$$\begin{array}{r} ? \\ \times 8 \\ \hline 56 \end{array}$$
25.
$$\begin{array}{r} ? \\ \times 7 \\ \hline 49 \end{array}$$

26.
$$\begin{array}{r} 4 \\ \times ? \\ \hline 36 \end{array}$$
27.
$$\begin{array}{r} 7 \\ \times ? \\ \hline 35 \end{array}$$
28.
$$\begin{array}{r} 9 \\ \times ? \\ \hline 9 \end{array}$$
29.
$$\begin{array}{r} 8 \\ \times ? \\ \hline 64 \end{array}$$
30.
$$\begin{array}{r} 6 \\ \times ? \\ \hline 0 \end{array}$$
31.
$$\begin{array}{r} 9 \\ \times ? \\ \hline 81 \end{array}$$
32.
$$\begin{array}{r} 7 \\ \times ? \\ \hline 56 \end{array}$$

Solve.

33. Mr. James collected $63 for selling 7 coins. How much was the average coin worth?

34. A package of Israeli stamps costs $7. Harry spent $42 for stamps. How many packages of Israeli stamps did he buy?

35. 9 coins fit in each page of Jim's coin album. Jim has 45 coins. How many pages can he fill?

36. Six students in the fourth grade are each building a race cart for the "Derby Race." They go to the town dump and find 24 wheels the right size. Do they have enough wheels to build the carts? Explain your answer.

37. How many wheels would they have to find for 5 carts? for 9 carts?

3-8 Number Patterns

Joseph used a number chart like this to find number patterns.

- He picked a number, 11, and circled it.

- He added 3 to 11, and circled his answer, 14.

- He kept doing this until he had these numbers:

  11, 14, 17, 20, 23, 26, 29.

If Joseph extended his chart to 59, he would have circled these numbers. Why?

  32, 35, 38, 41, 44, 47, 50, 53, 56

This is another way of showing what Joseph did:

Start	Operation	Number Pattern
11	+ 3	11, 14, 17, 20, 23, 26, 29, ... +3 +3

Study these.

Start	Operation	Number Pattern
2	Multiply by 2.	2, 4, 8, 16, ... ×2 ×2 ×2
3	Add 4. Then subtract 1.	3, 7, 6, 10, 9, 13, ... +4 −1 +4 −1 +4

Find the number pattern. (The first is done.)

1. 79, 76, 73, 70, 67 ⟶ Number Pattern—Subtract 3

2. 50, 54, 58, 62, 66

3. 59, 58, 57, 56, 55

4. 16, 8, 16, 8, 16

5. 25, 23, 27, 25, 29

Even and Odd Numbers

Even numbers are whole numbers that are multiples of 2.

Odd numbers are all other whole numbers.

0	1	2	3	4	5	6	7	8	9
10	11	12	13	14	15	16	17	18	19
20	21	22	23	24	25	26	27	28	29

Write *E* if the number is even, and *O* if the number is odd.

6. 19
7. 68
8. 20
9. 293
10. 796

11. 2912
12. 5141
13. 6768
14. 4095
15. 8472

16. 3334
17. 7477
18. 9103
19. 8006
20. 4449

Write the even numbers between:

21. 0 and 16
22. 66 and 82
23. 48 and 74

24. 116 and 130
25. 578 and 600
26. 3426 and 3440

Write the odd numbers between:

27. 1 and 21
28. 43 and 63
29. 95 and 113

30. 333 and 349
31. 801 and 835
32. 1021 and 1037

3-9 Dividing by 2

10 bunnies went canoeing. There were 2 bunnies in each canoe. How many canoes were there?

To find out how many canoes there were with 2 bunnies, ask, "How many sets of 2 make 10?"

| ? canoes with 2 bunnies is 10 bunnies. |
| ? twos = 10 |
| ? × 2 = 10 |

To find how many sets of 2 make 10, divide:

$$10 \div 2 = ? \quad or \quad ? \leftarrow \text{quotient}$$
$$2)\overline{10} \leftarrow \text{dividend}$$

Total number of bunnies — Number in each canoe — Number of canoes — divisor

Division is the opposite of multiplication.

To divide, find the missing factor:

$$10 \div 2 = ?$$

$$? \times 2 = 10 \longrightarrow 10 \div 2 = 5 \text{ because } 5 \times 2 = 10$$

Divide.

1. 8 ÷ 2 = ?
Think: ? × 2 = 8

2. 14 ÷ 2 = ?
Think: ? × 2 = 14

3. 6 ÷ 2 = ?
Think: ? × 2 = 6

4. 16 ÷ 2 = ?
Think: ? × 2 = 16

5. 12 ÷ 2 = ?
Think: ? × 2 = 12

6. 18 ÷ 2 = ?
Think: ? × 2 = 18

Divide.

7. $2 \div 2 = \underline{\ ?\ }$

Think: $\underline{\ ?\ } \times 2 = 2$

8. $10 \div 2 = \underline{\ ?\ }$

Think: $\underline{\ ?\ } \times 2 = 10$

9. $4 \div 2 = \underline{\ ?\ }$

Think: $\underline{\ ?\ } \times 2 = 4$

Divide.

10.

Dividing by 2
$2\overline{)2}$ $2\overline{)4}$ $2\overline{)6}$ $2\overline{)8}$ $2\overline{)10}$ $2\overline{)12}$ $2\overline{)14}$ $2\overline{)16}$ $2\overline{)18}$

Divide.

11. $2\overline{)14}$ **12.** $2\overline{)8}$ **13.** $2\overline{)2}$ **14.** $2\overline{)10}$ **15.** $2\overline{)6}$

16. $2\overline{)4}$ **17.** $2\overline{)18}$ **18.** $2\overline{)12}$ **19.** $2\overline{)16}$ **20.** $2\overline{)14}$

Solve.

21. 16 divided by 2 equals what number?

22. 2 is the divisor. 12 is the dividend. What is the quotient?

23. Write this division sentence as a multiplication sentence with a missing factor.

$18 \div 2 = \underline{\ ?\ }$

24. The quotient is 8. The divisor is 2. What is the dividend?

Make a division fact card!

25. • Use your multiplication card to divide:

$8 \div 2 = \underline{\ ?\ }$

• Find the factor 2 in the first **column.**
• Move right ⟶ to 8.
• Move up ↑ to 4 at the top of the column.

$8 \div 2 = 4$

×	1	2	3	4	5	6
1	1	2	3	4	5	6
2	2	4	6	8	10	12
3	3	6	9	12	15	18
4	4	8	12	16	20	24
5	5	10	15	20	25	30
6	6	12	18	24	30	36

3-10 Dividing by 3 and 4

The hen has 24 colored eggs.
She puts 4 eggs in every basket.
How many baskets does the
hen use?

To find how many baskets
the hen used, divide:
$24 \div 4 = \underline{\quad?\quad}$

Think: $\underline{\ ?\ } \times 4 = 24 \longrightarrow 6 \times 4 = 24$
So, $24 \div 4 = 6$ The hen uses 6 baskets.

If the hen put 3 eggs in a basket, how
many baskets does she use?
The hen uses 8 baskets.

Divide: $24 \div 3 = \underline{\ ?\ }$
Think: $\underline{\ ?\ } \times 3 = 24$
$8 \times 3 = 24$
So, $24 \div 3 = 8$

These multiplication and division facts form a fact family.

(3,4) Family	(2,3) Family	(2,4) Family
$3 \times 4 = 12$	$2 \times 3 = 6$	$2 \times 4 = 8$
$4 \times 3 = 12$	$3 \times 2 = 6$	$4 \times 2 = 8$
$12 \div 4 = 3$	$6 \div 3 = 2$	$8 \div 4 = 2$
$12 \div 3 = 4$	$6 \div 2 = 3$	$8 \div 2 = 4$

Divide.

1. $9 \div 3 = \underline{\ ?\ }$

Think: $\underline{\ ?\ } \times 3 = 9$

2. $20 \div 4 = \underline{\ ?\ }$

Think: $\underline{\ ?\ } \times 4 = 20$

3. $18 \div 3 = \underline{\ ?\ }$

Think: $\underline{\ ?\ } \times 3 = 18$

4. $16 \div 4 = \underline{\ ?\ }$

Think: $\underline{\ ?\ } \times 4 = 16$

5. $27 \div 3 = \underline{\ ?\ }$

Think: $\underline{\ ?\ } \times 3 = 27$

6. $32 \div 4 = \underline{\ ?\ }$

Think: $\underline{\ ?\ } \times 4 = 32$

Divide.

7. $15 \div 3 =$ _?_

Think: _?_ $\times 3 = 15$

8. $36 \div 4 =$ _?_

Think: _?_ $\times 4 = 36$

9. $28 \div 4 =$ _?_

Think: _?_ $\times 4 = 28$

10. $6 \div 3 =$ _?_

11. $12 \div 4 =$ _?_

12. $21 \div 3 =$ _?_

13. $24 \div 4 =$ _?_

14. $8 \div 4 =$ _?_

15. $3 \div 3 =$ _?_

Divide. (Check your answers using your division fact card.)

16.

Dividing by 3

$3\overline{)3}$ $3\overline{)6}$ $3\overline{)9}$ $3\overline{)12}$ $3\overline{)15}$ $3\overline{)18}$ $3\overline{)21}$ $3\overline{)24}$ $3\overline{)27}$

17.

Dividing by 4

$4\overline{)4}$ $4\overline{)8}$ $4\overline{)12}$ $4\overline{)16}$ $4\overline{)20}$ $4\overline{)24}$ $4\overline{)28}$ $4\overline{)32}$ $4\overline{)36}$

Find the quotient.

18. $3\overline{)12}$ **19.** $4\overline{)12}$ **20.** $4\overline{)24}$ **21.** $4\overline{)4}$ **22.** $3\overline{)9}$ **23.** $3\overline{)15}$

24. $4\overline{)32}$ **25.** $3\overline{)24}$ **26.** $4\overline{)28}$ **27.** $3\overline{)27}$ **28.** $4\overline{)20}$ **29.** $4\overline{)36}$

Solve.

30. 21 divided by 3 equals what number?

31. The dividend is 20. The divisor is 4. What is the quotient?

32. Write the fact family for the numbers (3,7).

33. The quotient is 6. The divisor is 3. What is the dividend?

85

Dividing by 5 and 6

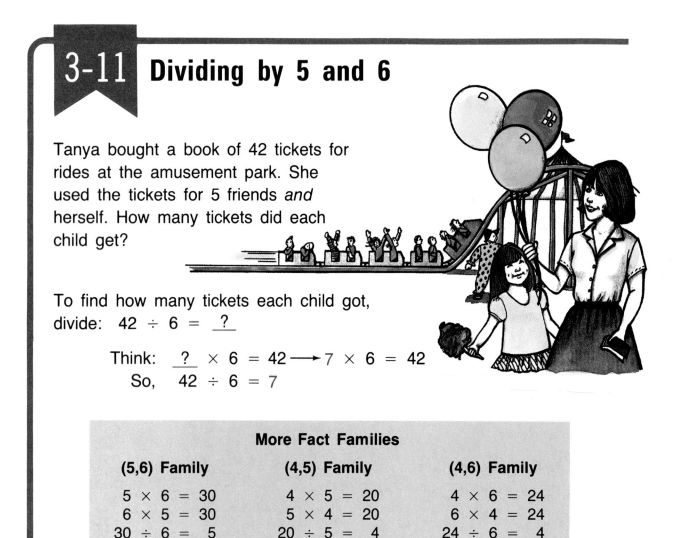

Tanya bought a book of 42 tickets for rides at the amusement park. She used the tickets for 5 friends *and* herself. How many tickets did each child get?

To find how many tickets each child got, divide: $42 \div 6 = \underline{\ ?\ }$

Think: $\underline{\ ?\ } \times 6 = 42 \longrightarrow 7 \times 6 = 42$
So, $42 \div 6 = 7$

More Fact Families		
(5,6) Family	**(4,5) Family**	**(4,6) Family**
$5 \times 6 = 30$	$4 \times 5 = 20$	$4 \times 6 = 24$
$6 \times 5 = 30$	$5 \times 4 = 20$	$6 \times 4 = 24$
$30 \div 6 = 5$	$20 \div 5 = 4$	$24 \div 6 = 4$
$30 \div 5 = 6$	$20 \div 4 = 5$	$24 \div 4 = 6$

Divide.

1. $15 \div 5 = \underline{\ ?\ }$

Think: $\underline{\ ?\ } \times 5 = 15$

2. $12 \div 6 = \underline{\ ?\ }$

Think: $\underline{\ ?\ } \times 6 = 12$

3. $6 \div 6 = \underline{\ ?\ }$

Think: $\underline{\ ?\ } \times 6 = 6$

4. $25 \div 5 = \underline{\ ?\ }$

Think: $\underline{\ ?\ } \times 5 = 25$

5. $40 \div 5 = \underline{\ ?\ }$

Think: $\underline{\ ?\ } \times 5 = 40$

6. $54 \div 6 = \underline{\ ?\ }$

Think: $\underline{\ ?\ } \times 6 = 54$

Divide. (Write your answers using your division fact card.)

Dividing by 5

7. $5\overline{)5}$ $5\overline{)10}$ $5\overline{)15}$ $5\overline{)20}$ $5\overline{)25}$ $5\overline{)30}$ $5\overline{)35}$ $5\overline{)40}$ $5\overline{)45}$

Dividing by 6

8. $6\overline{)6}$ $6\overline{)12}$ $6\overline{)18}$ $6\overline{)24}$ $6\overline{)30}$ $6\overline{)36}$ $6\overline{)42}$ $6\overline{)48}$ $6\overline{)54}$

Find the quotient.

9. $6\overline{)30}$ 10. $6\overline{)42}$ 11. $5\overline{)10}$ 12. $5\overline{)40}$ 13. $6\overline{)24}$ 14. $5\overline{)5}$

15. $6\overline{)18}$ 16. $5\overline{)35}$ 17. $6\overline{)36}$ 18. $5\overline{)25}$ 19. $5\overline{)15}$ 20. $6\overline{)12}$

21. $5\overline{)45}$ 22. $6\overline{)48}$ 23. $6\overline{)6}$ 24. $6\overline{)54}$ 25. $5\overline{)30}$ 26. $5\overline{)20}$

Write a fact family for each pair of numbers.

27. (2,5) 28. (2,6) 29. (3,5) 30. (3,6)

Solve.

31. 30 divided by 5 equals what number?

32. The dividend is 24. The divisor is 6. What is the quotient?

33. The quotient is 2. The divisor is 6. What is the dividend?

34. The dividend is 20. The quotient is 5. What is the divisor?

35. Tim bought 5 books of tickets. Each book contains 8 tickets. How many tickets did he buy?

36. There are 9 cars. Each car holds 6 people. How many people in all are there?

3-12 Dividing by 7 and 8

There are 7 pencil boxes.
There are 56 pencils in all.
There are the same number of
pencils in each box. How many
pencils are in each box?

To find how many pencils there are in each box, divide:

$$56 \div 7 = \underline{}$$

Total   Number   Number in
Number   of boxes   each box

56 pencils divided
among 7 boxes is
__?__ pencils in each box.

Think: __?__ $\times$ 7 = 56 $\longrightarrow$ 8 $\times$ 7 = 56
  so, 56 $\div$ 7 = 8

There are 8 pencils in each of the 7 boxes.

More Fact Families

(7,8) Family	(6,7) Family	(6,8) Family
7 $\times$ 8 = 56	6 $\times$ 7 = 42	6 $\times$ 8 = 48
8 $\times$ 7 = 56	7 $\times$ 6 = 42	8 $\times$ 6 = 48
56 $\div$ 8 = 7	42 $\div$ 7 = 6	48 $\div$ 8 = 6
56 $\div$ 7 = 8	42 $\div$ 6 = 7	48 $\div$ 6 = 8

Divide.

1. 49 $\div$ 7 = __?__

Think: __?__ $\times$ 7 = 49

2. 63 $\div$ 7 = __?__

Think: __?__ $\times$ 7 = 63

3. 64 $\div$ 8 = __?__

Think: __?__ $\times$ 8 = 64

Divide.

4. $16 \div 8 = \underline{\ ?\ }$ **5.** $21 \div 7 = \underline{\ ?\ }$ **6.** $14 \div 7 = \underline{\ ?\ }$

7. $8 \div 8 = \underline{\ ?\ }$ **8.** $28 \div 7 = \underline{\ ?\ }$ **9.** $32 \div 8 = \underline{\ ?\ }$

Divide. (Check your answers using your division fact card.)

Dividing by 7

10. $7\overline{)7}$ $7\overline{)14}$ $7\overline{)21}$ $7\overline{)28}$ $7\overline{)35}$ $7\overline{)42}$ $7\overline{)49}$ $7\overline{)56}$ $7\overline{)63}$

Dividing by 8

11. $8\overline{)8}$ $8\overline{)16}$ $8\overline{)24}$ $8\overline{)32}$ $8\overline{)40}$ $8\overline{)48}$ $8\overline{)56}$ $8\overline{)64}$ $8\overline{)72}$

Find the quotient.

12. $7\overline{)35}$ **13.** $8\overline{)24}$ **14.** $7\overline{)7}$ **15.** $7\overline{)21}$ **16.** $8\overline{)16}$ **17.** $8\overline{)64}$

18. $7\overline{)49}$ **19.** $8\overline{)56}$ **20.** $8\overline{)40}$ **21.** $8\overline{)72}$ **22.** $8\overline{)48}$ **23.** $7\overline{)63}$

Write a fact family for each pair of numbers.

24. (2,7)   **25.** (2,8)   **26.** (4,7)   **27.** (4,8)

Solve.

28. 8 divided by 8 equals what number?

29. The dividend is 28. The divisor is 7. What is the quotient?

30. Pedro has 40 tomatoes in several baskets. There are 8 in each basket. How many baskets are there?

31. The baseball coach had 24 baseballs. He gave 4 baseballs to each team. How many teams are there?

3-13 Dividing by 9

There are 9 Little League teams in Orange County. 81 new players are picked. They are equally divided among the 9 teams. How many new players does each team get?

To find how many each team got, divide: $81 \div 9 = \underline{\ ?\ }$

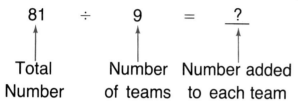

81	÷	9	=	?
↑		↑		↑
Total Number		Number of teams		Number added to each team

Think: $\underline{\ ?\ } \times 9 = 81 \longrightarrow 9 \times 9 = 81$

So, $81 \div 9 = 9$

There are 9 new players on each of the 9 teams.

81 players divided among 9 teams is $\underline{\ ?\ }$ new players on each team.

More Fact Families		
(8,9) Family	**(6,9) Family**	**(7,9) Family**
$8 \times 9 = 72$	$6 \times 9 = 54$	$7 \times 9 = 63$
$9 \times 8 = 72$	$9 \times 6 = 54$	$9 \times 7 = 63$
$72 \div 9 = 8$	$54 \div 9 = 6$	$63 \div 9 = 7$
$72 \div 8 = 9$	$54 \div 6 = 9$	$63 \div 7 = 9$

Divide.

1. $9 \div 9 = \underline{\ ?\ }$ **2.** $27 \div 9 = \underline{\ ?\ }$ **3.** $45 \div 9 = \underline{\ ?\ }$

90

Divide.

4. $18 \div 9 = $?   **5.** $54 \div 9 = $?   **6.** $36 \div 9 = $?

7. $63 \div 9 = $?   **8.** $81 \div 9 = $?   **9.** $72 \div 9 = $?

Divide. (Check your answers using your division fact card.)

Dividing by 9								
$9\overline{)9}$	$9\overline{)18}$	$9\overline{)27}$	$9\overline{)36}$	$9\overline{)45}$	$9\overline{)54}$	$9\overline{)63}$	$9\overline{)72}$	$9\overline{)81}$

10.

Find the quotient.

11. $9\overline{)27}$ **12.** $3\overline{)27}$ **13.** $6\overline{)36}$ **14.** $9\overline{)9}$ **15.** $4\overline{)36}$ **16.** $9\overline{)36}$

17. $2\overline{)14}$ **18.** $9\overline{)18}$ **19.** $5\overline{)35}$ **20.** $9\overline{)45}$ **21.** $8\overline{)64}$ **22.** $7\overline{)63}$

23. $9\overline{)63}$ **24.** $8\overline{)48}$ **25.** $9\overline{)54}$ **26.** $6\overline{)42}$ **27.** $4\overline{)32}$ **28.** $6\overline{)30}$

29. $8\overline{)72}$ **30.** $9\overline{)72}$ **31.** $8\overline{)56}$ **32.** $4\overline{)28}$ **33.** $9\overline{)81}$ **34.** $7\overline{)49}$

Write the fact family for each pair of numbers.

35. (2,9)   **36.** (5,9)   **37.** (3,9)   **38.** (4,9)

Solve.

39. 36 grapes are equally divided among 9 children. How many grapes does each child get?

40. A jacket has 8 buttons. There are 9 jackets in all. How many buttons in all are there?

3-14 Division Properties

These properties will help you divide quickly.

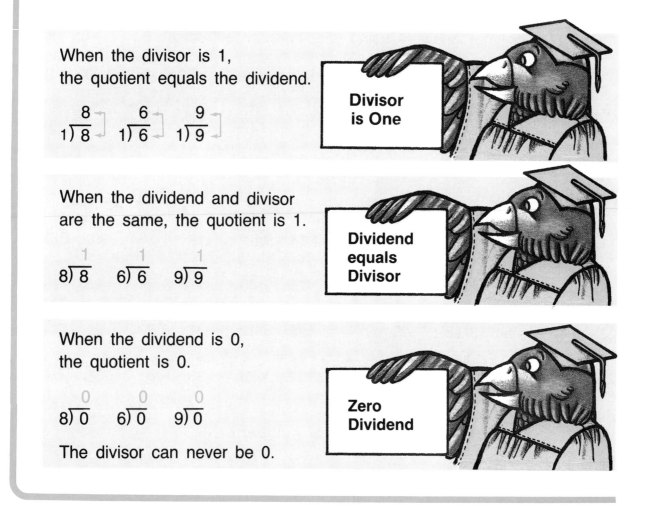

When the divisor is 1,
the quotient equals the dividend.

$$1)\overline{8} = 8 \quad 1)\overline{6} = 6 \quad 1)\overline{9} = 9$$

Divisor is One

When the dividend and divisor are the same, the quotient is 1.

$$8)\overline{8} = 1 \quad 6)\overline{6} = 1 \quad 9)\overline{9} = 1$$

Dividend equals Divisor

When the dividend is 0,
the quotient is 0.

$$8)\overline{0} = 0 \quad 6)\overline{0} = 0 \quad 9)\overline{0} = 0$$

The divisor can never be 0.

Zero Dividend

Divide.

1. $6)\overline{6}$ **2.** $5)\overline{0}$ **3.** $1)\overline{7}$ **4.** $3)\overline{3}$ **5.** $2)\overline{0}$ **6.** $9)\overline{9}$

7. $4)\overline{0}$ **8.** $2)\overline{2}$ **9.** $8)\overline{8}$ **10.** $4)\overline{4}$ **11.** $1)\overline{2}$ **12.** $1)\overline{6}$

13. $3)\overline{0}$ **14.** $1)\overline{4}$ **15.** $9)\overline{0}$ **16.** $7)\overline{7}$ **17.** $5)\overline{5}$ **18.** $7)\overline{0}$

Review

Compute. (Watch for $+, -, \times, \div$.)

1. 8×3
2. $6 - 4$
3. $49 \div 7$
4. $5 + 8$
5. 7×6

6. $36 \div 4$
7. $4 + 1$
8. $10 \div 5$
9. $8 - 7$
10. $3 \div 3$

11. 3×1
12. $54 \div 9$
13. $7 - 4$
14. 4×9
15. $12 \div 4$

16. $27 \div 3$
17. 5×7
18. $9 \div 9$
19. $2 + 5$
20. $72 \div 8$

21. 6×8
22. $81 \div 9$
23. $8 - 5$
24. 3×7
25. $9 - 1$

26. $36 \div 6$
27. 7×4
28. 9×7
29. 8×8
30. $12 \div 3$

Compare. Write $<$, $=$, or $>$.

31. $8 + 7$ _?_ $15 - 1$
32. 8×6 _?_ $48 \div 6$
33. $9 + 0$ _?_ $9 - 0$

34. $9 \div 3$ _?_ $12 \div 3$
35. $7 \div 1$ _?_ $7 + 0$
36. $6 + 9$ _?_ $9 + 6$

37. 9×0 _?_ $0 \div 9$
38. 7×8 _?_ 6×8
39. $63 \div 7$ _?_ $4 + 5$

Solve.

40. The subtrahend is 26. The minuend is 97. What is the difference?

41. The sum is 424. One addend is 103. What is the other addend?

42. 54 is a multiple for what two factors?

43. The quotient is 6. The divisor is 9. What is the dividend?

44. The dividend is 27. The divisor is 9. What is the quotient?

45. Ms. Jones had $25 in $5 bills. How many bills did she have?

3-16 Problem Solving: Choose the Operation

Operation	IMAGINE (Create a picture in your mind.)
+	Join equal or unequal groups or quantities.
−	Separate equal or unequal groups or quantities. Compare two groups or quantities.
×	Join only equal groups or quantities.
÷	Separate a group only into an equal number of objects or smaller groups. Separate only equal numbers of objects into groups.

To choose the correct operation:

- Read each problem.

- Imagine or create a picture in your mind.

- Draw a picture of what is happening.

- Think about the picture.

- The table above will help you choose the correct operation.

---

1. Tiffany buys 24 large balloons and 30 small balloons. How many balloons does Tiffany buy?

   Think: You are joining unequal groups.

   Choose the operation: Add.
   $$24 + 30 = \underline{\ ?\ }$$
   $$24 + 30 = 54$$
   Tiffany has 54 balloons.

   Imagine—Draw a picture.

   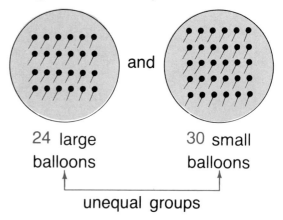

   24 large balloons and 30 small balloons

   unequal groups

2. How many more small balloons than large balloons does Tiffany have?

Think: The picture shows that you are comparing the size of unequal groups.

Choose the operation: Subtract.

    30 − 24 = ?
    30 − 24 = 6

Tiffany has 6 more small balloons.

Imagine—Draw a picture.

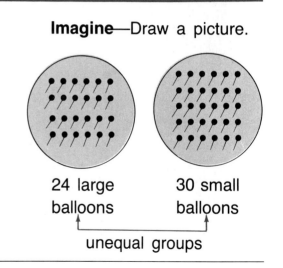

24 large   30 small
balloons   balloons

unequal groups

---

3. Tiffany wants to share her 54 balloons equally among her 9 friends. How many balloons does each friend get?

Imagine—Draw a picture.

Think: Separate 54 balloons into 9 equal groups.

Choose the operation:
The groups are equal, so divide.

    54 ÷ 9 = ?
    54 ÷ 9 = 6

Each of Tiffany's 9 friends got 6 balloons each.

4. Because Tiffany gave away her balloons, her Uncle Jim bought her three times the number of balloons that she gave each friend. How many balloons did he buy for Tiffany?

Imagine—Draw a picture.

Think: Join 3 equal groups of 6.

Choose the operation:
The groups are equal, so multiply.

    3 × 6 = ?
    3 × 6 = 18

He bought her 18 new balloons.

Choose the operation. Then solve.

5. Joshua collected 8 pounds of old newspapers every day. How many pounds had he collected at the end of 6 days?

6. Teresita decided to help Joshua collect newspapers. During the 6 days she collected: 9, 6, 7, 5, 6, and 8 pounds. How many pounds of paper had Teresita collected at the end of the 6 days?

95

More Practice

Multiply.

1. 3×8 2. 6×2 3. 2×2 4. 1×3 5. 7×2

6. 8×4 7. 9×6 8. 3×9 9. 8×7 10. 6×3

11. 8×0 12. 6×1 13. 5×9 14. 4×7 15. 7×7

16. 8×8 17. 8×5 18. 4×9 19. 5×0 20. 6×6

Find the missing factor.

21. $5 \times \underline{\ ?\ } = 40$ 22. $3 \times \underline{\ ?\ } = 9$ 23. $\underline{\ ?\ } \times 8 = 24$

24. $\underline{\ ?\ } \times 6 = 36$ 25. $7 \times \underline{\ ?\ } = 28$ 26. $\underline{\ ?\ } \times 3 = 21$

Divide.

27. $3\overline{)18}$ 28. $2\overline{)4}$ 29. $7\overline{)14}$ 30. $6\overline{)12}$ 31. $7\overline{)7}$ 32. $8\overline{)0}$

33. $72 \div 9$ 34. $45 \div 5$ 35. $16 \div 8$ 36. $18 \div 9$

Complete.

37. $6 \underline{\ ?\ } 8 = 48$ 38. $3 \underline{\ ?\ } 2 = 5$ 39. $12 \underline{\ ?\ } 5 = 7$

Solve.

40. Frances has 35 tulip bulbs to plant. She is going to put 5 bulbs in each pot. How many flower pots does she need?

41. In Ted's stamp book there are 8 stamps on each page. How many stamps are on 9 pages?

42. A singer recorded 63 songs. Each record has 7 songs. How many records are there?

(See *Still More Practice*, p. 359.)

Math Probe

FACTOR TREES

A **prime** number has exactly two factors, itself and 1.

$$5 = 1 \times 5$$

A **composite** number has more than two factors.

$$6 = 1 \times 6$$
$$= 1 \times 2 \times 3$$

A **factor tree** is made by finding the prime factors of a number.

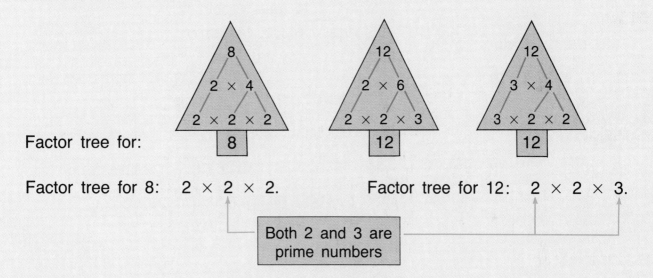

Factor tree for: 8 12 12

Factor tree for 8: $2 \times 2 \times 2$.   Factor tree for 12: $2 \times 2 \times 3$.

Both 2 and 3 are prime numbers

Complete these factor trees.

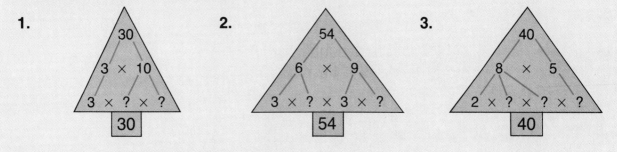

1. 30
   3×10
   $3 \times ? \times ?$
   30

2. 54
   6×9
   $3 \times ? \times 3 \times ?$
   54

3. 40
   8×5
   $2 \times ? \times ? \times ?$
   40

Draw a factor tree for each number.

4. 16   5. 10   6. 20   7. 27   8. 6

9. 32   10. 48   11. 56   12. 30   13. 64

Check Your Mastery

Multiply.

See pp. 68-75

1. 6×3 **2.** 4×8 **3.** 9×4 **4.** 7×8

5. 8×6 **6.** 7×9 **7.** 5×7 **8.** 6×7

Find the missing factor.

See pp. 78-79

9. $7 \times \underline{?} = 14$ **10.** $\underline{?} \times 4 = 36$ **11.** $\underline{?} \times 7 = 42$

Find each product. Write a division fact for each.

See pp. 84-91

12. 9×3 **13.** 5×9 **14.** 4×7 **15.** 6×8 **16.** 4×5

Divide.

See pp. 84-91

17. $4\overline{)24}$ **18.** $5\overline{)30}$ **19.** $7\overline{)49}$ **20.** $8\overline{)40}$ **21.** $6\overline{)36}$

22. $21 \div 3$ **23.** $63 \div 9$ **24.** $54 \div 6$ **25.** $56 \div 7$

Complete.

See pp. 70-71, 88-89

26. $9 \underline{\ ?\ } 4 = 13$ **27.** $6 \underline{\ ?\ } 9 = 54$ **28.** $72 \underline{\ ?\ } 8 = 9$

Solve.

See pp. 66-75

29. Blake has 56 books to place equally on 7 shelves. How many books will he place on each shelf?

30. Geri drives the school bus 9 miles each day. How many miles will she drive in 5 days?

4

More Addition and Subtraction

In this unit you will:

- Add and subtract numbers using regrouping
- Subtract with zero in the minuend
- Estimate sums and differences
- Solve problems using estimation

Do you remember:

The names used in addition are:

$$341 \longleftarrow \text{Addend}$$
$$+257 \longleftarrow \text{Addend}$$
$$598 \longleftarrow \text{Sum}$$

The names used in subtraction are:

$$478 \longleftarrow \text{Minuend}$$
$$-305 \longleftarrow \text{Subtrahend}$$
$$173 \longleftarrow \text{Difference}$$

To add or subtract, start with the ones column and work from right to left.

Regrouping

Rename.

2 tens 7 ones = _?_   3 tens 3 ones = _?_   1 ten 8 ones = _?_

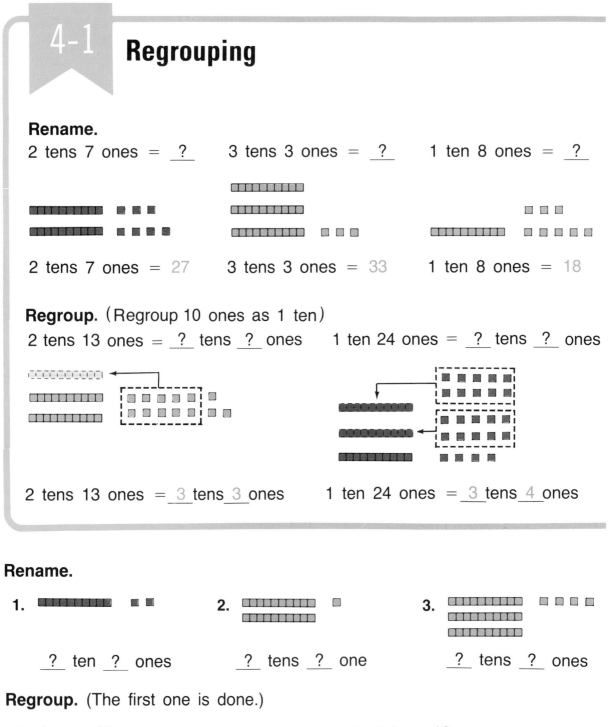

2 tens 7 ones = 27   3 tens 3 ones = 33   1 ten 8 ones = 18

Regroup. (Regroup 10 ones as 1 ten)

2 tens 13 ones = _?_ tens _?_ ones   1 ten 24 ones = _?_ tens _?_ ones

2 tens 13 ones = _3_ tens _3_ ones   1 ten 24 ones = _3_ tens _4_ ones

Rename.

1. _?_ ten _?_ ones

2. _?_ tens _?_ one

3. _?_ tens _?_ ones

Regroup. (The first one is done.)

4. 6 tens 26 ones =
   _8_ tens _6_ ones

5. 8 tens 13 ones =
   _?_ tens _?_ ones

6. 3 tens 18 ones =
   _?_ tens _?_ ones

7. 7 tens 11 ones =
   _?_ tens _?_ ones

4-2 Adding 2-Digit Numbers With Regrouping

There are 28 fruit bars without nuts
and 17 fruit bars with nuts.
How many fruit bars are there in all?

To find the number of fruit bars
in all, add: 28 + 17 = __?__

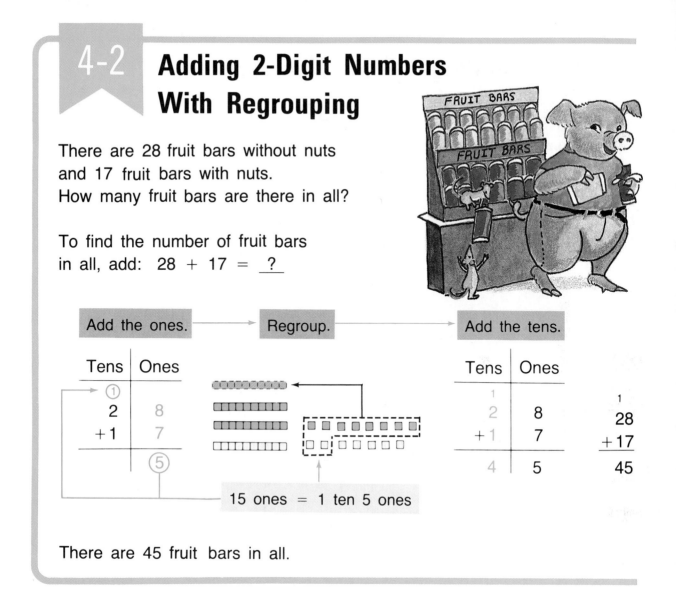

15 ones = 1 ten 5 ones

There are 45 fruit bars in all.

Add.

1.	48 + 18	**2.**	26 + 46	**3.**	49 + 27	**4.**	28 + 36	**5.**	39 + 46
6.	47 + 49	**7.**	55 + 38	**8.**	34 + 28	**9.**	18 + 66	**10.**	54 + 18
11.	86 + 9	**12.**	75 + 18	**13.**	63 + 7	**14.**	78 + 12	**15.**	31 + 59

4-3 Adding 3-Digit Numbers with Regrouping

Add: 142 + 275 = ?

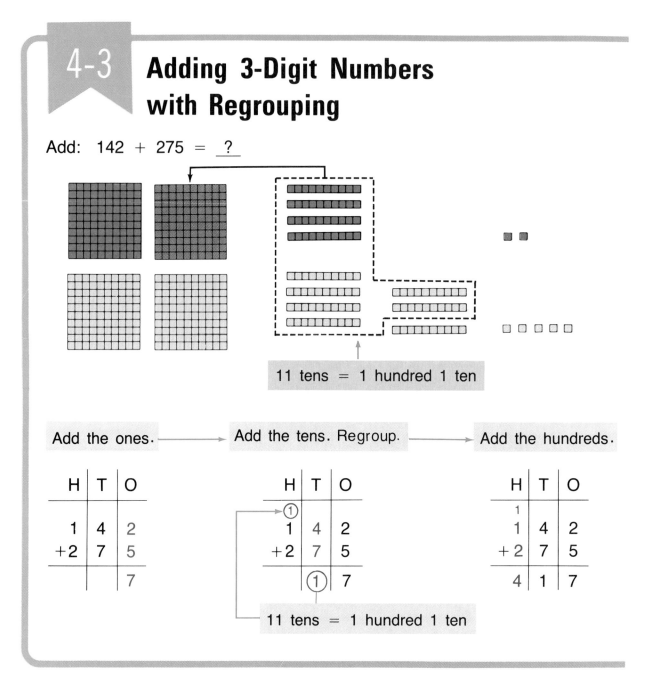

11 tens = 1 hundred 1 ten

Add the ones. ⟶ Add the tens. Regroup. ⟶ Add the hundreds.

H	T	O
1	4	2
+2	7	5
		7

H	T	O
	①	
1	4	2
+2	7	5
	①	7

11 tens = 1 hundred 1 ten

H	T	O
1		
1	4	2
+2	7	5
4	1	7

Regroup. (The first one is done.)

1. 6 hundreds 5 tens 18 ones = _6_ hundreds _6_ tens _8_ ones = 668

2. 4 hundreds 18 tens 7 ones = _?_ hundreds _?_ tens _?_ ones = _?_

3. 8 hundreds 7 tens 12 ones = _?_ hundreds _?_ tens _?_ ones = _?_

4. 3 hundreds 8 tens 25 ones = _?_ hundreds _?_ tens _?_ ones = _?_

102

Add. (Check your answers on a calculator.)

5.	329 +573	**6.**	375 +266	**7.**	489 +253	**8.**	389 +484
9.	688 +267	**10.**	724 +186	**11.**	668 +137	**12.**	486 +324
13.	224 +768	**14.**	389 +276	**15.**	342 +158	**16.**	211 +389

Arrange in columns. Add.

17. 269 + 641   **18.** 169 + 592   **19.** 275 + 136

20. 302 + 499   **21.** 581 + 229   **22.** 619 + 232

23. 114 + 388   **24.** 151 + 299   **25.** 397 + 403

Solve.

26. There are 187 cars in Parking Lot A. There are 236 cars in Parking Lot B. How many cars are parked?

27. In Todt Hill School there are 154 girls and 166 boys. How many children are in the Todt Hill School?

CHALLENGE

28. What are the largest and the smallest possible addends of two 3-digit numbers whose sum is 555? 999?

29. Find two 3-digit addends with the same digits in each number whose sum is 444.

4-4 Adding Three Addends with Regrouping

At the chicken farm there are 3 coops. Daniel counted 362 chickens in coop A, 422 in coop B, and 296 in coop C. How many chickens are there in all?

To find the number of chickens in all, add: 362 + 422 + 296 = _?_

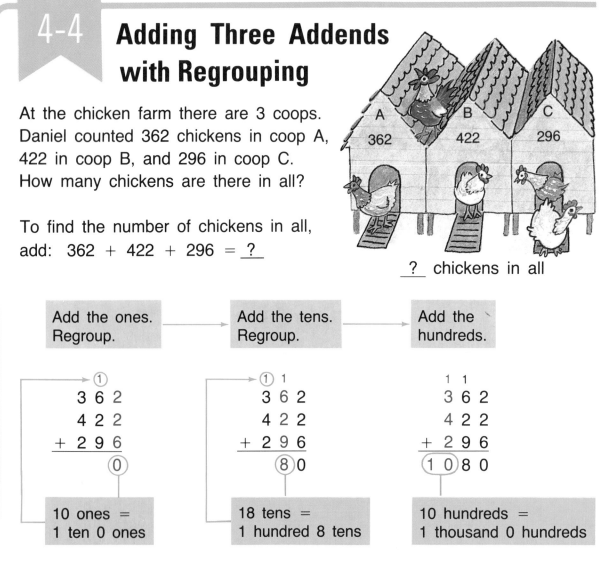

_?_ chickens in all

Add the ones. Regroup.	Add the tens. Regroup.	Add the hundreds.

```
    ①              ① 1           1  1
  3 6 2          3 6 2         3 6 2
  4 2 2          4 2 2         4 2 2
+ 2 9 6        + 2 9 6       + 2 9 6
    ⓪            ⑧ 0         ① 0 8 0
```

10 ones = 1 ten 0 ones	18 tens = 1 hundred 8 tens	10 hundreds = 1 thousand 0 hundreds

There are 1080 chickens in all.

Find the sum.

1.	247	2.	369	3.	267	4.	277
	191		431		124		406
	+322		+213		+539		+243

5.	423	6.	517	7.	293	8.	406
	492		197		312		173
	+175		+328		+409		+675

104

Add. Check your answers on a calculator.

9.	276	**10.**	27	**11.**	221	**12.**	144
	59		345		107		288
	+276		+456		+621		+437

13.	357	**14.**	516	**15.**	551	**16.**	514
	29		384		827		679
	+824		+967		+635		+823

Arrange in columns. Add.

17. 270 + 107 + 923

18. 426 + 346 + 99

19. 536 + 79 + 867

20. 51 + 276 + 429

Three of the four addends have a sum of 1000.
Write the addend that does *not* belong.

21. 421, 391, 198, 381

22. 510, 237, 253, 233

23. 173, 125, 225, 602

24. 345, 352, 303, 355

25. What is the number of bags of chicken feed used in the winter? spring? summer? and fall?

26. In which season was the most chicken feed used? the least?

27. How many more bags were used during the summer than were used during the winter?

Bags of Chicken Feed Used Each Month			
Winter		**Spring**	
December	361	March	451
January	217	April	214
February	345	May	346
Summer		**Fall**	
June	447	September	316
July	362	October	340
August	246	November	297

Subtracting 2-Digit Numbers with Regrouping

There are 34 monkeys on Monkey Island at the zoo. 18 monkeys are playing in the trees. How many monkeys are *not* playing in the trees?

To find how many are *not* in the trees, subtract: 34 − 18 = __?__

See if there are enough ones to subtract.	More ones are needed. Regroup the tens to get more ones.	Subtract the ones.

Tens	Ones
3	4
−1	8

34 = 3 tens   4 ones
= 2 tens 14 ones

Tens	Ones
2	14
3̸	4̸
−1	8
	6

Subtract the tens.	Check by adding.

Tens	Ones
2	14
3̸	4̸
−1	8
1	6

2 14
3̸ 4̸   minuend
−1 8   subtrahend
1 6   difference

16   difference
+18   subtrahend
34   minuend

There are 16 monkeys *not* playing in the trees.

Regroup for subtraction. (The first one is done.)

1. 56 = <u>5</u> tens <u>6</u> ones
    = <u>4</u> tens <u>16</u> ones

2. 63 = <u>?</u> tens <u>?</u> ones
    = <u>?</u> tens <u>?</u> ones

3. 82 = <u>?</u> tens <u>?</u> ones
    = <u>?</u> tens <u>?</u> ones

4. 60 = <u>?</u> tens <u>?</u> ones
    = <u>?</u> tens <u>?</u> ones

5. 95 = <u>?</u> tens <u>?</u> ones
    = <u>?</u> tens <u>?</u> ones

6. 80 = <u>?</u> tens <u>?</u> ones
    = <u>?</u> tens <u>?</u> ones

Find the difference.

7.
$$\begin{array}{r} \overset{8}{\cancel{9}}\ \overset{13}{\cancel{3}} \\ -7\ 8 \\ \hline \end{array}$$

8.
$$\begin{array}{r} \overset{4}{\cancel{5}}\ \overset{12}{\cancel{2}} \\ -1\ 9 \\ \hline \end{array}$$

9.
$$\begin{array}{r} \overset{2}{\cancel{3}}\ \overset{16}{\cancel{6}} \\ -2\ 9 \\ \hline \end{array}$$

10.
$$\begin{array}{r} 84 \\ -58 \\ \hline \end{array}$$

11.
$$\begin{array}{r} 50 \\ -24 \\ \hline \end{array}$$

12.
$$\begin{array}{r} 63 \\ -46 \\ \hline \end{array}$$

13.
$$\begin{array}{r} 82 \\ -17 \\ \hline \end{array}$$

14.
$$\begin{array}{r} 60 \\ -46 \\ \hline \end{array}$$

15.
$$\begin{array}{r} 80 \\ -34 \\ \hline \end{array}$$

16.
$$\begin{array}{r} 82 \\ -45 \\ \hline \end{array}$$

Arrange in columns. Subtract.

17. 92 − 34

18. 82 − 67

19. 52 − 34

20. 53 − 38

21. 75 − 67

22. 42 − 29

23. 63 − 45

24. 70 − 46

25. 60 − 18

Choose the difference which is not the same as the other three.

26. a.
$$\begin{array}{r} 63 \\ -29 \\ \hline \end{array}$$
  b.
$$\begin{array}{r} 51 \\ -17 \\ \hline \end{array}$$
  c.
$$\begin{array}{r} 92 \\ -48 \\ \hline \end{array}$$
  d.
$$\begin{array}{r} 100 \\ -66 \\ \hline \end{array}$$

27. a.
$$\begin{array}{r} 75 \\ -37 \\ \hline \end{array}$$
  b.
$$\begin{array}{r} 85 \\ -57 \\ \hline \end{array}$$
  c.
$$\begin{array}{r} 64 \\ -36 \\ \hline \end{array}$$
  d.
$$\begin{array}{r} 72 \\ -44 \\ \hline \end{array}$$

28. a.
$$\begin{array}{r} 82 \\ -39 \\ \hline \end{array}$$
  b.
$$\begin{array}{r} 80 \\ -47 \\ \hline \end{array}$$
  c.
$$\begin{array}{r} 62 \\ -29 \\ \hline \end{array}$$
  d.
$$\begin{array}{r} 90 \\ -57 \\ \hline \end{array}$$

Subtracting 3-Digit Numbers with Regrouping

A big brown bear weighs 363 pounds. A black bear weighs 147 pounds. How much heavier is the brown bear than the black bear?

To find how much heavier the brown bear is, subtract: 363 − 147 = __?__

See if there are enough ones to subtract.

$$
\begin{array}{r}
3\ 6\ 3 \\
-\ 1\ 4\ 7 \\
\hline
\end{array}
$$

More ones are needed. Regroup. Subtract ones.

$$
\begin{array}{r}
{\scriptstyle 5\ 13} \\
3\ 6\ 3 \\
-\ 1\ 4\ 7 \\
\hline
6
\end{array}
$$

6 tens 3 ones = 5 tens 13 ones

Subtract the tens.

$$
\begin{array}{r}
{\scriptstyle 5\ 13} \\
3\ 6\ 3 \\
-\ 1\ 4\ 7 \\
\hline
1\ 6
\end{array}
$$

Subtract the hundreds.

$$
\begin{array}{r}
{\scriptstyle 5\ 13} \\
3\ 6\ 3 \\
-\ 1\ 4\ 7 \\
\hline
2\ 1\ 6
\end{array}
$$

CHECK

$$
\begin{array}{r}
2\ 1\ 6 \\
+\ 1\ 4\ 7 \\
\hline
3\ 6\ 3
\end{array}
$$

The big brown bear is 216 pounds heavier.

Find the difference. Use the calculator to check your answers.

1. 527 −143	**2.** 264 −139	**3.** 826 −607	**4.** 518 −109	**5.** 273 −147
6. 666 −327	**7.** 586 −249	**8.** 384 −276	**9.** 262 −128	**10.** 963 − 27
11. 471 − 63	**12.** 590 −146	**13.** 516 −409	**14.** 263 − 47	**15.** 720 −418

Arrange in columns. Subtract.

16. 826 − 309 **17.** 727 − 308 **18.** 664 − 75

19. 921 − 316 **20.** 526 − 417 **21.** 814 − 306

22. 537 − 68 **23.** 351 − 22 **24.** 444 − 35

Solve.

25. Barky Kennels has 518 dogs. Ruffo Kennels has 479 dogs. How many more dogs does Barky Kennels have?

26. The kennels sold 173 cats last year and 489 dogs. How many more dogs than cats were sold?

27. Barky Kennels has 518 dogs. 193 dogs are pure breeds. How many dogs are mixed breeds?

28. The owners of Ruffo Kennels bought 545 pounds of cat food last year. They used 349 pounds. How many pounds of cat food are left?

More Subtraction of 3-Digit Numbers

524 people visited a fair on Saturday and 396 on Sunday. How many more people visited the fair on Saturday?

To find how many more visited on Saturday, subtract: 524 − 396 = __?__

More ones are needed. Regroup. Subtract.	More tens are needed. Regroup. Subtract.	Subtract.
$\begin{array}{r} 1\ 14 \\ 5\ \cancel{2}\ \cancel{4} \\ -3\ 9\ 6 \\ \hline 8 \end{array}$	$\begin{array}{r} 11 \\ 4\ \cancel{1}\ 14 \\ 5\ \cancel{2}\ \cancel{4} \\ -3\ 9\ 6 \\ \hline 2\ 8 \end{array}$	$\begin{array}{r} 11 \\ 4\ \cancel{1}\ 14 \\ 5\ \cancel{2}\ \cancel{4} \\ -3\ 9\ 6 \\ \hline 1\ 2\ 8 \end{array}$
2 tens 4 ones = 1 ten 14 ones	5 hundreds 1 ten = 4 hundreds 11 tens	

128 more people visited the fair on Saturday.

$\begin{array}{r} 11 \\ 4\ \cancel{1}\ 14 \\ 5\ \cancel{2}\ \cancel{4} \\ -3\ 9\ 6 \\ \hline 1\ 2\ 8 \end{array}$

Check

$\begin{array}{r} 1\ 2\ 8 \\ +3\ 9\ 6 \\ \hline 5\ 2\ 4 \end{array}$

Regroup the tens and hundreds for subtraction.

1. 845 = 7 hundreds 14 tens __?__ ones

   = __?__ hundreds __?__ tens __?__ ones

2. 278 = 1 hundred 17 tens __?__ ones

   = __?__ hundreds __?__ tens __?__ ones

3. 612 = 5 hundreds __?__ tens __?__ ones

   = __?__ hundreds __?__ tens __?__ ones

Find the difference. Use the calculator to check your answers.

4.	521 −347	**5.**	825 −169	**6.**	278 −139	**7.**	612 −476	**8.**	517 −248
9.	279 −189	**10.**	423 −347	**11.**	456 −389	**12.**	991 −197	**13.**	273 −189
14.	621 −535	**15.**	743 −467	**16.**	805 −476	**17.**	927 −368	**18.**	706 −197

Arrange in columns. Subtract.

19. 671 − 295   **20.** 837 − 488   **21.** 347 − 168

22. 936 − 759   **23.** 291 − 197   **24.** 542 − 67

Solve.

25. In the past, the zoo had 213 animals. Now it has 178. How many fewer animals does the zoo now have?

26. The zookeeper used 592 pounds of meat to feed the animals on Monday. On Tuesday he used 781 pounds. How many more pounds of meat did the zookeeper use on Tuesday?

CHALLENGE

Find the missing digits.

27.	923 −14☐ 776	**28.**	629 −☐8☐ 441	**29.**	231 −☐☐☐ 85	**30.**	856 −4☐8 ☐6☐

Zero in Subtraction

Subtraction with zeros in the minuend often requires regrouping more than once before starting to subtract.

Subtract: 208 − 29 = __?__

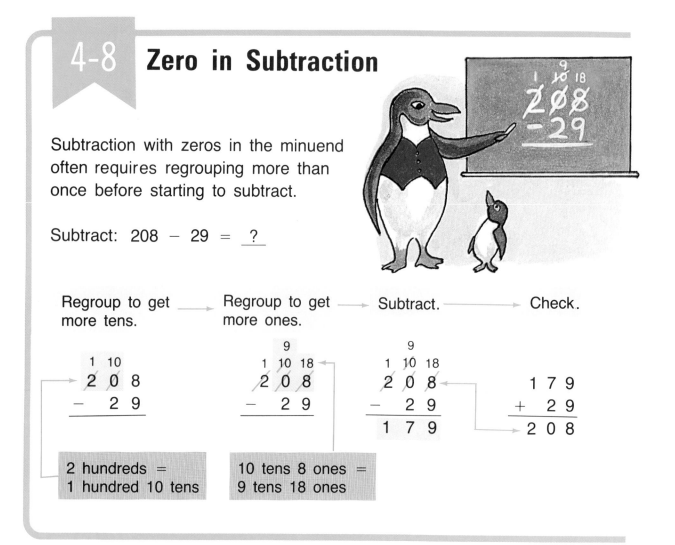

Regroup to get more tens. → Regroup to get more ones. → Subtract. → Check.

```
        1 10                9                    9
        2 0 8          1 10 18            1 10 18           1 7 9
      −   2 9            2 0 8              2 0 8          + 2 9
                       −   2 9            −   2 9            2 0 8
                                           1 7 9
```

2 hundreds =
1 hundred 10 tens

10 tens 8 ones =
9 tens 18 ones

Regroup hundreds and tens to subtract. (The first is done.)

1. 200 = 2 0 0 (with: 9 over, 1 10 10)

2. 500 = 5 0 0 (with: ?, 4 10 10)

3. 700 = 7 0 0 (with: ?, ? 10 ?)

4. 300 = 3 0 0 (with: ?, ? ? ?)

5. 900 = 9 0 0 (with: ?, ? ? ?)

6. 600 = 6 0 0 (with: ?, ? ? ?)

7. 806 = 8 0 6 (with: ?, ? ? 16)

8. 305 = 3 0 5 (with: ?, ? ? ?)

9. 508 = 5 0 8 (with: ?, ? ? ?)

Find the difference. (Use the calculator to check your answers.)

10.	500 −329	11.	600 −277	12.	407 −239	13.	806 −447	14.	205 −127

15.	800 −672	16.	900 −341	17.	400 −216	18.	700 −388	19.	200 −178

Arrange in columns. Subtract.

20. 600 − 428   21. 800 − 639   22. 700 − 485

23. 908 − 279   24. 706 − 98   25. 620 − 444

Solve.

26. 600 birds were in the old bird house. 423 birds were moved to the new bird house. How many birds were left in the old bird house?

27. Christopher jogged 200 miles in one month. Nicole jogged 178 miles in the same month. How many more miles did Christopher jog than Nicole?

28. Two planes flew from Los Angeles to New York. The RSA plane flew 605 miles an hour. The BBS plane flew 478 miles an hour. How much faster was the RSA plane than the BBS plane?

29. Find two 3-digit numbers that can be subtracted from each other and have a difference of 99.

Adding and Subtracting Larger Numbers

Study these examples. Add and subtract as usual.

Add: 5678 + 1234 = ___?___

$$\begin{array}{r} \overset{1\ \ 1}{5\ 6\ 7\ 8} \\ +\ 1\ 2\ 3\ 4 \\ \hline 6\ 9\ 1\ 2 \end{array}$$

Subtract: 8731 − 6542 = ___?___

$$\begin{array}{r} \overset{\overset{12}{6\ \ \ 2\ \ 11}}{8\ 7\ 3\ 1} \\ -\ 6\ 5\ 4\ 2 \\ \hline 2\ 1\ 8\ 9 \end{array}$$

Add: 6420 + 3981 + 463 = ___?___

$$\begin{array}{r} \overset{1\ \ 1}{6\ 4\ 2\ 0} \\ 3\ 9\ 8\ 1 \\ +\ \ \ 4\ 6\ 3 \\ \hline 1\ 0{,}8\ 6\ 4 \end{array}$$

Subtract: 9000 − 6788 = ___?___

$$\begin{array}{r} \overset{\overset{9\ \ \ 9}{8\ \ 10\ 10\ 10}}{9\ 0\ 0\ 0} \\ -\ 6\ 7\ 8\ 8 \\ \hline 2\ 2\ 1\ 2 \end{array}$$

Add or subtract. (Watch for + or −.)

1. $\begin{array}{r}2937\\+1426\end{array}$	2. $\begin{array}{r}2967\\+4828\end{array}$	3. $\begin{array}{r}5963\\+8279\end{array}$	4. $\begin{array}{r}6243\\+8079\end{array}$
5. $\begin{array}{r}4631\\-2087\end{array}$	6. $\begin{array}{r}5937\\-2649\end{array}$	7. $\begin{array}{r}8261\\-1494\end{array}$	8. $\begin{array}{r}6273\\-4099\end{array}$
9. $\begin{array}{r}6273\\+1592\end{array}$	10. $\begin{array}{r}3951\\-\ 997\end{array}$	11. $\begin{array}{r}4251\\-\ 879\end{array}$	12. $\begin{array}{r}6243\\-\ 975\end{array}$
13. $\begin{array}{r}3726\\+5192\end{array}$	14. $\begin{array}{r}3975\\+4632\end{array}$	15. $\begin{array}{r}6821\\+9429\end{array}$	16. $\begin{array}{r}7263\\+9904\end{array}$

Compute. (Use the calculator to check your answers.)

17. 3584 1592 + 437	**18.** 6420 3981 + 406	**19.** 8209 157 +7913	**20.** 267 5181 + 277
21. 3267 −1999	**22.** 8234 −2987	**23.** 5136 −4259	**24.** 8277 −1488
25. 627 5148 297 + 35	**26.** 8269 177 8243 + 625	**27.** 7091 8351 789 +2066	**28.** 4833 2160 497 +3003
29. 8000 −1962	**30.** 9000 −6788	**31.** 8003 −3667	**32.** 9050 −4789

Arrange in columns. Add or subtract.

33. 1863 + 2684 + 505 + 1326

34. 2010 + 300 + 1399 + 498

35. 5600 − 1592

36. 2090 − 1267

37. 956 − 667

38. 667 + 388

Complete the puzzles.

39.

40.

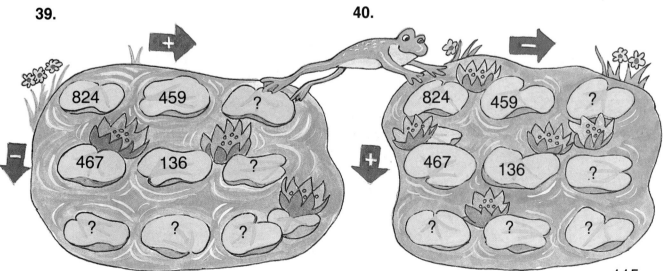

115

Estimating Sums

Estimate the sum: 562 + 388 = ?

To estimate the sum of two or more numbers:

- Round each addend to its greatest place-value position.
- Add the rounded numbers.

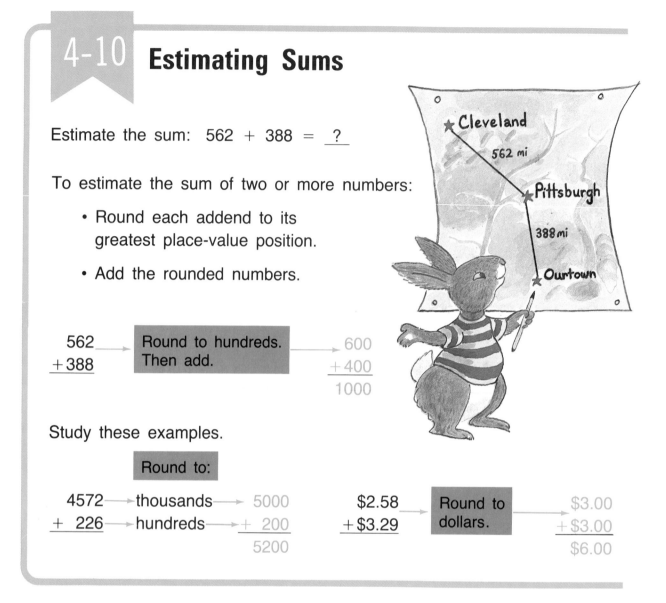

$$\begin{array}{r} 562 \\ +388 \end{array}$$ → Round to hundreds. Then add. → $$\begin{array}{r} 600 \\ +400 \\ \hline 1000 \end{array}$$

Study these examples.

Round to:

$$\begin{array}{r} 4572 \\ +\ 226 \end{array}$$ → thousands → hundreds → $$\begin{array}{r} 5000 \\ +\ 200 \\ \hline 5200 \end{array}$$

$$\begin{array}{r} \$2.58 \\ +\$3.29 \end{array}$$ → Round to dollars. → $$\begin{array}{r} \$3.00 \\ +\$3.00 \\ \hline \$6.00 \end{array}$$

Estimate each sum.

1. 46 + 73
2. 84 + 91
3. 67 + 38
4. 825 + 31
5. 656 + 124
6. 17 + 906
7. 827 + 763
8. 532 + 69
9. 260 + 577
10. 928 + 55
11. 637 + 862
12. 97 + 366
13. $5.62 + $3.98
14. $4.52 + $2.75
15. $8.27 + $7.63
16. $3.88 + $12.16
17. $72.79 + $8.62
18. $26.56 + $12.90

Estimating Differences

Estimate the difference: 623 − 372 = _?_

To estimate the difference of two numbers:

- Round each number to its greatest place-value position.

- Subtract the rounded numbers.

623   Round to hundreds.   600
−372   Then subtract.   −400
                                 200

Study these examples.

Round to:

813 ──→ hundreds ──→ 800 $9.25   Round to $9.00
− 85 ──→ tens ──→ − 90   −$4.98   dollars.   −$5.00
                    710                              $4.00

Estimate each difference.

1. 78 − 34

2. 659 − 394

3. 849 − 673

4. 555 − 230

5. 671 − 405

6. 813 − 490

7. 9204 − 3510

8. 7508 − 2170

9. 4910 − 2806

10. $5.16 − $3.25

11. $2.98 − $1.56

12. $18.46 − $7.92

13. $12.07 − $6.77

14. $24.36 − $12.15

15. $1.74 − $ .59

16. $10.94 − $8.96

17. $20.47 − $9.58

18. $19.95 − $10.99

Problem Solving: Using Estimation

Problem: Megan is saving to buy a tennis racket for $30. She has made deposits of $14.90, $4.78, $6.30, and $8.17. Estimate whether Megan has saved enough.

Needs	Saved (Deposits)
$30.00	$14.90
	4.78
	6.30
	8.17
Total	$?

1 IMAGINE

Draw a picture of how much Megan needs, and how much she has saved.

2 NAME

Facts: $30.00   needed

$14.90, $4.78, } deposits
$6.30, $8.17

Question: Does Megan have enough money?

3 THINK

Look at the picture.
You need to add the money Megan has saved to see if the sum is equal to or more than $30.
Estimate the sum.

4 COMPUTE

$14.90	⟶	Round to dollars. Then add.	⟶	$15.00
4.78			⟶	5.00
6.30			⟶	6.00
+ 8.17			⟶	+ 8.00
				$34.00

Megan has about $34. She has saved enough.

5 CHECK

Find the exact sum:
$14.90 + $4.78 + $6.30 + $8.17 = $34.15
The estimate, $34, is close to the exact sum.

Solve using estimation.

1. 4325 people in Somerville have pets.
2681 of these people have dogs. About how many people in Somerville have pets that are *not* dogs?

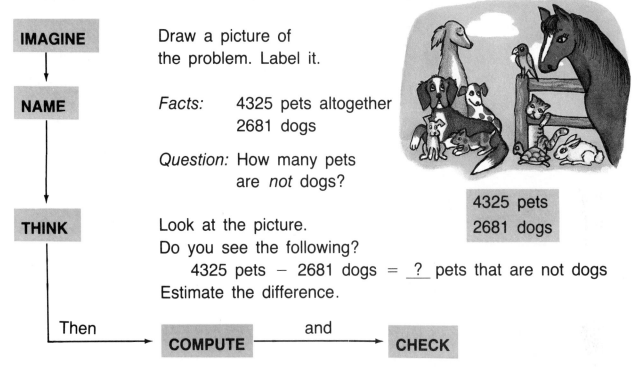

IMAGINE	Draw a picture of the problem. Label it.
NAME	*Facts:* 4325 pets altogether 2681 dogs *Question:* How many pets are *not* dogs?
THINK	Look at the picture. Do you see the following? 4325 pets − 2681 dogs = _?_ pets that are not dogs Estimate the difference.

4325 pets
2681 dogs

Then ——→ **COMPUTE** —— and ——→ **CHECK**

2. A Brite light bulb lasted for 4320 hours. A Superlight bulb lasted for 2942 hours. About how much longer did the Brite light bulb last?

3. Adam paid $27.83 for a new dog house for Frisky. He also paid $2.98 for a new collar and $3.57 for a new leash. His father had given him $30.00 to pay the bill. Estimate if Adam had enough money.

4. One horse weighed 3976 pounds. Another weighed 2835 pounds. Estimate the difference in their weights.

More Practice

Rename.

1. 13 = _?_ ten _?_ ones   **2.** 45 = _?_ tens _?_ ones

3. 32 = _?_ tens _?_ ones   **4.** 78 = _?_ tens _?_ ones

Regroup.

5. 4 tens 17 ones = _?_ tens _?_ ones

6. 6 tens 11 ones = _?_ tens _?_ ones

Add.

7. 55 + 19   **8.** 58 + 34   **9.** 476 + 438   **10.** 3172 + 3959

11.	**12.**	**13.**	**14.**	**15.**
346	340	176	459	227
928	129	83	209	482
+453	+232	+ 58	+1386	+1097

Subtract.

16. 42 − 15   **17.** 831 − 457   **18.** 715 − 159

19. 5361 − 1769   **20.** 700 − 179   **21.** 304 − 128

Estimate the sum or difference.

22. 1219 + 3708   **23.** $41.08 − $17.92

Solve.

24. A bag of fruit bars has 38 sweet fruit bars and 44 sour fruit bars. How many fruit bars are there in all?

(See *Still More Practice*, p. 360.)

Math Probe

NUMBER CODES

Complete each exercise.
Use the code to find the answer to the riddle.

WHAT IS "OLD" BUT CAN BE NEW
AND ALWAYS KEEPS UP WITH TIME?

Write the letter for each exercise on the
line above the correct answers, which
are shown below.

Exercises

A	7583	C	5269	D	4678
	− 7496		− 1376		+ 1532

E	4592	F	8000	G	1423
	− 3684		− 7891		+ 7890

H	5007	K	6081	L	5894
	− 2871		− 6058		+ 1278

O	2583	R	86	T	1334
	1119		24		567
	+ 367		+ 45		+ 1089

Answer

				N							
87	9313	155	87		6210	109	87	2990	2136	908	155

3893	7172	4069	3893	23

121

Check Your Mastery

Rename.

See pp. 100.

1. 82 = _?_ tens _?_ ones

2. 74 = _?_ tens _?_ ones

Regroup.

See pp. 100.

3. 4 tens 13 ones = _?_ tens _?_ ones

4. 6 tens 14 ones = _?_ tens _?_ ones

Add or Subtract.

See pp. 101-115.

5. 38 + 47

6. 324 + 579

7. 381 + 275

8. 2018 + 287

9. 52 − 19

10. 324 − 165

11. 269 − 147

12. 8004 − 4879

13.
$$423 + 534$$

14.
$$795 + 432$$

15.
$$2685 + 1319$$

16.
$$1378 + 702$$

17.
$$6925 - 3205$$

18.
$$545 - 375$$

19.
$$1485 - 598$$

20.
$$2195 - 1650$$

Estimate the sum or difference.

See pp. 116-117.

21.
$$1728 + 2342$$

22.
$$\$26.43 - 7.14$$

23.
$$\$4.83 + 2.17$$

Solve.

See pp. 104-105, 108-109.

24. A book has 231 pages. Anne has read 125 pages. How many more pages does she have to read?

25. The postman delivered 176 letters, 24 postcards, and 189 packages on Monday. How many pieces of mail in all did he deliver?

Cumulative Test I

Choose the correct answer.

1. The place value of the underlined digit in the number 2,3<u>4</u>5,798 is:
   a. hundreds   **b.** thousands   **c.** ten thousands   **d.** millions

2. The standard numeral for two hundred million, one thousand, forty-seven is:
   a. 201,000,047   **b.** 200,001,047   **c.** 201,047   **d.** 200,000,147

3. The standard numeral for thirty thousand, two hundred six is:
   a. 30,206   **b.** 300,206   **c.** 30,026   **d.** 30,000,205

4. When you round 763 to the nearest hundred, the answer is:
   a. 700   **b.** 800   **c.** 760   **d.** 770

5. When you round 87,923 to the nearest thousand, the answer is:
   a. 80,000   **b.** 90,000   **c.** 88,000   **d.** 87,000

6. The Roman numeral for 253 is:
   a. CCVIII   **b.** CCVII   **c.** CCLIV   **d.** CCLIII

7. The even numbers between 8 and 14 are:
   a. 10, 12   **b.** 8, 10, 12, 14   **c.** 9, 11, 13   **d.** 9, 10, 12

8. Which statement is true?
   a. $8207 > 8270$ **b.** $4391 < 4319$ **c.** $878 > 880$ **d.** $5386 > 5287$

9. The estimated sum of 385 and 425 is:
   a. 700   **b.** 800   **c.** 900   **d.** 1000

10. The estimated difference of 58 and 37 is:
    a. 10   **b.** 20   **c.** 30   **d.** 40

Add or subtract.

11.	45 +32	12.	95 +63	13.	731 +260	14.	882 +317	15.	7070 +2121
16.	38 +26	17.	468 +175	18.	$47.92 + 38.14	19.	53 −21	20.	83 −30
21.	987 −760	22.	8653 −3221	23.	91 −56	24.	709 −346	25.	634 −275
26.	980 −382	27.	400 −234	28.	780 −392	29.	$37.04 − 17.82	30.	$60.00 − 19.79

Find the missing addend or missing factor.

31. $5 + \underline{\ ?\ } = 13$ **32.** $6 \times \underline{\ ?\ } = 0$ **33.** $\underline{\ ?\ } \times 9 = 63$

Compute.

34. $12 + 43 + 20 + 73$ **35.** $230 + 421 + 246$

36. $2016 + 3520 + 3241$ **37.** $7660 + 115 + 8301 + 22$

38. $871 - 424$ **39.** $6985 - 2841$

40. $765 + 555 + 643$ **41.** $\$37.16 + \$8.60 + \$15.18$

Multiply.

42. $\begin{array}{r} 4 \\ \times 2 \\ \hline \end{array}$ **43.** $\begin{array}{r} 3 \\ \times 7 \\ \hline \end{array}$ **44.** $\begin{array}{r} 5 \\ \times 5 \\ \hline \end{array}$ **45.** $\begin{array}{r} 2 \\ \times 8 \\ \hline \end{array}$ **46.** $\begin{array}{r} 6 \\ \times 3 \\ \hline \end{array}$ **47.** $\begin{array}{r} 9 \\ \times 6 \\ \hline \end{array}$

48. $\begin{array}{r} 1 \\ \times 7 \\ \hline \end{array}$ **49.** $\begin{array}{r} 8 \\ \times 9 \\ \hline \end{array}$ **50.** $\begin{array}{r} 3 \\ \times 0 \\ \hline \end{array}$ **51.** $\begin{array}{r} 9 \\ \times 4 \\ \hline \end{array}$ **52.** $\begin{array}{r} 4 \\ \times 6 \\ \hline \end{array}$ **53.** $\begin{array}{r} 8 \\ \times 1 \\ \hline \end{array}$

Divide.

54. $12 \div 2$ **55.** $16 \div 4$ **56.** $49 \div 7$ **57.** $28 \div 4$ **58.** $12 \div 6$ **59.** $9 \div 9$

60. $7\overline{)21}$ **61.** $3\overline{)24}$ **62.** $9\overline{)45}$ **63.** $7\overline{)0}$ **64.** $8\overline{)72}$ **65.** $5\overline{)40}$

Solve.

66. In a bicycle race, Ernie rested after 6 miles, and then continued for 8 more miles. How far did he race?

67. The final score of the All-Star baseball game was 20-13. What was the difference in the number of runs?

68. School pennants are sold in 3 sizes. How many pennants were sold on Monday if 8 of each size were sold?

69. On Field Day, 63 boys were divided into 7 equal teams. How many boys were on each team?

70. Cal delivers 24 newspapers on Elm Street and 29 newspapers on Oak Street. How many papers does he deliver in all?

71. Bob squeezes 5 oranges for each glass of juice. How many glasses will he have if he squeezes 35 oranges?

72. Of 3424 books in a school library, 487 are fiction. How many are nonfiction?

73. 8 stamps fit on each page of a stamp collection. How many stamps fit on 9 pages?

74. Carlos bought 2 records for $7.98 and $5.98. What was the total cost?

75. An airplane rose from 2850 ft to 4175 ft above sea level. How far did the plane rise?

5

Measurement

In this unit you will:

- Use metric and customary units for length, capacity, and mass
- Estimate and measure lengths to the nearest centimeter
- Change units of measure (metric or customary)
- Read a thermometer and record temperatures (degrees Celsius)
- Estimate and measure lengths to the nearest inch
- Read dial and digital clocks and record times
- Determine the value of money using bills and coins
- Solve problems using time

Do you remember?

The standard metric units are:

meter: to measure length

liter: to measure capacity

gram: to measure weight

Metric Measurement

The Kane family spent their summer vacation in Europe. They learned how Europeans measured things using the **metric system**.

The metric system uses these basic units for measuring:

> **meter:** (m) to measure length
>
> **gram:** (g) to measure weight
>
> **liter:** (L) to measure capacity

Which metric unit—m, g, or L—is used to measure each?

1. the meat needed to make meatballs

2. the milk to put in a baby's bottle

3. the weight of a book

4. the height of a building

5. the juice left in a pitcher

6. the contents of a bag of sugar

7. the distance you can throw a ball

8. the gas needed to fill a car

9. the milk needed for pancake batter

10. the string needed for your kite

11. the thickness of a nickel

12. the weight of a football

Which metric unit—m, g, or L—is used to measure each?

13. 14. 15. 16.

17. 18. 19. 20.

Prefixes Tell How Large or How Small

Prefix	Symbol	Meaning			
1 **kilo**-	(k)	=	1000 units	1 **kilo**gram (kg) =	1000 grams
100 **centi**-	(c)	=	1 unit	100 **centi**meters (cm) =	1 meter
1000 **milli**-	(m)	=	1 unit	1000 **milli**liters (mL) =	1 liter

Write these measures in words.

21. 18 m	**22.** 23 cm	**23.** 68 km	**24.** 83 km
25. 27 cm	**26.** 114 g	**27.** 5 L	**28.** 41 mg
29. 75 km	**30.** 9 g	**31.** 3 kg	**32.** 78 cm
33. 125 m	**34.** 32 L	**35.** 48 cm	**36.** 11 kg
37. 184 mL	**38.** 14 m	**39.** 95 kg	**40.** 250 mL
41. 2 m	**42.** 3 km	**43.** 14 m	**44.** 4 kg
45. 36 m	**46.** 250 L	**47.** 14 L	**48.** 19 km
49. 4 L	**50.** 200 g	**51.** 200 cm	**52.** 9 mL

127

Centimeter

Small lengths and distances are measured by a metric unit called a **centimeter (cm).**

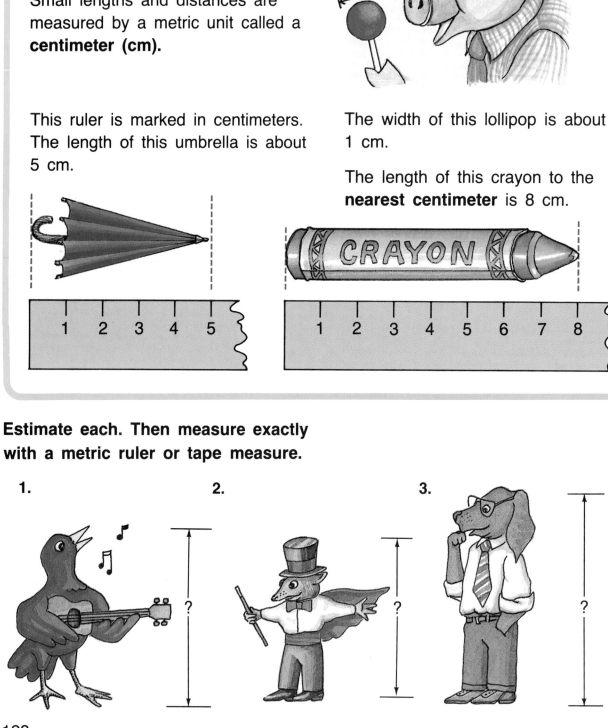

This ruler is marked in centimeters. The length of this umbrella is about 5 cm.

The width of this lollipop is about 1 cm.

The length of this crayon to the **nearest centimeter** is 8 cm.

1	2	3	4	5

1	2	3	4	5	6	7	8

Estimate each. Then measure exactly with a metric ruler or tape measure.

1.   2.   3.

?   ?   ?

Measure each picture to the nearest centimeter.

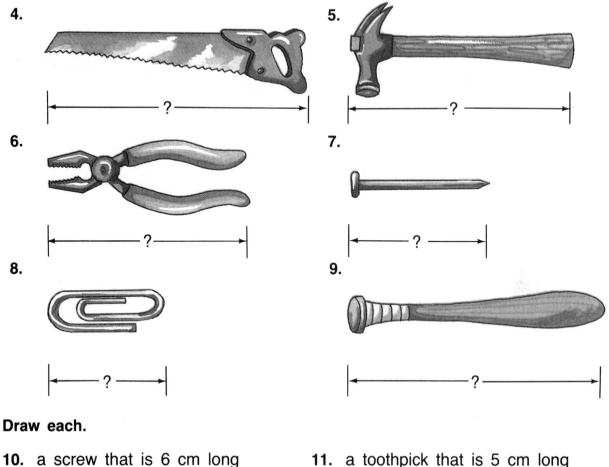

4. ?

5. ?

6. ?

7. ?

8. ?

9. ?

Draw each.

10. a screw that is 6 cm long

11. a toothpick that is 5 cm long

12. a ball whose width is 4 cm

13. a can whose height is 9 cm

14. a line that is 7 cm long

15. a nail that is 7 cm long

16. a bottle cap whose width is 2 cm

17. a thumb that is 6 cm long

Estimate each. Then measure to the nearest centimeter with a metric ruler or tape measure.

18. the length of your shoe

19. the length of your pencil

20. the width of your hand

21. the length of a dollar bill

22. the length of this book

23. the width of this book

24. the length of your thumb

25. the height of your desk

Meter and Kilometer

Another metric unit used to measure length or distance is the **meter** (m).

The height of the fence is about 1 m.

The metric unit for measuring long distances is the **kilometer** (km).

The distance from New York to Los Angeles is about 3900 km.

To change one unit to another, use the relations between metric units.

100 centimeters (cm) = 1 meter (m)	1000 meters = 1 kilometer (km)

- To change larger units into smaller ones, *multiply.*

25 m = __?__ cm   2 km = __?__ m

Think: 1 m = 100 cm	Think: 1 km = 1000 m

25 m = (25 × 100) cm   2 km = (2 × 1000) m
25 m = 2500 cm   2 km = 2000 m

- To change smaller units into larger ones, *divide.*

4000 m = __?__ km   500 cm = __?__ m

Think: 1000 m = 1 km	Think: 100 cm = 1 m

4000 m = (4000 ÷ 1000) km   500 cm = (500 ÷ 100) m
4000 m = 4 km   500 cm = 5 m

Write the best estimate of length for:

1. the distance between cities   **a.** meter   **b.** centimeter   **c.** kilometer

2. the width of a cup   **a.** meter   **b.** centimeter   **c.** kilometer

3. the length of a cane   **a.** meter   **b.** centimeter   **c.** kilometer

4. the length of a crayon   **a.** meter   **b.** centimeter   **c.** kilometer

5. the height of a door   **a.** meter   **b.** centimeter   **c.** kilometer

6. the width of a coin   **a.** meter   **b.** centimeter   **c.** kilometer

Complete

7. 2 km = _?_ m   **8.** 8 m = _?_ cm   **9.** 8000 m = _?_ km

10. 200 cm = _?_ m   **11.** 8 km = _?_ m   **12.** 2000 cm = _?_ m

Compare. Write <, =, or >.

13. 1 m _?_ 10 cm   **14.** 1 m _?_ 1000 cm   **15.** 30 cm _?_ 3m

16. 200 cm _?_ 2 m   **17.** 17 m _?_ 170 cm   **18.** 9000 m _?_ 8 km

19. 1000 m _?_ 1 km   **20.** 860 cm _?_ 9 m   **21.** 350 cm _?_ 3 m

Solve.

22. Joe swam 374 m during practice. Jan swam 389 m. How much farther did Jan swim?

23. Stu ran the 1200 m race and Jim ran the 1 km race. Who ran the longer distance?

24. Mrs. Waters placed twelve coins next to each other in a row. If each coin was 2 cm wide, how long were the coins?

Liters and Milliliters

The **liter** (L) is the unit used to measure liquid capacity.

Containers which hold 1 liter come in various shapes.

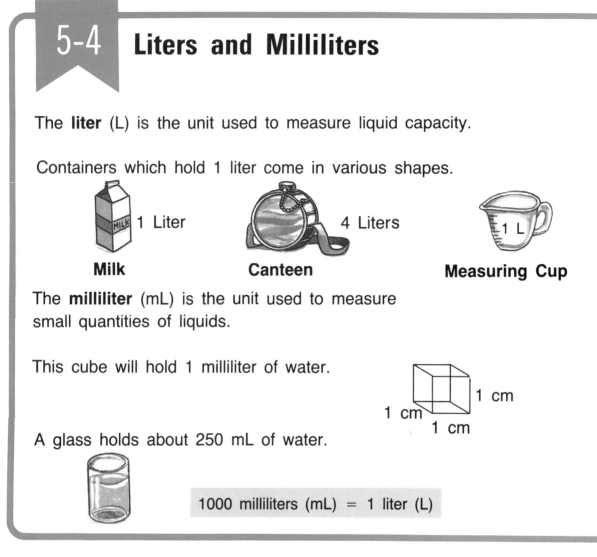

1 Liter
Milk

4 Liters
Canteen

1 L
Measuring Cup

The **milliliter** (mL) is the unit used to measure small quantities of liquids.

This cube will hold 1 milliliter of water.

1 cm
1 cm
1 cm

A glass holds about 250 mL of water.

1000 milliliters (mL) = 1 liter (L)

Choose the most reasonable measurement.

1.

1 mL or 1 L?

2.

48 mL or 48 L?

3.

250 mL or 250L?

4.

5 mL or 5L?

5.

20 mL or 20L?

6.

400 mL or 400 L?

Complete

	mL	L
7.	4000	?
8.	?	1
9.	9000	?

	mL	L
10.	?	5
11.	2000	?
12.	?	7

Arrange in order from least to greatest.

13. 4 L, 40 mL, 400 mL, 4 mL

14. 200 L, 20 mL, 20 L, 2 mL

15. 38 L, 380 mL, 380 L, 138 L

16. 24 L, 2400 mL, 240 mL, 240 L

Compare. Write <, =, or >.

17. 2000 mL _?_ 2 L

18. 2 L _?_ 1900 mL

19. 1100 mL _?_ L

20. 900 mL _?_ 1 L

21. 3 L _?_ 3500 mL

22. 4 L _?_ 4000 mL

Solve.

23. Mr. Woods filled the camper's gasoline tank before leaving. If the camper uses one liter of gasoline every 4 km, how much gas will be used when the camper has traveled 48 km?

24. Each drinking cup holds 200 mL of water. If each of the 5 people in the Woods family has one cupful, how much water is needed?

25. The water tank of the camper holds 150 L of water. If 114 L have been used, how much is left?

26. A glass holds 250 mL of water. If 24 glasses are filled, how many liters of water are needed?

133

5-5 Grams and Kilograms

The **gram** (g) is a unit used to measure weight.

Both a paper clip and a milliliter of water weigh about 1 g.

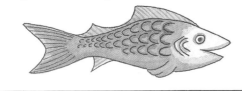

A **kilogram** (kg) is a unit used to measure heavy objects.

A large fish weighs about 10 kg.

Choose the most reasonable measurement.

1.

1000 g or 1000 kg?

2.

4 g or 4 kg?

3.

30 g or 30 kg?

4.

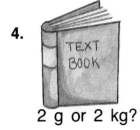

2 g or 2 kg?

5.

5 g or 5 kg?

6.

2 g or 2 kg?

Complete.

	g	kg
7.	1000	?
8.	?	2
9.	3000	?

	g	kg
10.	4000	?
11.	?	5
12.	?	6

Compare. Write $<$, $=$, or $>$.

13. 90 g _?_ 9 kg

14. 6 kg _?_ 5842 g

15. 7310 g _?_ 7 kg

16. 5000 g _?_ 5 kg

17. 200 g _?_ 1 kg

18. 40 kg _?_ 4811 g

Arrange in order from least to greatest.

19. 4 g, 40 mg, 400 mg, 4 mg

20. 20 g, 2 kg, 200 g, 20 kg

21. 380 g, 380 kg, 38 kg, 38 g

22. 2400 g, 240 kg, 24 kg, 240 g

Solve.

23. A sandwich has 150 g of meat. How much meat will 20 sandwiches have?

24. A penny weighs about 3 g. How much will a roll of 50 pennies weigh?

25. A ten-year old weighs about 40 kg. Is this weight more or less than 44 000 g? What is the difference?

26. A large fish weighs about 10 kg. How many kilograms will 12 large fish weigh?

27. A carton of sneakers weighs 48 kg. 24 pairs of sneakers are packed in a carton. What is the weight of one sneaker?

Celsius Temperature

The **degree Celsius (°C)** is a metric unit used to measure temperature. The symbol for Celsius is "C." The symbol for degrees is "°."

The number of degrees on a thermometer shows how hot or cold the weather is.

These thermometers show some common temperatures as measured in degrees Celsius.

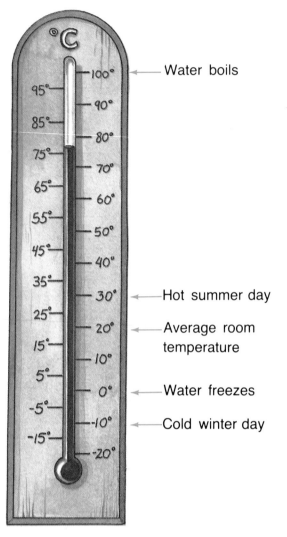

Water boils

Hot summer day

Average room temperature

Water freezes

Cold winter day

Choose the most reasonable measurement for each.

1. hot chocolate   **a.** 10 °C   **b.** 20 °C   **c.** 80 °C   **d.** 130 °C

2. ice skating   **a.** 30 °C   **b.** −10 °C   **c.** 40 °C   **d.** 60 °C

3. July 4th   **a.** 10 °C   **b.** −20 °C   **c.** 30 °C   **d.** 60 °C

4. baking a cake   **a.** 175 °C   **b.** −5 °C   **c.** 30 °C   **d.** 40 °C

5. swimming   **a.** 40 °C   **b.** 70 °C   **c.** 90 °C   **d.** 110 °C

Write "R" if the statement is *reasonable*.
Write "U" if it is *unreasonable*.

6. Bob will be unable to build a snowman at 36°C.

7. "I like to go swimming when the temperature reaches 39°C," Carol said.

8. At 43°C, the air conditioner is turned on.

9. We go ice skating when the temperature hits 14°C.

10. A heavy coat and gloves are needed when the thermometer reads 31°C.

Complete.

11.

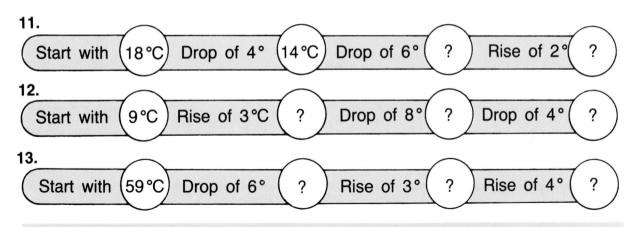

Start with (18°C) Drop of 4° (14°C) Drop of 6° (?) Rise of 2° (?)

12.

Start with (9°C) Rise of 3°C (?) Drop of 8° (?) Drop of 4° (?)

13.

Start with (59°C) Drop of 6° (?) Rise of 3° (?) Rise of 4° (?)

CHALLENGE

Use your Celsius thermometer to measure the temperature of:

14. a glass of tap water.

15. a glass of ice water.

16. the outdoors in the sun.

17. the outdoors in the shade.

18. the outdoors after the sun has set.

Customary Measurement

The guide told the group that the Washington Monument is 555 *feet* 5 *inches* tall. Gail explained to Maria that feet and inches are **customary measures** used in the United States.

The customary system uses these basic units for measuring.

Length	Weight	Capacity
inch (in.)	ounce (oz)	cup (c)
foot (ft)	pound (lb)	pint (pt)
yard (yd)		quart (qt)
mile (mi)		gallon (gal)

Which customary unit—in., yd, mi, oz, lb, pt, gal—is used to measure each?

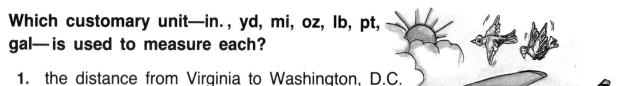

1. the distance from Virginia to Washington, D.C.
2. a walk around the block
3. the weight of a hamburger
4. a glass of milk
5. the weight of a panda
6. the length of a small bird
7. a large quantity of water

Complete. Use in., ft, lb, c, or gal.

8. The length of a fence is 150 _?_ long.

9. The weight of a person is 104 _?_ .

10. The length of a newborn infant is about 24 _?_ .

11. A _?_ of water is the approximate capacity of a pail.

12. Each girl had a _?_ of milk.

Which customary unit—in., yd, mi, oz, lb, pt, gal— is used to measure each?

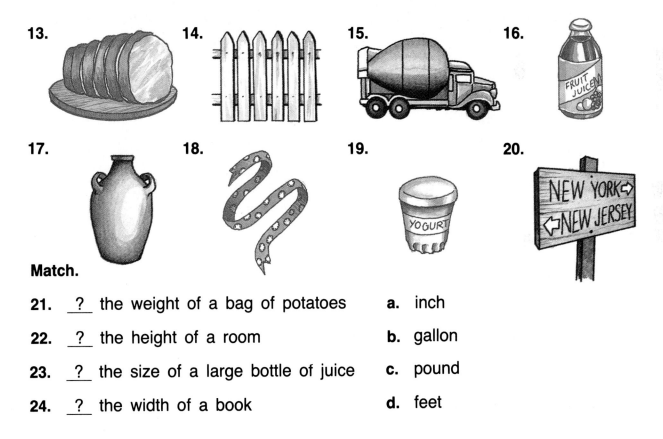

13.　　　14.　　　15.　　　16.

17.　　　18.　　　19.　　　20.

Match.

21. _?_ the weight of a bag of potatoes   **a.** inch

22. _?_ the height of a room   **b.** gallon

23. _?_ the size of a large bottle of juice   **c.** pound

24. _?_ the width of a book   **d.** feet

Solve.

25. By air, the distance from Chicago to Montreal is 745 mi and from Chicago to New York is 714 mi. How many miles less is it from Chicago to New York?

5-8 Customary Measures of Length

The **inch** (in.), the **foot** (ft), the **yard** (yd), and the **mile** (mi) are the customary units of length in the United States.

The width of this quarter is about 1 inch.

├─1 in.─┤

The length of a bed is about 7 ft.

A football field is 100 yd long.

inches 2

The distance from Atlanta to Dallas is about 820 mi.

Use the chart on the right to change one unit to another.

12 inches (in.) = 1 foot (ft)
3 feet (ft) = 1 yard (yd)
5280 feet (ft) = 1 mile (mi)
1760 yards (yd) = 1 mile (mi)

To change larger units into smaller ones, *multiply*

6 ft = _?_ in.

Think: 1 ft = 12 in.

6 ft = (6 × 12) in.
6 ft = 72 in.

To change smaller units into larger ones, *divide*.

12 ft = _?_ yd

Think: 3 ft = 1 yd

12 ft = (12 ÷ 3) yd
12 ft = 4 yd

Study these examples.

```
  4 ft   6 in.
+ 5 ft   9 in.
  9 ft  15 in.  =  10 ft. 3 in.
```
          ↑
15 in. = 1 ft 3 in.

```
  10 yd 2 ft
−  6 yd 1 ft
   4 yd 1 ft
```

Which customary unit—in., ft, yd, or mi—is used to measure each?

1. the length of a nail
2. a marathon distance
3. the height of a roof
4. the width of a paint brush
5. the height of a door
6. the length of a paper clip
7. the width of a tennis court
8. the height of a desk
9. the distance from New York to Mexico City
10. the width of a bottle cap

Complete.

11. 4 ft = __?__ in.
12. 2 yd = __?__ ft
13. 9 ft = __?__ yd
14. 24 in. = __?__ ft
15. 6 yd = __?__ ft
16. 36 in. = __?__ ft
17. 7 yd = __?__ ft
18. 6 ft = __?__ in.
19. 15 ft = __?__ yd

Add.

20. 3 ft 2 in.
    +5 ft 6 in.

21. 4 ft 7 in.
    +3 ft 9 in.

22. 8 yd 2 ft
    +7 yd 1 ft

Subtract

23. 8 ft 11 in.
    −2 ft 5 in.

24. 3 yd 2 ft
    −1 yd 1 ft

25. 12 ft 6 in.
    − 3 ft 3 in.

Solve.

26. Mrs. Long needs 3 yd of fabric for each curtain. She needs 4 curtains. How many yards in all will she need?

27. Dean painted 16 ft of fence. If the fence is 28 ft long, how many more feet must Dean paint?

5-9 Customary Measures of Capacity

The **cup** (c), the **pint** (pt), the **quart** (qt), and the **gallon** (gal) are the customary units used to measure liquid capacity.

2 cups = 1 pint   2 pints = 1 quart   4 quarts = 1 gallon

1 can of soup will fill 1 c.

Milk is usually sold in 1 pt and 1 qt containers.

Larger quantities of milk are sold in 1 gal bottles.

Which customary unit—c, pt, qt, gal—is used to measure each?

1.

2.

3.

4.

5.

6.

Match.

7. _?_ 8 c   **a.** 2 gal

8. _?_ 10 pt   **b.** 3 pt

9. _?_ 3 gal   **c.** 5 qt

10. _?_ 2 pt   **d.** 4 pt

11. _?_ 6 c   **e.** 12 qt

12. _?_ 8 qt   **f.** 4 c

Complete.

13. 2 pt = _?_ c   14. 5 qt = _?_ pt   15. 7 gal = _?_ qt

16. 8 c = _?_ pt   17. 2 gal = _?_ qt   18. 16 qt = _?_ gal

19. 5 pt = _?_ c   20. 8 pt = _?_ qt   21. 12 c = _?_ pt

22. 11 qt = _?_ pt   23. 16 pt = _?_ gal   24. 2 gal = _?_ qt

Compare. Write <, =, or >.

25. 5 qt _?_ 2 gal   26. 4 c _?_ 4 pt   27. 4 pt _?_ 2 qt

28. 3 gal _?_ 10 qt   29. 3 pt _?_ 6 c   30. 1 gal _?_ 7 qt

31. 6 qt _?_ 13 pt   32. 3 qt _?_ 1 gal   33. 7 c _?_ 3 pt

Solve.

34. If a car can travel for 30 miles on one gallon of gasoline, how far can it travel on 4 gallons?

35. If Tommy's pail holds 2 qt of water, how many gallons of water did he use if he filled it 6 times?

Customary Measures of Weight

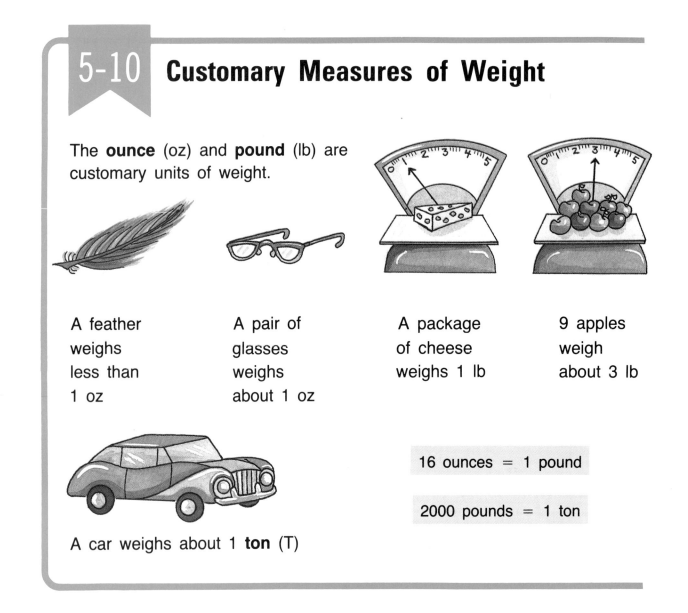

The **ounce** (oz) and **pound** (lb) are customary units of weight.

A feather weighs less than 1 oz

A pair of glasses weighs about 1 oz

A package of cheese weighs 1 lb

9 apples weigh about 3 lb

A car weighs about 1 **ton** (T)

16 ounces = 1 pound

2000 pounds = 1 ton

Which customary unit—oz, lb, T—is used to measure each?

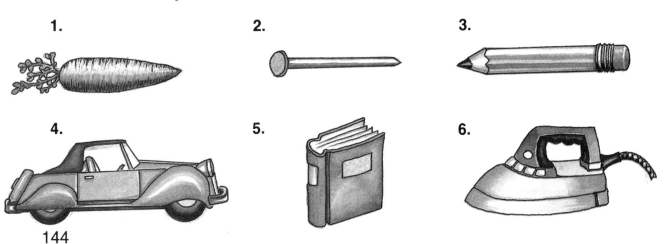

1.

2.

3.

4.

5.

6.

Which customary unit—oz, lb, T—would you use to measure the weight of each?

7. a dictionary   **8.** a pencil

9. a cat   **10.** one apple

11. an eraser   **12.** a flower

13. a moving van   **14.** a chair

Match. Choose the best unit to measure each.

15. _?_ a box of cereal   **a.** gallons

16. _?_ length of a pencil   **b.** miles

17. _?_ water in a bath tub   **c.** cups

18. _?_ distance from NY to Boston   **d.** ounces

19. _?_ a glass of water   **e.** pounds

20. _?_ weight of a person   **f.** inches

Solve.

21. If there are 4 oz in each stick of butter, how many sticks are needed to make 1 lb?

22. Mrs. Rhodes gave each of her 5 children a plum that weighed 4 oz. What was the total weight of the plums?

CHALLENGE

Complete.

23. 20 oz = _?_ lb _?_ oz

24. 13,500 lb = _?_ T _?_ lb

145

Time

The **digital** clock and the **dial** clock show 3:50. The time is read as minutes **past** the hour or as minutes **to** the next hour.

| 50 minutes **past** 3 | 10 minutes **to** 4 |

There are 60 minutes in one hour. The minute hand goes around the clock *once* in one hour.

There are 24 hours in one day. The hour hand goes around the clock *twice* in one day

| 12:00 MIDNIGHT | 10:00 A.M. | 12:00 NOON | 3:00 P.M. | 12:00 MIDNIGHT |

A.M. is used for times after 12:00 midnight and before 12:00 noon.

P.M. is used for times after 12:00 Noon and before 12:00 midnight.

Complete. Use A.M. or P.M.

1. Bill is eating his breakfast at 7 _?_ .

2. Lunch is served at 1 _?_ .

3. The boys come home from school at 3 _?_ .

4. Mrs. Day is preparing supper at 5 _?_ .

5. The alarm rings to wake us at 6 _?_ .

Write each time.

6.

7.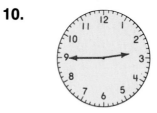

8.

9.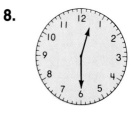

10.

11.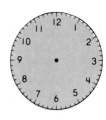

Match the times.

12. __?__ 35 minutes past 11

13. __?__ 15 minutes to 7

14. __?__ 5 minutes past 4

15. __?__ 5 minutes to 10

16. __?__ 12 midnight

17. __?__ 30 minutes past 4

18. __?__ 25 minutes past 1

19. __?__ 40 minutes past 8

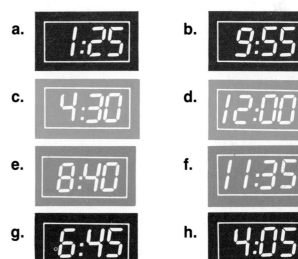

a. **1:25**

b. **9:55**

c. **4:30**

d. **12:00**

e. **8:40**

f. **11:35**

g. **6:45**

h. **4:05**

Copy. Then draw the hands of the clock to indicate the time.

20.

20 minutes past 1

21.

25 minutes to 6

22.

14 minutes past 11

147

Money

Bills

| twenty-dollar bill | ten-dollar bill | five-dollar bill | one-dollar bill |

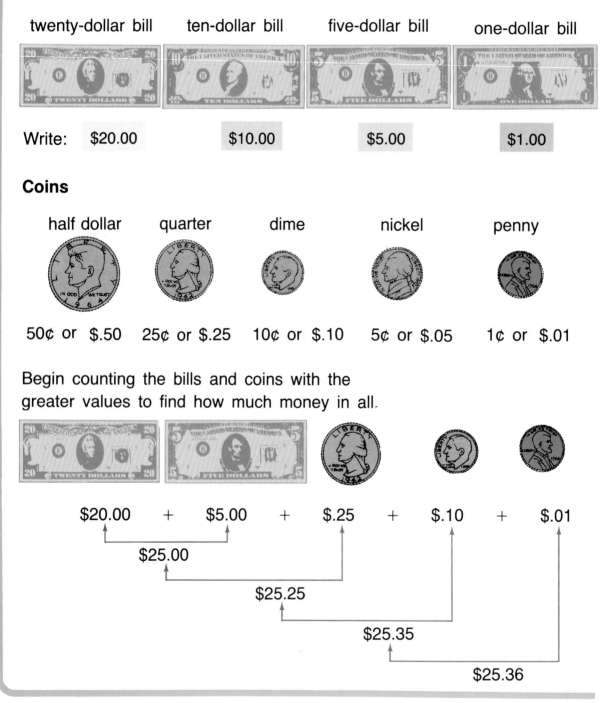

Write: $20.00 $10.00 $5.00 $1.00

Coins

| half dollar | quarter | dime | nickel | penny |

50¢ or $.50   25¢ or $.25   10¢ or $.10   5¢ or $.05   1¢ or $.01

Begin counting the bills and coins with the greater values to find how much money in all.

$20.00 + $5.00 + $.25 + $.10 + $.01

$25.00

$25.25

$25.35

$25.36

Write the amount of money for each using the dollar sign.

1.

2.

3.

4.

5.

6.

7. 1 dollar, 1 half dollar, 3 dimes, 1 nickel

8. 2 quarters, 6 dimes, 4 nickels, 8 pennies

9. 1 five-dollar bill, 3 quarters, 1 dime, 3 nickels, 2 pennies

10. 4 dollars, 1 quarter, 2 nickels

Complete.

	$10 bill	$5 bill	$1 bill	$.50	$.25	$.10	$.05	$.01	Total
11.	1	0	4	1	2	1	0	4	?
12.	0	3	2	0	3	2	2	6	?
13.	2	1	4	1	1	2	0	4	?

149

Problem Solving: Using Time

From   **To**

9:00 A.M.   11:15 A.M.

Problem: Todd arrived at the airport at 9:00 A.M. to meet his friend Raul. Raul's plane was scheduled to land at 11:15 A.M. How long did Todd wait for Raul?

1 IMAGINE

Draw and label a picture of the times.

2 NAME

Facts: 9:00 A.M.—Time Now
            11:15 A.M.—Plane Arrives

Question: How long did Todd wait?

3 THINK

Look at the times.
Count off how long it is between the two times.

2 h   15 min

4 COMPUTE

The hour hand has moved from 9 to 11. This is 2 hours.

The minute hand has moved 15 minutes ahead. This is 15 minutes.

Todd will have to wait 2 hr 15 min.

5 CHECK

From 9:00 A.M. to 10:00 A.M. : 1 hour
From 10:00 A.M. to 11:00 A.M. : 1 hour
From 11:00 A.M. to 11:15 A.M. : 15 minutes
    1 h + 1 h + 15 min = 2 h 15 min.

The answer checks.

Solve.

1. Todd and Raul started eating lunch at 11:45 A.M. and ended at 12:30 P.M. How long did they take to eat lunch?

START   END

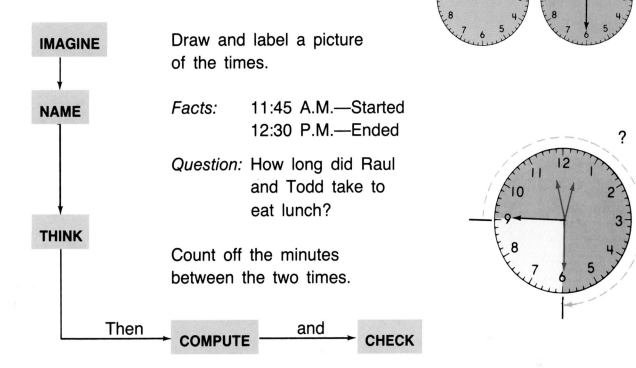

IMAGINE	Draw and label a picture of the times.
NAME	*Facts:* 11:45 A.M.—Started 12:30 P.M.—Ended *Question:* How long did Raul and Todd take to eat lunch?
THINK	Count off the minutes between the two times.

Then → **COMPUTE** — and → **CHECK**

2. Todd and Raul left the airport at 1:30 P.M. How long was Todd at the airport?

3. The plane that brought Raul was scheduled to leave at 2:20 P.M. How long was the airplane on the ground?

4. Todd and Raul arrived at Todd's house at 3:15 P.M. How long was the ride from the airport to Todd's house?

5. Raul said, "I have been visiting you now for 6 hours 25 minutes." What time is it?

More Practice

Choose the best unit of measure. Write m, g, or L.

1. the width of a door

2. the size of a soda bottle

3. the weight of a cookie

4. the distance run in a race.

Choose the most reasonable measure.

5. the length of a cat's tail   **a.** m   **b.** cm   **c.** km

6. the capacity of an eye dropper   **a.** m   **b.** mL   **c.** kL

7. the weight of a large chicken   **a.** kg   **b.** g   **c.** m

Complete.

8. 5 kL = _?_ L

9. 2 kg = _?_ g

10. 6 m = _?_ cm

11. 400 cm = _?_ m

12. 3000 m = _?_ km

13. 4000 g = _?_ kg

14. 2 ft = _?_ in.

15. 36 in. = _?_ ft

16. 3 ft = _?_ yd

Compute.

17.   2 ft 3 in.
    +4 ft 8 in.

18.   4 ft 8 in.
    +2 ft 6 in.

19.   6 ft 8 in.
    −2 ft 4 in.

Write the time.

20. 10 minutes to 5.

21. 35 minutes past 11.

Write the amount of money for each.

22.

23.

(See *Still More Practice*, p. 361.)

Math Probe

TIME ZONES

The map shows time zone divisions in the United
States. The clocks give the times when it is
5:00 P.M., Central Time.

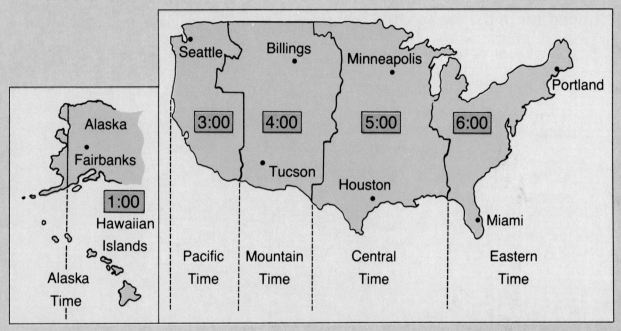

Complete.
1. When it is 9:00 P.M., Eastern Time, what time is it:

   a. Central Time   b. Mountain Time   c. Pacific Time

2. At 3:00 A.M. in Fairbanks, what time is it in:

   a. Seattle   b. Minneapolis   c. Portland

3. At midnight in Houston, what time is it in:

   a. Billings   b. Hawaii   c. Miami

   d. Seattle   e. Minneapolis   f. Tucson

4. Look up "Time Zone" in your encyclopedia.
   List 4 cities in each time zone.

Check Your Mastery

See pp. 126 - 127.

Choose the best unit of measure. Write m, g, or L.

1. the top of your desk
2. the amount of water in a pool
3. your weight
4. the soda in a can

Choose the most reasonable measure.

See pp. 126 - 135.

5. the size of a turkey   **a.** L   **b.** g   **c.** kg
6. the length of your foot   **a.** km   **b.** m   **c.** cm

Complete.

See pp. 130 - 135, 140 - 145.

7. 200 cm = __?__ m
8. 2 gal = __?__ qt
9. 3 yd = __?__ ft
10. 48 in. = __?__ ft
11. 4000 g = __?__ kg
12. 2 ft = __?__ in.
13. 16 pt = __?__ qt
14. 2 T = __?__ lb
15. 3 pt = __?__ c
16. 2 km = __?__ m
17. 6 ft = __?__ yd
18. 4 kL = __?__ L

Compute.

See pp. 140 - 141.

19.
```
  4 ft 9 in.
+2 ft 2 in.
```

20.
```
  11 ft 9 in.
-  4 ft 5 in.
```

21.
```
  6 ft 5 in.
+4 ft 9 in.
```

Write the time.

See pp. 146 - 147.

22. 20 minutes past 2
23. 15 minutes to 5

Write the amount of money for each.

See pp. 148 - 149.

24.

25.

Multiplication: 1- and 2-Digit Multipliers

In this unit you will:

- Multiply by one-digit
- Multiply by two-digits
- Multiply with money
- Estimate products
- Solve problems using the "working backwards" strategy

Do you remember?

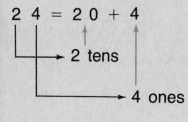

$$24 = 20 + 4$$

→ 2 tens

→ 4 ones

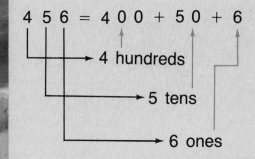

$$456 = 400 + 50 + 6$$

→ 4 hundreds

→ 5 tens

→ 6 ones

Multiplying by One Digit

The 3 members of the Scout troop made posters about the danger of forest fires. Each member made 12 posters. How many posters were made in all?

12　　12　　12 ⟶ 3 tens and 6 ones ⟶ 30 + 6 = 36

Look at the picture of the 3 twelves.

- Join 3 equal sets of two together.　　　$3 \times 2 = 6$

- Join 3 equal sets of ten together.　　　$3 \times 10 = 30$

- Add.　　　　　　　　　　　　　　　　$30 + 6 = 36$

To multiply by one digit:

Multiply the ones by 3. ⟶	Multiply the tens by 3.
$\begin{array}{r} 1\ 2 \\ \times\ \ 3 \\ \hline 6 \end{array}$	$\begin{array}{r} 1\ 2 \\ \times\ \ 3 \\ \hline 3\ 6 \end{array}$
3×2 ones $= 6$ ones	3×1 ten $= 3$ tens

36 posters were made in all.

Study these examples.

$\begin{array}{r} 2\ 2 \\ \times\ 4 \\ \hline 8 \end{array}$ ⟶ $\begin{array}{r} 2\ 2 \\ \times\ 4 \\ \hline 8\ 8 \end{array}$ 　　　　$\begin{array}{r} 4\ 3 \\ \times\ 2 \\ \hline 6 \end{array}$ ⟶ $\begin{array}{r} 4\ 3 \\ \times\ 2 \\ \hline 8\ 6 \end{array}$

Complete. (The first is done.)

1. 2 × 4 tens = 2 × 40 = 80   2. 3 × 2 tens = 3 × 20 = ___?

3. 5 × 1 ten = 5 × ___? = ___?   4. 4 × 2 tens = 4 × ___? = ___?

Multiply.

5.	12 ×2	6.	22 ×3	7.	13 ×3	8.	21 ×4	9.	14 ×2	10.	12 ×4

11.	11 ×9	12.	34 ×2	13.	23 ×3	14.	44 ×2	15.	11 ×6	16.	33 ×3

17.	32 ×3	18.	13 ×2	19.	43 ×2	20.	31 ×3	21.	26 ×1	22.	41 ×2

Solve.

23. At the Wilson School the fourth grade has 23 children. The Lane School has 3 times that number. How many fourth graders does the Lane School have?

24. Melissa can play 32 songs in an hour. How many songs can she play in 4 hours?

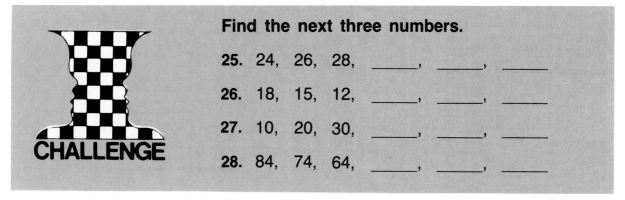

Find the next three numbers.

25. 24, 26, 28, _____, _____, _____

26. 18, 15, 12, _____, _____, _____

27. 10, 20, 30, _____, _____, _____

28. 84, 74, 64, _____, _____, _____

CHALLENGE

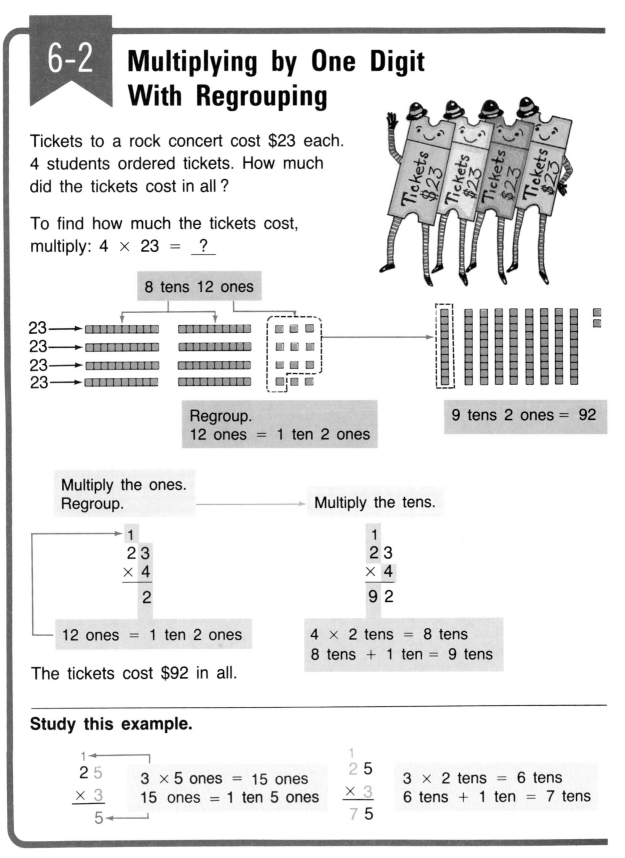

6-2 Multiplying by One Digit With Regrouping

Tickets to a rock concert cost $23 each. 4 students ordered tickets. How much did the tickets cost in all?

To find how much the tickets cost, multiply: $4 \times 23 = \underline{\ ?\ }$

8 tens 12 ones

23 →
23 →
23 →
23 →

Regroup.
12 ones = 1 ten 2 ones

9 tens 2 ones = 92

Multiply the ones. Regroup.

$$\begin{array}{r} 1\ \ \\ 2\ 3 \\ \times\ \ 4 \\ \hline 2 \end{array}$$

12 ones = 1 ten 2 ones

Multiply the tens.

$$\begin{array}{r} 1\ \ \\ 2\ 3 \\ \times\ \ 4 \\ \hline 9\ 2 \end{array}$$

4×2 tens $= 8$ tens
8 tens $+ 1$ ten $= 9$ tens

The tickets cost $92 in all.

Study this example.

$$\begin{array}{r} 1\ \ \\ 2\ 5 \\ \times\ 3 \\ \hline 5 \end{array}$$

3×5 ones $= 15$ ones
15 ones $= 1$ ten 5 ones

$$\begin{array}{r} 1\ \ \\ 2\ 5 \\ \times\ 3 \\ \hline 7\ 5 \end{array}$$

3×2 tens $= 6$ tens
6 tens $+ 1$ ten $= 7$ tens

158

Multiply.

1. 18 ×3	**2.** 16 ×5	**3.** 38 ×2	**4.** 24 ×3	**5.** 16 ×4	**6.** 25 ×2
7. 28 ×2	**8.** 17 ×3	**9.** 24 ×4	**10.** 19 ×3	**11.** 17 ×5	**12.** 19 ×4
13. 18 ×2	**14.** 25 ×3	**15.** 18 ×5	**16.** 16 ×5	**17.** 26 ×3	**18.** 45 ×2
19. 23 ×4	**20.** 36 ×2	**21.** 37 ×2	**22.** 14 ×5	**23.** 48 ×2	**24.** 27 ×3
25. 29 ×3	**26.** 49 ×2	**27.** 16 ×6	**28.** 14 ×7	**29.** 15 ×6	**30.** 12 ×8

Find the product.

31. 3 × 27

32. 2 × 46

33. 7 × 12

34. 4 × 23

35. 6 × 12

36. 6 × 14

37. 6 × 13

38. 4 × 23

39. 7 × 13

Solve.

40. There are 48 stickers on a sheet. How many stickers are there on 2 sheets?

41. Louisa has made only 17 base hits this year. She made 5 times that many last year. How many hits did she make last year?

42. This week Jon rode 13 miles on his bicycle. He will ride the same distance each week for 4 weeks. How many miles will he ride in all?

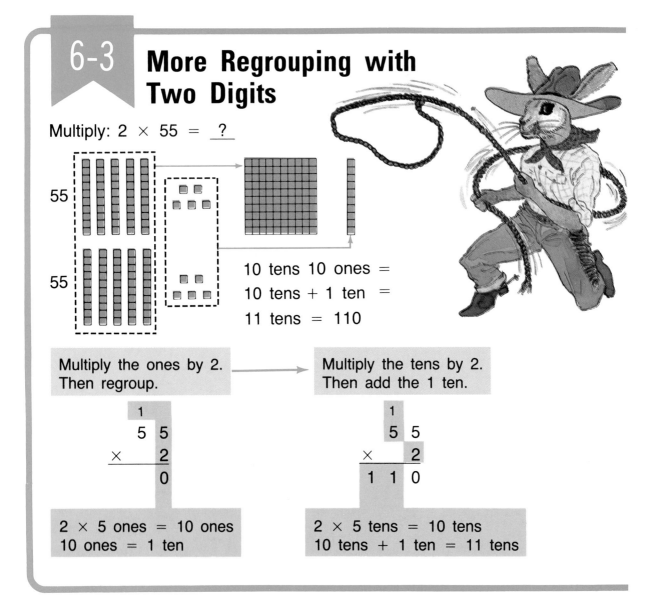

6-3 More Regrouping with Two Digits

Multiply: $2 \times 55 = $?

10 tens 10 ones =
10 tens + 1 ten =
11 tens = 110

Multiply the ones by 2.
Then regroup.

```
  1
  5 5
×   2
    0
```

2×5 ones = 10 ones
10 ones = 1 ten

Multiply the tens by 2.
Then add the 1 ten.

```
  1
  5 5
×   2
1 1 0
```

2×5 tens = 10 tens
10 tens + 1 ten = 11 tens

Multiply.

1. 24 ×6	**2.** 46 ×4	**3.** 68 ×5	**4.** 78 ×2	**5.** 36 ×3	**6.** 86 ×4
7. 74 ×3	**8.** 64 ×5	**9.** 37 ×6	**10.** 72 ×7	**11.** 82 ×8	**12.** 96 ×5
13. 43 ×9	**14.** 89 ×4	**15.** 77 ×3	**16.** 84 ×6	**17.** 79 ×8	**18.** 99 ×9

Find the products.

19. 76 ×4	**20.** 75 ×5	**21.** 89 ×4	**22.** 96 ×5	**23.** 57 ×5
24. 37 ×7	**25.** 42 ×9	**26.** 81 ×8	**27.** 45 ×6	**28.** 92 ×9

Multiply.

29. 4 × 63   **30.** 5 × 84   **31.** 3 × 76

32. 6 × 87   **33.** 9 × 58   **34.** 7 × 47

35. 8 × 79   **36.** 6 × 68   **37.** 9 × 78

Solve.

38. 7 times 84 is what number?

39. The factors are 65 and 9. What is the product?

40. What is the product of 3 times 18 times 2?

41. What is the product of 4 times 25 times 4?

42. There are 8 chicken legs in a box. How many chicken legs are there in 25 boxes?

43. A carton of grape-juice bottles holds 4 six-packs. How many bottles are there in 5 cartons?

44. Mary bought 2 chairs for $89 each. What was the total cost?

Calculator Activity

Compute on your calculator. 13 × 2 × 13 = __?__

Read the answer upside down to find a word that describes a honeymaker.

6-4 Multiplying Three-Digit Numbers

Danielle's family travel 146 mi to a picnic at the campgrounds. How far will they travel if they picnic there on two weekends?

To find the total distance,
multiply: $4 \times 146 = \underline{?}$

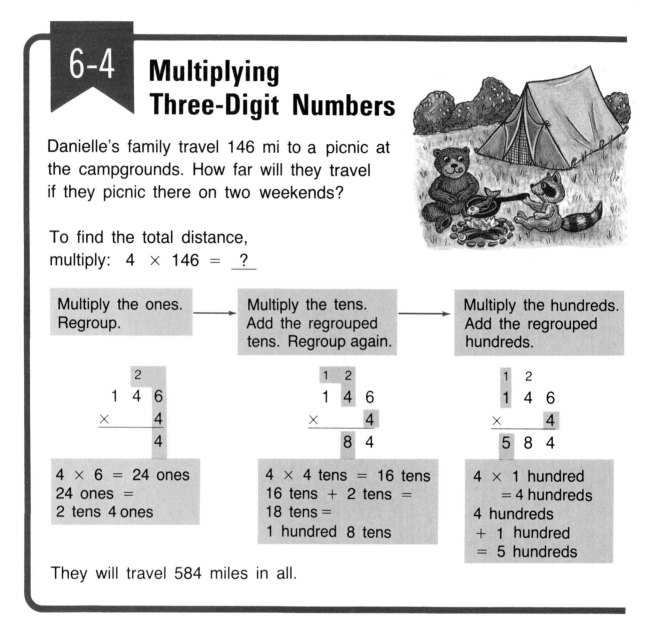

Multiply the ones. Regroup.	Multiply the tens. Add the regrouped tens. Regroup again.	Multiply the hundreds. Add the regrouped hundreds.
$\begin{array}{r} 2 \\ 1\ 4\ 6 \\ \times\ \ \ \ 4 \\ \hline 4 \end{array}$	$\begin{array}{r} 1\ 2 \\ 1\ 4\ 6 \\ \times\ \ \ \ 4 \\ \hline 8\ 4 \end{array}$	$\begin{array}{r} 1\ 2 \\ 1\ 4\ 6 \\ \times\ \ \ \ 4 \\ \hline 5\ 8\ 4 \end{array}$
$4 \times 6 = 24$ ones 24 ones = 2 tens 4 ones	4×4 tens $= 16$ tens 16 tens $+$ 2 tens $=$ 18 tens $=$ 1 hundred 8 tens	4×1 hundred $= 4$ hundreds 4 hundreds $+$ 1 hundred $= 5$ hundreds

They will travel 584 miles in all.

Copy and complete.

1. $\begin{array}{r} 3 \\ 117 \\ \times\ \ 5 \\ \hline ?85 \end{array}$

2. $\begin{array}{r} 3 \\ 219 \\ \times\ \ 4 \\ \hline ?76 \end{array}$

3. $\begin{array}{r} 3 \\ 106 \\ \times\ \ 5 \\ \hline ?30 \end{array}$

4. $\begin{array}{r} 1 \\ 316 \\ \times\ \ 2 \\ \hline ??2 \end{array}$

5. $\begin{array}{r} 1 \\ 213 \\ \times\ \ 6 \\ \hline ??? \end{array}$

6. $\begin{array}{r} 1\ 1 \\ 376 \\ \times\ \ 2 \\ \hline ?52 \end{array}$

7. $\begin{array}{r} 2\ 2 \\ 165 \\ \times\ \ 4 \\ \hline ?60 \end{array}$

8. $\begin{array}{r} 3\ 1 \\ 172 \\ \times\ \ 5 \\ \hline ?60 \end{array}$

9. $\begin{array}{r} ?\ 1 \\ 245 \\ \times\ \ 3 \\ \hline ??5 \end{array}$

10. $\begin{array}{r} ?\ ? \\ 134 \\ \times\ \ 5 \\ \hline ??? \end{array}$

Multiply.

11.	487 × 2	12.	234 × 3	13.	328 × 2	14.	115 × 4	15.	325 × 3

16.	256 × 3	17.	146 × 4	18.	287 × 3	19.	183 × 5	20.	123 × 6

21.	142 × 7	22.	276 × 3	23.	113 × 8	24.	126 × 6	25.	116 × 8

Find the products.

26. 4 × 249   27. 3 × 198   28. 2 × 376

29. 5 × 189   30. 3 × 279   31. 6 × 129

Solve.

32. Janet has collected 112 leaves for her science project. Darren has collected six times as many. How many leaves has Darren collected?

33. How many leaves do Janet and Darren have in all?

Complete. The pattern is given.

34. Add 5. Multiply by 2.

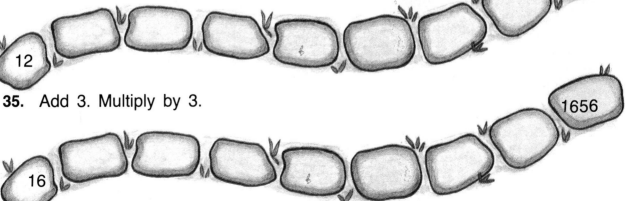

35. Add 3. Multiply by 3.

163

More Regrouping with Three Digits

Each section A, B, and C of the
Civic Center seats 456 people.
How many seats in all are there
in the 3 sections?

To find the number of seats in all,
multiply: 3 × 456 = __?__

Multiply the ones. Regroup.	Multiply the tens. Add the regrouped ten. Regroup again.	Multiply the hundreds. Add the regrouped hundred.

```
    1
  4 5 6
×     3
      8
```

```
  1 1
  4 5 6
×     3
    6 8
```

```
  1 1
  4 5 6
×     3
1 3 6 8
```

3 × 6 = 18
18 ones =
1 ten 8 ones

3 × 5 = 15 tens
15 tens + 1 ten = 16 tens
16 tens = 1 hundred 6 tens

There are 1 3 6 8 seats in all.

Multiply.

1.	565 × 2	2.	345 × 3	3.	659 × 2	4.	543 × 4	5.	567 × 5

6.	678 × 5	7.	432 × 8	8.	617 × 6	9.	345 × 9	10.	683 × 7

11.	679 × 6	12.	387 × 7	13.	426 × 4	14.	275 × 8	15.	146 × 5

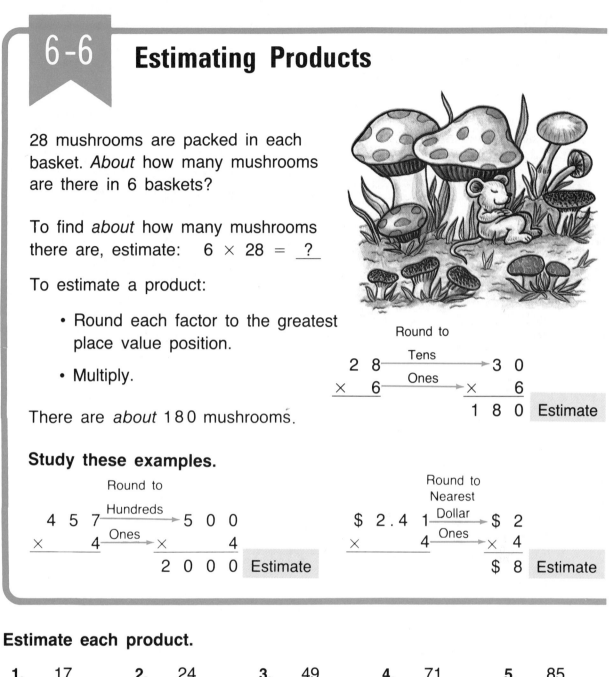

6-6 Estimating Products

28 mushrooms are packed in each basket. *About* how many mushrooms are there in 6 baskets?

To find *about* how many mushrooms there are, estimate: $6 \times 28 = \underline{\ ?\ }$

To estimate a product:

- Round each factor to the greatest place value position.

- Multiply.

There are *about* 180 mushrooms.

Round to

$$
\begin{array}{r}
2\ 8 \xrightarrow{\text{Tens}} 3\ 0 \\
\times\quad 6 \xrightarrow{\text{Ones}} \times\quad 6 \\
\hline
1\ 8\ 0
\end{array}
$$
Estimate

Study these examples.

Round to Hundreds

$$
\begin{array}{r}
4\ 5\ 7 \xrightarrow{\text{Hundreds}} 5\ 0\ 0 \\
\times\qquad 4 \xrightarrow{\text{Ones}} \times\qquad 4 \\
\hline
2\ 0\ 0\ 0
\end{array}
$$
Estimate

Round to Nearest Dollar

$$
\begin{array}{r}
\$\ 2\ .\ 4\ 1 \xrightarrow{\text{Dollar}} \$\ 2 \\
\times\qquad 4 \xrightarrow{\text{Ones}} \times\ 4 \\
\hline
\$\ 8
\end{array}
$$
Estimate

Estimate each product.

1. 17 $\times$ 5	**2.** 24 $\times$ 7	**3.** 49 $\times$ 8	**4.** 71 $\times$ 9	**5.** 85 $\times$ 6
6. 348 $\times$ 2	**7.** 551 $\times$ 4	**8.** 619 $\times$ 6	**9.** 809 $\times$ 9	**10.** 748 $\times$ 8
11. $3.15 $\times$ 3	**12.** $7.54 $\times$ 2	**13.** $4.49 $\times$ 5	**14.** $6.51 $\times$ 7	**15.** $8.76 $\times$ 9

6-7 Multiplying Four-Digit Numbers

A sweater company packs 4 sweaters in a carton. They packed 1760 cartons. How many sweaters are there in all?

To find the number of sweaters in all, multiply: 4 × 1760 = ?

```
  3 2
  1 7 6 0
×       4
  7 0 4 0
```

There are 7040 sweaters in all.

Study these examples.

```
  3   1
  9 5 1 2
×       6
5 7,0 7 2
```

```
  1 5 3
  5 2 7 5
×       7
3 6,9 2 5
```

```
  2 3 6
$ 7 3 4 8
×       8
$5 8,7 8 4
```

Multiply.

```
      1 1
1.  2134
  ×    4
   ?536
```

```
      1 1
2.  1234
  ×    4
   ??36
```

```
    ?  1
3.  3635
  ×    2
   ???0
```

```
    ? ? ?
4.  1254
  ×    7
   ???8
```

```
5.  1613
  ×    4
```

```
6.  1465
  ×    2
```

```
7.  2468
  ×    2
```

```
8. $2148
  ×    4
```

Multiply.

9. $\begin{array}{r} 1415 \\ \times\ \ \ 7 \\ \hline \end{array}$	10. $\begin{array}{r} \$2221 \\ \times\ \ \ 3 \\ \hline \end{array}$	11. $\begin{array}{r} 2423 \\ \times\ \ \ 4 \\ \hline \end{array}$	12. $\begin{array}{r} 1536 \\ \times\ \ \ 5 \\ \hline \end{array}$
13. $\begin{array}{r} 3341 \\ \times\ \ \ 2 \\ \hline \end{array}$	14. $\begin{array}{r} 1372 \\ \times\ \ \ 6 \\ \hline \end{array}$	15. $\begin{array}{r} 2179 \\ \times\ \ \ 4 \\ \hline \end{array}$	16. $\begin{array}{r} 1523 \\ \times\ \ \ 5 \\ \hline \end{array}$
17. $\begin{array}{r} \$1119 \\ \times\ \ \ 8 \\ \hline \end{array}$	18. $\begin{array}{r} 1468 \\ \times\ \ \ 7 \\ \hline \end{array}$	19. $\begin{array}{r} 1412 \\ \times\ \ \ 5 \\ \hline \end{array}$	20. $\begin{array}{r} \$1177 \\ \times\ \ \ 6 \\ \hline \end{array}$
21. $\begin{array}{r} 2421 \\ \times\ \ \ 3 \\ \hline \end{array}$	22. $\begin{array}{r} \$1258 \\ \times\ \ \ 7 \\ \hline \end{array}$	23. $\begin{array}{r} 1387 \\ \times\ \ \ 8 \\ \hline \end{array}$	24. $\begin{array}{r} 1119 \\ \times\ \ \ 9 \\ \hline \end{array}$

Find the products. Then find the sum of the products.

25. 3 × 1121   and   3 × 1525

26. 5 × 1556   and   2 × 3481

27. 6 × 1527   and   4 × 1398

28. 2 × $4197   and   6 × $1267

Solve.

29. Each day the postman delivers 3689 letters. How many letters does he deliver in 2 days?

30. Joe lives 1478 miles from Miami. He lives four times as far from Toronto. How far does Joe live from Toronto?

31. A small town spends $3650 a year for road repair. How much will it spend in all if the same amount is spent for 4 years?

167

6-8 Multiplying by Ten

Look for a pattern.

1 ten × 3 = 3 tens
10 × 3 = 30

1 ten × 6 = 6 tens
10 × 6 = 60

1 ten × 5 = 5 tens
10 × 5 = 50

1 ten × 8 = 8 tens
8 × 10 = 80

To multiply a number by 10:   10 × 27 = ?

• Write the number.

• Place 1 zero at the right of the number.

```
    2 7
×   1 0
    2 7 0
```

Study these examples.

```
    3 5          4 0          4 5 7          2 6 8 0
×   1 0      ×   1 0      ×       1 0      ×         1 0
    3 5 0        4 0 0        4 5 7 0        2 6 , 8 0 0
```

Multiply mentally. Write the products.

1. 18
   × 10

2. 24
   × 10

3. 57
   × 10

4. 61
   × 10

5. 50
   × 10

6. 345
   × 10

7. 638
   × 10

8. 999
   × 10

9. 450
   × 10

10. 690
    × 10

Multiplying by Multiples of Ten

There are 22 plums in a box. Mr. Pines orders 30 boxes of plums. How many plums did he order?

To find the number of plums, multiply: $30 \times 22 = $?

To multiply a number by a multiple of ten:

- Multiply the number by the number of tens.

- Place 1 zero at the right of the product.

$$\begin{array}{r} 2\ 2 \\ \times\ 3\ 0 \\ \hline 6\ 6\ 0 \end{array}$$

Mr. Pines ordered 660 plums.

Study these examples.

$$\begin{array}{r} 4\ 0 \\ \times\ 5\ 0 \\ \hline 2\ 0\ 0\ 0 \end{array} \qquad \begin{array}{r} 7\ 0 \\ \times\ 6\ 0 \\ \hline 4\ 2\ 0\ 0 \end{array} \qquad \begin{array}{r} 9\ 0\ 0 \\ \times\ 8\ 0 \\ \hline 7\ 2,0\ 0\ 0 \end{array}$$

Multiply.

1. $\begin{array}{r} 20 \\ \times\ 10 \\ \hline \end{array}$

2. $\begin{array}{r} 50 \\ \times\ 20 \\ \hline \end{array}$

3. $\begin{array}{r} 30 \\ \times\ 30 \\ \hline \end{array}$

4. $\begin{array}{r} 60 \\ \times\ 40 \\ \hline \end{array}$

5. $\begin{array}{r} 50 \\ \times\ 30 \\ \hline \end{array}$

6. $\begin{array}{r} 70 \\ \times\ 30 \\ \hline \end{array}$

7. $\begin{array}{r} 90 \\ \times\ 50 \\ \hline \end{array}$

8. $\begin{array}{r} 20 \\ \times\ 90 \\ \hline \end{array}$

9. $\begin{array}{r} 80 \\ \times\ 30 \\ \hline \end{array}$

10. $\begin{array}{r} 80 \\ \times\ 80 \\ \hline \end{array}$

Multiplying by Two Digits

In Riverbend Stadium, a section has 24 rows. Each row has 63 seats. How many seats are there in a section?

To find the number of seats, multiply: 24 × 63 = _?_

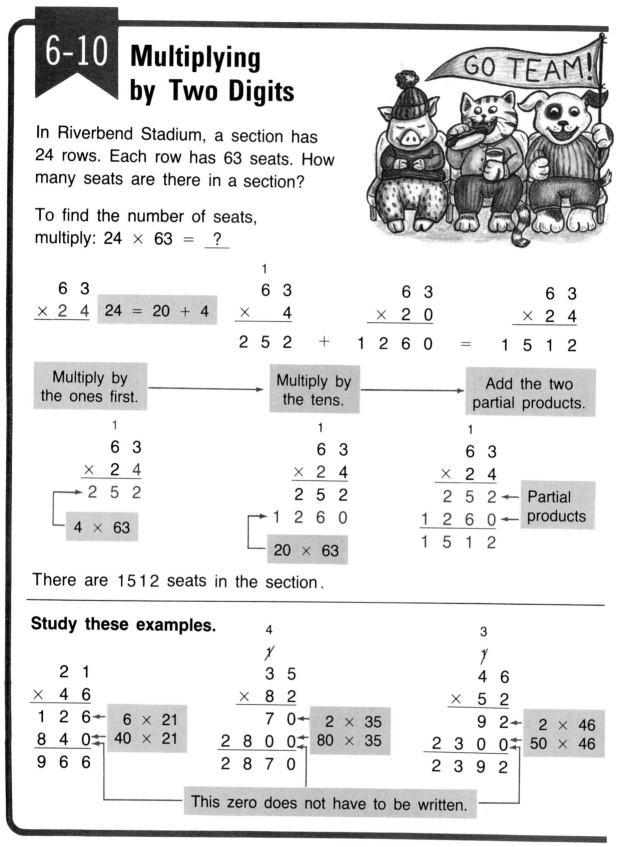

```
    6 3              1              6 3            6 3
  × 2 4    24 = 20 + 4    6 3      × 2 0        × 2 4
                        ×   4                
                        2 5 2  +  1 2 6 0  =  1 5 1 2
```

| Multiply by the ones first. | Multiply by the tens. | Add the two partial products. |

```
    1                    1              1
    6 3                  6 3            6 3
  × 2 4                × 2 4          × 2 4
  ┌→ 2 5 2              2 5 2          2 5 2 ← Partial
  │                  ┌→ 1 2 6 0        1 2 6 0 ← products
  └─ 4 × 63          │   20 × 63       1 5 1 2
                     └─
```

There are 1512 seats in the section.

Study these examples.

```
                          4              3
                          ⁄              ⁄
    2 1                  3 5            4 6
  × 4 6                × 8 2          × 5 2
  1 2 6 ←   6 × 21      7 0 ←  2 × 35  9 2 ←  2 × 46
  8 4 0 ←  40 × 21    2 8 0 0 ← 80 × 35  2 3 0 0 ← 50 × 46
  9 6 6                2 8 7 0          2 3 9 2
```

This zero does not have to be written.

Complete.

	1		1		1		?
1. 1 4		**2.** 5 2		**3.** 4 2		**4.** 9 3	

1.
```
   1
   1 4
 ×  2 3
     4 2
   ? 8 0
   ? ? 2
```

2.
```
      1
      5 2
    ×  3 5
      ? ? 0
    1 5 6 0
    ? ? ? 0
```

3.
```
      1
      4 2
    ×  4 9
      3 ? ?
    1 6 ? 0
    ? ? ? ?
```

4.
```
      ?
      9 3
    ×  2 4
      ? ? ?
    ? ? ? 0
    ? ? ? ?
```

5.
```
    14
 ×  43
    42
   560
```

6.
```
    56
 ×  24
   224
    20
```

7.
```
    42
 ×  55
   210
    00
```

8.
```
    84
 ×  38
   672
     0
```

9.
```
    53
 ×  63
     9
```

10.
```
    25
 ×  91
     5
```

Find the product.

11.
```
    82
 ×  67
```

12.
```
    91
 ×  42
```

13.
```
    88
 ×  16
```

14.
```
    27
 ×  72
```

15.
```
    36
 ×  63
```

16.
```
    93
 ×  18
```

Multiply.

17. 13 × 24

18. 31 × 42

19. 54 × 63

20. 75 × 86

21. 87 × 48

22. 48 × 37

23. 36 × 63

24. 45 × 54

25. 81 × 19

Calculator Activity

26. Multiply: 23 × 15 = _?_

27. Check the answer to exercise 26 on your calculator. Read the answer on your calculator upside down. It gives the answer to this question:
What pronoun is used to refer to a girl or a woman?

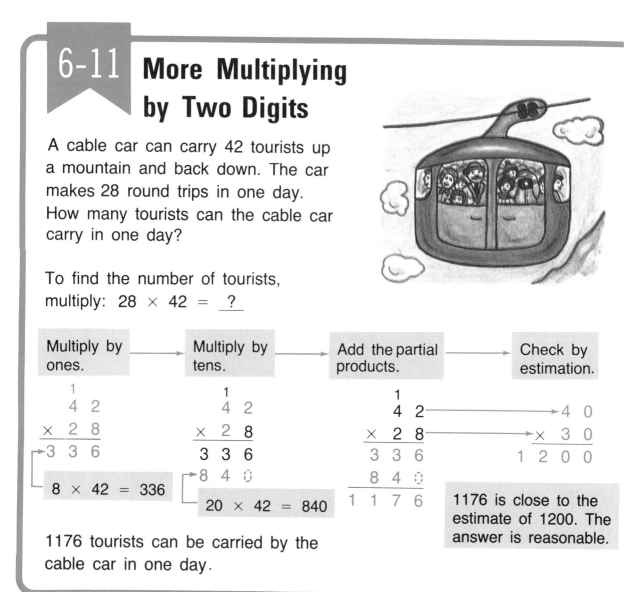

6-11 More Multiplying by Two Digits

A cable car can carry 42 tourists up a mountain and back down. The car makes 28 round trips in one day. How many tourists can the cable car carry in one day?

To find the number of tourists, multiply: 28 × 42 = _?_

Multiply by ones.	Multiply by tens.	Add the partial products.	Check by estimation.

Multiply by ones.

$$\begin{array}{r} 1 \\ 4\ 2 \\ \times\ 2\ 8 \\ \hline 3\ 3\ 6 \end{array}$$

8 × 42 = 336

Multiply by tens.

$$\begin{array}{r} 1 \\ 4\ 2 \\ \times\ 2\ 8 \\ \hline 3\ 3\ 6 \\ 8\ 4\ 0 \end{array}$$

20 × 42 = 840

Add the partial products.

$$\begin{array}{r} 1 \\ 4\ 2 \\ \times\ 2\ 8 \\ \hline 3\ 3\ 6 \\ 8\ 4\ 0 \\ \hline 1\ 1\ 7\ 6 \end{array}$$

Check by estimation.

$$\begin{array}{r} 4\ 0 \\ \times\ 3\ 0 \\ \hline 1\ 2\ 0\ 0 \end{array}$$

1176 is close to the estimate of 1200. The answer is reasonable.

1176 tourists can be carried by the cable car in one day.

Multiply. Check by estimation.

1. 13 ×24

2. 57 ×68

3. 58 ×67

4. 37 ×48

5. 38 ×47

6. 54 ×63

7. 68 ×22

8. 82 ×25

9. 64 ×52

10. 43 ×36

11. 51 ×73

12. 36 ×67

13. 75 ×23

14. 86 ×42

15. 94 ×57

16. 43 ×63

17. 54 ×74

18. 62 ×82

Find the product.

19. 36 ×37	**20.** 27 ×12	**21.** 29 ×24	**22.** 45 ×22	**23.** 26 ×32	**24.** 45 ×12
25. 28 ×34	**26.** 89 ×47	**27.** 78 ×63	**28.** 59 ×64	**29.** 89 ×35	**30.** 95 ×45

Multiply. Check by estimation.

31. 78 × 54　　　　　**32.** 83 × 76　　　　　**33.** 97 × 86

34. 45 × 39　　　　　**35.** 59 × 84　　　　　**36.** 57 × 77

Solve.

37. What is the product of 49 and 36?

38. The factors are 63 and 24. What is the product?

39. In the auditorium there are 36 rows of chairs with 48 chairs in each row. How many chairs are there?

40. Andrew has 90 rolls of nickels. Each roll has 20 nickels in it. How many nickels does Andrew have in all?

41. A plumber is replacing pieces of pipe. Each piece measures 96 inches. Find the length in inches of 38 pieces of pipe.

42. Find the length in feet of the 38 pieces of pipe.

6-12 Multiplying with Two and Three Digits

Louise has a flock of hens on her farm. They lay about 175 eggs a week. About how many eggs will the hens lay in a year (52 weeks)?

To find the number of eggs, multiply: $52 \times 175 = \underline{?}$

Multiply by the ones.	Multiply by the tens.	Add partial products.	Check by estimation

```
                         3 2              3 2
      1 1                ⨯ ⨯              ⨯ ⨯
    1 7 5              1 7 5            1 7 5 ⟶    2 0 0
    ×  5 2             ×  5 2           ×  5 2 ⟶  ×  5 0
    3 5 0              3 5 0            3 5 0       1 0,0 0 0
                       8 7 5 ◌          8 7 5 ◌
   2 × 175 = 350                        9 1 0 0
                       50 × 175 = 8750
```

9100 is close to the estimate of 10,000. The answer is reasonable.

The hens lay about 9100 eggs in a year.

Complete.

```
      3 1               2 1                             1
                         ⨉                            2 �slash5
1.    142          2.    263         3.    607     4.    149
    ×  28              ×  43             ×  18          ×  26
    1136               789             4856            894
    284◌              1052◌            607◌            ???◌
    ??? 6             ?????            ?????           ????
```

```
5.    156          6.    567         7.    429     8.    427
    ×  21              ×  17             ×  16          ×  53
```

Multiply. Check by estimation.

9.	10.	11.	12.	13.
234 × 51	629 × 43	827 × 16	206 × 43	362 × 91

14.	15.	16.	17.	18.
436 × 82	427 × 53	449 × 72	107 × 24	808 × 83

19.	20.	21.	22.	23.
883 × 34	623 × 71	861 × 41	523 × 22	526 × 37

24.	25.	26.	27.	28.
609 × 43	704 × 65	430 × 36	817 × 32	525 × 28

Use the information in the chart to solve the problems.

29. *The Flight of the Kitty Hawk* was one of the most popular books read during the week. 68 children read it. How many pages were read in all?

30. 23 children read *Small Home in the Forest*. How many pages were read in all?

31. How many pages would be used to print 325 copies of *Here Comes the King?*

32. *The Billsey Triplets* was a favorite of 16 children. How many pages were read in all?

33. Mabel read all of the four books. How many pages did she read in all?

34. 16 children read *The Billsey Triplets* and 68 children read *The Flight of Kitty Hawk.* How many pages were read in all?

Reading Club
Weekly Book List

Title	Pages
Small House in the Forest	237
The Billsey Triplets	146
Here Comes the King	86
The Flight of the Kitty Hawk	112

Multiplication and Money

Multiply: 45 × $4.85 = __?__

| Multiply as with whole numbers. | Put a decimal point in the product two places from the right. Write a $. | Check by estimation. |

```
    $ 4 . 8  5
    ×     4  5
    2 4 2  5   ←  5 × 485
    1 9 4 0    ←  40 × 485
    2 1 8 2 5
```

```
    $ 4 . 8  5  ─────────→ $ 5 . 0 0
    ×     4  5  ─────────→ ×   5 0
    2 4 2  5              $ 2 5 0 . 0 0
    1 9 4 0
  $ 2 1 8 . 2 5  ←
```

$218.25 is close to the estimate of $250. The answer is reasonable.

Study these examples.

```
       1    1
    $ 3 5 . 1 6
    ×         3
  $ 1 0 5 4 8
```

```
    $ 6 . 0 0
    ×     8 0
  $ 4 8 0 . 0 0
```

```
          2
    $ 8 . 4 0
    ×     5 0
  $ 4 2 0 . 0 0
```

```
       2   2
       2   2
    $ 0 . 7 9
    ×     3 4
      3 1 6
    2 3 7 0
  $ 2 6 . 8 6
```

Multiply. Check by estimation.

1. $5.21
   × 7

2. $7.20
   × 6

3. $8.00
   × 9

4. $6.00
   × 73

5. $4.00
   × 65

6. $7.64
   × 47

7. $3.27
   × 38

8. $6.19
   × 92

9. $2.97
   × 75

10. $4.26
    × 63

11. $4.59
    × 24

12. $8.80
    × 54

13. $5.91
    × 42

14. $1.49
    × 39

15. $7.79
    × 81

176

Multiply. Check by estimation.

16. $8.00 × 39	**17.** $6.20 × 30	**18.** $8.60 × 90	**19.** $9.40 × 80	**20.** $8.20 × 70
21. $7.54 × 26	**22.** $5.25 × 47	**23.** $4.91 × 36	**24.** $8.25 × 48	**25.** $7.75 × 54
26. $3.98 × 26	**27.** $7.54 × 68	**28.** $2.99 × 88	**29.** $8.51 × 55	**30.** $9.25 × 99

Choose the correct answer.

31. 40 stamps at $.22 each   **a.** $.88   **b.** $8.80   **c.** $88.00   **d.** $8.08

32. 7 coins at $1.80 each   **a.** $126.00   **b.** $12.60   **c.** $1.26   **d.** $12.06

33. 50 pins at $.04 each   **a.** $200   **b.** $2   **c.** $.20   **d.** $20

34. 6 books at $2.95 each   **a.** $17.07   **b.** $177   **c.** $17.70   **d.** $7.77

35. 30 cards at $.95 each   **a.** $2.85   **b.** $285   **c.** $28.50   **d.** $28.05

Solve.

36. A T.V. costs $329.95. What is the cost of 6 T.V.'s?

37. The price of a cassette deck is $79.95. Jim purchased one as a gift and one for himself. What is the total price?

38. Mary wants to buy 3 compact disc players for $449.95 each. She has saved $1000. How much more must she save to buy the 3 compact disc players?

39. The price of cassettes is 4 for $9.99. What is the cost of 12 cassettes?

Problem Solving: Working Backwards

Problem: After shopping, Stephanie has $3.25 left. She spent $10.80 for balloons, horns, and favors for her party. She spent $24.55 for a pair of sneakers. With how much money did Stephanie start?

1 IMAGINE You are Stephanie and want to know with how much money you started.

2 NAME *Facts:* $10.80 for party, $24.55 for sneakers, $3.25 left.

Question: With how much money did Stephanie start?

3 THINK Work backwards to find with how much Stephanie started. Add all she spent and what she had left to find this amount.

Left: $3.25
Party: $10.80
Sneakers: $24.55

4 COMPUTE

```
    1 1
$   3. 2 5
   1 0. 8 0
+  2 4. 5 5
$  3 8. 6 0
```

Stephanie had $38.60 when she started shopping.

5 CHECK Check by estimation.

```
$    3. 2 5 ──→ $    3
    1 0. 8 0 ──→     1 1
+   2 4. 5 5 ──→ +   2 5
                $   3 9
```

$38.60 is close to the estimate of $39.

The answer is reasonable.

Solve by working backwards.

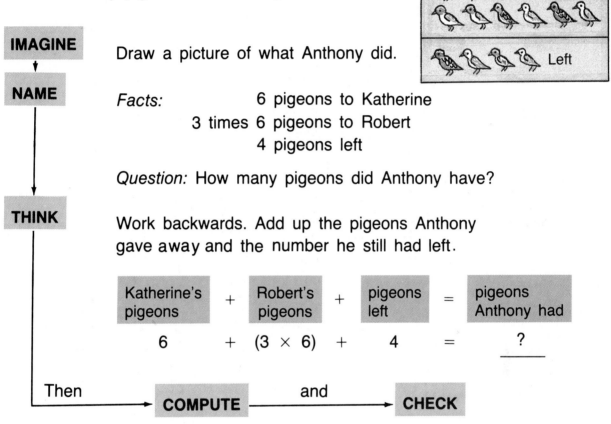

1. Anthony was moving away. He gave 6 pigeons to Katherine. He gave three times that number to Robert. He kept only 4 pigeons. How many pigeons did Anthony have?

IMAGINE

Draw a picture of what Anthony did.

NAME

Facts: 6 pigeons to Katherine
3 times 6 pigeons to Robert
4 pigeons left

Question: How many pigeons did Anthony have?

THINK

Work backwards. Add up the pigeons Anthony gave away and the number he still had left.

Katherine's pigeons	+	Robert's pigeons	+	pigeons left	=	pigeons Anthony had
6	+	(3 × 6)	+	4	=	?

Then → **COMPUTE** — and → **CHECK**

2. Matthew gave each of his 5 friends 16 of his marbles. He gave his sister 8 marbles. Matthew still had 20 marbles. With how many marbles did Matthew start?

3. Hector baked cupcakes. He gave 3 to William and 4 each to fifteen of his other friends. Hector took 8 cupcakes home. How many cupcakes did Hector bake?

179

More Practice

Find the product.

1. 3 × 56

2. 5 × 214

3. 6 × 82

4. 5 × 95

5. 3 × 5129

6. 7 × 6071

7. 6 × 5034

8. 9 × 6207

9. 51
  × 72

10. 83
  × 83

11. 76
  × 24

12. 29
  × 38

13. 639
  × 24

14. 428
  × 34

15. 723
  × 75

16. 515
  × 76

17. 10 × 25

18. 10 × 463

19. 70 × 83

20. 40 × 30

21. $5.20
  × 15

22. $3.40
  × 29

23. $8.69
  × 46

24. $9.08
  × 34

Estimate the product.

25. 9 × 283

26. 3 × 658

27. 8 × 712

Solve.

28. Mr. King travels 328 miles each day. How many miles does he travel in 6 days?

29. Jill spent 4 weeks at camp. If she spent $7.45 each week at the canteen, how much did she spend altogether?

30. Records cost $6.99 each. Find the cost of 5 records.

(See *Still More Practice,* p. 362.)

Math Probe

Order Forms

Frank is going to spend his summer vacation in a tennis camp. He completes the **order form** by carefully completing each line.

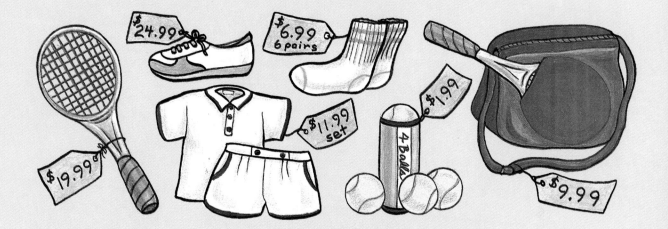

Item	Quantity	Price		Total Price	
Tennis Racket	1	$19	99	$19	99
Tennis Shoes	1	24	99	24	99
Tennis Balls (can)	4	1	99	7	96
Tops and Shorts	2	11	99	23	98
Socks (6-pr. Pack)	3	6	99	20	97
		Total		$97	89

Copy and complete this order form.

Item	Quantity	Price		Total Price	
Racquetsports bag	1	$ 9	99	$ 9	99
Tennis Racket	1	??	??	??	??
Tennis Balls (can)	2	?	??	?	??
Tops and Shorts	2	11	99	??	??
		Total		$??	??

Check Your Mastery

Find the product.

See pp. 156-177.

1. 3 × 43

2. 6 × 47

3. 8 × 207

4. 3 × 27

5. 5 × 503

6. 5 × 2063

7. 6 × 279

8. 4 × 6351

9.
27
× 32

10.
54
× 26

11.
46
× 83

12.
82
× 37

13.
238
× 16

14.
453
× 62

15.
$7.51
× 35

16.
$5.07
× 94

17. 10 × 56

18. 20 × 73

19. 60 × 84

20. 50 × 70

21. 78 × 47

22. 56 × 39

23. 212 × 57

24. 197 × 38

Estimate the product.

See p. 165.

25. 6 × 279

26. 8 × 327

27. 7 × 473

Solve.

See pp. 162-163, 170-171, 176-177.

28. Each week Mr. Garcia earns $272. How much does he earn in 4 weeks?

29. There are 175 pages in each notebook. How many pages are there in 16 notebooks of the same size?

30. Traveling by automobile we can cover 325 miles each day. About how many miles can we travel in 7 days?

182

7

Division: One-Digit Divisors

In this unit you will:

- Divide by one digit
- Compute two- and three-digit quotients
- Check division by multiplication
- Divide with money
- Estimate quotients
- Find averages
- Solve problems by making up questions

Do you remember?

Division is the opposite of multiplication.

$$35 \div 7 = \underline{\ ?\ }$$

is the same as:

$$\underline{\ ?\ } \times 7 = 35$$

The parts of a division problem have special names.

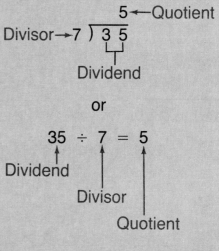

$$\text{Divisor} \rightarrow 7\overline{)3\,5} \quad \begin{array}{c} 5 \leftarrow \text{Quotient} \end{array}$$

Dividend

or

$$35 \div 7 = 5$$

Dividend   Divisor   Quotient

183

7-1 Division Facts Review

Do You Remember?

$$42 \div 6 = \underline{\ ?\ } \longrightarrow \underline{\ ?\ } \times 6 = 42 \longrightarrow 6\overline{)42}^{\,7}$$

$$63 \div 7 = \underline{\ ?\ } \longrightarrow \underline{\ ?\ } \times 7 = 63 \longrightarrow 7\overline{)63}^{\,9}$$

Divide mentally.

1. $9\overline{)63}$
2. $2\overline{)12}$
3. $6\overline{)30}$
4. $4\overline{)32}$
5. $9\overline{)36}$

6. $5\overline{)35}$
7. $6\overline{)36}$
8. $9\overline{)54}$
9. $7\overline{)49}$
10. $8\overline{)32}$

11. $8\overline{)56}$
12. $7\overline{)14}$
13. $8\overline{)48}$
14. $5\overline{)15}$
15. $9\overline{)45}$

16. $4\overline{)24}$
17. $3\overline{)24}$
18. $4\overline{)20}$
19. $5\overline{)40}$
20. $3\overline{)15}$

21. $8\overline{)40}$
22. $3\overline{)18}$
23. $8\overline{)64}$
24. $7\overline{)28}$
25. $6\overline{)48}$

26. $7\overline{)42}$
27. $3\overline{)21}$
28. $8\overline{)24}$
29. $2\overline{)10}$
30. $4\overline{)28}$

31. $7\overline{)56}$
32. $6\overline{)24}$
33. $2\overline{)12}$
34. $9\overline{)81}$
35. $4\overline{)20}$

36. $4\overline{)12}$
37. $9\overline{)72}$
38. $7\overline{)35}$
39. $6\overline{)42}$
40. $4\overline{)16}$

41. $3\overline{)12}$
42. $2\overline{)16}$
43. $2\overline{)14}$
44. $9\overline{)27}$
45. $5\overline{)25}$

46. $6\overline{)18}$
47. $5\overline{)30}$
48. $7\overline{)21}$
49. $9\overline{)9}$
50. $7\overline{)0}$

51. $9\overline{)18}$
52. $5\overline{)20}$
53. $6\overline{)12}$
54. $7\overline{)63}$
55. $8\overline{)8}$

56. $3\overline{)27}$
57. $4\overline{)36}$
58. $8\overline{)16}$
59. $2\overline{)0}$
60. $6\overline{)54}$

Dividends with Multiples of Ten

Look for a pattern.

6 tens ÷ 2 = 3 tens

60 ÷ 2 = 30

Divide: 40 ÷ 2 = ?

Think:
Divide 4 by 2.
Place 1 zero at the right in the quotient.

40 ÷ 2 = 20

8 tens ÷ 4 = 2 tens

80 ÷ 4 = 20

Divide: 300 ÷ 6 = ?

Think:
Divide 30 by 6.
Place 1 zero at the right in the quotient.

300 ÷ 6 = 50

Study these examples.

$$240 \div 6 = 40$$

$$\begin{array}{r} 6\;0 \\ 8\overline{)4\;8\;0} \end{array}$$

$$800 \div 8 = 100$$

$$\begin{array}{r} 5\;0 \\ 8\overline{)4\;0\;0} \end{array}$$

Divide.

1. 50 ÷ 5

2. 60 ÷ 2

3. 30 ÷ 3

4. 80 ÷ 2

5. 240 ÷ 6

6. 560 ÷ 8

7. 200 ÷ 4

8. 700 ÷ 7

9. 2)80

10. 3)120

11. 4)80

12. 8)640

13. 6)540

14. 7)490

15. 5)400

16. 9)720

17. 8)480

18. 3)270

19. 4)320

20. 7)210

One-Digit Divisors

The counselors at Middle Camp wanted to divide 31 children into equal groups of 7. How many equal groups of 7 children can the counselors form? How many children will be left over?

Since the 31 children are being separated into *equal* groups, divide:

$$31 \div 7 = \text{?}$$

Total   Number in   Number of
each group   groups

31 children in all

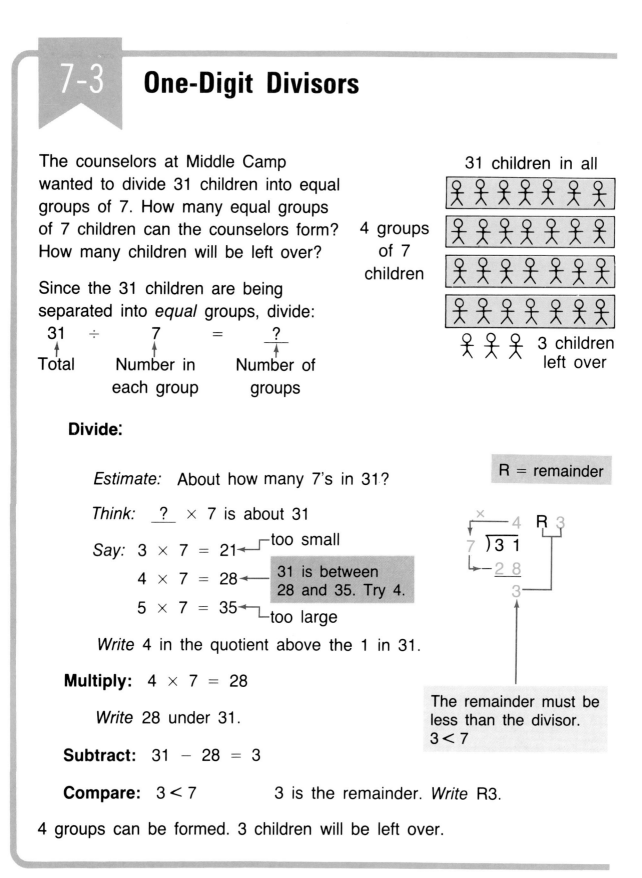

4 groups
of 7
children

3 children
left over

Divide:

Estimate: About how many 7's in 31?

Think: ___?___ × 7 is about 31

Say: 3 × 7 = 21 ——too small

4 × 7 = 28 ← 31 is between 28 and 35. Try 4.

5 × 7 = 35 ——too large

Write 4 in the quotient above the 1 in 31.

Multiply: 4 × 7 = 28

Write 28 under 31.

Subtract: 31 − 28 = 3

Compare: 3 < 7   3 is the remainder. *Write* R3.

R = remainder

$$\begin{array}{r} 4 \text{ R } 3 \\ 7\overline{)31} \\ -28 \\ \hline 3 \end{array}$$

The remainder must be less than the divisor. 3 < 7

4 groups can be formed. 3 children will be left over.

Complete.

1.
```
    6
4)2 4
 -2 4
    0
```
↑ There is no remainder.

2.
```
    5 R ?
3)1 9
 -1 5
    4
```

3.
```
    9 R ?
5)4 8
 -4 5
    ?
```

4.
```
    ? R ?
2)1 3
 -? ?
    ?
```

Divide.

5. 2)15

6. 4)35

7. 3)23

8. 5)17

9. 6)27

10. 6)14

11. 5)26

12. 4)37

13. 7)50

14. 4)33

15. 6)55

16. 5)38

17. 8)68

18. 2)19

19. 7)45

20. 8)17

21. 3)26

22. 4)15

23. 7)29

24. 8)38

25. 9)64

26. 8)52

27. 6)45

28. 5)33

29. 9)82

Find the quotient and the remainder.

30. 19 ÷ 6

31. 23 ÷ 7

32. 84 ÷ 9

33. 50 ÷ 8

34. 38 ÷ 4

35. 57 ÷ 6

Solve.

36. Ted wants to place 4 hanging baskets on each rod. If he has 33 baskets, how many rods will he need? How many baskets will be left over?

37. At Pine's Nursery plants are packed in groups of 6. Katherine has 46 plants. How many plants can she pack? How many plants will she have left?

187

Two-Digit Quotients

A loaf of bread has 56 slices. How many sandwiches can be made from the loaf?

To find the number of sandwiches, divide: $56 \div 2 = \underline{\ ?\ }$

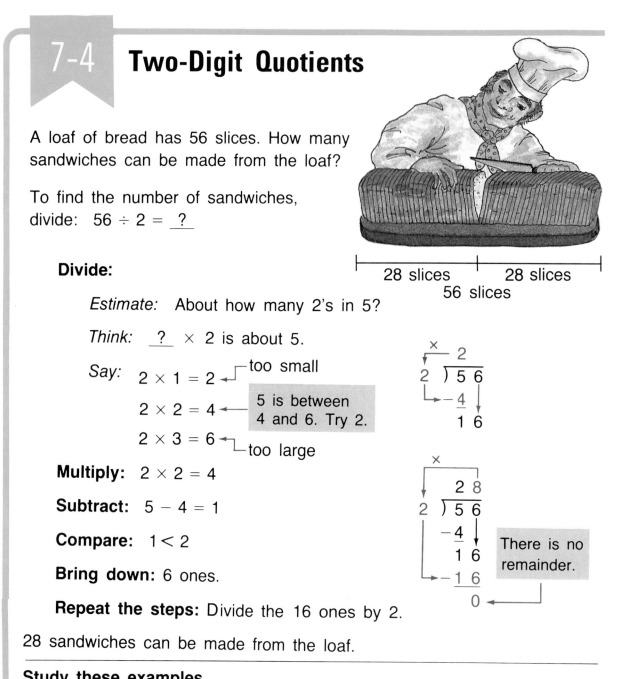

28 slices	28 slices

56 slices

Divide:

Estimate: About how many 2's in 5?

Think: $\underline{\ ?\ } \times 2$ is about 5.

Say: $2 \times 1 = 2$ ⟵ too small

$2 \times 2 = 4$ ⟵ 5 is between 4 and 6. Try 2.

$2 \times 3 = 6$ ⟵ too large

Multiply: $2 \times 2 = 4$

Subtract: $5 - 4 = 1$

Compare: $1 < 2$

Bring down: 6 ones.

There is no remainder.

Repeat the steps: Divide the 16 ones by 2.

28 sandwiches can be made from the loaf.

Study these examples.

$$
\begin{array}{r}
1\,8 \\
3\,\overline{)\,5\,4} \\
-3 \\
\hline
2\,4 \\
-2\,4 \\
\hline
0
\end{array}
\qquad
\begin{array}{r}
2\,3 \\
4\,\overline{)\,9\,2} \\
-8 \\
\hline
1\,2 \\
-1\,2 \\
\hline
0
\end{array}
\qquad
\begin{array}{r}
3\,2 \\
3\,\overline{)\,9\,6} \\
-9 \\
\hline
0\,6 \\
-\,6 \\
\hline
0
\end{array}
$$

This 0 need not be written.

Complete.

1.
```
      1 4
  4 ) 5 6
    − 4 ↓
      1 6
    − ? ?
        ?
```

2.
```
      2 ?
  4 ) 8 4
    − 8 ↓
      ⊙ 4
    −   ?
        ?
```

3.
```
      1 ?
  6 ) 7 2
    − ? ↓
      ? ?
    − ? ?
        ?
```

4.
```
      ? ?
  2 ) 3 4
    − ? ↓
      ? ?
    − ? ?
        ?
```

Divide.

5. 2)76 6. 5)85 7. 3)78 8. 7)98 9. 4)68

10. 3)57 11. 4)76 12. 2)46 13. 5)65 14. 5)95

15. 3)42 16. 4)48 17. 2)50 18. 3)75 19. 2)64

20. 5)60 21. 4)64 22. 6)84 23. 3)48 24. 3)69

25. 8)96 26. 4)92 27. 6)96 28. 7)91 29. 9)99

Find the quotient.

30. 84 ÷ 3   31. 90 ÷ 5   32. 56 ÷ 4

33. 45 ÷ 3   34. 90 ÷ 2   35. 88 ÷ 2

36. 70 ÷ 2   37. 66 ÷ 6   38. 99 ÷ 3

Solve.

39. There are 75 bolts. If a package holds 3 bolts, how many packages are there?

40. Farmer Lavelle picked 79 ears of corn. He put 6 ears of corn in each basket. How many baskets did he fill? How many ears of corn were left over?

More Two-Digit Quotients

A tailor has 74 buttons. He wants to sew 3 buttons on the front of each jacket. How many jackets can he complete? How many buttons will be left over?

To find the number of jackets,
divide: $74 \div 3 = \underline{\ ?\ }$

Divide:

Estimate: About how many 3's in 7?

Think: $\underline{\ ?\ } \times 3$ is about 7.

Say: $2 \times 3 = 6 \longleftarrow$ Try 2.

$3 \times 3 = 9 \longleftarrow$ too large

Multiply: $2 \times 3 = 6$

Subtract: $7 - 6 = 1$

Compare: $1 < 3$

Bring down: 4

Repeat the steps: Divide 14 ones by 3.

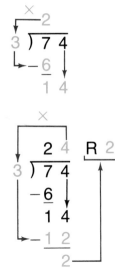

Check your division.

- *Multiply* the quotient by the divisor.

- *Add* the remainder.

- The answer is the dividend.

The tailor can complete 24 jackets. 2 buttons will be left over.

$$\begin{array}{r} 2\,4 \quad \text{Quotient} \\ \times \quad 3 \quad \text{Divisor} \\ \hline 7\,2 \\ +\quad 2 \quad \text{Remainder} \\ \hline 7\,4 \quad \text{Dividend} \end{array}$$

The answer checks!

Complete.

1.

```
      1 2  R ?        Check
  8 ) 9 8               1 2
    − 8                ×  8
      1 8              ? ?
    − ? ?            +    2
        2              9 8
```

2.

```
      2 ?  R 3        Check
  4 ) 9 9               2 ?
    − 8                ×  4
      1 ?              ? ?
    − ? ?            +    3
        3              9 9
```

Division Steps

- Divide.
- Multiply.
- Subtract.
- Compare.
- Bring down.
- Repeat the steps.
- Check your answer.

Divide and check.

3. 4)49   **4.** 2)63   **5.** 5)92   **6.** 6)83   **7.** 3)34

8. 8)91   **9.** 7)87   **10.** 3)58   **11.** 4)89   **12.** 2)74

13. 3)37   **14.** 5)63   **15.** 7)94   **16.** 6)67   **17.** 8)89

18. 5)86   **19.** 2)93   **20.** 4)51   **21.** 2)47   **22.** 7)79

23. 6)97   **24.** 4)86   **25.** 6)99   **26.** 5)87   **27.** 4)98

Solve.

28. The divisor is 4. The quotient is 23. What is the dividend?

29. Cars are parked 4 in a row in the *Dents-on-Us* Parking Lot. There are 86 cars. How many rows are there? How many cars are *not* in a row of 4?

191

7-6   **Three-Digit Quotients**

Divide: 936 ÷ 4 = <u> ? </u>

Use the division steps. Estimate the
quotient as shown.

- Divide the 9 hundreds by 4.

$$\underline{\;?\;} \times 4 = 9$$

$$2 \times 4 = 8$$

Try 2

```
      2
4 ) 9 3 6
   -8 ↓
    1 3
```

- Divide the 13 tens by 4.

$$\underline{\;?\;} \times 4 = 13$$

$$3 \times 4 = 12$$

Try 3

```
      2 3
4 ) 9 3 6
   -8
    1 3
   -1 2 ↓
       1 6
```

- Divide the 16 ones by 4.

$$\underline{\;?\;} \times 4 = 16$$

$$4 \times 4 = 16$$

Try 4

```
      2 3 4
4 ) 9 3 6
   -8
    1 3
   -1 2
       1 6
      -1 6
         0
```

Check: 4 × 234 = 936

Complete.

1.
```
        1 2 5  R 3
   5 ) 6 2 8
     − 5 ↓
       1 2
     − ? ?
         2 8
       − ? ?
           3
```
Check
```
      1 2 5
   ×      5
      6 2 5
   +      ?
      6 2 8
```

2.
```
        2 4 3  R 2
   3 ) 7 3 1
     − 6 ↓
       1 3
     − 1 2 ↓
           1 1
         −   ?
             2
```
Check
```
      2 4 3
   ×      3
      7 2 9
   +      ?
      7 3 1
```

3.
```
        2 6 ?
   3 ) 8 0 7
     − ? ↓
       2 0
     − ? ?
         2 7
       − ? ?
           0
```
Check
```
      2 6 ?
   ×      3
      ? ? ?
   +      0
      8 0 7
```

4.
```
        ? 2 ?  R  ?
   2 ) 6 5 1
     − 6 ↓
       ⓪ 5
       − ?
           1 1
         − 1 0
             ?
```
Check
```
      ? 2 ?
   ×      2
      ? ? ?
   +      ?
      6 5 1
```

Divide and check.

5. 2)632 **6.** 4)976 **7.** 3)936 **8.** 6)762 **9.** 7)931

10. 8)968 **11.** 7)868 **12.** 4)907 **13.** 6)918 **14.** 4)772

15. 8)936 **16.** 5)960 **17.** 7)924 **18.** 7)802 **19.** 2)922

20. 6)918 **21.** 3)537 **22.** 6)714 **23.** 5)815 **24.** 8)984

Solve.

25. 336 ducklings were shipped to 2 farms. If each farm received the same number of ducklings, how many were shipped to each farm?

7-7 More Difficult Quotients

Divide: $3\overline{)254}$ ──→ 254 = 2 hundreds 5 tens 4 ones

= 25 tens 4 ones

Think: 3 > 2. So divide the 25 tens by 3.

25 tens ÷ 3 = _?_ tens, or _?_ tens × 3 = 25 tens

8 × 3 = 24 ←┐

9 × 3 = 27 └─ Try 8.

```
      8                   8 4  R 2            Check
  3 ) 2 5 4           3 ) 2 5 4                  8 4
    - 2 4 ↓             - 2 4 ↓               ×    3
        1 4                 1 4               2 5 2
                          - 1 2              +    2   The answer
                              2              2 5 4   checks.
```

Study these examples.

```
                        5 2                                    8 2  R 6
  8 ) 4 1 6         8 ) 4 1 6         7 ) 5 8 0          7 ) 5 8 0
  └──┘                - 4 0 ↓         └──┘                 - 5 6 ↓
                          1 6                                  2 0
    8 > 4, so            - 1 6           7 > 5, so           - 1 4
    divide the 41 tens.                  divide the 58 tens.     6
```

Complete.

```
1.        7 ?      2.        8 ?  R ?    3.        ? ?  R 4    4.        ? ?  R ?
      8 ) 6 0 8        5 ) 4 3 3             6 ) 3 5 8             9 ) 4 7 2
        - 5 6 ↓          - ? ? ↓              - 3 0 ↓              - 4 ? ↓
            ? 8              3 ?                  ? 8                  ? 2
          - ? ?            - ? ?                - ? ?                - ? ?
              ?                3                    4                    ?
```

194

Divide and check.

5. $3\overline{)105}$ 6. $4\overline{)231}$ 7. $6\overline{)258}$ 8. $3\overline{)188}$ 9. $5\overline{)130}$

10. $6\overline{)236}$ 11. $3\overline{)201}$ 12. $5\overline{)359}$ 13. $4\overline{)354}$ 14. $7\overline{)182}$

15. $9\overline{)756}$ 16. $3\overline{)202}$ 17. $9\overline{)337}$ 18. $6\overline{)276}$ 19. $8\overline{)197}$

20. $6\overline{)220}$ 21. $4\overline{)328}$ 22. $7\overline{)195}$ 23. $5\overline{)295}$ 24. $8\overline{)735}$

25. $7\overline{)308}$ 26. $9\overline{)823}$ 27. $8\overline{)692}$ 28. $8\overline{)666}$ 29. $9\overline{)717}$

Divide.

30. $657 \div 9$ 31. $267 \div 8$ 32. $396 \div 4$

33. $462 \div 5$ 34. $498 \div 6$ 35. $391 \div 7$

Match.

36. $288 \div 6 = \underline{\ ?\ }$ a. 45

37. $204 \div 4 = \underline{\ ?\ }$ b. 51

38. $405 \div 9 = \underline{\ ?\ }$ c. 47

39. $441 \div 9 = \underline{\ ?\ }$ d. 50

40. $368 \div 8 = \underline{\ ?\ }$ e. 48

41. $416 \div 8 = \underline{\ ?\ }$ f. 49

42. $141 \div 3 = \underline{\ ?\ }$ g. 52

43. $350 \div 7 = \underline{\ ?\ }$ h. 46

Solve.

44. 275 tomatoes are to be packed equally into 8 baskets. How many tomatoes will there be in each basket? How many will be left over?

195

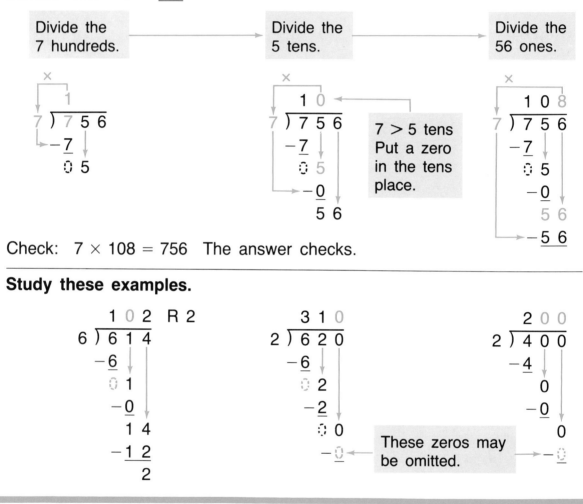

7-8 Zeros in the Quotient

Divide: 756 ÷ 7 = ?

Divide the 7 hundreds.	Divide the 5 tens.	Divide the 56 ones.

×

```
      1
7 ) 7 5 6
   − 7
     0 5
```

×

```
      1 0
7 ) 7 5 6
   − 7
     0 5
     − 0
       5 6
```

7 > 5 tens
Put a zero
in the tens
place.

×

```
      1 0 8
7 ) 7 5 6
   − 7
     0 5
     − 0
       5 6
     − 5 6
```

Check: 7 × 108 = 756   The answer checks.

Study these examples.

```
      1 0 2  R 2
6 ) 6 1 4
   − 6
     0 1
     − 0
       1 4
     − 1 2
         2
```

```
      3 1 0
2 ) 6 2 0
   − 6
     0 2
     − 2
       0 0
     − 0
```

These zeros may
be omitted.

```
      2 0 0
2 ) 4 0 0
   − 4
       0
     − 0
         0
       − 0
```

Complete.

1.
```
      3 0 4
3 ) 9 1 2
   − 9
     0 1
     − 0
       1 2
     − ? ?
```

2.
```
      2 0 ?
4 ) 8 3 6
   − 8
     0 3
     − 0
       3 6
     − ? ?
```

3.
```
      1 ? 0
3 ) 4 2 0
   − 3
     1 2
   − 1 2
       0 0
     − 0
```

4.
```
      ? 0 ?
5 ) 5 0 0
   − 5
     0 0
     − 0
       0 ?
     − ?
```

196

Divide and check.

5. $3\overline{)918}$ 6. $4\overline{)824}$ 7. $6\overline{)609}$ 8. $2\overline{)817}$ 9. $5\overline{)506}$

10. $8\overline{)832}$ 11. $7\overline{)745}$ 12. $9\overline{)954}$ 13. $6\overline{)654}$ 14. $4\overline{)833}$

15. $7\overline{)707}$ 16. $9\overline{)909}$ 17. $6\overline{)642}$ 18. $8\overline{)866}$ 19. $9\overline{)900}$

Divide.

20. $922 \div 9$ 21. $267 \div 8$ 22. $847 \div 8$

23. $462 \div 5$ 24. $744 \div 7$ 25. $555 \div 6$

26. $620 \div 6$ 27. $888 \div 9$ 28. $985 \div 9$

29. $280 \div 7$ 30. $972 \div 9$ 31. $850 \div 5$

Solve.

32. The dividend is 615. The divisor is 3. What is the quotient?

33. 654 hams were sold in 6 stores. If each store sold the same number of hams, how many did each store sell?

34. 763 balloons were given out at the Children's Hospital by 7 fourth graders. If each fourth grader gave out the same number, how many balloons did each one give?

35. One spring these birds flew into a bird sanctuary: 212 robins, 356 cardinals, and 256 bluejays. All of these birds were equally divided among 4 bird houses. How many birds were in each house?

197

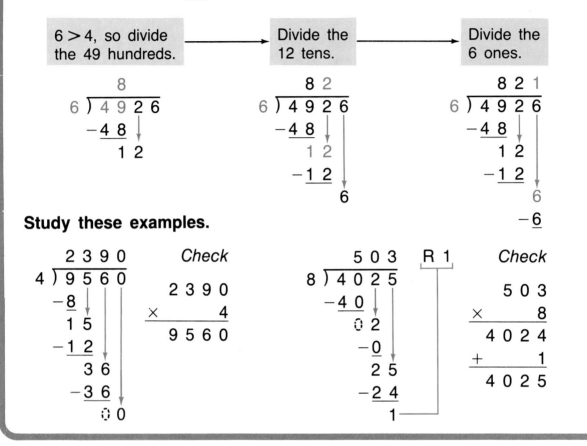

7-9 Four-Digit Dividends

Divide: 4926 ÷ 6 = _?_

6 > 4, so divide the 49 hundreds.	Divide the 12 tens.	Divide the 6 ones.

```
        8
  6 ) 4 9 2 6
     - 4 8
       1 2
```

```
        8 2
  6 ) 4 9 2 6
     - 4 8
       1 2
     - 1 2
          6
```

```
        8 2 1
  6 ) 4 9 2 6
     - 4 8
       1 2
     - 1 2
          6
        - 6
```

Study these examples.

```
      2 3 9 0
  4 ) 9 5 6 0
     - 8
       1 5
     - 1 2
         3 6
       - 3 6
           0 0
```

Check
```
      2 3 9 0
  ×         4
      9 5 6 0
```

```
      5 0 3   R 1
  8 ) 4 0 2 5
     - 4 0
       0 2
       - 0
         2 5
       - 2 4
           1
```

Check
```
      5 0 3
  ×       8
    4 0 2 4
  +       1
    4 0 2 5
```

Complete.

1.
```
        5 6 ?  R  ?
  4 ) 2 2 4 2
     - ? ?
       2 4
     - ? ?
         2
       - ?
         ?
```

2.
```
      2 6 ? ?  R 1
  3 ) 7 9 4 8
     - ?
       1 9
     - ? ?
         1 4
       - 1 2
           ? 8
         - 2 7
             1
```

3.
```
      3 ? ?  R  ?
  7 ) 2 5 0 1
     - ? ?
       4 0
     - 3 5
         5 1
       - 4 9
           ?
```

198

Divide and check.

4. $4\overline{)7576}$ 5. $6\overline{)1344}$ 6. $3\overline{)8217}$ 7. $7\overline{)2982}$ 8. $5\overline{)7870}$

9. $8\overline{)4336}$ 10. $2\overline{)5566}$ 11. $9\overline{)1962}$ 12. $3\overline{)4545}$ 13. $7\overline{)4361}$

14. $6\overline{)2418}$ 15. $8\overline{)7249}$ 16. $9\overline{)4567}$ 17. $7\overline{)5320}$ 18. $8\overline{)3600}$

19. $4\overline{)6204}$ 20. $6\overline{)5043}$ 21. $5\overline{)9990}$ 22. $3\overline{)8181}$ 23. $3\overline{)1311}$

24. $9\overline{)2884}$ 25. $7\overline{)3225}$ 26. $9\overline{)2772}$ 27. $8\overline{)2884}$ 28. $9\overline{)3675}$

Find the quotient and any remainder.

29. $1332 \div 6$ 30. $2562 \div 4$ 31. $2454 \div 5$

32. $1753 \div 7$ 33. $4638 \div 6$ 34. $6834 \div 7$

Solve.

35. 5445 divided by 9 equals what number?

36. The dividend is 2880. The divisor is 9. What is the quotient?

37. The factors are 49 and 8. What is the product?

38. The quotient is 509. The divisor is 7. What is the dividend?

39. In 9 months the girls made 941 toys and the boys made 931. The total number of toys made each month was the same. How many toys were made each month?

199

Division, Money, and Unit Prices

Henry bought 4 matching lawn chairs for $63.80. How much does one chair cost?

To find the cost of one item or the **unit price**, divide: $63.80 ÷ 4 = ?

| Write the dollar and cent signs in the quotient above the signs in the dividend. | → | Divide as usual. (Remember: $63.80 is 6380 cents.) Check. |

```
        $    .                      $ 1 5 . 9 5              Check
   4 ) $ 6 3 . 8 0            4 ) $ 6 3 . 8 0             $ 1 5 . 9 5
                                  - 4                       ×        4
                                    2 3                   $ 6 3 . 8 0
                                  - 2 0
                                      3  8
                                    - 3  6
                                       2 0
                                     - 2 0
```

Each chair costs $15.95.

Divide: $63 ÷ 4 = ?

```
     $ 1 5 . 7 5           Check
 4 ) $ 6 3 . 0 0       $ 1 5 . 7 5
    - 4                   ×        4
      2 3             $ 6 3 . 0 0 = $ 6 3
    - 2 0
        3  0
      - 2  8
         2 0
       - 2 0
```

Before dividing, write a decimal point and 2 zeros in the dividend.

Divide: $.49 ÷ 7 = ?

```
      $ . 0 7             Check
 7 ) $ . 4 9            $ . 0 7
    - 4 9                ×      7
                       $ . 4 9
```

There are no dimes in the quotient. Write a zero.

Complete.

1.
```
      $ 2 . 0 1
  4 ) $ 8 . 0 4
    − 8
        0
      − ?
        ?
      − ?
```

2.
```
      $   5 . ? ?
  9 ) $ 4 9 . 9 5
    − ? ?
        4   9
      − 4   5
          ? ?
        − ? ?
```

3.
```
      $ . 1 ?
  7 ) $ . 8 4
    − ?
      1 4
    − ? ?
```

4.
```
      $   . 0 ?
  8 ) $ 0 . 5 6
      − 5 6
          0
```

Divide and check.

5. 5)$1.35   6. 2)$4.94   7. 4)$2.44   8. 7)$2.31   9. 2)$8.58

10. 4)$20.84   11. 8)$24.16   12. 7)$14.28   13. 3)$24.72   14. 5)$18.10

15. 9)$49.77   16. 6)$14.82   17. 7)$27.93   18. 8)$20.88   19. 5)$26.00

20. 7)$21.63   21. 7)$17.01   22. 4)$24.96   23. 9)$73.53   24. 6)$22.20

Find the unit price of each item.

	Quantity Bought	Total Price	Unit Price
25.	3	$7.41	?
26.	2	$9.78	?
27.	6	$10.68	?
28.	9	$31.50	?
29.	4	$20.48	?
30.	8	$48.40	?
31.	7	$36.12	?
32.	5	$55.15	?
33.	9	$81.72	?

7-11 Estimating Quotients

Margo has 583 stamps in 6 albums. About how many stamps are there in each album?

To find about how many stamps are in each album, estimate the quotient: $583 \div 6 = \underline{?}$

To estimate a quotient:

- Round the dividend to its greatest place value.

$583 \xrightarrow{\text{rounds to}} 600$

- Find the first digit of the quotient.

$$6\overline{)600}\quad 1$$

- Write zeros for the other digits.

$$6\overline{)600}\quad 100$$

Each album has about 100 stamps.

Estimate the quotient.
$\$15.25 \div 2 = \underline{?}$

$\$15.25 \xrightarrow{\text{rounds to}} \$15.00$

$$2\overline{)\$15.00}\quad \$7.$$

For money, round the dividend to the nearest dollar.

$$2\overline{)\$15.00}\quad \$7.00$$

Estimate each quotient.

1. $5\overline{)322}$ 2. $6\overline{)63}$ 3. $3\overline{)87}$ 4. $7\overline{)143}$ 5. $9\overline{)448}$

6. $4\overline{)213}$ 7. $5\overline{)385}$ 8. $8\overline{)351}$ 9. $6\overline{)3594}$ 10. $7\overline{)4225}$

11. $2\overline{)\$23.97}$ 12. $4\overline{)\$15.75}$ 13. $8\overline{)\$32.19}$ 14. $9\overline{)\$53.50}$ 15. $7\overline{)\$41.65}$

16. $6\overline{)\$38.41}$ 17. $8\overline{)\$52.35}$ 18. $9\overline{)\$40.23}$ 19. $7\overline{)\$38.48}$ 20. $5\overline{)\$31.82}$

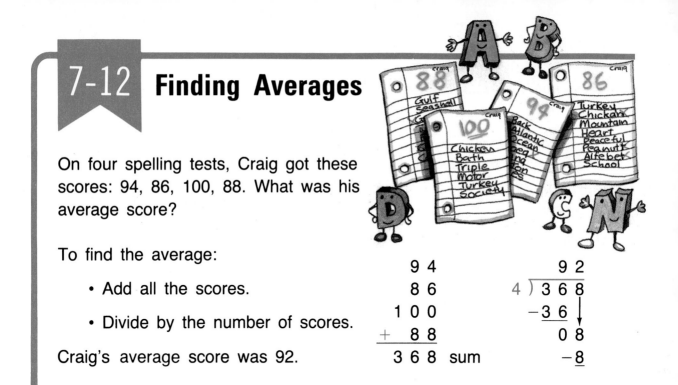

7-12 Finding Averages

On four spelling tests, Craig got these scores: 94, 86, 100, 88. What was his average score?

To find the average:

• Add all the scores.

• Divide by the number of scores.

Craig's average score was 92.

```
    9 4           9 2
    8 6        4 ) 3 6 8
  1 0 0         -3 6 ↓
+   8 8            0 8
  3 6 8  sum      -8
```

Find the average.

1. 23, 37, 41, 19

2. 62, 71, 58, 85, 44

3. 98, 81, 76

4. 235, 417, 338

5. $224, $219, $313

6. $39, $52, $43, $50

Solve.

7. Andrew spent a total of $6.25 for lunch for 5 school days. On the average how much did he spend for lunch each day?

8. On four days the store sold these numbers of books: 156, 274, 856 and 306. What was the average number sold each day?

9. In 7 hours 392 cars crossed the bridge. About how many cars crossed every hour?

10. In 6 basketball games, Andrew scored a total of 168 points. What was his average score?

203

7-13 Problem Solving: Make up a Question

When solving problems, it is sometimes difficult to know whether to add, subtract, multiply, or divide. Play the "Making up 4 Questions" game to help you decide.

1 IMAGINE

You have these words. | has or have / need or needs / more | You have these numbers. | 2 or $2 / 6 or $6

2 NAME

Facts: Use these words and numbers to make up:

1. an addition question   2. a subtraction question
3. a multiplication question   4. a division question

3 THINK

Read pp. 94–95 again to review the 4 operations.

1. *Addition Question*
Jason *has $6.*
He gets *$2 more.*
How many dollars does Jason *have?*
Compute: $6 + $2 = $8
Check: $8 − $2 = $6

2. *Subtraction Question*
Tiffany *needs $6.*
She *has $2.*
How many *more* dollars does she *need*?
Compute: $6 − $2 = $4
Check: $4 + $2 = $6

3. *Multiplication Question*
To make his quota, Mike *needs 2 more* customers for his paper route. Each customer pays Mike *$6* a month. How much money does Mike *need* to make his quota?
Compute: 2 × $6 = $12
Check: $12 ÷ 6 = $2

4. *Division Question*
Sarah *has $2* to buy her ticket to the game. She *needs $6 more* to buy tickets for her friends. For how many friends does Sarah want to buy tickets?
Compute: $6 ÷ $2
       = 3 friends
Check: 3 × $2 = $6

Play the "Make Up 4 Questions" Game

1.

WORD CARD	– Use each word at least once in each problem.	was or were sum
NUMBER CARD	– Use each number at least once in each problem.	4 or fourth 356
ONCE CARD	– Each number can be used in only *one* of the questions.	87, 92, 96

IMAGINE — You have to make up 4 questions or problems using the cards above.

NAME — *Facts:* See the cards above.

Questions: Make up 4 questions.

THINK

2. *Subtraction*

The *sum* of Tanya's scores *was 356*. On three tests her scores were *87, 92, and 96*. What did Tanya get on her *fourth* test?

4. *Division*

The *sum* of George's scores on *4* tests *was 356*. What was his average score?

Make up your own word problems for addition and multiplication.

Then → **COMPUTE** — and → **CHECK**

2. WORD CARD: was or were; and; left
NUMBER CARD: 8 and 16
ONCE CARD: 4

3. WORD CARD: was or were; difference
NUMBER CARD: 12 and 24
ONCE CARD: 3

4. WORD CARD: was or were; product
NUMBER CARD: 6 and 24
ONCE CARD: 12

5. Make up your own word and number cards.

More Practice

Divide.

1. $7\overline{)31}$

2. $3\overline{)28}$

3. $5\overline{)48}$

4. $5\overline{)75}$

5. $4\overline{)96}$

6. $6\overline{)85}$

7. $2\overline{)75}$

8. $6\overline{)82}$

9. $4\overline{)980}$

10. $3\overline{)813}$

11. $5\overline{)457}$

12. $8\overline{)263}$

13. $7\overline{)2828}$

14. $9\overline{)8163}$

15. $4\overline{)\$16.92}$

16. $3\overline{)\$18.54}$

In each group write the quotients in order from least to greatest.

17. $4\overline{)852}$ $7\overline{)819}$ $9\overline{)1107}$ $6\overline{)942}$

18. $7\overline{)602}$ $5\overline{)390}$ $8\overline{)704}$ $6\overline{)522}$

19. $6\overline{)672}$ $2\overline{)228}$ $3\overline{)309}$ $7\overline{)791}$

Estimate the quotient.

20. $336 \div 7$

21. $5663 \div 8$

22. $6572 \div 9$

Solve.

23. Betty gathered 54 flowers. She put them in bunches of 6. How many bunches did she have?

24. The 4th-grade classes sent 25, 30, 17, 24, and 19 children to the circus. What was the average number of students sent per class?

(See *Still More Practice*, p. 363.)

Math Probe

FACT FAMILIES

A geometric model can be used to show a
fact family for multiplication and division facts.

9 columns
8 in each column

8 rows
9 in each
row

Number of Columns	×	Number in Each Column	=	Total		Number of Rows	×	Number in Each Row	=	Total
9	×	8	=	72		8	×	9	=	72

Total	÷	Number in Each Column	=	Number of Columns		Total	÷	Number in Each Row	=	Number of Rows
72	÷	8	=	9		72	÷	9	=	8

Write the fact family for each.

1.

2.

Draw a model to show the fact family for each:

3. 7×2

4. 8×4

5. 9×1

6. $18 \div 6$

7. $27 \div 3$

8. $30 \div 5$

Check Your Mastery

Divide.

See pp. 184-201

1. 3)23

2. 6)48

3. 4)27

4. 5)39

5. 7)98

6. 6)91

7. 2)83

8. 7)93

9. 4)872

10. 5)985

11. 7)849

12. 6)344

13. 9)3636

14. 7)2856

15. 4)$8.56

16. 3)$16.92

In each group write the quotients in order from least to greatest.

See pp. 188-189

17. 9)216   5)180   6)228   7)259

18. 4)116   6)168   8)216   5)180

19. 6)510   7)581   8)856   9)864

Estimate the quotient.

See p. 202

20. 2473 ÷ 8

21. 1904 ÷ 9

22. 2257 ÷ 6

Solve.

See pp. 185-189, 198-199

23. Marina has 37 flowers. She divided them equally among 5 vases. How many are in each vase? How many flowers are left over?

24. 84 boys were divided equally into 7 teams. How many boys were on each team?

25. There are 2347 books in a library. If each shelf holds 8 books, about how many shelves are needed to hold all the books?

Cumulative Test II

Multiply.

1. 7 × 10

2. 6 × 100

3. 5 × 400

4. 6 × 42

5. 7 × 250

6. 4 × 2354

Complete.

7. 6 ft = _?_ in.

8. 3 yd = _?_ ft

9. 12 ft = _?_ yd

10. 40 km = _?_ m

11. 4000 g = _?_ kg

12. 6 pt = _?_ c

13. 16 kL = _?_ L

14. 6 L = _?_ mL

15. 7 m = _?_ cm

16. 200 cm = _?_ m

17. 2 mi = _?_ ft

18. 30 kg = _?_ g

Write the time.

19.
  a. 5 minutes to 6
  b. 15 minutes to 4
  c. 10 minutes to 3
  d. 20 minutes to 5

20.
  a. 40 minutes past 9
  b. 5 minutes past 6
  c. 12 midnight
  d. 12 noon

Multiply.

21. 69 × 58

22. 39 × 41

23. 35 × 63

24. 43 × 29

25. 12 × 254

26. 24 × 149

27. 62 × 483

28. 37 × 590

29. 8 × $8.67

30. 60 × $9.50

31. 24 × $9.45

32. 39 × $6.19

Divide.

33. 4)83

34. 7)50

35. 3)426

36. 5)515

37. 9)6273

38. 6)8906

39. 4)2754

40. 6)19

Write the total amount of money.

41.
  a. 2 dollars, 4 dimes, 3 pennies
  b. 3 dollars, 2 quarters, 1 nickel
  c. 12 dollars, 2 dimes, 2 pennies
  d. 15 dollars, 4 quarters, 4 pennies

42.
  a. 2 quarters, 2 nickels, 4 pennies
  b. 5 dimes, 5 nickels, 5 pennies
  c. 1 quarter, 2 dimes, 1 nickel
  d. 2 quarters, 6 nickels, 9 pennies

Estimate the length to the nearest centimeter.

43. 44. 45. 46.

Which metric unit (cm, m, g, kg, mL, L) should be used to measure each item?

47. a carton of milk

48. gas in a car

49. a bag of potatoes

50. a bunch of grapes

51. the weight of a banana

52. the length of a comb

53. the width of a window frame

54. water in a pool

Compare. Write <, =, or >.

55. 6 qt ? 3 gal

56. 3 c ? 1 pt

57. 40 mL ? 6 L

58. 3000 mL ? 3 L

59. 3 mL ? 30 L

60. 2 m ? 200 cm

61. 950 mL ? 2 L

62. 4800 mL ? 48 L

63. 4 km ? 4000 m

64. 18 cm ? 180 m

Arrange in order from the least to the greatest.

65. 3 g, 3 kg, 30 kg, 300 g

66. 470 g, 47 g, 47 kg, 470 kg

67. 3,300 L, 3 mL, 30 mL

68. 51,500 mL, 50 L, 500 L

Solve.

69. Pam needs 3 yd of fabric for one tablecloth. How much must she buy for 4 tablecloths?

70. Miguel's scores for 5 games were 28, 32, 33, 41, and 16 points. What was his average score?

71. A car travels 25 mi on a gallon of gas. How far does it travel on 13 gallons of gas?

72. Brian fed each of 16 chickens 7 oz of ground corn and soybean. How much of the mixture did the chickens eat?

73. Jill's thermos jug holds 2 L of soup. How many mL of soup can it hold?

74. Mary's change from a $5 purchase was 45¢. If she received 3 coins, which coins were they?

75. Girls' blouses are on sale for 4 for $50. How much is each blouse?

8

Geometry

In this unit you will:

- Learn about parallel, perpendicular, and intersecting lines
- Identify simple closed curves
- Learn about quadrilaterals and other polygons
- Find the perimeter of a polygon
- Name the parts of a circle
- Solve problems by using formulas

Do you remember?

circle

square

rectangle

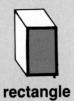

triangle

Points, Lines, and Line Segments

A **plane** is a never-ending flat surface.
The surface of your desk is part of a plane.

A and B are points: A.   B.
Write: A or B

Each edge of your desk is a **line segment**. A line segment has two **endpoints**.

You name a line segment by using its endpoints.

A————B

Write: $\overline{AB}$ or $\overline{BA}$

A————B
write:
$\overline{AB}$ $\overline{BA}$

end point   line segment   end point

A line segment is part of a **line**.

$\longleftarrow$————X————Y——Z$\longrightarrow$

The arrows tell you the line goes on and on in opposite directions. You name a line by naming any two points on it.

Write: $\overleftrightarrow{XY}$, $\overleftrightarrow{XZ}$, $\overleftrightarrow{YZ}$, $\overleftrightarrow{YX}$, $\overleftrightarrow{ZX}$, or $\overleftrightarrow{ZY}$

Identify each.

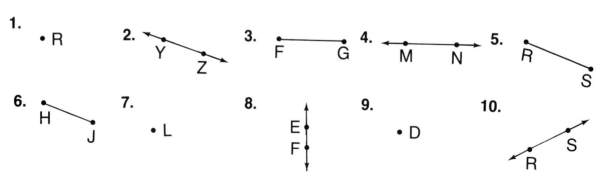

1. • R

2. Y Z

3. F G

4. M N

5. R S

6. H J

7. • L

8. E F

9. • D

10. R S

Draw these.

11. $\overline{TV}$ **12.** point K   **13.** $\overleftrightarrow{ST}$ **14.** $\overline{FG}$

15. point T   **16.** $\overrightarrow{PQ}$ **17.** $\overline{AB}$ **18.** point R

Solve.

19. Which are line segments?

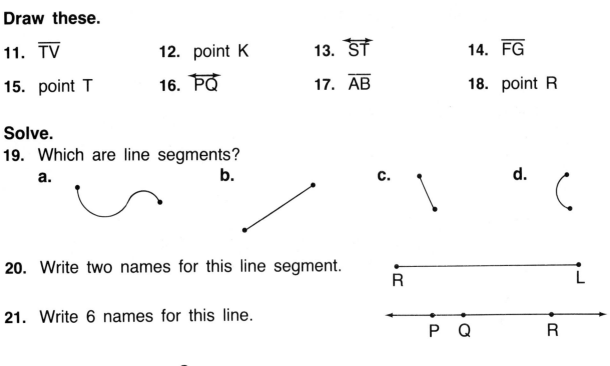

a.　　　b.　　　c.　　　d.

20. Write two names for this line segment.

R ———————————— L

21. Write 6 names for this line.

←——•——•————•——→
　　　P　Q　　　R

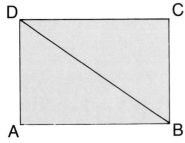

D ———————— C
| ╲ |
A ———————— B

22. Name the four points in this figure.

23. Write 2 names for each line segment in this figure.

24. How many line segments are there in the figure below?

25. Write two names for each line segment.

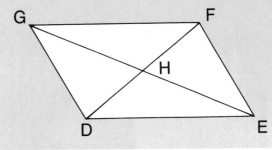

G　　　　　　　F

H

D　　　　　　　E

213

Rays and Angles

If a line segment goes on and on in one direction, a **ray** is formed. A ray has only one endpoint.

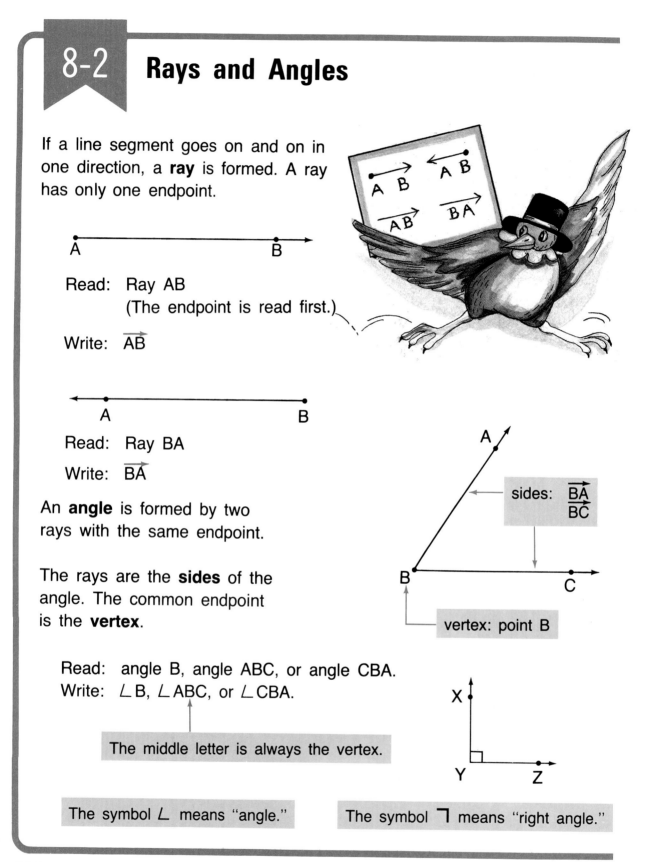

A •————————————→ B

Read: Ray AB
        (The endpoint is read first.)

Write: $\overrightarrow{AB}$

←————————————• B
A

Read: Ray BA

Write: $\overrightarrow{BA}$

An **angle** is formed by two rays with the same endpoint.

The rays are the **sides** of the angle. The common endpoint is the **vertex**.

sides: $\overrightarrow{BA}$
        $\overrightarrow{BC}$

vertex: point B

Read: angle B, angle ABC, or angle CBA.
Write: ∠B, ∠ABC, or ∠CBA.

The middle letter is always the vertex.

The symbol ∠ means "angle."

The symbol ⌐ means "right angle."

Write the name for each ray.

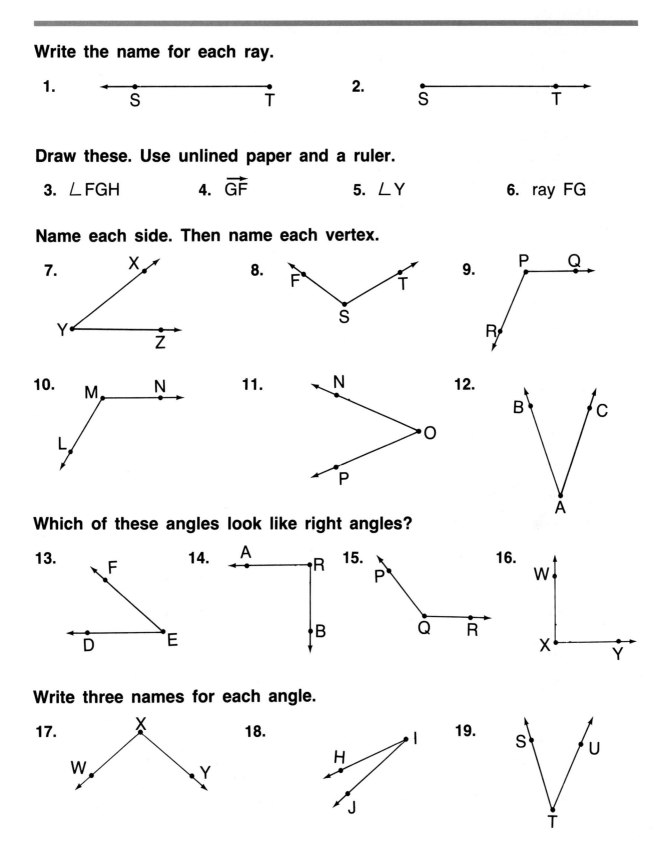

1. ●————————● S   T

2. S ●————————● T →

Draw these. Use unlined paper and a ruler.

3. ∠FGH   4. $\overrightarrow{GF}$ 5. ∠Y   6. ray FG

Name each side. Then name each vertex.

7.   8.   9.

10.   11.   12.

Which of these angles look like right angles?

13.   14.   15.   16.

Write three names for each angle.

17.   18.   19.

215

8-3 Parallel and Perpendicular Lines

$\overleftrightarrow{AB}$ and $\overleftrightarrow{CD}$ cross at point P. Lines that cross are **intersecting lines.**

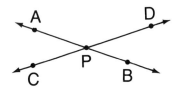

$\overleftrightarrow{MN}$ and $\overleftrightarrow{PQ}$ do not cross. Lines that do not cross are **parallel lines**.

Write: $\overleftrightarrow{MN} \parallel \overleftrightarrow{PQ}$. The symbol ∥ means "is parallel to".

$\overleftrightarrow{DE}$ and $\overleftrightarrow{FG}$ are intersecting lines. They form right angles where they cross. $\overleftrightarrow{DE}$ and $\overleftrightarrow{FG}$ are **perpendicular** lines.

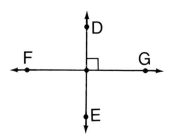

Write: $\overleftrightarrow{DE} \perp \overleftrightarrow{FG}$. The symbol ⊥ means "is perpendicular to."

Write "intersecting" or "parallel" to describe each pair of green lines

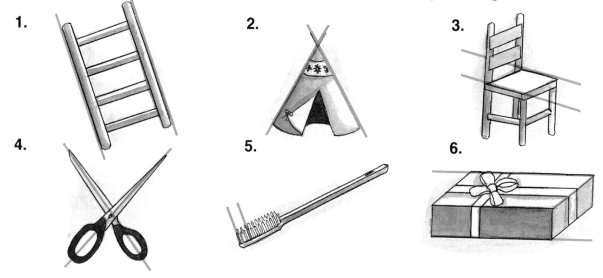

1.

2.

3.

4.

5.

6.

216

Write "parallel" or "perpendicular" to describe the lines formed.

7. The corner of a page.

8. The ties of a railroad track.

9. The top and side of a window.

10. The legs of a chair.

11. A flagpole and its shadow.

12. The lines on notebook paper.

13. The top and side of a doorway.

14. The stripes of the U.S. flag.

Solve.

Columns 1 through 7 each contain a series of letters.

15. Decide which letters contain parallel or perpendicular lines.

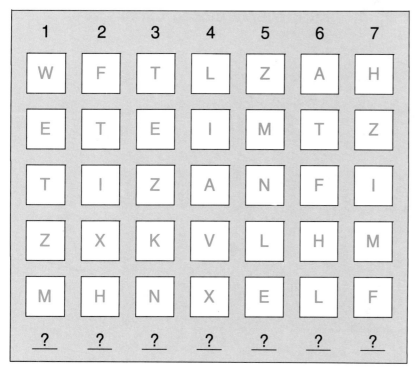

Example:
L perpendicular lines = 2 points
N parallel lines = 1 point

Score letters with:

- parallel lines as 1 point

- perpendicular lines as 2 points

- parallel and perpendicular lines as 3 points

1	2	3	4	5	6	7
W	F	T	L	Z	A	H
E	T	E	I	M	T	Z
T	I	Z	A	N	F	I
Z	X	K	V	L	H	M
M	H	N	X	E	L	F
?	?	?	?	?	?	?

8-4 Closed Curves

Mr. Garcia showed the Washington family the latest designs for swimming pools. Each design was a simple closed curve.

A **simple closed curve** begins and ends at the same point and does *not* cross itself.

Swimming Pool Designs

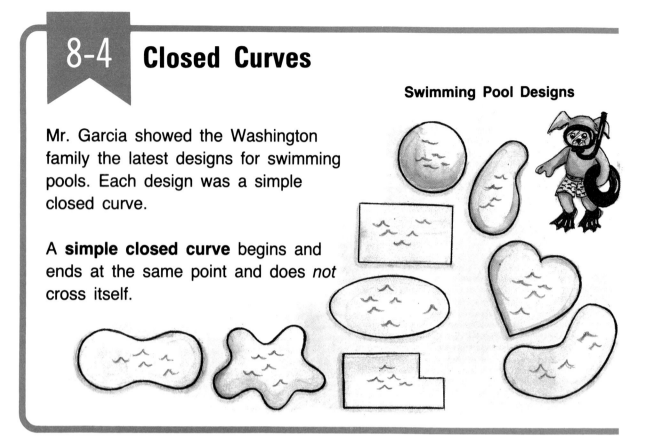

Write "simple closed curve" or "not a simple closed curve" to describe each figure.

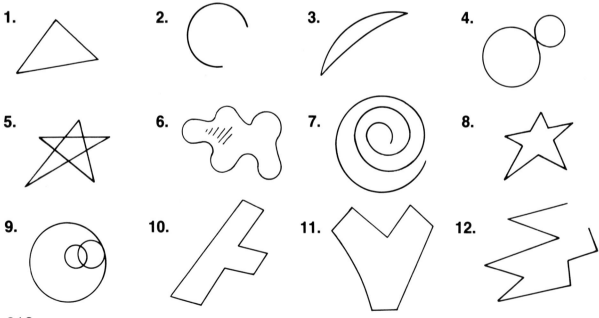

1.

2.

3.

4.

5.

6.

7.

8.

9.

10.

11.

12.

218

Quadrilaterals

A simple closed curve formed by four sides and four angles is a **quadrilateral**.

Quadrilaterals

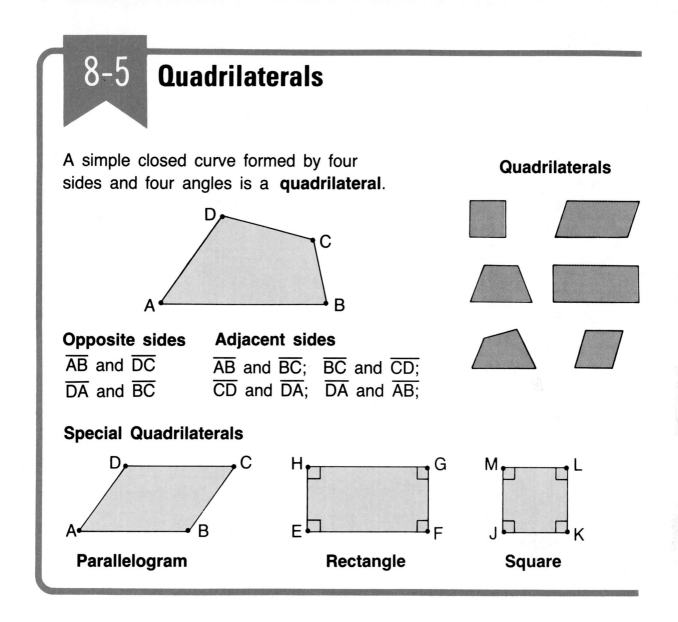

Opposite sides

$\overline{AB}$ and $\overline{DC}$
$\overline{DA}$ and $\overline{BC}$

Adjacent sides

$\overline{AB}$ and $\overline{BC}$; $\overline{BC}$ and $\overline{CD}$;
$\overline{CD}$ and $\overline{DA}$; $\overline{DA}$ and $\overline{AB}$;

Special Quadrilaterals

Parallelogram   **Rectangle**   **Square**

Decide if each figure is a quadrilateral. Write "Yes" or "No."

1.   2.   3.   4.

Complete.

5. Which of the figures above are parallelograms?

6. Which are rectangles?

7. Which are squares?

Polygons

A simple closed curve formed by line segments is a **polygon**. Its sides are line segments. A pair of sides meet to form an angle.

Polygons

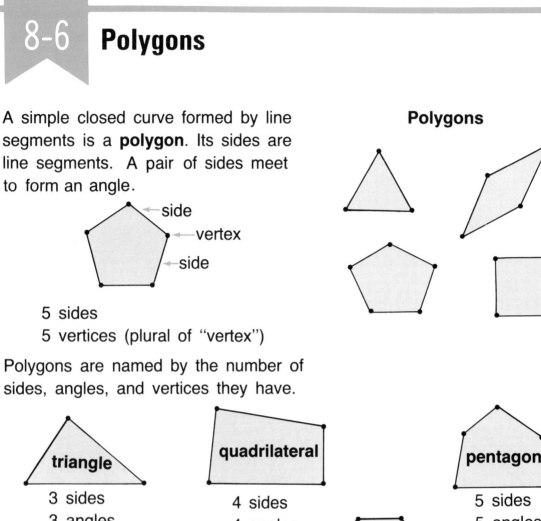

5 sides
5 vertices (plural of "vertex")

Polygons are named by the number of sides, angles, and vertices they have.

triangle
3 sides
3 angles

quadrilateral
4 sides
4 angles

pentagon
5 sides
5 angles

hexagon
6 sides
6 angles

octagon
8 sides
8 angles

Decide if each figure is a polygon. Write "Yes" or "No."

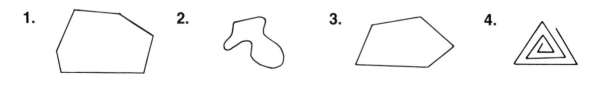

1.　　　　　2.　　　　　3.　　　　　4.

Identify each polygon.

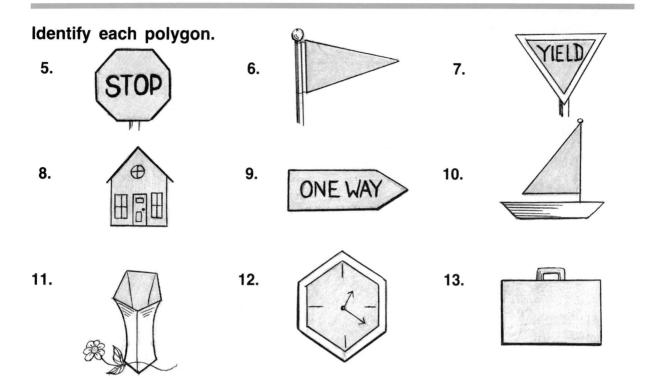

5.

6.

7.

8.

9.

10.

11.

12.

13.

Complete the table.

	Figure	Name	Number of angles	Number of sides
14.	▭	?	?	?
15.	?	hexagon	?	?
16.	?	?	8	?
17.	△	?	?	?
18.	?	?	?	5

CHALLENGE

Make a pattern using the polygons above. Make your own picture. You can:

19. Use the same polygon in different sizes.

20. Use different polygons in different sizes.

8-7 Perimeter

Farmer Jim wants to enclose his chickens in a yard. The yard is in the shape of a hexagon. Each side of the yard is 8 ft. How much fencing does he need?

The distance around a polygon is its **perimeter**.

To find the perimeter of a polygon, add the lengths of all its sides.

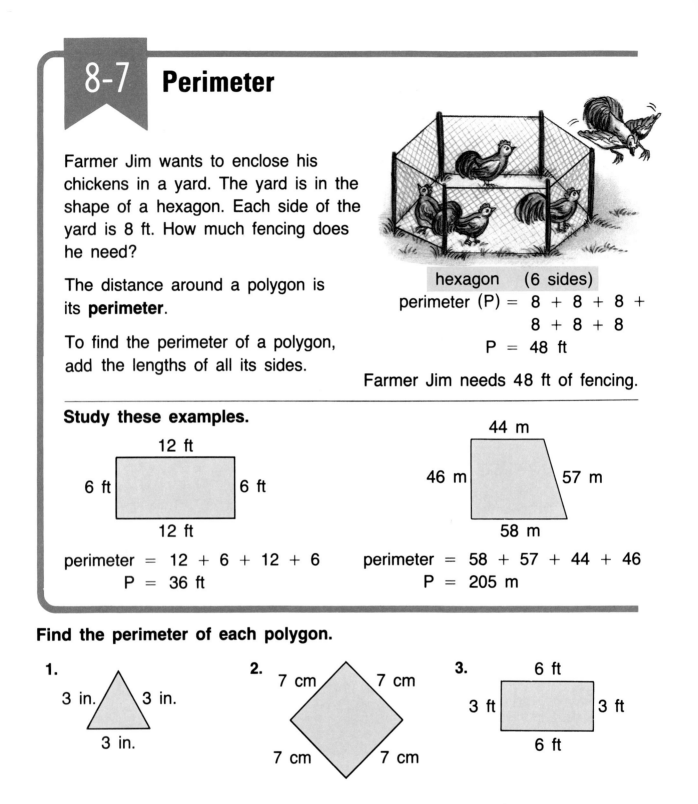

hexagon   (6 sides)

perimeter (P) = 8 + 8 + 8 + 8 + 8 + 8

P = 48 ft

Farmer Jim needs 48 ft of fencing.

Study these examples.

12 ft

6 ft   6 ft

12 ft

perimeter = 12 + 6 + 12 + 6

P = 36 ft

44 m

46 m   57 m

58 m

perimeter = 58 + 57 + 44 + 46

P = 205 m

Find the perimeter of each polygon.

1.

3 in.   3 in.

3 in.

2.

7 cm   7 cm

7 cm   7 cm

3.

6 ft

3 ft   3 ft

6 ft

4. a square whose side measures 12 m.

5. a triangle with sides of 14 yd, 11 yd, and 19 yd.

Find the perimeter of each polygon.

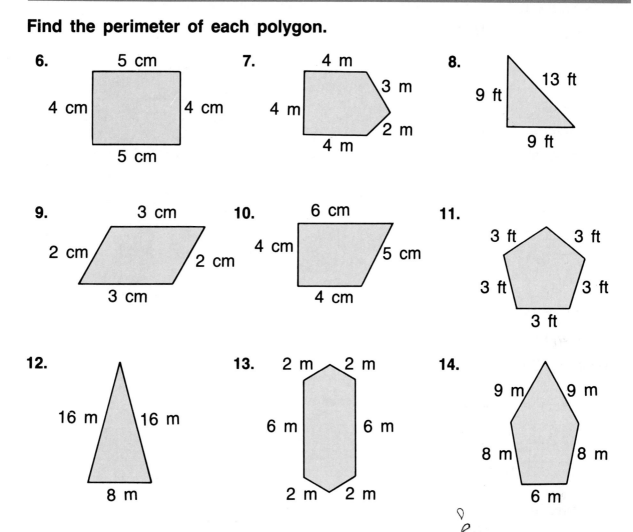

6. 5 cm, 4 cm, 4 cm, 5 cm

7. 4 m, 3 m, 2 m, 4 m, 4 m

8. 13 ft, 9 ft, 9 ft

9. 3 cm, 2 cm, 2 cm, 3 cm

10. 6 cm, 4 cm, 5 cm, 4 cm

11. 3 ft, 3 ft, 3 ft, 3 ft, 3 ft

12. 16 m, 16 m, 8 m

13. 2 m, 2 m, 6 m, 6 m, 2 m, 2 m

14. 9 m, 9 m, 8 m, 8 m, 6 m

Solve. Draw a diagram for each problem.

15. A jogger ran once around a rectangular park 280 ft long and 150 ft wide. How far did the jogger run?

16. A playground is shaped like a pentagon with sides measuring 49 m, 36 m, 42 m, 38 m, and 45 m. Find the perimeter of the playground.

17. How many inches of tape will it take to bind a triangular pennant with sides measuring 16 in., 16 in., and 6 in.?

223

Circles

Luz drew this design in the **circle**.

A simple closed curve with all points the same distance from the center is a **circle**.

O is the **center** point. This figure is named circle O.

A line segment which connects two points on a circle *and* passes through its center is a **diameter**. $\overline{BC}$ is a diameter.

A line segment from the center to any point on the circle is a **radius**. $\overline{OA}$, $\overline{OB}$, and $\overline{OC}$ are radii (plural of "radius").

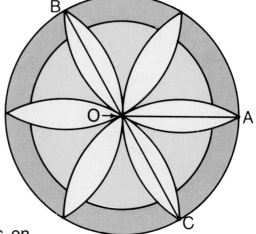

Which are in the shape of a circle? Write "Yes" or "No."

1. a penny

2. a book

3. the sun

4. a chair

5. a door

6. a jar lid

7. a ring

8. a basketball hoop

9. an egg

10. a hockey puck

11. a tire

12. a football

Write the name of the radius for each.

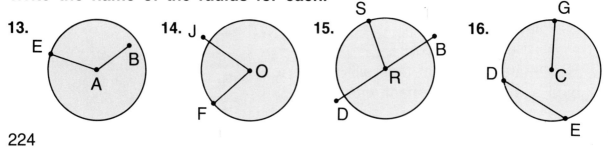

13.

14.

15.

16.

Write the name of the diameter for each.

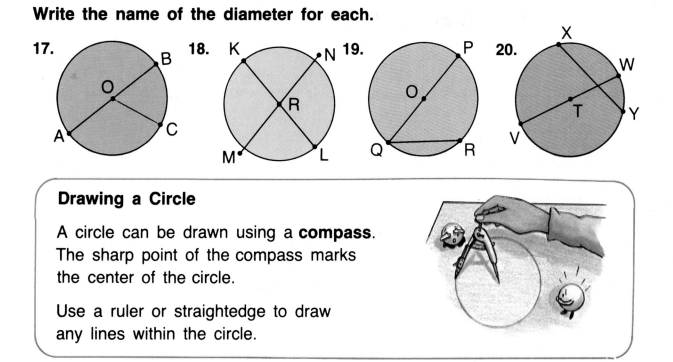

17. **18.** **19.** **20.**

Drawing a Circle

A circle can be drawn using a **compass**.
The sharp point of the compass marks
the center of the circle.

Use a ruler or straightedge to draw
any lines within the circle.

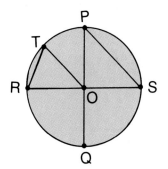

Use your compass to draw a circle. Then draw:

21. center X   **22.** diameter $\overline{TV}$ **23.** radius $\overline{XR}$

Identify each for the circle at the right.

24. Name the center of the circle.

25. Name two diameters.

26. Name five radii.

CHALLENGE

**27. You can draw many
lovely designs with
your compass.**

Draw this design or a
design of your own.

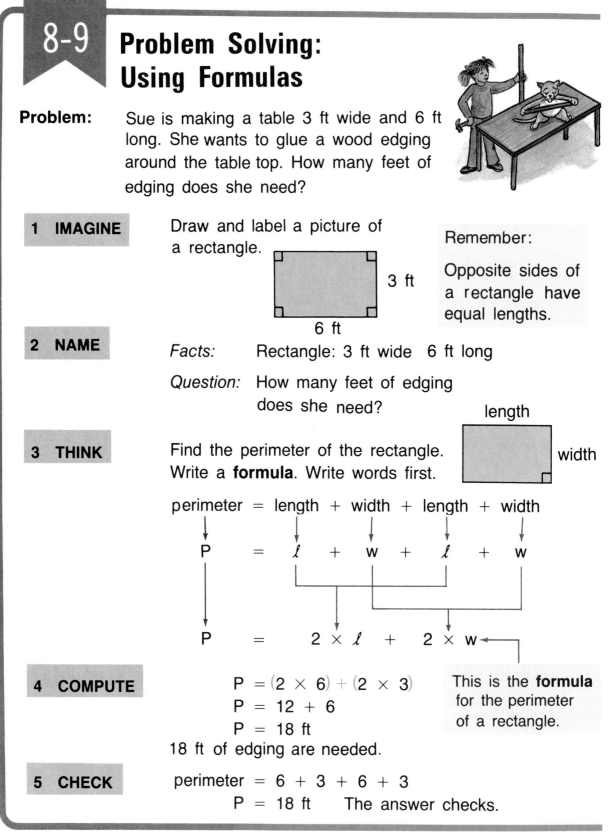

8-9 Problem Solving: Using Formulas

Problem: Sue is making a table 3 ft wide and 6 ft long. She wants to glue a wood edging around the table top. How many feet of edging does she need?

1 IMAGINE

Draw and label a picture of a rectangle.

3 ft

6 ft

Remember:

Opposite sides of a rectangle have equal lengths.

2 NAME

Facts: Rectangle: 3 ft wide   6 ft long

Question: How many feet of edging does she need?

length

width

3 THINK

Find the perimeter of the rectangle. Write a **formula**. Write words first.

perimeter = length + width + length + width

$P = \ell + w + \ell + w$

$P = 2 \times \ell + 2 \times w$

4 COMPUTE

$P = (2 \times 6) + (2 \times 3)$
$P = 12 + 6$
$P = 18$ ft
18 ft of edging are needed.

This is the **formula** for the perimeter of a rectangle.

5 CHECK

perimeter = 6 + 3 + 6 + 3
$P = 18$ ft   The answer checks.

Solve. Use a formula for each.

1. A company receives an order to make 25,000 gold pennants with black edging for the upcoming elections. The two equal sides of the pennant are 18 in. long and the third side is 7 in. long. How much edging is needed for one pennant?

IMAGINE	Draw and label the pennant.
NAME	*Facts:* Triangle: two sides 18 in. long one side 7 in. long *Question:* How much edging is needed for one pennant?
THINK	Write a formula for the perimeter of the triangle. Write words first. perimeter = side + side + side P = 18 + 18 + 7

Then → **COMPUTE** → and → **CHECK**

2. A flower bed is shaped like a hexagon. The measure of each of its equal sides is 4 m. Find the perimeter.

3. A "STOP" sign is shaped like an octagon. The measure of each of its equal sides is 14 in. Find its perimeter.

4. The base of the Washington Monument is shaped like a square. Each side of the square is about 55 ft long. How far would you travel if you walked twice around the monument?

More Practice

Identify each.

1. __?__ ray
2. __?__ line segment
3. __?__ perpendicular lines
4. __?__ pentagon
5. __?__ line
6. __?__ simple closed curve
7. __?__ circle
8. __?__ parallel lines
9. __?__ point

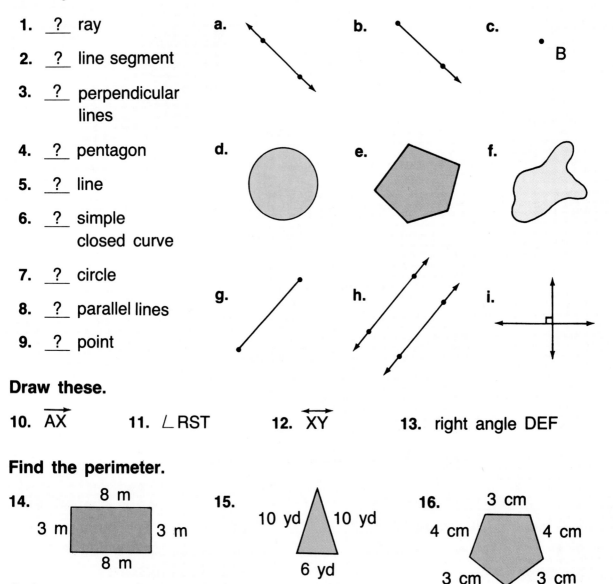

Draw these.

10. $\overrightarrow{AX}$ 11. ∠RST   12. $\overleftrightarrow{XY}$ 13. right angle DEF

Find the perimeter.

14.
8 m
3 m   3 m
8 m

15.
10 yd   10 yd
6 yd

16.
3 cm
4 cm   4 cm
3 cm   3 cm

Solve.

17. How many feet of molding is needed to go around a room 12 ft long and 10 ft wide?

18. Find the cost of edging a table top 7 ft long and 3 ft wide at $3 a foot.

(See *Still More Practice*, p. 364)

Math Probe

MATH WORD MEANINGS

The word *Polygon* can be traced back to two Greek words.

"poly" means "many"   "gonia" means "angle"

A *polygon* is a simple closed figure with three or more angles.

- Penta means *five*. What is a *pentagon*?

- A *hexagon* has 6 angles. What does "hexa" mean?

- An *octagon* has 8 angles. What does "octa" mean?

- *Deca* means *ten*. What is a *decagon*?

Answer these.

1. How many events would an athletic PENTATHLON have?

2. Would a POLYGLOT know only one language?

3. In poetry, how many measures would a HEXAMETER have?

4. How many meters are in a DECAMETER?

5. How many people would sing in an OCTET?

6. What is a POLYSYLLABIC word?

7. How many sides does the PENTAGON building have?

8. How many liters are in a DECALITER?

9. How many arms does an OCTOPUS have?

10. How many events would an athletic DECATHLON have?

Check Your Mastery

Identify each.

See pp. 212-221, 224-225.

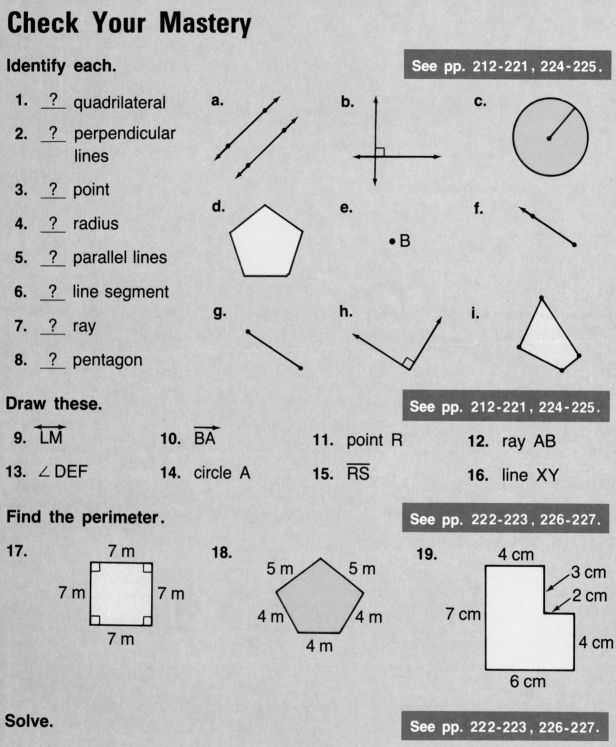

1. __?__ quadrilateral
2. __?__ perpendicular lines
3. __?__ point
4. __?__ radius
5. __?__ parallel lines
6. __?__ line segment
7. __?__ ray
8. __?__ pentagon

Draw these.

See pp. 212-221, 224-225.

9. $\overleftrightarrow{LM}$
10. $\overrightarrow{BA}$
11. point R
12. ray AB
13. $\angle$ DEF
14. circle A
15. $\overline{RS}$
16. line XY

Find the perimeter.

See pp. 222-223, 226-227.

17. 7 m, 7 m, 7 m, 7 m

18. 5 m, 5 m, 4 m, 4 m, 4 m

19. 4 cm, 3 cm, 2 cm, 7 cm, 4 cm, 6 cm

Solve.

See pp. 222-223, 226-227.

20. How many feet of fencing are needed to enclose a garden 30 ft long and 25 ft wide?

Fractions

In this unit you will:

- Learn about fractions as equal parts of regions and sets
- Write equivalent fractions
- Reduce fractions to lowest terms
- Compare fractions
- Add and subtract fractions with like denominators
- Write mixed numbers
- Change fractions greater than one to mixed numbers
- Add and subtract mixed numbers with like denominators
- Add and subtract fractions with unlike denominators
- Find parts of numbers
- Solve problems by using models

Do you remember?

A **factor** is one of two or more numbers that are multiplied to form a product.

Factors of:
- 4: 1, 2, 4
- 6: 1, 2, 3, 6
- 8: 1, 2, 4, 8
- 9: 1, 3, 9

Parts of Regions

Look at these.

Cut into 2 equal parts.   Cut into 3 equal parts.   Cut into 4 equal parts.
Each part is $\frac{1}{2}$ Each part is $\frac{1}{3}$ Each part is $\frac{1}{4}$

$\frac{1}{2}$, $\frac{1}{3}$, and $\frac{1}{4}$ are fractions.

A **fraction** names one or more equal parts of a whole.
A fraction has a **numerator** and a **denominator**.

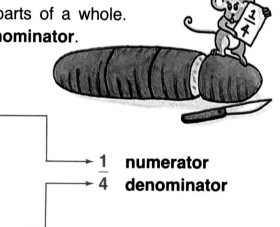

The **numerator** names the number of
equal parts described by the fraction.
(1 of 4 equal parts of the bread is
cut. So one fourth is the fraction.)

$\frac{1}{4}$ **numerator**
   denominator

The **denominator** names the number
of equal parts into which the whole is
divided. (The bread is divided
into 4 equal parts.)

Study these examples.

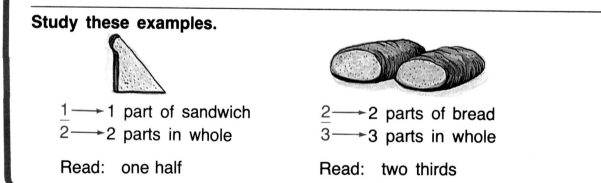

$\frac{1}{2}$ ⟶ 1 part of sandwich
⟶ 2 parts in whole

Read: one half

$\frac{2}{3}$ ⟶ 2 parts of bread
⟶ 3 parts in whole

Read: two thirds

Write a fraction that names the shaded region.

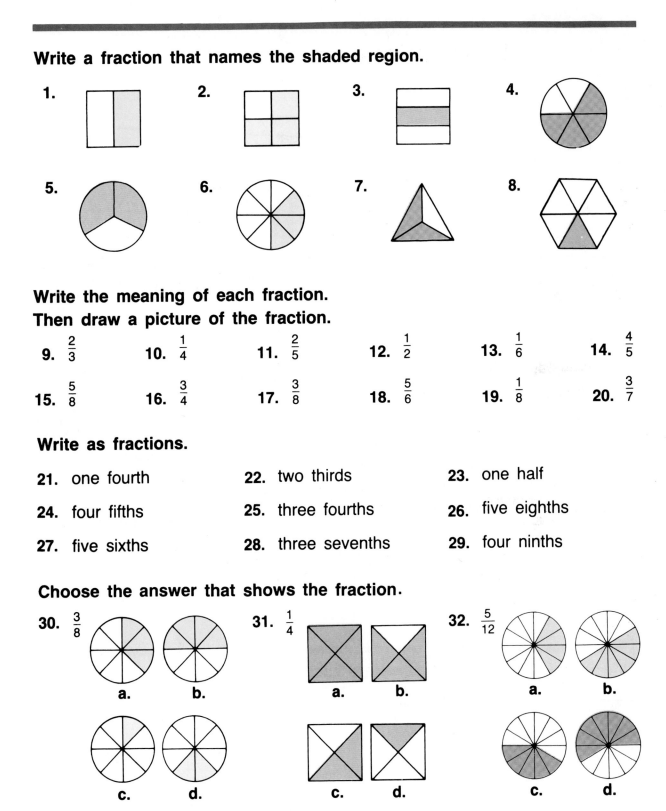

1.

2.

3.

4.

5.

6.

7.

8.

Write the meaning of each fraction.
Then draw a picture of the fraction.

9. $\frac{2}{3}$ 10. $\frac{1}{4}$ 11. $\frac{2}{5}$ 12. $\frac{1}{2}$ 13. $\frac{1}{6}$ 14. $\frac{4}{5}$

15. $\frac{5}{8}$ 16. $\frac{3}{4}$ 17. $\frac{3}{8}$ 18. $\frac{5}{6}$ 19. $\frac{1}{8}$ 20. $\frac{3}{7}$

Write as fractions.

21. one fourth

22. two thirds

23. one half

24. four fifths

25. three fourths

26. five eighths

27. five sixths

28. three sevenths

29. four ninths

Choose the answer that shows the fraction.

30. $\frac{3}{8}$

a.   b.

c.   d.

31. $\frac{1}{4}$

a.   b.

c.   d.

32. $\frac{5}{12}$

a.   b.

c.   d.

233

Parts of Sets

A fraction may also be one or more equal parts of a group or a set of objects.

5 of the 6 rabbits are in the hutch.

$\frac{5}{6}$ are in the hutch.

$\frac{1}{6}$ are on the grass.

2 of the 5 rabbits are in the hutch.

$\frac{2}{5}$ are in the hutch.

$\frac{3}{5}$ are on the grass.

There are 8 carrots.
3 are on the plate.
$\frac{3}{8}$ are on the plate.

There are 7 tomatoes.
2 are on the plate.
$\frac{2}{7}$ are on the plate.

There are 8 peppers.
5 are *not* on the plate.
$\frac{5}{8}$ are *not* on the plate.

Use the picture above to complete each.

1. __?__ carrots are *not* on the plate.

2. __?__ tomatoes are *not* on the plate.

3. What part of the vegetables on each plate are carrots? tomatoes? peppers?

4. What part of all the vegetables *not* on the plate begin with "p?"

Write the correct fraction.

5. What part of a pair of shoes is your right shoe?

6. What part of all your fingers are your left thumb and left pinky?

7. What part of a dozen eggs are five eggs?

8. What part of all your toes are your two big toes and one little toe?

9. A set of checker pieces has 12 red pieces and 12 black pieces.

   a. What part of the set of checkers are the red pieces?

   b. What part of the set of checkers are 5 red and 5 black pieces?

   c. What part of the set of checkers are 1 red and 4 black pieces?

10. A set of silverware has 6 knives, 6 forks, and 6 spoons.

    a. What part of the silverware are 5 knives?

    b. What part of the silverware are 3 knives, 3 forks, and 3 spoons?

    c. What part of the silverware are 1 knife, 2 forks, and 5 spoons?

CHALLENGE

Try a little logic!
Use the picture of vegetables on p. 234 to answer these.

11. If $\frac{3}{8}$ of the carrots are on the plate, what part is *not* on the plate?

12. If $\frac{5}{8}$ of the peppers are *not* on the plate, what part is on the plate?

13. What part of the tomatoes is *not* not on the plate?

14. What part of all the vegetables is *not* on the plate?

15. What part of all the vegetables is *not* not on the plate?

9-3 Equivalent Fractions

Equivalent fractions name the *same* part of a region, object, or set of objects.

Ed had 9 strips of wood of equal size. He made this "Fraction Chart" for the school's Math Fair.

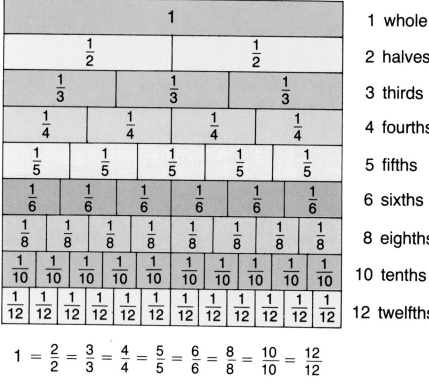

1		1 whole
$\frac{1}{2}$ $\frac{1}{2}$		2 halves
$\frac{1}{3}$ $\frac{1}{3}$ $\frac{1}{3}$		3 thirds
$\frac{1}{4}$ $\frac{1}{4}$ $\frac{1}{4}$ $\frac{1}{4}$		4 fourths
$\frac{1}{5}$ $\frac{1}{5}$ $\frac{1}{5}$ $\frac{1}{5}$ $\frac{1}{5}$		5 fifths
$\frac{1}{6}$ $\frac{1}{6}$ $\frac{1}{6}$ $\frac{1}{6}$ $\frac{1}{6}$ $\frac{1}{6}$		6 sixths
$\frac{1}{8}$ $\frac{1}{8}$ $\frac{1}{8}$ $\frac{1}{8}$ $\frac{1}{8}$ $\frac{1}{8}$ $\frac{1}{8}$ $\frac{1}{8}$		8 eighths
$\frac{1}{10}$ $\frac{1}{10}$ $\frac{1}{10}$ $\frac{1}{10}$ $\frac{1}{10}$ $\frac{1}{10}$ $\frac{1}{10}$ $\frac{1}{10}$ $\frac{1}{10}$ $\frac{1}{10}$		10 tenths
$\frac{1}{12}$ $\frac{1}{12}$ $\frac{1}{12}$ $\frac{1}{12}$ $\frac{1}{12}$ $\frac{1}{12}$ $\frac{1}{12}$ $\frac{1}{12}$ $\frac{1}{12}$ $\frac{1}{12}$ $\frac{1}{12}$ $\frac{1}{12}$		12 twelfths

$$1 = \frac{2}{2} = \frac{3}{3} = \frac{4}{4} = \frac{5}{5} = \frac{6}{6} = \frac{8}{8} = \frac{10}{10} = \frac{12}{12}$$

Compare Ed's halves, fourths and eighths bars. Notice that:

$$\frac{1}{2} = \frac{2}{4} = \frac{4}{8}$$

and

$$\frac{3}{4} = \frac{6}{8}$$

These are called **equivalent fractions.**

Use the fraction chart to find equivalent fractions.

1. $\frac{1}{2} = \frac{?}{6}$

2. $\frac{1}{4} = \frac{?}{8}$

3. $\frac{2}{5} = \frac{?}{10}$

4. $\frac{4}{8} = \frac{?}{4}$

5. $\frac{2}{3} = \frac{?}{12}$

6. $\frac{5}{10} = \frac{?}{2}$

7. $\frac{3}{12} = \frac{?}{4}$

8. $\frac{4}{5} = \frac{?}{10}$

9. $\frac{1}{3} = \frac{?}{6}$

10. $\frac{2}{4} = \frac{?}{8}$

11. $\frac{2}{3} = \frac{?}{6}$

12. $\frac{1}{5} = \frac{?}{10}$

13. $\frac{1}{3} = \frac{?}{12}$

14. $\frac{1}{2} = \frac{?}{6}$

15. $\frac{3}{4} = \frac{?}{8}$

16. $\frac{3}{5} = \frac{?}{10}$

17. $\frac{1}{2} = \frac{?}{10}$

18. $\frac{3}{4} = \frac{?}{12}$

19. $\frac{1}{2} = \frac{?}{8}$

20. $\frac{2}{5} = \frac{?}{10}$

Choose the two figures whose shaded parts show equivalent fractions. Write the equivalent fractions. (The first one is done.)

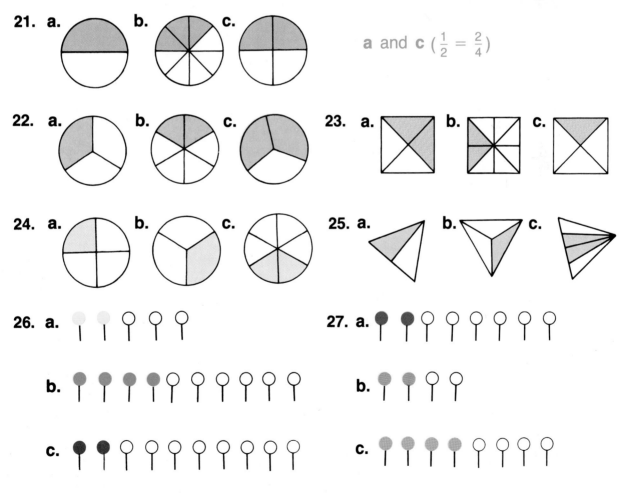

21. **a.** **b.** **c.** a and c ($\frac{1}{2} = \frac{2}{4}$)

22. **a.** **b.** **c.** 23. **a.** **b.** **c.**

24. **a.** **b.** **c.** 25. **a.** **b.** **c.**

26. **a.**

b.

c.

27. **a.**

b.

c.

Writing Equivalent Fractions

$\frac{2}{3} = \frac{?}{6}$

To find equivalent fractions, multiply the numerator and denominator of the fraction by the same number.

$\frac{1}{3}$		$\frac{1}{3}$		$\frac{1}{3}$	
$\frac{1}{6}$	$\frac{1}{6}$	$\frac{1}{6}$	$\frac{1}{6}$	$\frac{1}{6}$	$\frac{1}{6}$

$\frac{2 \times 2}{3 \times 2} = \frac{4}{6}$

Remember:
$\frac{2}{2} = \frac{1}{1}$

These are equivalent fractions. $\longrightarrow \frac{2}{3} = \frac{4}{6}$

Study these examples.

$\frac{3}{8} = \frac{3 \times 2}{8 \times 2} = \frac{6}{16}$

$\frac{3}{8} = \frac{3 \times 3}{8 \times 3} = \frac{9}{24}$

$\frac{3}{8} = \frac{3 \times 4}{8 \times 4} = \frac{12}{32}$

$\frac{3}{8} = \frac{3 \times 5}{8 \times 5} = \frac{15}{40}$

$\frac{3}{4} = \frac{3 \times 3}{4 \times 3} = \frac{9}{12}$

$\frac{3}{5} = \frac{3 \times 4}{5 \times 4} = \frac{12}{20}$

$\frac{2}{5} = \frac{2 \times 2}{5 \times 2} = \frac{4}{10}$

$\frac{4}{5} = \frac{4 \times 5}{5 \times 5} = \frac{20}{25}$

So, $\frac{3}{8} = \frac{6}{16} = \frac{9}{24} = \frac{12}{32} = \frac{15}{40}$

Complete.

1. $\frac{1 \times 2}{3 \times 2} = \frac{?}{?}$

2. $\frac{5 \times 3}{6 \times 3} = \frac{?}{?}$

3. $\frac{2 \times 2}{5 \times 2} = \frac{?}{?}$

4. $\frac{3 \times 4}{4 \times 4} = \frac{?}{?}$

5. $\frac{1 \times 3}{8 \times 3} = \frac{?}{?}$

6. $\frac{3 \times 2}{10 \times 2} = \frac{?}{?}$

7. $\frac{1 \times 3}{7 \times ?} = \frac{3}{?}$

8. $\frac{3 \times ?}{8 \times 2} = \frac{?}{?}$

9. $\frac{2 \times 4}{3 \times ?} = \frac{?}{?}$

Write an equivalent fraction.

10. $\dfrac{3 \times ?}{5 \times 2} = \dfrac{?}{10}$

11. $\dfrac{1 \times ?}{3 \times 3} = \dfrac{?}{9}$

12. $\dfrac{2 \times ?}{4 \times 4} = \dfrac{?}{16}$

13. $\dfrac{1 \times ?}{3 \times ?} = \dfrac{?}{9}$

14. $\dfrac{5 \times ?}{6 \times ?} = \dfrac{?}{12}$

15. $\dfrac{2 \times ?}{9 \times ?} = \dfrac{?}{27}$

16. $\dfrac{4 \times ?}{5 \times ?} = \dfrac{?}{20}$

17. $\dfrac{1 \times ?}{2 \times ?} = \dfrac{?}{10}$

18. $\dfrac{3 \times ?}{8 \times ?} = \dfrac{?}{32}$

19. $\dfrac{7 \times ?}{10 \times ?} = \dfrac{?}{30}$

20. $\dfrac{2 \times ?}{9 \times ?} = \dfrac{?}{18}$

21. $\dfrac{4 \times ?}{7 \times ?} = \dfrac{?}{21}$

Change each to an equivalent fraction.

22. $\dfrac{3}{4} = \dfrac{?}{8}$

23. $\dfrac{4}{5} = \dfrac{?}{10}$

24. $\dfrac{1}{3} = \dfrac{?}{9}$

25. $\dfrac{1}{2} = \dfrac{?}{10}$

26. $\dfrac{5}{6} = \dfrac{?}{12}$

27. $\dfrac{3}{8} = \dfrac{?}{24}$

28. $\dfrac{2}{9} = \dfrac{?}{27}$

29. $\dfrac{1}{4} = \dfrac{?}{16}$

30. $\dfrac{3}{7} = \dfrac{?}{14}$

31. $\dfrac{2}{5} = \dfrac{?}{25}$

32. $\dfrac{2}{3} = \dfrac{?}{18}$

33. $\dfrac{2}{4} = \dfrac{?}{12}$

34. $\dfrac{1}{6} = \dfrac{?}{30}$

35. $\dfrac{5}{8} = \dfrac{?}{40}$

36. $\dfrac{7}{9} = \dfrac{?}{27}$

37. $\dfrac{6}{10} = \dfrac{?}{20}$

38. $\dfrac{2}{4} = \dfrac{?}{12}$

39. $\dfrac{4}{6} = \dfrac{?}{18}$

40. $\dfrac{6}{8} = \dfrac{18}{?}$

41. $\dfrac{2}{7} = \dfrac{4}{?}$

42. $\dfrac{1}{9} = \dfrac{3}{?}$

43. $\dfrac{2}{3} = \dfrac{?}{12}$

44. $\dfrac{3}{10} = \dfrac{6}{?}$

45. $\dfrac{1}{8} = \dfrac{3}{?}$

46. $\dfrac{1}{5} = \dfrac{?}{15}$

47. $\dfrac{4}{9} = \dfrac{?}{18}$

48. $\dfrac{7}{10} = \dfrac{21}{?}$

CHALLENGE

Complete each set of equivalent fractions.

49. $\dfrac{2}{7} = \dfrac{?}{14} = \dfrac{6}{?} = \dfrac{8}{?} = \dfrac{?}{35} = \dfrac{?}{42} = \dfrac{14}{?}$

50. $\dfrac{4}{9} = \dfrac{8}{?} = \dfrac{12}{?} = \dfrac{16}{?} = \dfrac{?}{45} = \dfrac{?}{63} = \dfrac{36}{?}$

Lowest Terms Fractions

A fraction is written in **lowest terms**, or in **simplest form**, when the numerator and the denominator have no common factors other than 1.

$\frac{2}{3}$ is written in lowest terms.

Factors of 2: 1, 2
Factors of 3: 1, 3
Common factor of 2 and 3: 1
Greatest common factor (GCF): 1

$\frac{6}{8}$ is *not* written in lowest terms.

Factors of 6: 1, 2, 3, 6
Factors of 8: 1, 2, 4, 8
Common factors of 6 and 8: 1 and
Greatest common factor (GCF): 2

To change a fraction to an equivalent fraction written in lowest terms, divide both the numerator and the denominator by their greatest common factor (GCF).

$$\frac{6 \div 2}{8 \div 2} = \frac{3}{4}$$

2 is the greatest common factor of 6 and 8

Study these examples.

$\frac{6}{18}$ Factors of 6:   1, 2, 3, 6
Factors of 18:   1, 2, 3, 6, 9, 18

    GCF: 6

$$\frac{6 \div 6}{18 \div 6} = \frac{1}{3}$$

$\frac{15}{20}$ Factors of 15:   1, 3, 5 15
Factors of 20:   1, 2, 4, 5 10, 20

    GCF: 5

$$\frac{15 \div 5}{20 \div 5} = \frac{3}{4}$$

Write the factors of both numbers. Then write the common factors for both.

1. 2 and 6   2. 4 and 24   3. 9 and 18   4. 9 and 12

5. 6 and 10   6. 12 and 20   7. 6 and 18   8. 10 and 20

9. 8 and 24   10. 8 and 12   11. 4 and 12   12. 9 and 15

Find the greatest common factor (GCF).

13. 4 and 12   14. 2 and 8   15. 10 and 20   16. 9 and 15

17. 12 and 16   18. 5 and 10   19. 6 and 9   20. 4 and 8

21. 10 and 15   22. 9 and 12   23. 12 and 20   24. 6 and 12

Write as a lowest–terms fraction.

25. $\frac{2}{6}$ 26. $\frac{4}{24}$ 27. $\frac{9}{18}$ 28. $\frac{3}{12}$ 29. $\frac{6}{10}$

30. $\frac{12}{20}$ 31. $\frac{6}{18}$ 32. $\frac{10}{20}$ 33. $\frac{8}{24}$ 34. $\frac{8}{12}$

35. $\frac{15}{20}$ 36. $\frac{4}{10}$ 37. $\frac{6}{24}$ 38. $\frac{6}{14}$ 39. $\frac{3}{15}$

40. $\frac{9}{12}$ 41. $\frac{6}{9}$ 42. $\frac{5}{15}$ 43. $\frac{8}{18}$ 44. $\frac{9}{27}$

45. $\frac{15}{18}$ 46. $\frac{10}{15}$ 47. $\frac{8}{16}$ 48. $\frac{9}{15}$ 49. $\frac{12}{18}$

Find each fraction written in lowest terms.
The letters of these fractions spell out a secret message!

50. $\frac{4}{6}$ **M**   51. $\frac{3}{8}$ **Y**   52. $\frac{2}{5}$ **O**   53. $\frac{2}{6}$ **T**   54. $\frac{1}{4}$ **U**

55. $\frac{3}{7}$ **A**   56. $\frac{4}{8}$ **L**   57. $\frac{3}{4}$ **R**   58. $\frac{5}{10}$ **M**   59. $\frac{4}{5}$ **E**

60. $\frac{7}{8}$ **R**   61. $\frac{2}{9}$ **I**   62. $\frac{2}{3}$ **G**   63. $\frac{9}{10}$ **H**   64. $\frac{10}{33}$ **T**

The message is _?_ _?_ _?_   _?_ _?_ _?_   _?_ _?_ _?_ _?_ _?_ .

Comparing Fractions

Compare: $\frac{3}{4}$? $\frac{1}{4}$

To compare fractions with *like* denominators, compare the numerators.

$$3 > 1 \longrightarrow \frac{3}{4} > \frac{1}{4}$$

Compare: $\frac{3}{4}$? $\frac{3}{8}$

To compare fractions with *unlike* denominators: Write equivalent fractions with like denominators. Then compare the numerators.

Change to eighths. $\longrightarrow \frac{3 \times 2}{4 \times 2} = \frac{6}{8}$

$$\frac{3}{8} = \frac{3}{8}$$

$$6 > 3 \longrightarrow \frac{6}{8} > \frac{3}{8}$$

or, $\frac{3}{4} > \frac{3}{8}$

Study these examples.

$$\frac{4}{5} \ ? \ \frac{7}{10}$$

Change to tenths. $\frac{4 \times 2}{5 \times 2} \ ? \ \frac{7}{10}$

$\longrightarrow \frac{8}{10} \ ? \ \frac{7}{10}$

Since $8 > 7$, then

$$\frac{8}{10} \text{ or } \frac{4}{5} > \frac{7}{10}$$

$$\frac{2}{3} \ ? \ \frac{5}{6}$$

Change to sixths. $\longrightarrow \frac{2 \times 2}{3 \times 2} \ ? \ \frac{5}{6}$

$\longrightarrow \frac{4}{6} \ ? \ \frac{5}{6}$

Since $4 < 5$, then

$$\frac{4}{6} \text{ or } \frac{2}{3} < \frac{5}{6}$$

Compare. Write $<$, $=$, or $>$.

1. $\frac{5}{8}$? $\frac{7}{8}$

2. $\frac{3}{7}$? $\frac{4}{7}$

3. $\frac{2}{3}$? $\frac{1}{3}$

Equivalent Fraction Table

X	$\frac{2}{2}$	$\frac{3}{3}$	$\frac{4}{4}$	$\frac{5}{5}$
$\frac{1}{2}$	$\frac{2}{4}$	$\frac{3}{6}$	$\frac{4}{8}$	$\frac{5}{10}$
$\frac{1}{3}$	$\frac{2}{6}$	$\frac{3}{9}$	$\frac{4}{12}$	$\frac{5}{15}$
$\frac{1}{4}$	$\frac{2}{8}$	$\frac{3}{12}$	$\frac{4}{16}$	$\frac{5}{20}$
$\frac{1}{5}$	$\frac{2}{10}$	$\frac{3}{15}$	$\frac{4}{20}$	$\frac{5}{25}$
$\frac{1}{6}$	$\frac{2}{12}$	$\frac{3}{18}$	$\frac{4}{24}$	$\frac{5}{30}$

X	$\frac{2}{2}$	$\frac{3}{3}$	$\frac{4}{4}$	$\frac{5}{5}$
$\frac{1}{8}$	$\frac{2}{16}$	$\frac{3}{24}$	$\frac{4}{32}$	$\frac{5}{40}$
$\frac{2}{3}$	$\frac{4}{6}$	$\frac{6}{9}$	$\frac{8}{12}$	$\frac{10}{15}$
$\frac{2}{5}$	$\frac{4}{10}$	$\frac{6}{15}$	$\frac{8}{20}$	$\frac{10}{25}$
$\frac{3}{4}$	$\frac{6}{8}$	$\frac{9}{12}$	$\frac{12}{16}$	$\frac{15}{20}$
$\frac{3}{5}$	$\frac{6}{10}$	$\frac{9}{15}$	$\frac{12}{20}$	$\frac{15}{25}$

X	$\frac{2}{2}$	$\frac{3}{3}$	$\frac{4}{4}$	$\frac{5}{5}$
$\frac{3}{8}$	$\frac{6}{16}$	$\frac{9}{24}$	$\frac{12}{32}$	$\frac{15}{40}$
$\frac{4}{5}$	$\frac{8}{10}$	$\frac{12}{15}$	$\frac{16}{20}$	$\frac{20}{25}$
$\frac{5}{6}$	$\frac{10}{12}$	$\frac{15}{18}$	$\frac{20}{24}$	$\frac{25}{30}$
$\frac{5}{8}$	$\frac{10}{16}$	$\frac{15}{24}$	$\frac{20}{32}$	$\frac{25}{40}$
$\frac{7}{8}$	$\frac{14}{16}$	$\frac{21}{24}$	$\frac{28}{32}$	$\frac{35}{40}$

4. Copy the Equivalent Fraction Table. Write other equivalent fractions in it as you continue studying fractions.

Compare. Write $<$, $=$, or $>$. Use the Equivalent Fraction Table. (The first one is done.)

5. $\frac{1}{4}$? $\frac{3}{8}$ $\longrightarrow$ $\frac{2}{8} < \frac{3}{8}$ $\longrightarrow$ So, $\frac{1}{4} < \frac{3}{8}$.

6. $\frac{5}{8}$? $\frac{3}{8}$

7. $\frac{1}{2}$? $\frac{1}{8}$

8. $\frac{3}{4}$? $\frac{5}{12}$

9. $\frac{4}{5}$? $\frac{12}{20}$

10. $\frac{2}{3}$? $\frac{6}{9}$

11. $\frac{2}{3}$? $\frac{9}{12}$

12. $\frac{2}{5}$? $\frac{8}{20}$

13. $\frac{2}{12}$? $\frac{4}{24}$

14. $\frac{7}{8}$? $\frac{35}{40}$

15. $\frac{5}{8}$? $\frac{14}{24}$

16. $\frac{5}{6}$? $\frac{17}{18}$

17. $\frac{3}{4}$? $\frac{10}{12}$

18. $\frac{5}{10}$? $\frac{1}{2}$

19. $\frac{1}{6}$? $\frac{2}{18}$

20. $\frac{7}{8}$? $\frac{21}{24}$

Solve.

21. Walnuts filled $\frac{3}{4}$ of a jar. The cook needed $\frac{5}{8}$ of a jar. Does she have enough walnuts? Explain.

Adding Fractions with Like Denominators

Dave weeds $\frac{5}{8}$ of his garden before breakfast. He weeds another $\frac{1}{8}$ after supper. How much of his garden does he weed in all?

To find the total, add: $\frac{5}{8} + \frac{1}{8} = \underline{\quad?\quad}$

↑   ↑

like denominators

To add fractions with like denominators, add the numerators and keep the same denominator.

$\frac{5}{8} + \frac{1}{8} = \frac{6}{8} \longrightarrow \frac{6}{8} = \frac{3}{4}$ ← Always write in lowest terms.

Dave weeds $\frac{3}{4}$ of his garden.

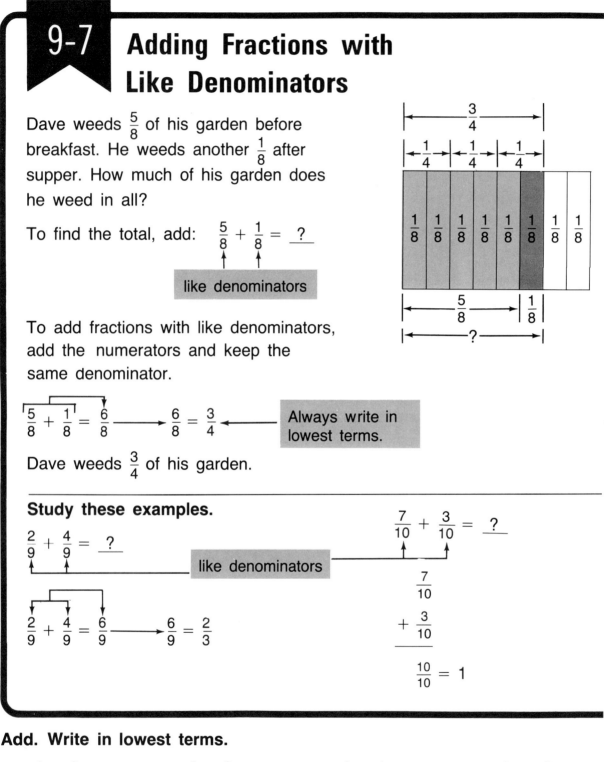

Study these examples.

$\frac{2}{9} + \frac{4}{9} = \underline{\quad?\quad}$

↑   ↑   like denominators

$\frac{2}{9} + \frac{4}{9} = \frac{6}{9} \longrightarrow \frac{6}{9} = \frac{2}{3}$

$\frac{7}{10} + \frac{3}{10} = \underline{\quad?\quad}$

↑   ↑

$\frac{7}{10}$

$+\ \frac{3}{10}$

$\overline{\phantom{+\ \frac{3}{10}}}$

$\frac{10}{10} = 1$

Add. Write in lowest terms.

1. $\frac{1}{4} + \frac{2}{4}$

2. $\frac{5}{8} + \frac{2}{8}$

3. $\frac{2}{9} + \frac{1}{9}$

4. $\frac{2}{7} + \frac{3}{7}$

5. $\frac{1}{3} + \frac{1}{3}$

6. $\frac{2}{6} + \frac{4}{6}$

7. $\frac{2}{5} + \frac{1}{5}$

8. $\frac{3}{10} + \frac{2}{10}$

Add.

9.
$$\frac{3}{9}$$
$$+\frac{1}{9}$$

10.
$$\frac{2}{10}$$
$$+\frac{4}{10}$$

11.
$$\frac{2}{8}$$
$$+\frac{5}{8}$$

12.
$$\frac{4}{7}$$
$$+\frac{2}{7}$$

13.
$$\frac{1}{6}$$
$$+\frac{3}{6}$$

14.
$$\frac{1}{10}$$
$$+\frac{4}{10}$$

15.
$$\frac{3}{15}$$
$$+\frac{2}{15}$$

16.
$$\frac{7}{12}$$
$$+\frac{3}{12}$$

17.
$$\frac{5}{18}$$
$$+\frac{3}{18}$$

18.
$$\frac{6}{24}$$
$$+\frac{10}{24}$$

19.
$$\frac{1}{7}$$
$$\frac{2}{7}$$
$$+\frac{4}{7}$$

20.
$$\frac{1}{5}$$
$$\frac{1}{5}$$
$$+\frac{2}{5}$$

21.
$$\frac{3}{9}$$
$$\frac{1}{9}$$
$$+\frac{2}{9}$$

22.
$$\frac{1}{6}$$
$$\frac{2}{6}$$
$$+\frac{3}{6}$$

23.
$$\frac{2}{8}$$
$$\frac{3}{8}$$
$$+\frac{1}{8}$$

Find the fractions with like denominators. Then add them.

24. $\frac{2}{8}$, $\frac{1}{5}$, $\frac{4}{8}$

25. $\frac{1}{5}$, $\frac{2}{5}$, $\frac{2}{3}$

26. $\frac{4}{5}$, $\frac{2}{7}$, $\frac{4}{7}$

27. $\frac{2}{9}$, $\frac{4}{6}$, $\frac{7}{9}$

28. $\frac{3}{8}$, $\frac{3}{10}$, $\frac{5}{10}$

29. $\frac{1}{12}$, $\frac{1}{2}$, $\frac{8}{12}$

30. $\frac{2}{7}$, $\frac{1}{6}$, $\frac{2}{6}$

31. $\frac{3}{20}$, $\frac{4}{10}$, $\frac{5}{20}$

Solve.

32. What is the sum of $\frac{1}{8}$ and $\frac{3}{8}$?

33. How much is $\frac{2}{6}$ and $\frac{1}{6}$?

34. If you add $\frac{3}{7}$ and $\frac{2}{7}$, what is the sum?

35. One eighth plus three eighths is _?_

36. Ruth plants $\frac{2}{6}$ of the garden with tomatoes, and $\frac{3}{6}$ with corn. How much of the garden did Ruth plant in all?

37. On Monday Dave fertilized $\frac{2}{5}$ of the garden. On Tuesday he fertilized $\frac{3}{5}$ of the garden. How much of the garden did he fertilize in all?

9-8 Subtracting Fractions with Like Denominators

Donald drinks $\frac{3}{4}$ cup of milk.
Helen drinks $\frac{1}{4}$ cup of milk.
How much more milk does
Donald drink than Helen?

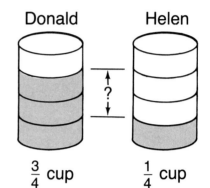

Donald   Helen

$\frac{3}{4}$ cup $\frac{1}{4}$ cup

To find how much more milk Donald drinks,

subtract: $\frac{3}{4} - \frac{1}{4} = \underline{\ ?\ }$

like denominators

To subtract fractions with like denominators,
subtract the numerators and keep the
same denominator.

$\frac{3}{4} - \frac{1}{4} = \frac{2}{4} \longrightarrow \frac{2}{4} = \frac{1}{2}$ Always write in lowest terms.   Donald drinks $\frac{1}{2}$ cup more than Helen.

Study these examples.

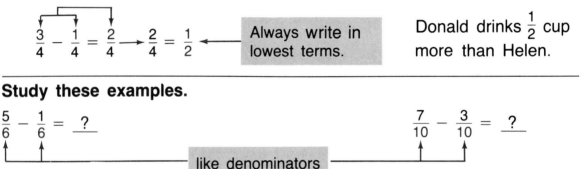

$\frac{5}{6} - \frac{1}{6} = \underline{\ ?\ }$ $\frac{7}{10} - \frac{3}{10} = \underline{\ ?\ }$

like denominators

$\frac{5}{6} - \frac{1}{6} = \frac{4}{6} \longrightarrow \frac{4}{6} = \frac{2}{3}$

$\begin{array}{r} \frac{7}{10} \\ - \frac{3}{10} \\ \hline \frac{4}{10} = \frac{2}{5} \end{array}$

Subtract. Write in lowest terms.

1. $\frac{7}{8} - \frac{4}{8}$ 2. $\frac{5}{6} - \frac{4}{6}$ 3. $\frac{7}{9} - \frac{1}{9}$ 4. $\frac{3}{6} - \frac{1}{6}$

5. $\frac{8}{9} - \frac{5}{9}$ 6. $\frac{7}{8} - \frac{3}{8}$ 7. $\frac{9}{12} - \frac{3}{12}$ 8. $\frac{12}{15} - \frac{3}{15}$

246

Subtract.

9. $\dfrac{5}{7}$ $-\dfrac{2}{7}$

10. $\dfrac{4}{5}$ $-\dfrac{2}{5}$

11. $\dfrac{8}{9}$ $-\dfrac{6}{9}$

12. $\dfrac{6}{8}$ $-\dfrac{2}{8}$

13. $\dfrac{5}{6}$ $-\dfrac{2}{6}$

14. $\dfrac{8}{10}$ $-\dfrac{2}{10}$

15. $\dfrac{3}{4}$ $-\dfrac{1}{4}$

16. $\dfrac{10}{12}$ $-\dfrac{2}{12}$

17. $\dfrac{8}{15}$ $-\dfrac{3}{15}$

18. $\dfrac{12}{20}$ $-\dfrac{2}{20}$

19. $\dfrac{7}{9}$ $-\dfrac{4}{9}$

20. $\dfrac{7}{8}$ $-\dfrac{1}{8}$

21. $\dfrac{9}{10}$ $-\dfrac{4}{10}$

22. $\dfrac{15}{18}$ $-\dfrac{3}{18}$

23. $\dfrac{20}{24}$ $-\dfrac{4}{24}$

Add or subtract. (Watch for + or −!)

24. $\dfrac{5}{9} - \dfrac{2}{9}$

25. $\dfrac{3}{7} + \dfrac{2}{7}$

26. $\dfrac{1}{5} + \dfrac{2}{5}$

27. $\dfrac{7}{12} - \dfrac{1}{12}$

28. $\dfrac{1}{10} + \dfrac{1}{10}$

29. $\dfrac{1}{8} + \dfrac{5}{8}$

30. $\dfrac{9}{10} - \dfrac{2}{10}$

31. $\dfrac{7}{10} + \dfrac{1}{10}$

32. $\dfrac{11}{12} - \dfrac{9}{12}$

33. $\dfrac{4}{6} - \dfrac{1}{6}$

34. $\dfrac{2}{12} + \dfrac{4}{12}$

35. $\dfrac{7}{16} - \dfrac{3}{16}$

Solve.

36. Subtract one third from two thirds.

37. What is the difference between $\dfrac{8}{9}$ and $\dfrac{5}{9}$?

38. A melon was cut into six equal pieces. $\dfrac{5}{6}$ of the melon was on the dish. Jean ate $\dfrac{1}{6}$. How much melon was left?

39. A large turnip weighs $\dfrac{7}{8}$ of a pound. A piece weighing $\dfrac{1}{8}$ of a pound is cut off. How much does the turnip now weigh?

Mixed Numbers

Cheryl's mother gives her 3 apple tarts to share equally with her brother, Chris. Cheryl divides the tarts:

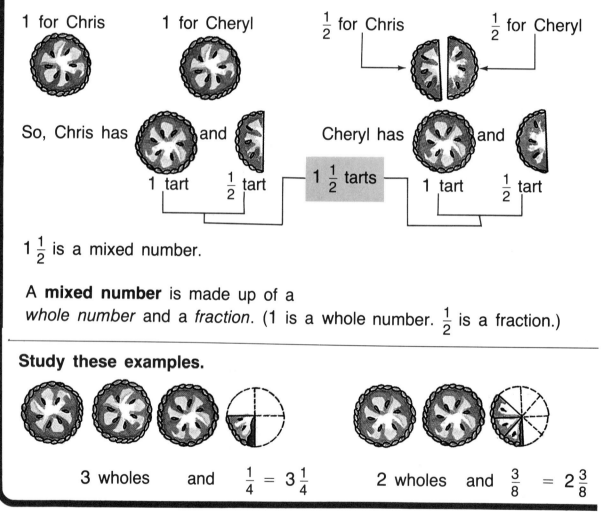

1 for Chris   1 for Cheryl $\frac{1}{2}$ for Chris $\frac{1}{2}$ for Cheryl

So, Chris has ⬤ and ◗   Cheryl has ⬤ and ◗

1 tart $\frac{1}{2}$ tart $1\frac{1}{2}$ tarts   1 tart $\frac{1}{2}$ tart

$1\frac{1}{2}$ is a mixed number.

A **mixed number** is made up of a *whole number* and a *fraction*. (1 is a whole number. $\frac{1}{2}$ is a fraction.)

Study these examples.

3 wholes   and $\frac{1}{4} = 3\frac{1}{4}$ 2 wholes   and $\frac{3}{8} = 2\frac{3}{8}$

Write whether each is a fraction, a whole number, or a mixed number. Draw a picture of each mixed number.

1. 8   2. $\frac{3}{8}$ 3. $8\frac{3}{8}$ 4. $\frac{5}{6}$ 5. $7\frac{2}{5}$

6. $2\frac{1}{2}$ 7. $3\frac{3}{4}$ 8. $4\frac{1}{6}$ 9. $2\frac{5}{8}$ 10. $7\frac{4}{5}$

9-10 Fractions Equal To or Greater Than One

A **fraction** is *greater than one* when the numerator is greater than the denominator.

$$\frac{3}{4} + \frac{3}{4} = \frac{6}{4}$$

To change a fraction greater than 1 to a mixed number: $\frac{6}{4} = \underline{\ ?\ }$

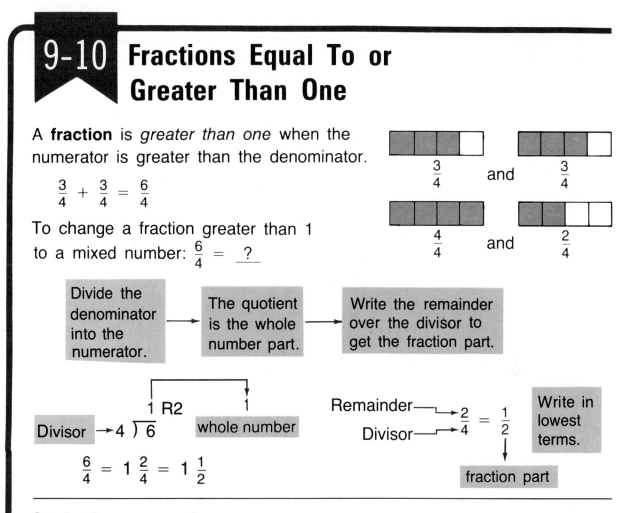

$$\frac{3}{4} \quad \text{and} \quad \frac{3}{4}$$

$$\frac{4}{4} \quad \text{and} \quad \frac{2}{4}$$

Divide the denominator into the numerator. → The quotient is the whole number part. → Write the remainder over the divisor to get the fraction part.

Divisor → 4$\overline{)6}$ 1 R2 — whole number

Remainder → $\frac{2}{4} = \frac{1}{2}$ ← Divisor — Write in lowest terms.

fraction part

$$\frac{6}{4} = 1\frac{2}{4} = 1\frac{1}{2}$$

Study these examples.

Whole Number Sums

$$\frac{6}{9} + \frac{3}{9} = \frac{9}{9} = 1 \qquad 9\overline{)9}\ ^1$$

Mixed Number Sums

$$\frac{9}{8} + \frac{5}{8} = \frac{14}{8} \longrightarrow \frac{14}{8} = 1\frac{6}{8} = 1\frac{3}{4}$$

Write the sum as a whole number or a mixed number.

1. $\frac{3}{5} + \frac{4}{5}$
2. $\frac{2}{3} + \frac{2}{3}$
3. $\frac{4}{6} + \frac{2}{6}$
4. $\frac{3}{4} + \frac{7}{4}$

5. $\frac{2}{6} + \frac{4}{6}$
6. $\frac{15}{8} + \frac{3}{8}$
7. $\frac{12}{5} + \frac{3}{5}$
8. $\frac{3}{2} + \frac{3}{2}$

9. $\frac{13}{7} + \frac{6}{7}$
10. $\frac{1}{6} + \frac{5}{6}$
11. $\frac{14}{5} + \frac{10}{5}$
12. $\frac{14}{8} + \frac{20}{8}$

13. $\frac{8}{4} + \frac{4}{4}$
14. $\frac{7}{3} + \frac{3}{3}$
15. $\frac{5}{2} + \frac{5}{2}$
16. $\frac{3}{7} + \frac{4}{7}$

Adding and Subtracting Mixed Numbers

Joshua buys $3\frac{5}{8}$ lb of cheese.
Maria buys $2\frac{1}{8}$ lb of cheese.

Joshua   Maria

How many pounds of cheese do Joshua and Maria buy in all? How much more cheese does Joshua buy than Maria?

To find how many pounds Joshua and Maria buy in all, add: $3\frac{5}{8} + 2\frac{1}{8} = \underline{\ ?\ }$

Are the denominators the same?	Add the fraction parts.	Add the whole number parts.	Write in lowest terms.
$3\frac{5}{8}$ $+ 2\frac{1}{8}$	$3\frac{5}{8}$ $+ 2\frac{1}{8}$ $\overline{\frac{6}{8}}$	$3\frac{5}{8}$ $+ 2\frac{1}{8}$ $\overline{5\frac{6}{8}}$	$3\frac{5}{8}$ $+ 2\frac{1}{8}$ $\overline{5\frac{6}{8} = 5\frac{3}{4}}$

$5\frac{3}{4}$ pounds were bought in all.

To find how much more cheese Joshua buys than Maria, subtract: $3\frac{5}{8} - 2\frac{1}{8} = \underline{\ ?\ }$

Are the denominators the same?	Subtract the fraction parts.	Subtract the whole number parts.	Write in lowest terms.
$3\frac{5}{8}$ $- 2\frac{1}{8}$	$3\frac{5}{8}$ $- 2\frac{1}{8}$ $\overline{\frac{4}{8}}$	$3\frac{5}{8}$ $- 2\frac{1}{8}$ $\overline{1\frac{4}{8}}$	$3\frac{5}{8}$ $- 2\frac{1}{8}$ $\overline{1\frac{4}{8} = 1\frac{1}{2}}$

Joshua buys $1\frac{1}{2}$ more pounds of cheese than Maria.

Add. Write the sum in lowest terms.

1. $6\frac{2}{6}$
$+ 7\frac{1}{6}$

2. $8\frac{1}{4}$
$+ 5\frac{1}{4}$

3. $6\frac{3}{5}$
$+ 18\frac{1}{5}$

4. $27\frac{4}{10}$
$+ 17\frac{5}{10}$

5. $16\frac{3}{8}$
$+ 24\frac{1}{8}$

Subtract. Write the differences in lowest terms.

6. $6\frac{4}{9}$
$- 4\frac{1}{9}$

7. $8\frac{4}{5}$
$- 6\frac{3}{5}$

8. $9\frac{7}{9}$
$- 5\frac{1}{9}$

9. $7\frac{5}{6}$
$- 4\frac{1}{6}$

10. $12\frac{3}{4}$
$- 9\frac{1}{4}$

11. $38\frac{7}{8}$
$- 17\frac{3}{8}$

12. $43\frac{2}{3}$
$- 28\frac{1}{3}$

13. $64\frac{7}{8}$
$- 47\frac{1}{8}$

14. $86\frac{6}{7}$
$- 79\frac{3}{7}$

15. $57\frac{5}{9}$
$- 49\frac{2}{9}$

Add or subtract. (Watch for + and −!)

16. $17\frac{3}{8}$
$+ 2\frac{1}{8}$

17. $26\frac{1}{7}$
$+ 8\frac{3}{7}$

18. $12\frac{2}{4}$
$+ 19\frac{1}{4}$

19. $18\frac{5}{6}$
$- 9\frac{1}{6}$

20. $25\frac{3}{4}$
$- 17\frac{1}{4}$

21. $81\frac{7}{9}$
$- 19\frac{1}{9}$

22. $74\frac{3}{5}$
$+ 59\frac{1}{5}$

23. $65\frac{7}{8}$
$- 38\frac{3}{8}$

24. $59\frac{3}{6}$
$+ 73\frac{1}{6}$

25. $98\frac{6}{8}$
$- 89\frac{4}{8}$

Add or subtract.

26. $9\frac{8}{10} - 3\frac{4}{10}$

27. $6\frac{9}{12} - 4\frac{3}{12}$

28. $8\frac{7}{15} + 9\frac{5}{15}$

29. $18\frac{15}{18} - 9\frac{3}{18}$

30. $24\frac{12}{20} + 36\frac{3}{20}$

31. $45\frac{21}{24} - 15\frac{3}{24}$

Solve.

32. Letitia buys $3\frac{3}{4}$ gallons of oil. She uses $1\frac{1}{4}$ gallons to oil a floor. How many gallons of oil does Letitia have left?

33. Warren has a pile of records $4\frac{1}{8}$ feet high. He adds more records and makes the pile $2\frac{3}{8}$ feet higher. How high is the pile now?

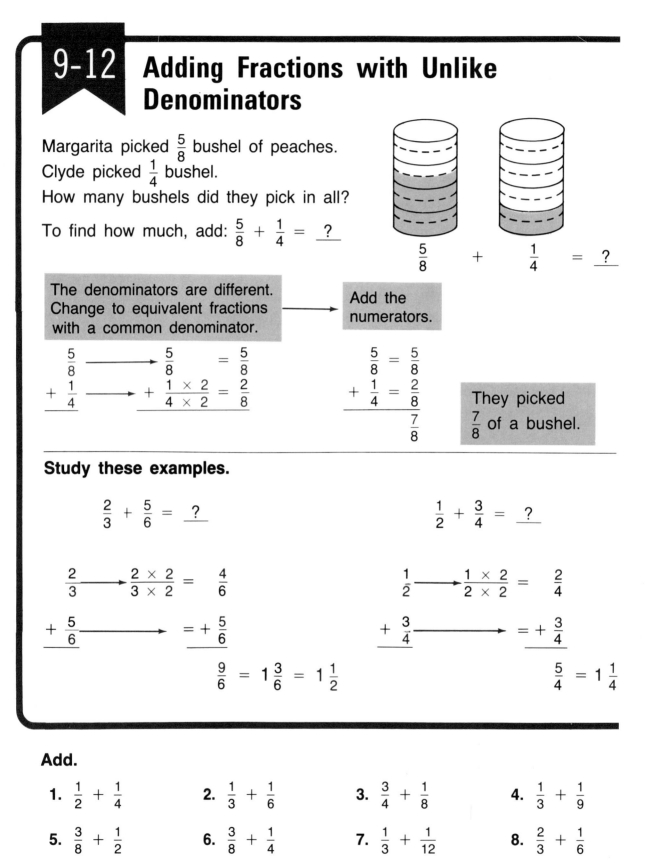

9-12 Adding Fractions with Unlike Denominators

Margarita picked $\frac{5}{8}$ bushel of peaches.
Clyde picked $\frac{1}{4}$ bushel.
How many bushels did they pick in all?

To find how much, add: $\frac{5}{8} + \frac{1}{4} = \underline{\ ?\ }$

$\frac{5}{8}$ + $\frac{1}{4}$ = $\underline{\ ?\ }$

The denominators are different. Change to equivalent fractions with a common denominator. → Add the numerators.

$\frac{5}{8} \longrightarrow \frac{5}{8} = \frac{5}{8}$

$+ \frac{1}{4} \longrightarrow + \frac{1 \times 2}{4 \times 2} = \frac{2}{8}$

$\frac{5}{8} = \frac{5}{8}$

$+ \frac{1}{4} = \frac{2}{8}$

$\frac{7}{8}$

They picked $\frac{7}{8}$ of a bushel.

Study these examples.

$\frac{2}{3} + \frac{5}{6} = \underline{\ ?\ }$

$\frac{2}{3} \longrightarrow \frac{2 \times 2}{3 \times 2} = \frac{4}{6}$

$+ \frac{5}{6} \longrightarrow\ \ = + \frac{5}{6}$

$\frac{9}{6} = 1\frac{3}{6} = 1\frac{1}{2}$

$\frac{1}{2} + \frac{3}{4} = \underline{\ ?\ }$

$\frac{1}{2} \longrightarrow \frac{1 \times 2}{2 \times 2} = \frac{2}{4}$

$+ \frac{3}{4} \longrightarrow\ \ = + \frac{3}{4}$

$\frac{5}{4} = 1\frac{1}{4}$

Add.

1. $\frac{1}{2} + \frac{1}{4}$

2. $\frac{1}{3} + \frac{1}{6}$

3. $\frac{3}{4} + \frac{1}{8}$

4. $\frac{1}{3} + \frac{1}{9}$

5. $\frac{3}{8} + \frac{1}{2}$

6. $\frac{3}{8} + \frac{1}{4}$

7. $\frac{1}{3} + \frac{1}{12}$

8. $\frac{2}{3} + \frac{1}{6}$

Find the sum.

9. $\frac{1}{3}$
   $+\frac{1}{6}$

10. $\frac{3}{4}$
    $+\frac{1}{8}$

11. $\frac{2}{3}$
    $+\frac{1}{9}$

12. $\frac{1}{2}$
    $+\frac{2}{8}$

13. $\frac{1}{2}$
    $+\frac{1}{4}$

14. $\frac{1}{4}$
    $+\frac{5}{8}$

15. $\frac{3}{10}$
    $+\frac{1}{5}$

16. $\frac{1}{2}$
    $+\frac{3}{8}$

17. $\frac{1}{4}$
    $+\frac{2}{8}$

18. $\frac{1}{12}$
    $+\frac{3}{4}$

19. $\frac{1}{8}$
    $+\frac{2}{4}$

20. $\frac{2}{7}$
    $+\frac{1}{14}$

21. $\frac{1}{10}$
    $+\frac{3}{5}$

22. $\frac{1}{6}$
    $+\frac{2}{3}$

23. $\frac{2}{9}$
    $+\frac{2}{3}$

24. $\frac{3}{9}$
    $+\frac{2}{3}$

25. $\frac{7}{8}$
    $+\frac{1}{4}$

26. $\frac{5}{8}$
    $+\frac{3}{4}$

27. $\frac{3}{4}$
    $+\frac{1}{2}$

28. $\frac{3}{16}$
    $+\frac{1}{4}$

Solve.

29. What is the sum of $\frac{3}{4}$ and $\frac{1}{2}$?

30. Three eighths and one fourth equals what number?

31. Karen needed $\frac{5}{8}$ of a yard of cloth for her costume in the school play. Jon needed $\frac{1}{2}$ yards. How much cloth did they need altogether?

32. In a question game William answered $\frac{1}{3}$ of the questions correctly. Harry answered $\frac{1}{6}$ correctly. What part of all the questions did William and Harry answer correctly?

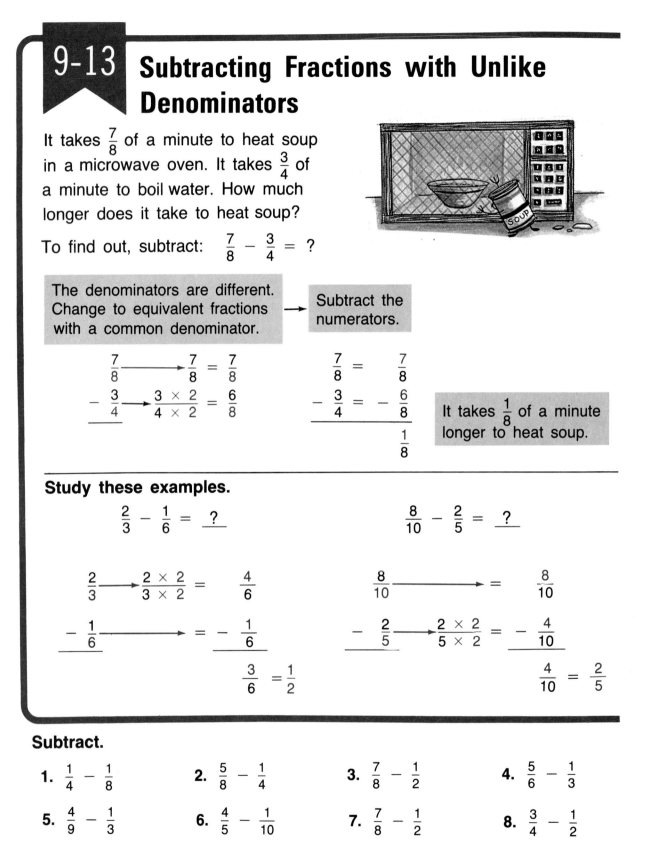

9-13 Subtracting Fractions with Unlike Denominators

It takes $\frac{7}{8}$ of a minute to heat soup in a microwave oven. It takes $\frac{3}{4}$ of a minute to boil water. How much longer does it take to heat soup?

To find out, subtract: $\frac{7}{8} - \frac{3}{4} = ?$

The denominators are different. Change to equivalent fractions with a common denominator. → Subtract the numerators.

$$\frac{7}{8} \longrightarrow \frac{7}{8} = \frac{7}{8}$$
$$-\frac{3}{4} \longrightarrow \frac{3 \times 2}{4 \times 2} = \frac{6}{8}$$

$$\frac{7}{8} = \frac{7}{8}$$
$$-\frac{3}{4} = -\frac{6}{8}$$
$$\frac{1}{8}$$

It takes $\frac{1}{8}$ of a minute longer to heat soup.

Study these examples.

$$\frac{2}{3} - \frac{1}{6} = \underline{\quad ?\quad}$$

$$\frac{2}{3} \longrightarrow \frac{2 \times 2}{3 \times 2} = \frac{4}{6}$$
$$-\frac{1}{6} \longrightarrow = -\frac{1}{6}$$
$$\frac{3}{6} = \frac{1}{2}$$

$$\frac{8}{10} - \frac{2}{5} = \underline{\quad ?\quad}$$

$$\frac{8}{10} \longrightarrow = \frac{8}{10}$$
$$-\frac{2}{5} \longrightarrow \frac{2 \times 2}{5 \times 2} = -\frac{4}{10}$$
$$\frac{4}{10} = \frac{2}{5}$$

Subtract.

1. $\frac{1}{4} - \frac{1}{8}$

2. $\frac{5}{8} - \frac{1}{4}$

3. $\frac{7}{8} - \frac{1}{2}$

4. $\frac{5}{6} - \frac{1}{3}$

5. $\frac{4}{9} - \frac{1}{3}$

6. $\frac{4}{5} - \frac{1}{10}$

7. $\frac{7}{8} - \frac{1}{2}$

8. $\frac{3}{4} - \frac{1}{2}$

Find the difference.

9. $\dfrac{2}{3}$
    $-\dfrac{1}{6}$

10. $\dfrac{6}{8}$
    $-\dfrac{1}{2}$

11. $\dfrac{8}{9}$
    $-\dfrac{1}{3}$

12. $\dfrac{1}{3}$
    $-\dfrac{1}{6}$

13. $\dfrac{4}{7}$
    $-\dfrac{1}{7}$

14. $\dfrac{4}{9}$
    $-\dfrac{1}{3}$

15. $\dfrac{3}{4}$
    $-\dfrac{2}{8}$

16. $\dfrac{5}{6}$
    $-\dfrac{3}{12}$

17. $\dfrac{6}{7}$
    $-\dfrac{2}{14}$

18. $\dfrac{7}{8}$
    $-\dfrac{2}{4}$

19. $\dfrac{2}{3}$
    $-\dfrac{2}{9}$

20. $\dfrac{4}{5}$
    $-\dfrac{3}{10}$

21. $\dfrac{5}{6}$
    $-\dfrac{1}{12}$

22. $\dfrac{5}{6}$
    $-\dfrac{3}{12}$

23. $\dfrac{5}{8}$
    $-\dfrac{1}{2}$

24. $\dfrac{4}{5}$
    $-\dfrac{1}{10}$

25. $\dfrac{6}{8}$
    $-\dfrac{1}{2}$

26. $\dfrac{2}{3}$
    $-\dfrac{1}{6}$

27. $\dfrac{7}{8}$
    $-\dfrac{3}{4}$

28. $\dfrac{7}{10}$
    $-\dfrac{1}{5}$

Solve.

29. What is the difference between $\dfrac{8}{9}$ and $\dfrac{2}{3}$?

30. The difference between three fourths and three eighths is what number?

31. $\dfrac{9}{10}$ minus $\dfrac{4}{5}$ equals what number?

32. The sum of $\dfrac{3}{4}$ and $\dfrac{1}{8}$ is what number?

33. Carlos uses the microwave to bake $\dfrac{1}{2}$ of of his cakes and $\dfrac{1}{4}$ of his pies. Does he use the microwave more for cakes or pies? How much more?

34. Mr. Santos drove $\dfrac{1}{2}$ of the distance to Florida, and Mrs. Santos drove $\dfrac{1}{8}$ of the distance. Paulo drove the rest of the way. What part of the distance did Paulo drive?

255

9-14 Finding Parts of Numbers

Juanita has 16 balloons for her party.
$\frac{1}{2}$ of the balloons have stripes, $\frac{1}{4}$ have
polka dots, and $\frac{2}{8}$ are plain.
How many of each does Juanita have?

Look at the picture.

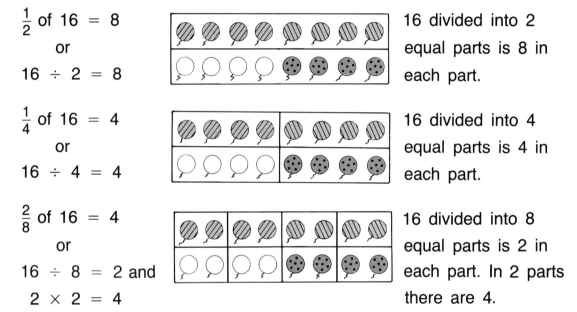

$\frac{1}{2}$ of 16 = 8

or

16 ÷ 2 = 8

16 divided into 2 equal parts is 8 in each part.

$\frac{1}{4}$ of 16 = 4

or

16 ÷ 4 = 4

16 divided into 4 equal parts is 4 in each part.

$\frac{2}{8}$ of 16 = 4

or

16 ÷ 8 = 2 and

2 × 2 = 4

16 divided into 8 equal parts is 2 in each part. In 2 parts there are 4.

Study these examples:

Divide the whole number by the denominator. →	Multiply by the numerator.

$\frac{3}{4}$ of 12 = $\underline{\ ?\ }$ 12 ÷ 4 = 3 ⟶ 3 × 3 = 9 $\frac{3}{4}$ of 12 = 9

$\frac{5}{8}$ of 24 = $\underline{\ ?\ }$ 24 ÷ 8 = 3 ⟶ 5 × 3 = 15 $\frac{5}{8}$ of 24 = 15

$\frac{3}{5}$ of 10 = $\underline{\ ?\ }$ 10 ÷ 5 = 2 ⟶ 3 × 2 = 6 $\frac{3}{5}$ of 10 = 6

Draw a picture showing each.

1. $\frac{1}{2}$ of 12

2. $\frac{1}{3}$ of 9

3. $\frac{1}{4}$ of 16

4. $\frac{2}{3}$ of 9

5. $\frac{3}{4}$ of 16

6. $\frac{6}{8}$ of 16

Find the missing number.

7. $\frac{1}{5}$ of 15 = ___?___

8. $\frac{1}{6}$ of 18 = ___?___

9. $\frac{1}{8}$ of 40 = ___?___

10. $\frac{2}{3}$ of 12 = ___?___

11. $\frac{3}{8}$ of 16 = ___?___

12. $\frac{4}{5}$ of 20 = ___?___

13. $\frac{3}{4}$ of 8 = ___?___

14. $\frac{1}{9}$ of 18 = ___?___

15. $\frac{4}{7}$ of 14 = ___?___

16. $\frac{2}{9}$ of 18 = ___?___

17. $\frac{5}{8}$ of 32 = ___?___

18. $\frac{1}{9}$ of 9 = ___?___

19. $\frac{7}{9}$ of 27 = ___?___

20. $\frac{5}{8}$ of 48 = ___?___

21. $\frac{2}{9}$ of 36 = ___?___

Solve.

22. Juan buys 15 paper hats for the party. $\frac{1}{3}$ of the hats are red and $\frac{2}{3}$ are striped. How many of each kind did Juan buy?

23. 18 children are invited to the party but only $\frac{1}{6}$ accept. How many children accept?

24. 8 hot dogs and 8 hamburgers are cooked. Jason's puppy ate $\frac{1}{4}$ of each. How many of each did the puppy eat?

Problem Solving: Using Models

Problem: Make a model of a Fraction Slide Rule.

1 IMAGINE You want to make your own fraction slide rule so you can discover some interesting things about fractions.

2 NAME The materials you will need:
2 different colored pieces of construction paper each 15 in. long and 2 in. wide.

3 THINK Fold each piece in half so that each piece is now 1 inch wide. Mark off each piece in 1-inch units from 0 to 16. (See the illustration.) Label one piece the numerator, and the other the denominator.

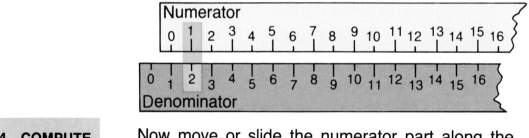

4 COMPUTE Now move or slide the numerator part along the denominator part so that the 1 is directly over the 2 in the denominator.
Look at the "slide rule." Do you see these fractions?

$$\cdots \; \frac{1}{2}, \; \frac{2}{3}, \; \frac{3}{4}, \; \frac{4}{5}, \; \frac{5}{6}, \; \frac{6}{7}, \; \frac{7}{8}, \; \frac{8}{9}, \; \frac{9}{10} \; \cdots$$

Choose $\frac{3}{4}$. $\frac{3}{4}$ is greater than every fraction to the left of it, and smaller than every fraction to the right of it.

$$\frac{3}{4} > \frac{1}{2}, \frac{2}{3} \qquad \frac{3}{4} < \frac{4}{5}, \frac{5}{6}, \frac{6}{7}, \frac{7}{8}, \frac{8}{9}, \frac{9}{10}$$

5 CHECK Compare: $\frac{3}{4} \underline{\; ? \;} \frac{1}{2} \longrightarrow \frac{3}{4} > \frac{2}{4} \longrightarrow \frac{3}{4} > \frac{1}{2}$

Solve using models.

1. Does Brian ever get home again? He leaves his house and walks $3\frac{1}{2}$ blocks east. He then walks $1\frac{1}{2}$ blocks west. Brian then decides to walk $4\frac{3}{4}$ blocks north and $3\frac{3}{4}$ blocks south. Finally, he walks 2 blocks west and 1 block south.

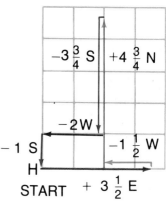

$-3\frac{3}{4}$ S $+4\frac{3}{4}$ N

-2 W

-1 S $-1\frac{1}{2}$ W

H

START $+3\frac{1}{2}$ E

IMAGINE

Draw a model of Brian's walk on a piece of graph paper.

NAME

Facts: Label the facts on the model.

Question: Does Brian get home again?

THINK

Look at the model. Let H be Brian's Home.
Let going east and north be addition.
Let going west and south be subtraction.
These are Brian's stops:

Stop 1: $+3\frac{1}{2}$ E   Stop 4: $-3\frac{3}{4}$ S

Stop 2: $-1\frac{1}{2}$ W   Stop 5: -2 W

Stop 3: $+4\frac{3}{4}$ N   Stop 6: -1 S

Then   ⟶   **COMPUTE**   and   ⟶   **CHECK**

2. If Brian had traveled $4\frac{3}{4}$ blocks north, $2\frac{3}{4}$ blocks south, 1 block east, and 3 blocks west, where would Brian be in relation to his home?

3. Make up your own trip. Ask your friends if you ever get home.

4. Use the slide rule. What fractions are greater than $\frac{2}{5}$? Less than $\frac{2}{5}$?

More Practice

Write an equivalent fraction.

1. $\frac{1}{2} = \frac{?}{10}$

2. $\frac{3}{4} = \frac{?}{12}$

3. $\frac{7}{8} = \frac{?}{16}$

4. $\frac{3}{4} = \frac{?}{8}$

5. $\frac{3}{7} = \frac{?}{14}$

Write in simplest form.

6. $\frac{3}{24}$

7. $\frac{5}{20}$

8. $\frac{10}{16}$

9. $\frac{6}{12}$

10. $\frac{18}{27}$

Compare. Write <, =, or >.

11. $\frac{1}{5}$ __?__ $\frac{1}{3}$

12. $\frac{1}{7}$ __?__ $\frac{1}{12}$

13. $\frac{2}{3}$ __?__ $\frac{2}{5}$

14. $\frac{3}{6}$ __?__ $\frac{2}{4}$

15. $\frac{3}{5}$ __?__ $\frac{3}{4}$

Change to a whole or mixed number.

16. $\frac{16}{8}$

17. $\frac{13}{4}$

18. $\frac{15}{6}$

19. $\frac{20}{5}$

20. $\frac{17}{3}$

Add or Subtract.

21. $\begin{array}{r} \frac{1}{5} \\ + \frac{2}{5} \\ \hline \end{array}$

22. $\begin{array}{r} \frac{5}{8} \\ - \frac{3}{8} \\ \hline \end{array}$

23. $\begin{array}{r} \frac{5}{6} \\ + \frac{1}{2} \\ \hline \end{array}$

24. $\begin{array}{r} \frac{8}{9} \\ - \frac{2}{3} \\ \hline \end{array}$

25. $\begin{array}{r} \frac{7}{10} \\ - \frac{2}{20} \\ \hline \end{array}$

26. $\begin{array}{r} 4\frac{1}{2} \\ + 3\frac{1}{2} \\ \hline \end{array}$

27. $\begin{array}{r} 8\frac{5}{6} \\ - 4\frac{2}{3} \\ \hline \end{array}$

28. $\begin{array}{r} 5\frac{7}{8} \\ - 3\frac{3}{16} \\ \hline \end{array}$

29. $\begin{array}{r} 12\frac{12}{25} \\ + 2\frac{2}{5} \\ \hline \end{array}$

30. $\begin{array}{r} 5\frac{3}{16} \\ + 4\frac{5}{8} \\ \hline \end{array}$

Solve.

31. Sal climbed $7\frac{1}{2}$ feet up a rope. He slipped back $1\frac{1}{4}$ feet. How high on the rope is he now?

(See *Still More Practice*, p. 365)

Math Probe

FINDING FRACTION PATTERNS

X	1	2	3	4	5	6	7	8	9
1	1	2	3	4	5	6	7	8	9
2	2	4	6	8	10	12	14	16	18
3	3	6	9	12	15	18	21	24	27
4	4	8	12	16	20	24	28	32	36
5	5	10	15	20	25	30	35	40	45
6	6	12	18	24	30	36	42	48	54
7	7	14	21	28	35	42	49	56	63
8	8	16	24	32	40	48	56	64	72
9	9	18	27	36	45	54	63	72	81

Finding Equivalent Fractions.

Look at Rows 3 and 5. Imagine row 3 as the numerator and row 5 the denominator of a fraction.

Do you find a pattern for equivalent fractions?

$$\frac{3}{5} = \frac{6}{10} = \frac{9}{15} = \frac{12}{20} = \frac{15}{25}$$

1. Do this for Rows 3 and 8.

Finding Common Denominators

Find a common denominator for $\frac{3}{5}$ and $\frac{3}{8}$.
Look at the rows for each denominator.

$\frac{3}{5}$ ⌐→ 5   10   15   20   25   30   35   (40)   45

$\frac{3}{8}$ ⌐→ 8   16   20   32   (40)   48   56   64   72

40 is a common denominator. It is also the least common denominator LCD.

Use the Multiplication Table to find the LCD of:

2. $\frac{1}{2}$ and $\frac{2}{3}$ **3.** $\frac{7}{8}$ and $\frac{3}{4}$ **4.** $\frac{3}{4}$ and $\frac{2}{3}$ **5.** $\frac{5}{6}$ and $\frac{7}{8}$

Check Your Mastery

Write an equivalent fraction.

See pp. 236-239

1. $\frac{2}{3} = \frac{?}{9}$

2. $\frac{4}{7} = \frac{?}{14}$

3. $\frac{3}{5} = \frac{?}{10}$

4. $\frac{3}{4} = \frac{?}{12}$

Write in simplest form.

See pp. 240-241

5. $\frac{4}{10}$

6. $\frac{18}{27}$

7. $\frac{6}{8}$

8. $\frac{2}{20}$

9. $\frac{5}{15}$

Compare. Write <, =, or >.

See pp. 242-243

10. $\frac{5}{8}$? $\frac{1}{2}$

11. $\frac{1}{6}$? $\frac{1}{3}$

12. $\frac{4}{5}$? $\frac{3}{10}$

13. $\frac{2}{3}$? $\frac{12}{18}$

Change to a whole or mixed number.

See pp. 248-249

14. $\frac{14}{8}$

15. $\frac{13}{3}$

16. $\frac{12}{6}$

17. $\frac{18}{4}$

Add or Subtract.

See pp. 244-255

18. $\frac{3}{5} + \frac{2}{5}$

19. $\frac{9}{11} + \frac{5}{11}$

20. $\frac{5}{8} + \frac{1}{8}$

21. $\frac{3}{10} + \frac{5}{10}$

22. $\frac{1}{2} - \frac{5}{12}$

23. $\frac{3}{4} - \frac{1}{8}$

24. $\frac{5}{8} - \frac{1}{2}$

25. $\frac{5}{6} - \frac{1}{2}$

26. $4\frac{3}{4} + 3\frac{1}{2}$

27. $10\frac{1}{6} + 7\frac{2}{3}$

28. $8\frac{2}{3} - 4\frac{1}{6}$

29. $9\frac{9}{10} - 7\frac{3}{10}$

Solve.

See pp. 254-255

30. The speed of a horse is $47\frac{1}{2}$ mph. The speed of a greyhound is $39\frac{7}{20}$ mph. How much faster is a horse than a greyhound?

Division: Two-Digit Divisors

10

In this unit you will:

- Divide 2- and 3-digit dividends by 2 digits
- Use trial quotients in division
- Divide dividends with 4 digits
- Divide when zero is in the quotient
- Divide when the dividend is money
- Solve problems by comparing prices

Do you remember?

The steps for long division:

- Divide.
- Multiply.
- Subtract.
- Compare.
- Bring down.
- Repeat the steps.
- Check.

Divisors: Multiples of Ten

Look for a pattern.

$$2\,0\,\overline{)\,8\,0\,} = 8 \text{ tens} \div 2 \text{ tens} = 4 \longrightarrow 2\,0\,\overset{4}{\overline{)\,8\,0\,}}$$

$$3\,0\,\overline{)\,1\,5\,0\,} = 15 \text{ tens} \div 3 \text{ tens} = 5 \longrightarrow 3\,0\,\overset{5}{\overline{)\,1\,5\,0\,}}$$

Now study these.

$$2\,0\,\overline{)\,8\,5\,} = 8 \text{ tens } 5 \text{ ones} \div 2 \text{ tens} = \underline{\ ?\ }$$

Begin where? $\longrightarrow$	Divide the ones. $\longrightarrow$	Complete. $\longrightarrow$	Check.

$2\,0\,\overline{)\,8\,5\,}$
20 > 8. So divide the 85 ones to find the first digit.

$85 \div 20 = \underline{\ ?\ }$
$\underline{\ ?\ } \times 20 = 85$

Think: $8 \div 2 = \underline{\ ?\ }$

Try 4.

$2\,0\,\overset{4}{\overline{)\,8\,5\,}}$

$$\begin{array}{r} \overset{\times}{}4 \text{ R } 5 \\ 2\,0\,\overline{)\,8\,5\,} \\ -8\,0 \\ \hline 5 \end{array}$$

$$\begin{array}{r} 2\,0 \\ \times\ \ 4 \\ \hline 8\,0 \\ +\ \ 5 \\ \hline 8\,5 \end{array}$$

Begin where? $\longrightarrow$	Divide the ones. $\longrightarrow$	Complete. $\longrightarrow$	Check.

$3\,0\,\overline{)\,1\,5\,7\,}$
30 > 1, 30 > 15
So divide the 157 ones.

$157 \div 30 = \underline{\ ?\ }$
$\underline{\ ?\ } \times 30 = 157$

Think: $15 \div 3 = \underline{\ ?\ }$

Try 5.

$0\,\overset{5}{\overline{)\,1\,5\,7\,}}$

$$\begin{array}{r} \overset{\times}{}5 \text{ R } 7 \\ 3\,0\,\overline{)\,1\,5\,7\,} \\ -1\,5\,0 \\ \hline 7 \end{array}$$

$$\begin{array}{r} 3\,0 \\ \times\ \ \ 5 \\ \hline 1\,5\,0 \\ +\ \ \ 7 \\ \hline 1\,5\,7 \end{array}$$

Divide mentally.

1. $20\overline{)40}$ 2. $30\overline{)60}$ 3. $30\overline{)90}$ 4. $40\overline{)80}$ 5. $30\overline{)120}$

6. $90\overline{)90}$ 7. $60\overline{)120}$ 8. $80\overline{)720}$ 9. $70\overline{)280}$ 10. $50\overline{)400}$

Multiply mentally.

11. 20×4 12. 60×7 13. 40×5 14. 80×6

15. 30×9 16. 70×3 17. 60×8 18. 90×5

Complete.

19.
```
          6
  9 0 ) 5 4 0
  − ? ? ?
        ?
```

20.
```
          6 R  ?
  9 0 ) 5 4 8
  − ? ? ?
        8
```

21.
```
          9 R  ?
  7 0 ) 6 3 5
  − ? ? ?
        ?
```

22.
```
          ?
  8 0 ) 6 4 0
  − ? ? ?
        ?
```

23.
```
          ? R  ?
  6 0 ) 4 2 5
  − ? ? ?
        ?
```

24.
```
          ? R  ?
  5 0 ) 4 5 3
  − ? ? ?
        ?
```

Divide and check.

25. $30\overline{)180}$ 26. $50\overline{)350}$ 27. $60\overline{)300}$ 28. $70\overline{)420}$ 29. $90\overline{)810}$

30. $40\overline{)363}$ 31. $80\overline{)486}$ 32. $20\overline{)181}$ 33. $50\overline{)254}$ 34. $30\overline{)272}$

35. $70\overline{)356}$ 36. $90\overline{)548}$ 37. $80\overline{)567}$ 38. $40\overline{)283}$ 39. $50\overline{)453}$

40. $90\overline{)365}$ 41. $70\overline{)145}$ 42. $60\overline{)364}$ 43. $30\overline{)122}$ 44. $90\overline{)635}$

45. $80\overline{)647}$ 46. $60\overline{)485}$ 47. $90\overline{)278}$ 48. $40\overline{)163}$ 49. $70\overline{)498}$

Two-Digit Divisors: Two-Digit Dividends

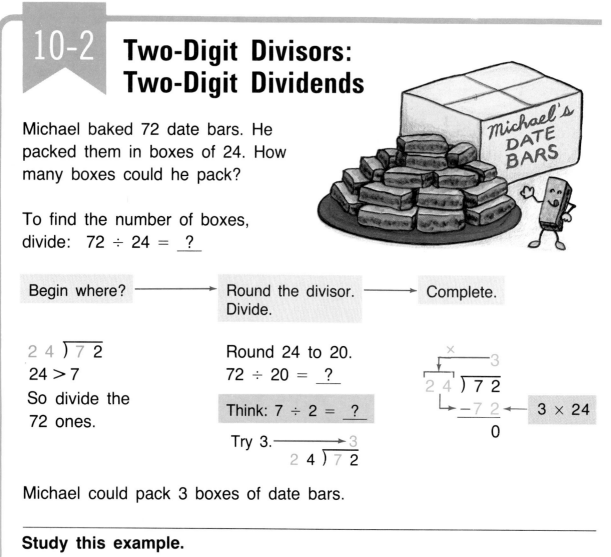

Michael baked 72 date bars. He packed them in boxes of 24. How many boxes could he pack?

To find the number of boxes, divide: $72 \div 24 = \underline{\ ?\ }$

Begin where?	→	Round the divisor. Divide.	→	Complete.

$$2\,4\,\overline{)7\,2}$$

$24 > 7$

So divide the 72 ones.

Round 24 to 20.

$72 \div 20 = \underline{\ ?\ }$

Think: $7 \div 2 = \underline{\ ?\ }$

Try 3. ⟶ $\overset{3}{2\,4\,\overline{)7\,2}}$

$$\overset{\times \qquad\quad 3}{2\,4\,\overline{)7\,2}}$$
$$\underline{-7\,2} \leftarrow 3 \times 24$$
$$0$$

Michael could pack 3 boxes of date bars.

Study this example.

Divide: $98 \div 32 = \underline{\ ?\ }$

Begin where?	→	Round the divisor. Divide.	→	Complete.	→	Check.

$$3\,2\,\overline{)9\,8}$$

$32 > 9$

So divide the 98 ones.

Round 32 to 30.

$98 \div 30 = \underline{\ ?\ }$

Think: $9 \div 3 = \underline{\ ?\ }$

Try 3. ⟶ $\overset{3}{3\,2\,\overline{)9\,8}}$

$$\overset{\times \qquad\quad 3\ \text{R } 2}{3\,2\,\overline{)9\,8}}$$
$$\underline{-9\,6}$$
$$2$$

$$\begin{array}{r} 3\,2 \\ \times\ \ 3 \\ \hline 9\,6 \\ +\ \ 2 \\ \hline 9\,8 \end{array}$$

Round to the nearest ten.

1. 21   **2.** 35   **3.** 43   **4.** 27   **5.** 42

6. 54   **7.** 28   **8.** 33   **9.** 48   **10.** 26

Complete.

11.
$$\begin{array}{r} 2 \\ 24\overline{)48} \\ -48 \\ \hline ? \end{array}$$

12.
$$\begin{array}{r} 3 \\ 32\overline{)96} \\ -?? \\ \hline ? \end{array}$$

13.
$$\begin{array}{r} 2\ R\ ? \\ 44\overline{)89} \\ -88 \\ \hline ? \end{array}$$

14.
$$\begin{array}{r} ?\ R\ ? \\ 33\overline{)67} \\ -66 \\ \hline ? \end{array}$$

Divide and check.

15. $31\overline{)62}$ **16.** $23\overline{)46}$ **17.** $42\overline{)84}$ **18.** $33\overline{)99}$ **19.** $31\overline{)93}$

20. $32\overline{)64}$ **21.** $33\overline{)66}$ **22.** $41\overline{)82}$ **23.** $34\overline{)68}$ **24.** $43\overline{)86}$

25. $22\overline{)45}$ **26.** $42\overline{)88}$ **27.** $31\overline{)96}$ **28.** $23\overline{)49}$ **29.** $34\overline{)69}$

30. $21\overline{)48}$ **31.** $44\overline{)89}$ **32.** $31\overline{)95}$ **33.** $24\overline{)79}$ **34.** $42\overline{)50}$

35. $33\overline{)70}$ **36.** $24\overline{)52}$ **37.** $22\overline{)88}$ **38.** $41\overline{)91}$ **39.** $32\overline{)69}$

Solve.

40. If 26 chairs were made in a day, how many days did it take to make 78 chairs?

41. Ms. David divided 50 pencils among her 24 students. How many pencils did each receive? How many were left over?

42. The dividend is 97. The divisor is 32. What is the quotient? Is there a remainder? If so, what is it?

10-3 Two-Digit Divisors: Three-Digit Dividends

Divide: 102 ÷ 34 = ?

34 > 1, 34 > 10,
so divide the 102 ones.

Round the divisor 34 to 30.

Estimate: About how many 30's in 102?

     Think: 10 ÷ 3 = ?
       Try 3.

Multiply: 3 × 34 = 102

Subtract: 102 − 102 = 0

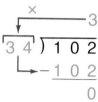

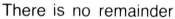

There is no remainder

Divide: 161 ÷ 37 = ?

37 > 1; 37 > 16,
so divide the 161 ones.

Round the divisor 37 to 40.

Estimate: About how many 40's in 161?

     Think: 16 ÷ 4 = ?
       Try 4.

Multiply: 4 × 37 = 148

Subtract: 161 − 148 = 13

Compare: 13 < 37

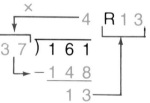

Write the remainder as R13

Complete.

1.
$$\begin{array}{r} 4 \text{ R } \underline{?} \\ 32\overline{)129} \\ -128 \\ \hline ? \end{array}$$

2.
$$\begin{array}{r} 5 \\ 51\overline{)255} \\ -??? \\ \hline ? \end{array}$$

3.
$$\begin{array}{r} 4 \text{ R } \underline{?} \\ 36\overline{)148} \\ -??? \\ \hline ? \end{array}$$

4.
$$\begin{array}{r} 5 \\ 61\overline{)305} \\ -??? \\ \hline ? \end{array}$$

Divide and check.

5. $22\overline{)176}$
6. $32\overline{)160}$
7. $43\overline{)258}$
8. $33\overline{)132}$
9. $53\overline{)265}$

10. $22\overline{)133}$
11. $42\overline{)252}$
12. $21\overline{)126}$
13. $62\overline{)248}$
14. $81\overline{)324}$

15. $42\overline{)126}$
16. $31\overline{)186}$
17. $51\overline{)153}$
18. $21\overline{)147}$
19. $43\overline{)129}$

20. $62\overline{)187}$
21. $52\overline{)106}$
22. $41\overline{)329}$
23. $42\overline{)169}$
24. $71\overline{)289}$

25. $21\overline{)149}$
26. $31\overline{)157}$
27. $91\overline{)366}$
28. $81\overline{)486}$
29. $63\overline{)190}$

Solve.

30. The dividend is 294. The divisor is 42. What is the quotient?

31. What number is 128 divided by 32?

32. The dividend is 156. The divisor is 52. What is the quotient?

33. The Wood Factory uses 21 pieces of lumber for each set of picnic tables and benches. One day, the factory had 129 pieces of lumber. How many picnic sets could be made? How many pieces of lumber were left over?

Two-Digit Quotients

Divide: 768 ÷ 24 = _?_

24 > 7, so divide the 76 tens.

Round the divisor 24 to 20.

Estimate: About how many 20's in 76?

Think: 7 ÷ 2 = _?_ Try 3.

Multiply: 3 × 24 = 72

Subtract: 76 − 72 = 4

Compare: 4 < 24

Bring down: 8

```
      × ────── 3
  2 4 ) 7 6 8
      └→ − 7 2 ↓
           4 8 ←
```

The partial dividend is 48.

Divide: 48 ÷ 24 = _?_

Estimate: About how many 20's in 48?

Think: 4 ÷ 2 = _?_ Try 2.

Multiply: 2 × 24 = 48

Subtract: 48 − 48 = 0

Check: 32 × 24 = 768

```
      ×          3 2
  2 4 ) 7 6 8
         − 7 2 ↓
            4 8
          → − 4 8
               0
```

Study these examples.

```
        2 3 ←
  3 4 ) 7 8 2      Think: 7 ÷ 3
      − 6 8
        1 0 2      Think: 10 ÷ 3
      − 1 0 2
```

```
          1 9 R 9
  4 9 ) 9 4 0      Think: 9 ÷ 5
      − 4 9
        4 5 0      Think: 45 ÷ 5
      − 4 4 1
            9
```

Complete.

1.
```
      26
34)884
   -??
    204
   -??
```

2.
```
       2? R ?
42)890
   -??
     50
   -??
      ?
```

3.
```
       ?? R ?
52)629
   -??
    ??9
  -???
      ?
```

Divide and check.

4. 42)882 5. 23)552 6. 34)721 7. 44)968 8. 31)899

9. 52)729 10. 45)670 11. 24)988 12. 31)994 13. 22)682

14. 24)990 15. 43)993 16. 23)972 17. 21)695 18. 32)769

19. 24)552 20. 33)830 21. 31)750 22. 44)975 23. 72)794

24. 41)943 25. 38)801 26. 33)835 27. 63)882 28. 29)673

Find the quotient.

29. 704 ÷ 32 = _?_   30. 770 ÷ 33 = _?_   31. 902 ÷ 82 = _?_

32. 900 ÷ 64 = _?_   33. 910 ÷ 41 = _?_   34. 984 ÷ 54 = _?_

Solve.

Find the age of Scottie!

To find out, divide each. Then
add the sum of any remainders.

35. 22)529   36. 43)646

37. 52)938   38. 33)827   39. 43)606

271

Trial Quotients

If the estimated quotient is too big
or too small, change the estimate.

Divide: 148 ÷ 36 = _?_

36 > 1; 36 > 14,
so divide the 148 ones.

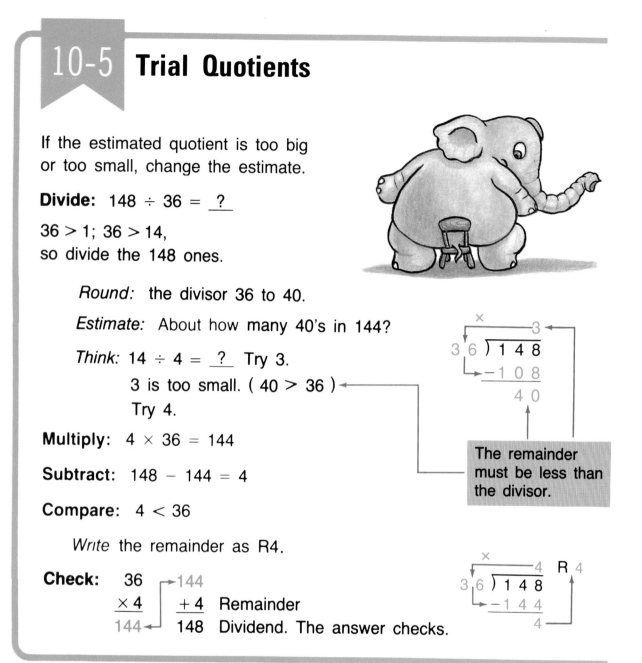

Round: the divisor 36 to 40.

Estimate: About how many 40's in 144?

Think: 14 ÷ 4 = _?_ Try 3.
3 is too small. (40 > 36)
Try 4.

Multiply: 4 × 36 = 144

Subtract: 148 − 144 = 4

Compare: 4 < 36

Write the remainder as R4.

The remainder
must be less than
the divisor.

Check: 36 ⟶ 144
×4   +4 Remainder
144 ⟵ 148 Dividend. The answer checks.

$$36 \overline{)148} \quad R\,4$$
$$-144$$
$$4$$

Complete.

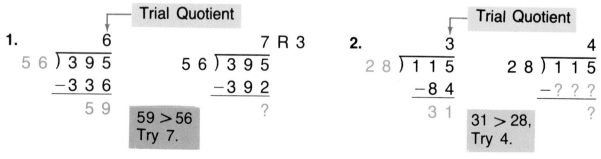

Trial Quotient

1.   6   7 R 3
    56) 3 9 5   56) 3 9 5
    − 3 3 6   − 3 9 2
        5 9   ?

59 > 56
Try 7.

Trial Quotient

2.   3   4
    28) 1 1 5   28) 1 1 5
    − 8 4   − ? ? ?
        3 1   ?

31 > 28,
Try 4.

Divide and check.

3. 27)203   **4.** 28)224   **5.** 82)483   **6.** 43)417   **7.** 38)229

8. 59)177   **9.** 29)265   **10.** 39)273   **11.** 54)259   **12.** 33)627

13. 38)308   **14.** 21)609   **15.** 75)365   **16.** 27)166   **17.** 48)248

18. 39)275   **19.** 62)208   **20.** 82)440   **21.** 58)244   **22.** 73)238

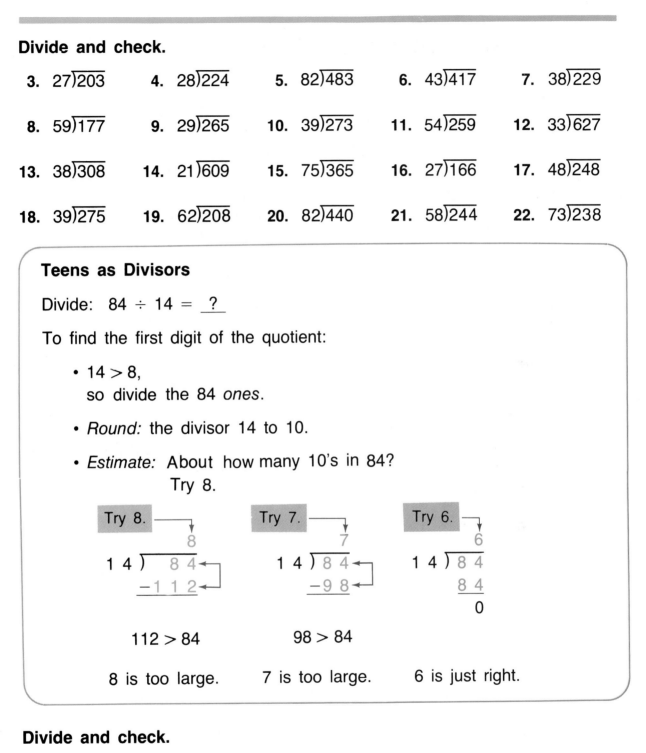

Teens as Divisors

Divide: $84 \div 14 = \underline{\quad ? \quad}$

To find the first digit of the quotient:

- $14 > 8$,
  so divide the 84 *ones*.

- *Round:* the divisor 14 to 10.

- *Estimate:* About how many 10's in 84?
  Try 8.

Try 8.
```
        8
  1 4 )  8 4
      -1 1 2
```
$112 > 84$

8 is too large.

Try 7.
```
        7
  1 4 )  8 4
      -9 8
```
$98 > 84$

7 is too large.

Try 6.
```
        6
  1 4 )  8 4
        8 4
          0
```
6 is just right.

Divide and check.

23. 12)91   **24.** 19)79   **25.** 18)165   **26.** 17)140   **27.** 16)135

28. 14)112   **29.** 18)162   **30.** 15)115   **31.** 17)104   **32.** 19)117

273

More Trial Quotients

Divide: 2346 ÷ 64 = _?_

64 > 2, 64 > 23,
so divide the 234 tens.

    Round: the divisor 64 to 60.
    Estimate: About how many 60's
             in 234?
    Think: 23 ÷ 6 = _?_   Try 3.

```
      ×          3
  6 4 ) 2 3 4 6
         -1 9 2
           4 2 6  ← Partial
                    Dividend
```

Divide: 426 ÷ 64 = _?_
    Think: 42 ÷ 6 = _?_   Try 7.
          7 is too large (448 > 426).
          Try 6.

```
      ×              3 7
  6 4 ) 2 3 4 6
         -1 9 2
           4 2 6 ←
          -4 4 8 ─── too large
```

Check:

```
              3 6 ← Quotient
          ×   6 4 ← Divisor
            1 4 4
          2 1 6
          2 3 0 4
        +     4 2 ← Remainder
          2 3 4 6 ← Dividend
```

```
      ×            3 6 R 4 2
  6 4 ) 2 3 4 6
         -1 9 2
           4 2 6
          -3 8 4
             4 2
```

The answer checks.

Complete.

1.
```
         24 R _?_
   51)1273
    -102
     253
    -???
      ?
```

2.
```
         46 R _?_
   24)1107
    -96
     147
    -???
      ?
```

3.
```
         ?? R _?_
   33)2179
    -198
     199
    -???
      ?
```

Divide and check.

4. 34)1180   **5.** 33)1110   **6.** 44)2106   **7.** 63)4914

8. 72)2808   **9.** 76)2128   **10.** 72)3550   **11.** 84)3285

12. 64)5084   **13.** 48)4128   **14.** 38)2242   **15.** 42)2226

16. 22)1810   **17.** 33)2808   **18** 41)1284   **19.** 41)1200

Magic Numbers to Find Trial Quotients Quickly

	1	2	3	4	5	6	7	8	9
How many 6's?	6)6	12	18	24	30	36	42	48	54
How many 7's?	7)7	14	21	28	35	42	49	56	63
How many 8's?	8)8	16	24	32	40	48	56	64	72
How many 9's?	9)9	18	27	36	45	54	63	72	81

Divide. Use the magic numbers.

20. 62)1488   **21.** 64)1664   **22.** 61)4392   **23.** 63)2646

24. 24)1992   **25.** 65)5465   **26.** 67)5628   **27.** 35)1649

28. 23)1314   **29.** 84)2271   **30.** 12)458   **31.** 24)674

Solve.

32. There are 34 pages of stamps. Each page contains the same number of stamps. If the total number of stamps is 1292, how many stamps are on a page?

33. Dick has 1634 pennies. 50 pennies fit in a roll. How many rolls of pennies can Dick make? How many are left over?

275

10-7 Zero in the Quotient

Don't forget to put a zero in the quotient!

Leaving out 0 can change:

601 to 61   and   470 to 47

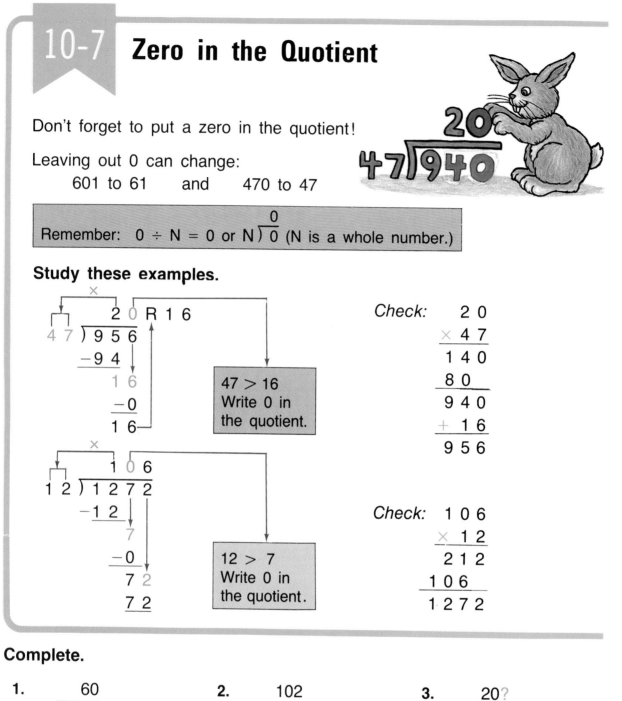

Remember: $0 \div N = 0$ or $N\overline{)\,0}^{\,0}$ (N is a whole number.)

Study these examples.

```
       × 
      2 0  R 1 6
4 7 )9 5 6
    -9 4
      1 6
     - 0
      1 6
```

47 > 16
Write 0 in
the quotient.

```
Check:    2 0
        × 4 7
        1 4 0
        8 0
        9 4 0
      +   1 6
        9 5 6
```

```
        × 
      1 0 6
1 2 )1 2 7 2
    -1 2
        7
      - 0
        7 2
        7 2
```

12 > 7
Write 0 in
the quotient.

```
Check:   1 0 6
       ×   1 2
         2 1 2
         1 0 6
       1 2 7 2
```

Complete.

1.
```
        60
35)2100
   210
       ?
```

2.
```
        102
57)5814
    57
    11
     ?
    1?4
    ???
```

3.
```
        20?
18)3690
    36
     9
     ?
    ?0
    ??
```

Divide and check.

4. $5 \overline{)200}$ 5. $7 \overline{)210}$ 6. $9 \overline{)630}$ 7. $3 \overline{)241}$

8. $6 \overline{)544}$ 9. $8 \overline{)406}$ 10. $7 \overline{)563}$ 11. $31 \overline{)1550}$

12. $42 \overline{)2940}$ 13. $63 \overline{)1260}$ 14. $47 \overline{)1880}$ 15. $56 \overline{)4480}$

16. $35 \overline{)2100}$ 17. $36 \overline{)1802}$ 18. $57 \overline{)3421}$ 19. $82 \overline{)4712}$

20. $21 \overline{)2247}$ 21. $19 \overline{)5852}$ 22. $32 \overline{)9856}$ 23. $46 \overline{)9246}$

Solve.

24. 720 free pamphlets are distributed among the eight 4th-grade classes. They are distributed equally to each class. How many does each class receive?

25. The 4th–grade class collected 1040 aluminum cans. Each student brought in 26 cans. How many students are in the class?

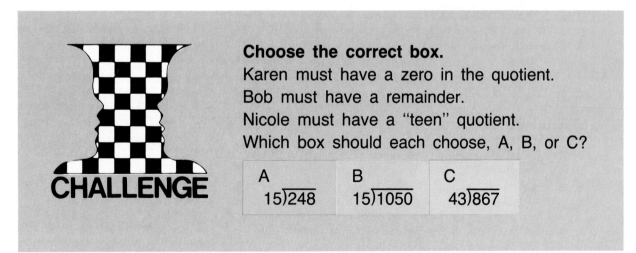

CHALLENGE

Choose the correct box.
Karen must have a zero in the quotient.
Bob must have a remainder.
Nicole must have a "teen" quotient.
Which box should each choose, A, B, or C?

A	B	C
$15 \overline{)248}$	$15 \overline{)1050}$	$43 \overline{)867}$

Dividing with Money

Ray puts 14 gallons of gasoline into his car.
It costs him $16.38. What is the price of
the gasoline per gallon?

To find the price of one gallon or the **unit
price**, divide: $16.38 ÷ 14 = ?

| Write the decimal point and the dollar sign in the quotient. | → | Divide as usual. | → | Check. |

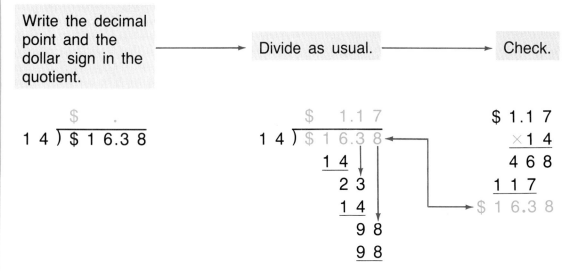

$$\begin{array}{r} \$. \\ 14\overline{)\$16.38} \end{array}$$

$$\begin{array}{r} \$1.17 \\ 14\overline{)\$16.38} \\ \underline{14} \\ 23 \\ \underline{14} \\ 98 \\ \underline{98} \end{array}$$

Check.
$$\begin{array}{r} \$1.17 \\ \times14 \\ \hline 468 \\ 117 \\ \hline \$16.38 \end{array}$$

Ray pays $1.17 per gallon for gasoline.

Study these examples.

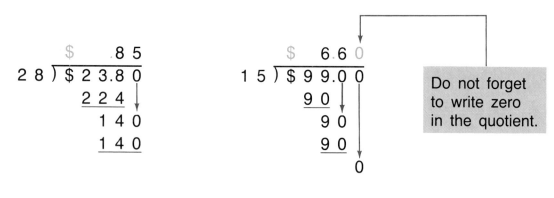

$$\begin{array}{r} \$.85 \\ 28\overline{)\$23.80} \\ \underline{224} \\ 140 \\ \underline{140} \end{array}$$

$$\begin{array}{r} \$6.60 \\ 15\overline{)\$99.00} \\ \underline{90} \\ 90 \\ \underline{90} \\ 0 \end{array}$$

Do not forget
to write zero
in the quotient.

Write a dollar sign and decimal point in the correct place in each quotient. Then check each quotient.

1.
$$\begin{array}{r} 7\ 56 \\ 6\overline{)\$45.36} \end{array}$$

2.
$$\begin{array}{r} 2\ 15 \\ 27\overline{)\$58.05} \end{array}$$

3.
$$\begin{array}{r} 85 \\ 36\overline{)\$30.60} \end{array}$$

4.
$$\begin{array}{r} 3\ 40 \\ 24\overline{)\$81.60} \end{array}$$

Divide and check.

5. $6\overline{)\$2.10}$

6. $15\overline{)\$99.45}$

7. $25\overline{)\$26.25}$

8. $27\overline{)\$58.05}$

9. $92\overline{)\$36.80}$

10. $34\overline{)\$8.16}$

11. $46\overline{)\$17.02}$

12. $68\overline{)\$74.12}$

Find the cost of one or the unit price.

13. 3 pairs of socks for $3.96

14. 2 batteries for $1.56

15. 4 books for $9.00

16. 9 tickets for $29.25

17. 5 pennants for $7.25

18. 4 records for $7.32

19. 6 pens for $8.94

20. 5 balloons for $1.85

21. 3 notebooks for $7.50

22. 4 calculators for $50.00

Solve.

23. Jacqueline pays $7.12 for 8 pounds of peaches. How much is a pound of peaches?

24. Roberto saves $54.00 in 24 weeks. On the average how much does he save each week?

25. 12 bushels of apples cost $234.00. Find the cost of 1 bushel.

APPLES FOR SALE

Problem Solving: Comparing Prices

Problem: The smart shopper looks for the best buy. Are you a smart shopper? Will you select the best buy from a group of pens?

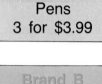

Brand A
Triple Good
Pens
3 for $3.99

1 IMAGINE

You can buy Brand A, Brand B, or Brand C pens.
You want to select the best buy.

Brand B
Top Quality
Pens
6 for $8.16

2 NAME

Facts:
3 for $3.99	Brand A
6 for $8.16	Brand B
10 for $13.50	Brand C

Brand C
Best Ever
Pens
10 for $13.50

Question: Which is the best buy?
To find the best buy, find the **unit price.**

3 THINK

To find the unit price of each, divide.
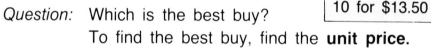
Brand A: $3.99 ÷ 3 = ?
Brand B: $8.16 ÷ 6 = ?
Brand C: $13.50 ÷ 10 = ?

4 COMPUTE

Brand A: $3.99 ÷ 3 = $1.33
Brand B: $8.16 ÷ 6 = $1.36
Brand C: $13.50 ÷ 10 = $1.35

The unit price of Brand A is the lowest. If the pen is of equal quality to Brands B and C, it is the best buy.

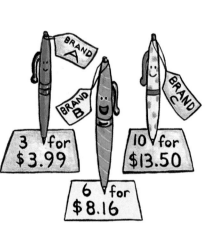

5 CHECK

$1.33	$1.36	$1.35
× 3	× 6	× 10
$3.99	$8.16	$13.50

Solve by comparing prices.

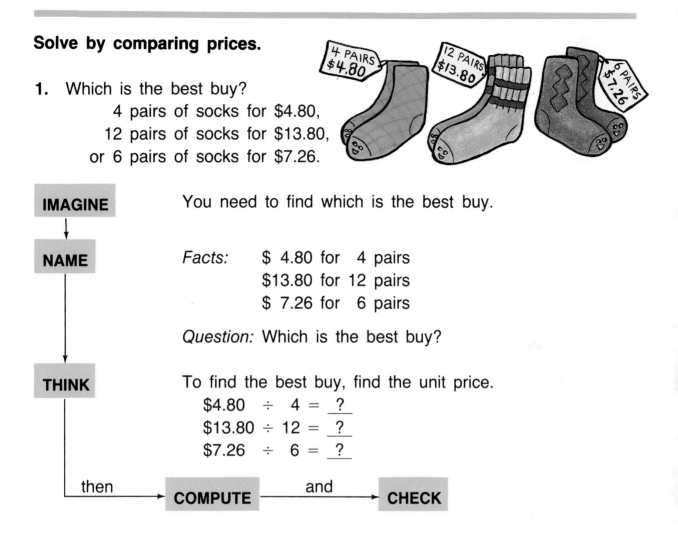

1. Which is the best buy?
       4 pairs of socks for $4.80,
      12 pairs of socks for $13.80,
      or 6 pairs of socks for $7.26.

IMAGINE   You need to find which is the best buy.

NAME   *Facts:* $ 4.80 for 4 pairs
                         $13.80 for 12 pairs
                         $ 7.26 for 6 pairs

             Question: Which is the best buy?

THINK   To find the best buy, find the unit price.
                $4.80 ÷ 4 = _?_
                $13.80 ÷ 12 = _?_
                $7.26 ÷ 6 = _?_

    then   ⟶   **COMPUTE**   and   ⟶   **CHECK**

2. Which size toothpaste is the better buy?
7 oz for $1.54 or 13 oz for $2.73

3. Which size jar is the better buy?
4 oz for $4.76 or 6 oz for $7.08

4. Which is the best buy? 3 notebooks
for $4.50, 6 notebooks for $8.40,
or 12 notebooks for $14.40

5. The fruit and nut shop sells nuts at:
2 lb for $2.98, 5 lb for $6.95, or
8 lb for $11.60. Which is the best buy?

More Practice

Divide and check.

1. $80\overline{)320}$ 2. $20\overline{)80}$ 3. $30\overline{)160}$ 4. $90\overline{)372}$ 5. $30\overline{)111}$

6. $27\overline{)83}$ 7. $36\overline{)87}$ 8. $16\overline{)39}$ 9. $37\overline{)93}$ 10. $11\overline{)36}$

11. $87\overline{)360}$ 12. $39\overline{)160}$ 13. $93\overline{)372}$ 14. $36\overline{)111}$ 15. $21\overline{)109}$

Find each quotient.

16. $21\overline{)378}$ 17. $21\overline{)669}$ 18. $47\overline{)555}$ 19. $73\overline{)4088}$ 20. $84\overline{)3025}$

21. $25\overline{)675}$ 22. $17\overline{)544}$ 23. $58\overline{)1508}$ 24. $65\overline{)4424}$ 25. $14\overline{)1206}$

26. $33\overline{)1650}$ 27. $52\overline{)3642}$ 28. $34\overline{)1020}$ 29. $56\overline{)3930}$ 30. $42\overline{)2646}$

31. $21\overline{)7770}$ 32. $47\overline{)8460}$ 33. $73\overline{)4088}$ 34. $84\overline{)3025}$ 35. $58\overline{)1508}$

36. $65\overline{)4424}$ 37. $14\overline{)1204}$ 38. $33\overline{)1650}$ 39. $52\overline{)3642}$ 40. $35\overline{)2170}$

Solve.

41. Twelve part-time workers earned $281.40. How much did each worker get if the money was divided equally?

42. The cost of 24 hammers is $162.96. How much does one hammer cost?

Which is the better buy?

43. 7 oz for $3.43 or 11 oz for $5.28

44. 6 bottles for $5.34 or 12 bottles for $10.80

(See *Still More Practice*, p.366)

Math Probe

RULES FOR DIVISIBILITY

The dividend is **divisible** by the divisor when the remainder is zero.

Make a list of numbers from 1 to 50.

1. Cross out all the numbers that are *multiples of 2.* Look at the digits in the *ones* place. What pattern do you see? ————————————→

> Any number ending in 0, 2, 4, 6, or 8 is *divisible by 2.*

2. Cross out all the numbers that are *multiples of 5.* Look at the digits in the *ones* place. What pattern do you see? ————————→

> Any number ending in 0 or 5 is *divisible by 5.*

3. Do you see a pattern for *multiples of 10?* ——————————

> Any number ending in 0 is *divisible by 10.*

4. Cross out all the numbers that are *multiples of 3.* Add the digits of each number and divide by 3:

$$27 \longrightarrow 2 + 7 = 9 \longrightarrow 9 \div 3 = 3$$
So, 27 is *divisible by 3.*

$$42 \longrightarrow 4 + 2 = 6 \longrightarrow 6 \div 3 = 2$$
So, 42 is *divisible by 3.*

> If the *sum* of the digits of a number is *divisible by 3,* the number is *divisible by 3.*

What pattern do you see? ————————————

Complete. Tell whether the first number is divisible by the second number. Write "Yes," or "No."

1. 38; 2   2. 75; 2   3. 40; 10   4. 39; 3   5. 57; 2

6. 86; 3   7. 90; 10   8. 354; 3   9. 468; 2   10. 715; 5

Check Your Mastery

Choose the correct answer.

See pp. 263 - 269.

1. 70)280   a. 3   b. 3 R1   c. 4 R1   d. 4

2. 32)64   a. 3   b. 2   c. 2 R2   d. 2 R1

3. 24)49   a. 2 R1   b. 3 R2   c. 1 R2   d. 3

4. 41)328   a. 8 R7   b. 7   c. 8   d. 7 R8

5. 51)308   a. 5 R6   b. 6 R5   c. 6 R2   d. 6 R8

6. 37)74   a. 3   b. 2 R3   c. 4   d. 2

7. 22)51   a. 2 R7   b. 2 R6   c. 1 R6   d. 1 R7

Divide and check.

See pp. 270 - 279.

8. 73)876   9. 62)936   10. 44)2772   11. 32)1728

12. 52)3120   13. 64)1924   14. 23)759   15. 73)2045

16. 35)630   17. 23)625   18. 56)2409   19. 86)3354

20. 66)1984   21. 58)3480   22. 32)$241.92   23. 18)$179.10

Solve.

See pp. 272 - 73, 280 - 81.

24. There are 24 cans of juice in a case. How many cases are needed for 1968 cans?

25. Tara paid $141.00 for 6 music lessons. Mike paid $252.00 for 12 lessons. Who got the better buy?

Cumulative Test III

Tell the number of sides for each.

1. triangle
2. rectangle
3. pentagon
4. octagon

Tell the number of vertices for each.

5. triangle
6. quadrilateral
7. hexagon
8. octagon

Choose the correct answer.

9. A simple closed curve formed by line segments is a:
   a. ray
   b. polygon
   c. circle
   d. point

10. The distance around a polygon is the:
    a. perimeter
    b. diameter
    c. center
    d. area

11. Lines that do not cross are:
    a. perpendicular
    b. intersecting
    c. right
    d. parallel

12. An angle that forms a square corner is a:
    a. ray
    b. radius
    c. right angle
    d. rectangle

13. A rectangle is a special type of:
    a. pentagon
    b. square
    c. hexagon
    d. quadrilateral

Draw these.

14. right angle ABC
15. circle T
16. $\angle$ XYZ
17. point Q
18. $\overrightarrow{MN}$
19. $\overline{RS}$

Find the perimeter.

20.

2 in.   4 in.   5 in.

21.

6 yd   3 yd   3 yd   6 yd

22.

4 ft   5 ft   2 ft   4 ft   6 ft   3 ft

Write as fractions.

23. two thirds
24. three eighths
25. seven ninths

Write the correct fraction.

26. What part of a week is one day?
27. What part of a dollar is a quarter?
28. What part of a yard is one foot?

Write an equivalent fraction.

29. $\frac{1}{2} = \frac{?}{6}$ 30. $\frac{3}{4} = \frac{?}{8}$ 31. $\frac{1}{5} = \frac{?}{10}$ 32. $\frac{2}{3} = \frac{?}{9}$ 33. $\frac{4}{5} = \frac{?}{20}$

Write in simplest form.

34. $\frac{3}{15}$ 35. $\frac{4}{24}$ 36. $\frac{4}{12}$ 37. $\frac{25}{35}$ 38. $\frac{9}{18}$

Change to a whole or mixed number.

39. $\frac{9}{2}$ 40. $\frac{17}{5}$ 41. $\frac{23}{4}$ 42. $\frac{18}{7}$ 43. $\frac{32}{5}$

Add or subtract.

44. $\begin{array}{r} \frac{1}{3} \\ + \frac{2}{3} \\ \hline \end{array}$ 45. $\begin{array}{r} \frac{5}{6} \\ + \frac{1}{6} \\ \hline \end{array}$ 46. $\begin{array}{r} \frac{3}{5} \\ + \frac{1}{2} \\ \hline \end{array}$ 47. $\begin{array}{r} \frac{7}{8} \\ + \frac{3}{8} \\ \hline \end{array}$ 48. $\begin{array}{r} \frac{7}{10} \\ - \frac{2}{5} \\ \hline \end{array}$

49. $\begin{array}{r} 5\frac{1}{2} \\ + 2\frac{1}{2} \\ \hline \end{array}$ 50. $\begin{array}{r} 5\frac{5}{6} \\ + 4\frac{1}{3} \\ \hline \end{array}$ 51. $\begin{array}{r} 6\frac{3}{8} \\ - 4\frac{1}{3} \\ \hline \end{array}$ 52. $\begin{array}{r} 7\frac{3}{7} \\ + \frac{3}{14} \\ \hline \end{array}$ 53. $\begin{array}{r} 9\frac{3}{16} \\ + 5\frac{5}{8} \\ \hline \end{array}$

Divide.

54. $20\overline{)80}$ 55. $30\overline{)180}$ 56. $11\overline{)34}$ 57. $62\overline{)930}$ 58. $23\overline{)761}$

59. $17\overline{)527}$ 60. $18\overline{)415}$ 61. $58\overline{)1566}$ 62. $42\overline{)2100}$ 63. $31\overline{)1395}$

Find the cost of one.

64. 3 pens for $2.37   65. 6 apples for $1.26   66. 2 tapes for $13.98

67. 5 notebooks for $7.95   68. 10 postcards for $2.30   69. 8 books for $24.00

Solve.

70. Find the perimeter of a square measuring 6 in. on a side.

71. Mae read $\frac{1}{4}$ of a book, and then $\frac{1}{3}$ of the book. What part of the book has she read?

72. If a diameter of a circle measures 6 cm, what is the measure of one of its radii?

73. Peter grew $\frac{7}{8}$ in. and John grew $\frac{5}{6}$ in. How much more did Peter grow than John?

74. If Sally runs 15 laps every day, how many days will it take her to run 270 laps?

75. If the divisor is 36 and the dividend is 144, what is the quotient?

286

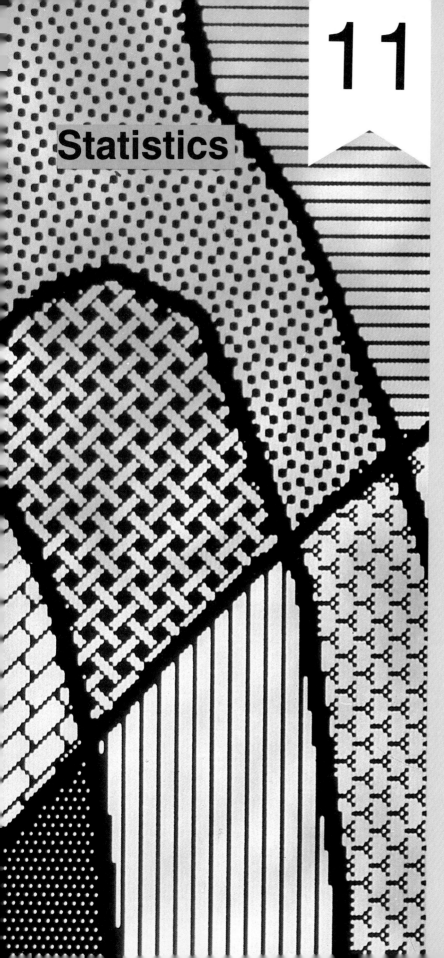

Statistics

11

In this unit you will:

- Read and interpret pictographs, bar graphs, line graphs, and circle graphs
- Use a calendar to determine a date a number of days after a given date
- Find probabilities
- Solve two-step problems

Do you remember?

2 of the 5 figures are triangles.

$\frac{2}{5}$ of the set are triangles.

3 of the 5 figures are circles.

$\frac{3}{5}$ of the set are circles.

287

11-1 Pictographs

A graph is an interesting and attractive way of showing information. A **pictograph** uses pictures to show "how many" or "how much."

Sophia took a survey to find out what the favorite snacks were of the 4th grade students.

Sophia used a pictograph to report her results to the students.

Favorite Snacks of 4th Grade Students	
Fruit	🧍 🧍 🧍 🧍 🧍
Pretzels	🧍 🧍
Carrot Sticks	🧍 🧍 🧍
Milk	🧍 🧍 🧍 🧍 🧍 🧍
Peanut Butter on Crackers	🧍 🧍 🧍 🧍 🧍
Key: Each 🧍 stands for 2 students.	

4 students chose pretzels.

Use the pictograph above to answer each question.

1. How many votes does 🧍 stand for?

2. Which snack is the favorite?

3. How many students prefer peanut butter on crackers?

4. Which snack is the least favorite?

5. How many students voted in this survey?

Use the pictograph to answer each question.

Numbers of Ice Cream Cones Sold	
Monday	🍦 🍦 🍦 🍦
Tuesday	🍦 🍦
Wednesday	🍦 🍦 🍦 🍦 🍦 🍦
Thursday	🍦 🍦 🍦 🍦 🍦 🍦 🍦 🍦 🍦 🍦
Friday	🍦 🍦 🍦 🍦 🍦 🍦 🍦

Key: Each 🍦 stands for 20 cones.

6. How many cones does 🍦 stand for?

7. How many cones were sold on Monday?

8. How many more cones were sold on Friday than on Tuesday?

9. On what day were the most cones sold? How many were sold?

Students Who Bought Stationery		
📓📓	Copybooks	👤 👤 👤 👤 👤 👤 👤 👤
📏📏	Rulers	👤 👤 👤 👤
✏️✏️✏️	Crayons	👤 👤 👤 👤 👤 👤 👤 👤 👤
✏️✏️✏️	Pencils	👤 👤 👤 👤 👤 👤 👤
▭ ▭	Erasers	👤 👤 👤 👤 👤

Key: Each 👤 stands for 9 students.

10. How many students bought copybooks?

11. How many more students bought crayons than rulers?

12. How many bought erasers and pencils?

13. Which item did the fewest students buy?

289

11-2 Bar Graphs

A **bar graph** is helpful to use when reporting or comparing information.

Ms. Cook asked the students for their favorite sport.

She made a vertical bar graph to record the results.

The tallest bar was for football. Football was the most popular sport. 60 students chose football.

Favorite Sport

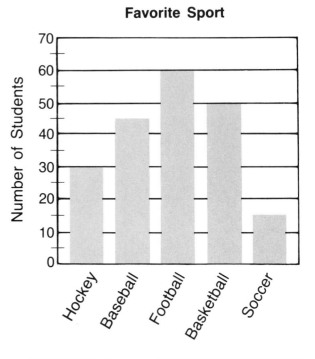

Use the bar graph above to answer each.

1. Name the title of the **vertical** bar graph.

2. How many students chose hockey?

3. Which sport was the least popular?

4. Which sport was chosen by 50 students?

5. How many more students chose football than baseball?

6. How many fewer students chose baseball than basketball?

7. There are 200 students in the school. Did they all choose a favorite sport?

8. How many sports were less favored than baseball? Which sports were they?

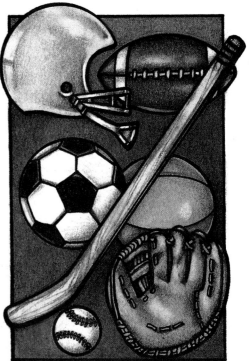

Use the horizontal bar graph to answer each question.

9. What is the title of the **horizontal** bar graph?

10. How many students come to school by:

   a. walking?   **b.** bicycle?

   c. bus?   **d.** car?

11. How many more students walk than come by car?

12. How many students were included in the survey?

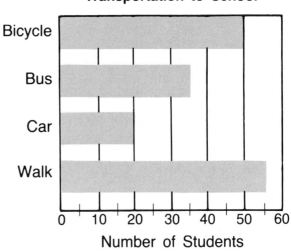

Transportation to School

Number of Students

Use the vertical bar graph to answer each question.

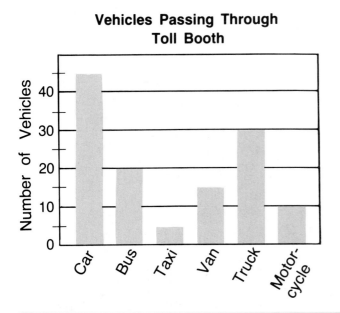

Vehicles Passing Through Toll Booth

13. What does the mark between 0 and 10 stand for?

14. How many trucks passed through the toll booth?

15. How many more cars than buses were there?

16. Which type of vehicle passed through most often?

17. How many vehicles in all passed through?

Mental Math
Do these calculations as rapidly as possible.

1. 9 × 8	**2.** 6 × 7	**3.** 4 × 9	**4.** 7 × 8	**5.** 6 × 9	**6.** 9 × 7
7. 8 × 6	**8.** 9 × 9	**9.** 7 × 5	**10.** 5 × 9	**11.** 7 × 6	**12.** 8 × 8

Line Graphs

A **line graph** is used to show change over a period of time.

This line graph shows John's grades in his 7 math exams this year.

What was John's grade on the 5th exam?

To read a line graph:

- Locate the number of the exam on the horizontal scale.

- Follow the vertical line upward to the dot.

- Follow the horizontal line left to the vertical scale.

John's grade was 80.

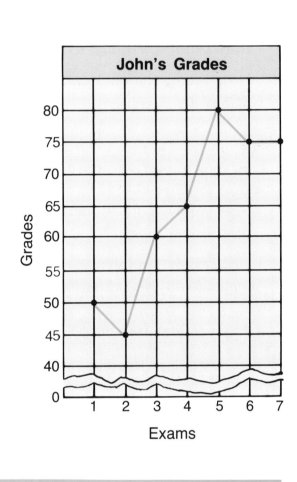

John's Grades

Grades

Exams

Use the line graph above to answer each question.

1. How many exams are listed on the graph?

2. What was the highest grade John received on any math exam?

3. Which grade did he receive more than once?

4. What was his lowest grade?

Compare grades. Write <, =, or >.

5. Exam 4 _?_ Exam 6

6. Exam 1 _?_ Exam 4

7. Exam 3 _?_ Exam 1

8. Exam 7 _?_ Exam 5

Use the line graph to answer each question.

9. When was the temperature 10°?

10. What was the temperature the third week it was measured?

11. When was the temperature 20°? 30°?

12. What was the difference in temperatures between Week 1 and Week 5?

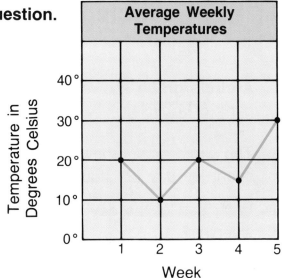

Average Weekly Temperatures

Temperature in Degrees Celsius

Week

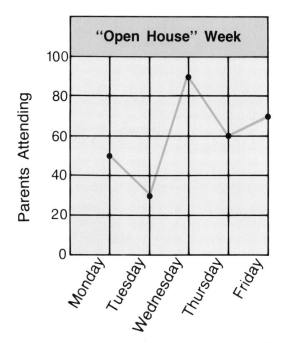

"Open House" Week

Parents Attending

Monday   Tuesday   Wednesday   Thursday   Friday

Use the line graph to answer each.

13. How many parents came to "Open House" on Tuesday?

14. On what day did 60 parents come?

15. When was the attendance the poorest?

16. What was the increase in "Open House" attendance from Tuesday to Wednesday?

17. When did more than 40 parents come?

CHALLENGE

The 4th grade students averaged their spelling grades for 6 months.

Jan.	80
Feb.	85
Mar.	80

Apr.	90
May	80
June	95

Draw a line graph to show the results.

293

Circle Graphs

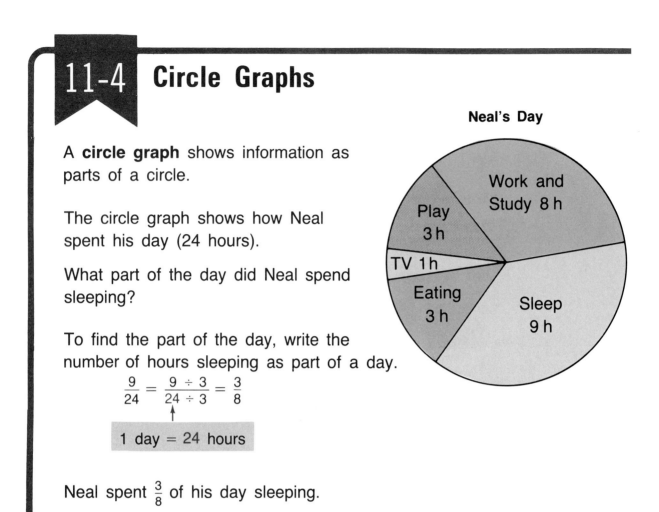

A **circle graph** shows information as parts of a circle.

The circle graph shows how Neal spent his day (24 hours).

What part of the day did Neal spend sleeping?

To find the part of the day, write the number of hours sleeping as part of a day.

$$\frac{9}{24} = \frac{9 \div 3}{24 \div 3} = \frac{3}{8}$$

↑

1 day = 24 hours

Neal spent $\frac{3}{8}$ of his day sleeping.

Neal's Day

Work and Study 8 h

Play 3 h

TV 1 h

Eating 3 h

Sleep 9 h

Use the circle graph above to find the part of the day Neal spent in each activity.

1. Work and Study

2. Play

3. Watching Television

4. Eating

Use the circle graph above to answer each.

5. Was more time spent eating or watching TV? How much more?

6. How many hours were spent eating and sleeping? What part of a day is this?

7. How many hours a day is Neal not working or studying? What part of a day is this?

Use the circle graph to answer each.

1. What part of the students:

   a. rode a bus? **b.** walked?

   c. rode a van? **d.** rode a bike?

2. How many more students used a bus than walked?

3. What part of the students did *not* use wheeled transportation?

4. What part of the students either walk or ride by van?

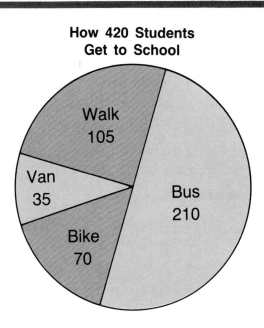

How 420 Students Get to School

Walk 105

Van 35

Bus 210

Bike 70

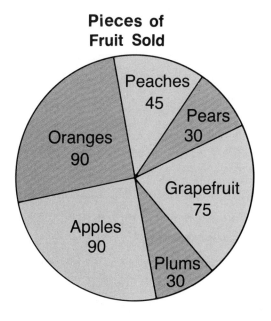

Pieces of Fruit Sold

Peaches 45

Pears 30

Oranges 90

Grapefruit 75

Apples 90

Plums 30

A fruit vendor made a circle graph to show the number of fruits he sold at his fruit stand on a certain day. Use his circle graph to answer each question.

5. Which two fruits sold the most?

6. Which two fruits sold the least?

7. How many more apples did he sell than peaches?

8. How many pieces of fruit did he sell in all?

9. What part of the total number of fruit sold were:

   a. oranges   **b.** grapefruit

   c. plums   **d.** peaches

   e. pears   **f.** apples

10. What part of the total number of fruits sold were peaches and pears?

295

Using a Calendar

A **calendar** organizes the days of the week into months and years.

July						
					1	2
3	4	5	6	7	8	9
10	11	12	13	14	15	16
17	18	19	20	21	22	23
24	25	26	27	28	29	30
31						

August						
	1	2	3	4	5	6
7	8	9	10	11	12	13
14	15	16	17	18	19	20
21	22	23	24	25	26	27
28	29	30	31			

September						
				1	2	3
4	5	6	7	8	9	10
11	12	13	14	15	16	17
18	19	20	21	22	23	24
25	26	27	28	29	30	

Elena needs $15 to buy gifts. She saves
$.20 each day starting after Bastille Day, July 14.
On what day will she have $15?

To find on what day she will have $15, divide: $15 ÷ $.20 = 75

Elena will have $15 on the 75th day after July 14.

July	August	September
17 days	31 days	30 days

To find the 75th day, add: $17 + 31 +$ _?_ $= 75$
$48 +$ _?_ $= 75$
$75 - 48 = 27$ days in September.

On September 27, Martha will have $15.

Use the calendar above to answer each question.

1. School opens on September 6. You will
   receive your first progress report card 17
   days after September 6. What is that date?

2. The Fall Fair is on September 24. How
   many days after September 6 is this?

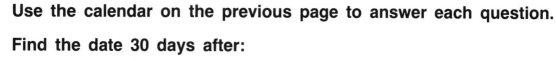

Use the calendar on the previous page to answer each question.

Find the date 30 days after:

3. July 4

4. August 18

5. September 1

6. July 31

7. August 30

8. July 16

9. Find the date on the:

    a. 50th day of the year.

    b. 75th day of the year.

    c. 40th day after February 22.

    d. 50th day after February 12.

    e. 70th day after January 1.

    f. 70th day after July 4.

Can you find the date on the 60th day of the year? Leap year?

Turn the 🔑 to learn about our calendar.

    60 days
  −31 days in January
    29 days

    29 days
  −28 days in February
     1 day in March

30 days have September, April, June, and November. All the rest have 31, except February, which has 28 (or 29 every leap year).

The 60th day of the year is March 1.
The 60th day of the leap year is February 29, one day earlier.

---

10. Find the date in the leap year 40 days after:

    a. January 25

    b. February 15

    c. May 30

    d. September 5

11-6 Probability

To select a ball **at random** means you select a ball without looking so that the chance of getting any one is the same.

This box contains a set of 6 balls. The balls are all the same size and shape, but are colored differently.

1 ball is colored black. $\frac{1}{6}$ of the set is black.

2 balls are dotted. $\frac{2}{6}$ of the set are dotted.

3 balls are striped. $\frac{3}{6}$ of the set are striped.

The chance of choosing a certain ball is called the **probability**.

The probability that a random selection will give a striped ball is $\frac{3}{6}$.

Write: $P(\text{striped ball}) = \frac{3}{6}$

What is the probability of choosing a dotted or striped ball?

$P(\text{dotted or striped ball}) = \frac{2+3}{6} = \frac{5}{6}$

Use the set of balls above to find the probability of each event.

1. $P(\text{dotted ball})$

2. $P(\text{black ball})$

3. $P(\text{black or striped ball})$

4. $P(\text{black or dotted ball})$

5. $P(\text{not black})$

6. $P(\text{not striped})$

Use this set of blocks to find the probability of each event.

7. $P(A)$ 8. $P(B)$

9. $P(C)$ 10. $P(A \text{ or } B)$

11. $P(\text{not } A)$ 12. $P(A \text{ or } C)$

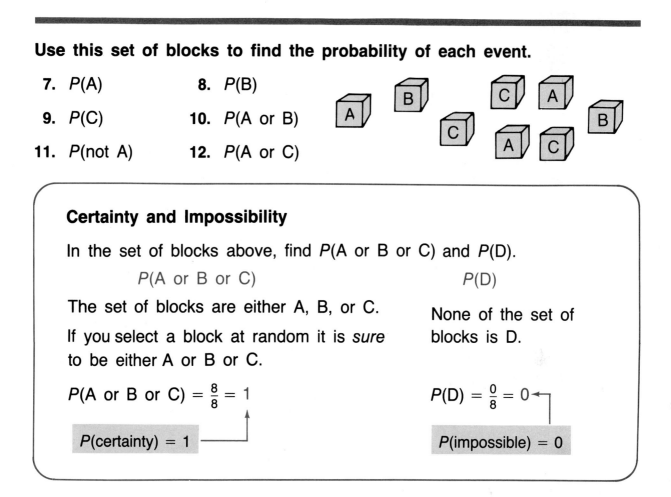

Certainty and Impossibility

In the set of blocks above, find $P(A \text{ or } B \text{ or } C)$ and $P(D)$.

$P(A \text{ or } B \text{ or } C)$ $P(D)$

The set of blocks are either A, B, or C.

If you select a block at random it is *sure* to be either A or B or C.

None of the set of blocks is D.

$P(A \text{ or } B \text{ or } C) = \frac{8}{8} = 1$

$P(\text{certainty}) = 1$

$P(D) = \frac{0}{8} = 0$

$P(\text{impossible}) = 0$

Use the set of balls on page 298 to find the probability of each event.

13. $P(\text{white ball})$ 14. $P(\text{black or dotted or striped})$

Use the spinner at the right to find the probability of each event.

15. $P(5)$ 16. $P(2)$ 17. $P(3)$

18. $P(4)$ 19. $P(1)$ 20. $P(2 \text{ or } 3)$

21. $P(3 \text{ or } 4)$ 22. $P(2 \text{ or } 5)$ 23. $P(3 \text{ or } 4 \text{ or } 5)$

Use this set of cards to find the probability of each event.

24. $P(\text{circle})$ 25. $P(\text{triangle})$

26. $P(\text{square})$ 27. $P(\text{diamond})$

299

Problem Solving:
Two-Step Problems

Problem: Mrs. O'Shaughnessy dialed Dublin, Ireland on
Sunday at 4:00 P.M. She spoke to her brother for
10 minutes. How much will she be charged?

1   IMAGINE   You use this rate table for overseas calls.

Overseas Rates		Initial Period Rate			Additional Minute Rate
		1 Minute	3 Minute	3 Minute	
Rate Levels	Hours	Dial	Station	Person	All Calls
Economy	6PM-7AM	1.17	5.35	9.48	.71
Discount	1PM-6PM	1.46	5.35	9.48	.89
Standard	7AM-1PM	1.95	5.35	9.48	1.18

2   NAME   *Facts:*   10-minute call at 4:00 P.M.

Question: What is the charge?

3   THINK   Look at the table.
Since she dialed at 4:00 P.M., she qualifies
for the discount rate of $1.46 for the first
minute plus $.89 for each additional minute.

4   COMPUTE   **Total Cost = Cost for first minute**
**   + Cost for 9 additional minutes**
Cost of 9 additional minutes
        $= 9 \times \$.89 = \$8.01$
Total Cost $= \$1.46 + \$8.01 = \$9.47$

Mrs. O'Shaughnessy will be charged $9.47 for her call.

5   CHECK $\begin{array}{r} \$\ .89 \\ \hline 9)\overline{\$8.01} \end{array}$ The answer for the cost of 9
additional minutes checks.

Solve each. (Use the rate table on page 300.)

1. Suppose Mrs. O'Shaughnessy wanted the minimum charge for a 10-minute call to Dublin, Ireland. When and how should she call?

IMAGINE
You are Mrs. O'Shaughnessy reading the rates for overseas calls.

NAME
Facts: 10-minute call to Dublin, Ireland.

Question: What is the minimum charge?

THINK
Look at the table to find the economy rate for dialing direct. (1 minute = $1.17)
Cost = Cost of 1 minute ($1.17)
          + Cost of 9 additional minutes.
Cost of 9 additional minutes = 9 × $.71

Add: $1.17 + cost of 9 additional minutes

Then → **COMPUTE** — and → **CHECK**

2. Pierre called his parents in Paris, France at 8:30 P.M. He dialed direct and spoke for 13 minutes. How much will he be charged?

3. Mr. and Mrs. Samuels are planning a trip to Spain this summer and need a hotel reservation. Mr. Samuels calls station-to-station at 10:00 A.M. and speaks for 5 minutes. How much will he be charged?

4. The A and Z Company called London, England at noon. The owner spoke person-to-person with Mr. Scott for 10 minutes. How much will the company be charged?

More Practice

Use the pictograph to answer each.

1. How many records were sold on Friday?

2. What were the total record sales for Thursday and Saturday?

3. On what day were the most records sold?

4. How many more records were sold on Saturday than on Monday?

5. How many records in all were sold during the entire week?

Record Sales

Monday	◉◉◉
Tuesday	◉◉◉◉
Wednesday	◉
Thursday	◉◉◉
Friday	◉◉
Saturday	◉◉◉◉◉

Each ◉ stands for 10 records

Numbers of Students Drinking Each Beverage

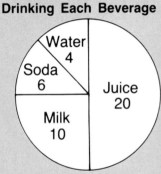

Water 4
Soda 6
Juice 20
Milk 10

Use the circle graph to answer each question.

6. What part of the class drank:
   a. milk?   **b.** juice?

7. What part of the class drank milk or soda?

8. What part of the class drank water or juice?

Use the bar graph to answer each question.

9. How many marbles does each boy have?

10. Who has the most? The fewest?

11. How many more marbles does Max have than Ray?

12. How many fewer marbles does Bob have than Mark?

13. How many marbles are there in all?

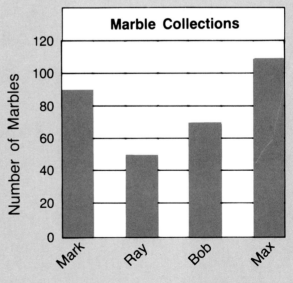

Marble Collections

Number of Marbles

Mark Ray Bob Max

(See *Still More Practice*, p.367.)

302

Math Probe

LOCATING POINTS ON A GRID

The boys and girls used this grid to name their favorite sports. **Ordered number pairs** are used to locate points on a grid.

Point E is: 5 units to the *right* and 4 units *up* from 0.

The ordered number pair (5, 4) gives the location of point E.

(4, 5) gives the location of point N. The order of the numbers is important. Changing the order locates different points.

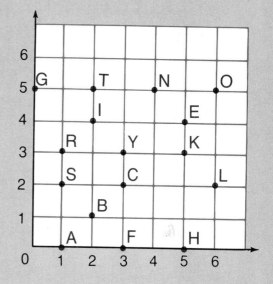

Locate these points on the grid. Name each sport.

1. (5, 0) (6, 5) (3, 2) (5, 3) (5, 4) (3, 3)

2. (3, 0) (6, 5) (6, 5) (2, 5) (2, 1) (1, 0) (6, 2) (6, 2)

3. (2, 5) (5, 4) (4, 5) (4, 5) (2, 4) (1, 2)

4. (0, 5) (6, 5) (6, 2) (3, 0)

5. (1, 2) (5, 3) (2, 4) (2, 4) (4, 5) (0, 5)

6. (2, 1) (1, 0) (1, 2) (5, 4) (2, 1) (1, 0) (6, 2) (6, 2)

7. (1, 2) (5, 3) (1, 0) (2, 5) (2, 4) (4, 5) (0, 5)

8. (1, 2) (6, 5) (3, 2) (3, 2) (5, 4) (1, 3)

9. (2, 5) (1, 3) (1, 0) (3, 2) (5, 3)

10. (1, 3) (1, 0) (3, 2) (2, 4) (4, 5) (0, 5)

Check Your Mastery

Use the pictograph to answer each question.

See pp. 288-289.

1. Who had the most strikes?

2. Who had the fewest strikes?

3. How many strikes were there in all?

4. How many strikes did each girl have?

5. How many more strikes did Helen have than Bernadette?

6. How many more strikes did Anita have than Rose?

Bowling Strikes	
Theresa	🎳 🎳 🎳 🎳
Helen	🎳 🎳 🎳 🎳 🎳
Rose	🎳 🎳 🎳
Bernadette	🎳 🎳
Anita	🎳 🎳 🎳 🎳

Each 🎳 represents 4.

See pp. 292-293.

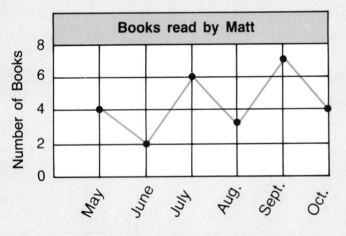

Books read by Matt

Use the line graph to answer each question.

7. When did Matt read 6 books?

8. How many books did he read in May?

9. When did Matt read the fewest books?

10. Did Matt read more books in July or September?

Use the spinner to find the probability of each event.

See pp. 298-299.

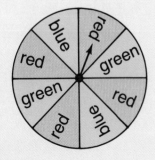

11. *P*(red)

12. *P*(green)

13. *P*(blue)

14. *P*(red or green)

15. *P*(blue or green)

16. *P*(red or blue)

17. *P*(not green)

18. *P*(black)

19. *P*(not blue)

20. *P*(not red)

12

Decimals

In this unit you will:

- Read and write decimals to hundredths
- Study decimals greater than one
- Add and subtract decimals
- Round decimals to a given place
- Estimate sums and differences of decimals
- Solve multi-step problems

Do you remember?

A fraction is one or more equal parts of a whole.

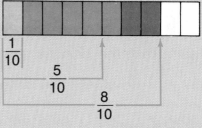

$\dfrac{1}{10}$

$\dfrac{5}{10}$

$\dfrac{8}{10}$

Tenths

A fraction with a denominator of 10 can be written as a **decimal**.

Study these regions and their values:

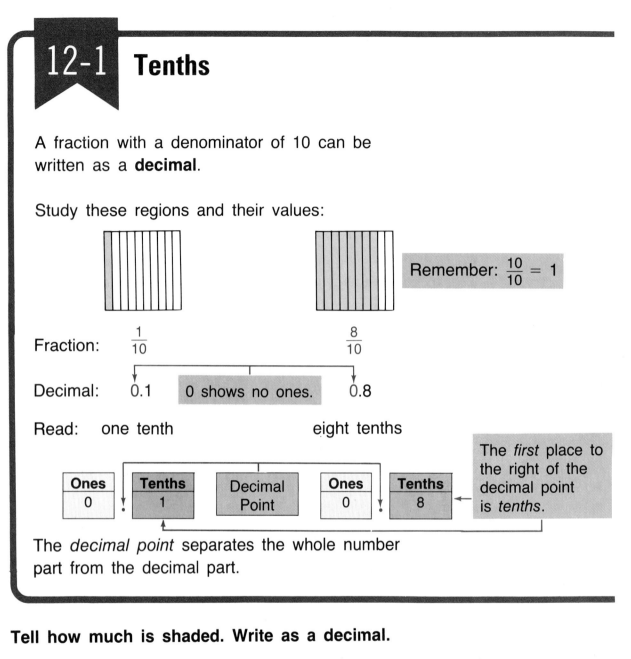

Remember: $\frac{10}{10} = 1$

Fraction: $\frac{1}{10}$ $\frac{8}{10}$

Decimal: 0.1 0 shows no ones. 0.8

Read: one tenth eight tenths

Ones	Tenths	Decimal Point	Ones	Tenths
0	1		0	8

The *first* place to the right of the decimal point is *tenths*.

The *decimal point* separates the whole number part from the decimal part.

Tell how much is shaded. Write as a decimal.

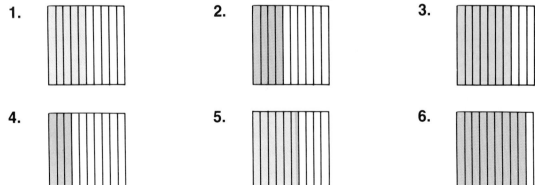

1.

2.

3.

4.

5.

6.

Write the word name for each.

7. 0.8   **8.** 0.3   **9.** 0.7   **10.** 0.4   **11.** 0.2

Write as a decimal. (Remember: Write a zero to the left of the decimal point.)

12. $\frac{3}{10}$ **13.** $\frac{7}{10}$ **14.** $\frac{9}{10}$ **15.** $\frac{1}{10}$ **16.** $\frac{5}{10}$

17. six tenths   **18.** two tenths   **19.** eight tenths   **20.** four tenths

Write each answer as a decimal.
(Use the information in the diagram.)

What part of the flavors are:

21. lime?   **22.** lemon?

23. raspberry?   **24.** orange?

25. lemon or lime?   **26.** orange or lime?

27. lime or raspberry?   **28.** lemon or orange?

Juice Flavors

Write the underlined word as a decimal.

29. A penny is <u>one tenth</u> of a dime.

30. Margo answered <u>eight tenths</u> of the questions.

31. One millimeter is <u>one tenth</u> of a centimeter.

32. The gas tank is <u>seven tenths</u> full.

33. Brad and his friend finished <u>six tenths</u> of a pie.

34. Saul ran <u>four tenths</u> of a mile.

35. Pat read <u>nine tenths</u> of the book.

36. 30 cents is <u>three tenths</u> of a dollar.

Hundredths

Study these regions and these values:

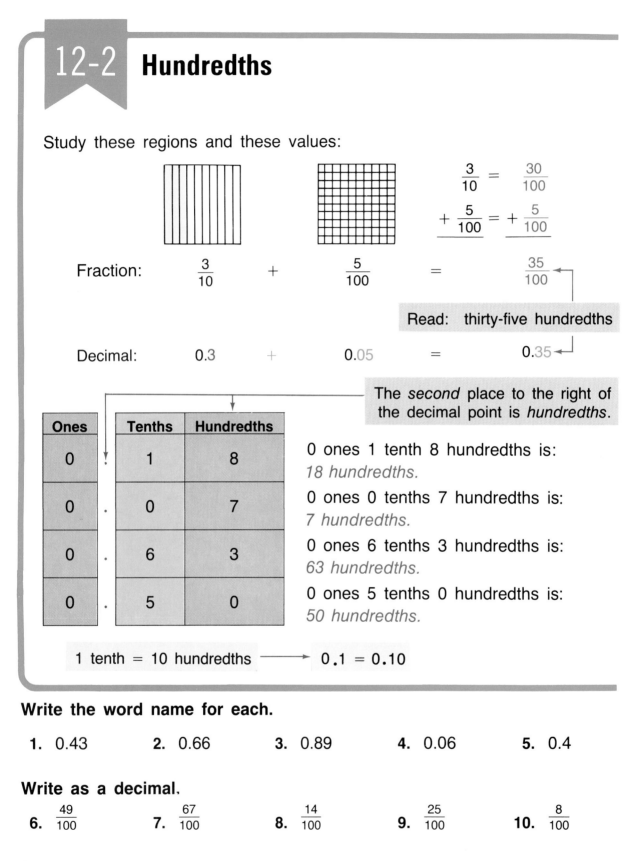

$$\frac{3}{10} = \frac{30}{100}$$

$$+ \frac{5}{100} = + \frac{5}{100}$$

Fraction: $\frac{3}{10}$ + $\frac{5}{100}$ = $\frac{35}{100}$

Read: thirty-five hundredths

Decimal: 0.3 + 0.05 = 0.35

The *second* place to the right of the decimal point is *hundredths*.

Ones	Tenths	Hundredths
0	1	8
0	0	7
0	6	3
0	5	0

0 ones 1 tenth 8 hundredths is:
18 hundredths.

0 ones 0 tenths 7 hundredths is:
7 hundredths.

0 ones 6 tenths 3 hundredths is:
63 hundredths.

0 ones 5 tenths 0 hundredths is:
50 hundredths.

1 tenth = 10 hundredths $\longrightarrow$ 0.1 = 0.10

Write the word name for each.

1. 0.43 **2.** 0.66 **3.** 0.89 **4.** 0.06 **5.** 0.4

Write as a decimal.

6. $\frac{49}{100}$ **7.** $\frac{67}{100}$ **8.** $\frac{14}{100}$ **9.** $\frac{25}{100}$ **10.** $\frac{8}{100}$

Tell how much is shaded. Write as a decimal.

11.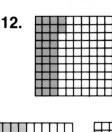

12.

13.

14.

15.

16.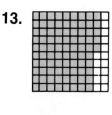

Write as a decimal.

17. eighty-two hundredths
18. fifty-three hundredths
19. eleven hundredths

20. seven hundredths
21. seventy hundredths
22. one hundredth

Write the underlined word as a decimal.

23. A quarter is <u>twenty-five hundredths</u> of a dollar.

24. A centimeter is <u>one hundredth</u> of a meter.

25. The length of a paper clip is about <u>three hundredths</u> of a meter.

26. The star Tan Ceta is <u>forty-four hundredths</u> the brightness of the sun.

27. The diameter of a penny is about <u>two hundredths</u> of a meter.

Choose the correct answer.

28. $0.8 = \underline{\ ?\ }$ a. 8   b. 0.08   c. $\frac{8}{100}$ d. $\frac{8}{10}$

29. $0.09 = \underline{\ ?\ }$ a. 9   b. 0.9   c. $\frac{9}{10}$ d. $\frac{9}{100}$

30. $0.1 = \underline{\ ?\ }$ a. 1   b. $\frac{1}{10}$ c. 0.01   d. $\frac{1}{100}$

31. $0.14 = \underline{\ ?\ }$ a. 14   b. 1.4   c. $\frac{14}{100}$ d. $\frac{14}{10}$

12-3 Decimals Greater Than One

Decimals can show numbers greater than one.
Study these regions and their values.

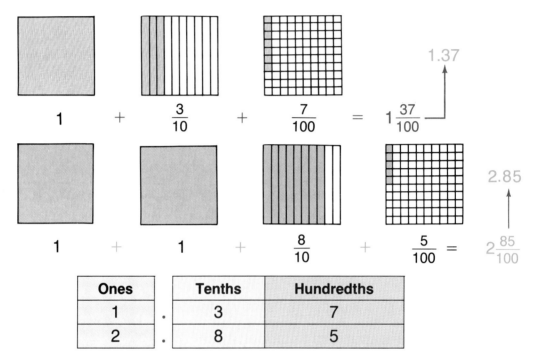

$$1 \quad + \quad \frac{3}{10} \quad + \quad \frac{7}{100} \quad = \quad 1\frac{37}{100} \quad \rightarrow \quad 1.37$$

$$1 \quad + \quad 1 \quad + \quad \frac{8}{10} \quad + \quad \frac{5}{100} = \quad 2\frac{85}{100} \quad \rightarrow \quad 2.85$$

Ones		Tenths	Hundredths
1	.	3	7
2	.	8	5

The place-value chart below includes
whole numbers and decimals.

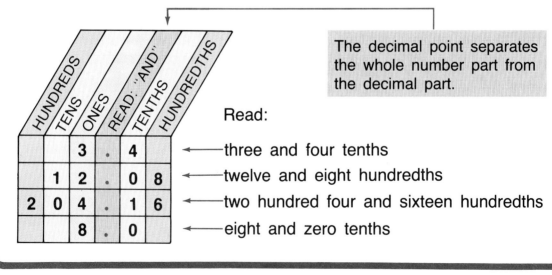

The decimal point separates
the whole number part from
the decimal part.

Read:

three and four tenths

twelve and eight hundredths

two hundred four and sixteen hundredths

eight and zero tenths

Read the numeral.

1. 1.4   2. 3.32   3. 9.03   4. 29.7   5. 7.0

6. 4.50   7. 4.5   8. 87.34   9. 42.05   10. 25.18

Tell how much is shaded. Write as a decimal.

11.

12.

13.

14.

Write as a decimal.

15. $5\frac{3}{10}$ 16. $8\frac{7}{10}$ 17. $4\frac{4}{10}$ 18. $6\frac{13}{100}$

19. $49\frac{21}{100}$ 20. $28\frac{37}{100}$ 21. $16\frac{8}{100}$ 22. $9\frac{9}{100}$

23. $17\frac{17}{100}$ 24. $25\frac{5}{100}$ 25. $25\frac{5}{10}$ 26. $25\frac{50}{100}$

Write in decimal form.

27. three and five tenths

28. fifteen and four hundredths

29. nine and sixteen hundredths

30. twelve and thirty hundredths

Write the value of the underlined digit.

31. 0.3<u>6</u>   32. 0.<u>4</u>9   33. <u>8</u>.91   34. 30.<u>5</u>

Complete. Write a decimal that is:

35. between 2 and 3.

36. less than 10 and greater than 9.

37. greater than 5 and less than 6.

38. between 8 and 9.

12-4 Comparing and Ordering Decimals

Carl Lewis ran 60 yards in 6.02 seconds. Evelyn Ashford ran 60 yards in 6.54 seconds. Which runner is faster?

To find which runner is faster, compare: 6.02 _?_ 6.54

To compare decimals:

- Write the numbers. Be sure the decimal points line up.

- Start at the left and compare the digits in each place.

- Continue until you find the first digits that are different.

- Compare these digits. The decimal with the greater digit is greater.

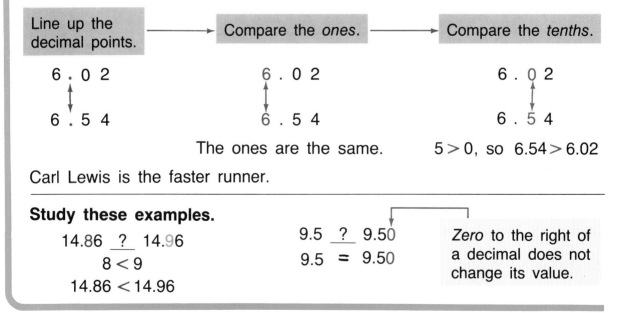

Line up the decimal points.	Compare the *ones*.	Compare the *tenths*.
6 . 0 2 ↕ 6 . 5 4	6 . 0 2 ↕ 6 . 5 4 The ones are the same.	6 . 0 2 ↕ 6 . 5 4 5 > 0, so 6.54 > 6.02

Carl Lewis is the faster runner.

Study these examples.

14.86 _?_ 14.96
8 < 9
14.86 < 14.96

9.5 _?_ 9.50
9.5 = 9.50

Zero to the right of a decimal does not change its value.

Compare. Write <, =, or >.

1. 0.4 _?_ 0.9
2. 0.22 _?_ 0.29
3. 3.9 _?_ 3.90

4. 5.36 _?_ 5.4
5. 0.35 _?_ 0.31
6. 2.58 _?_ 2.57

7. 2.7 _?_ 1.8
8. 6.60 _?_ 6.6
9. 9.17 _?_ 9.27

10. 4.05 _?_ 4.50
11. 4.73 _?_ 4.33
12. 6.81 _?_ 6.87

13. 10.7 _?_ 10.71
14. 8.85 _?_ 8.8
15. 9.0 _?_ 9

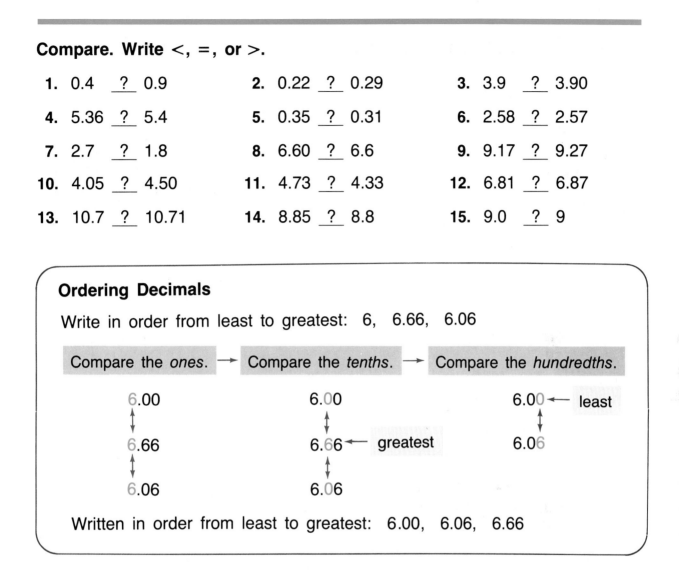

Ordering Decimals

Write in order from least to greatest: 6, 6.66, 6.06

Compare the *ones*. →	Compare the *tenths*. →	Compare the *hundredths*.
6.00	6.00	6.00 ← least
↕	↕	↕
6.66	6.66 ← greatest	6.06
↕	↕	
6.06	6.06	

Written in order from least to greatest: 6.00, 6.06, 6.66

Write in order from least to greatest.

16. 0.2, 0.9, 0.5
17. 3.5, 3.33, 3.35

18. 1.12, 1.19, 1.4
19. 5, 0.05, 0.5

20. 0.5, 0.53, 0.51
21. 0.8, 0.6, 0.84

22. 0.16, 0.4, 0.24
23. 1, 0.1, 0.01

Solve.

24. Karen ran 2.71 km and Charles ran 2.17 km. Who ran farther?

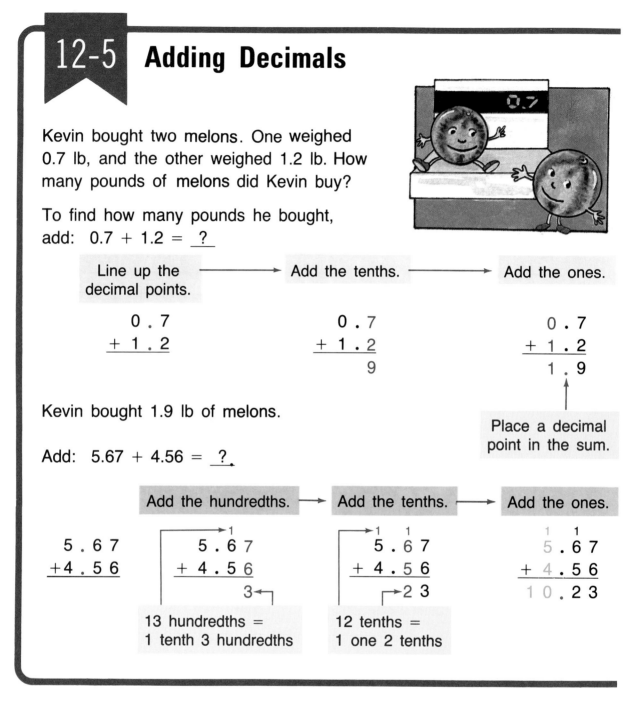

12-5 Adding Decimals

Kevin bought two melons. One weighed 0.7 lb, and the other weighed 1.2 lb. How many pounds of melons did Kevin buy?

To find how many pounds he bought, add: $0.7 + 1.2 =$ __?__

Line up the decimal points.	→	Add the tenths.	→	Add the ones.

$$
\begin{array}{r}
0.7 \\
+\ 1.2 \\
\end{array}
\qquad
\begin{array}{r}
0.7 \\
+\ 1.2 \\
\hline
9 \\
\end{array}
\qquad
\begin{array}{r}
0.7 \\
+\ 1.2 \\
\hline
1.9 \\
\end{array}
$$

Place a decimal point in the sum.

Kevin bought 1.9 lb of melons.

Add: $5.67 + 4.56 =$ __?__

Add the hundredths.	→	Add the tenths.	→	Add the ones.

$$
\begin{array}{r}
5.67 \\
+4.56 \\
\end{array}
\qquad
\begin{array}{r}
\overset{1}{}\ \ \ \\
5.67 \\
+\ 4.56 \\
\hline
3 \\
\end{array}
\qquad
\begin{array}{r}
\overset{1}{}\ \ \overset{1}{} \\
5.67 \\
+\ 4.56 \\
\hline
23 \\
\end{array}
\qquad
\begin{array}{r}
\overset{1}{}\ \ \overset{1}{} \\
5.67 \\
+\ 4.56 \\
\hline
10.23 \\
\end{array}
$$

13 hundredths = 1 tenth 3 hundredths

12 tenths = 1 one 2 tenths

Regroup as tenths and hundredths.

1. 15 hundredths   **2.** 23 hundredths   **3.** 10 hundredths

Regroup as ones and tenths.

4. 12 tenths   **5.** 24 tenths   **6.** 30 tenths

314

Add.

7.   0.4
    +0.7

8.   1.6
    +2.4

9.   3.6
    +4.7

10.   4.4
    +2.8

11.   12.4
    + 1.9

12.   0.21
    +0.89

13.   1.43
    +0.42

14.   1.56
    +1.24

15.   0.34
    +0.27

16.   1.37
    +2.15

17.   3.46
    +5.54

18.   6.25
    +2.86

19.   5.34
    +3.72

20.   4.61
    +5.62

21.   7.63
    +1.62

22.   25.64
    +14.88

23.   34.56
    +47.85

24.   19.45
    +23.88

25.   44.63
    +40.61

26.   99.99
    +11.11

Solve.

27. It took the computer 2.08 s to solve the first problem and 1.42 s to solve a second problem. What was the total time used?

28. In a running exercise Frank ran 0.59 mi the first five minutes and 0.43 mi the next five minutes. How far did he run in ten minutes?

29. Jo drove 40.5 mi the first hour and 59.5 mi the next hour. How far did she drive during the two hours?

30. Joe bicycled 13.43 km and 11.78 km in two days. How many kilometers did he bicycle in all?

31. On Monday, 13.4 gallons of gas were put in the car. On Friday the tank was filled with 18.2 gallons. How many gallons were put in the car altogether?

12-6 Subtracting Decimals

The distance around Grass Lake is 6.8 mi. If 4.3 mi is unpaved roads, how much is paved?

To find how much is paved, subtract: 6.8 − 4.3 = __?__

| Line up the decimal points. | → | Subtract the tenths. | → | Subtract the ones. |

```
  6 . 8            6 . 8            6 . 8
− 4 . 3          − 4 . 3          − 4 . 3
                       5          2 . 5
```

Place a decimal point in the difference.

2.5 mi is paved roads.

Subtract: 36.88 − 5.95 = __?__

| Subtract the hundredths. | → | Subtract the tenths. | → | Subtract the ones and tens. |

```
 3 6 . 8 8         3 6 . 8 8        3 ⁵6 . ¹⁸8 8      3 ⁵6 . ¹⁸8 8
−  5 . 9 5        −  5 . 9 5       −  5 . 9 5        −  5 . 9 5
                            3              9 3      3 0 . 9 3
```

6 ones = 5 ones 10 tenths
10 tenths + 8 tenths = 18 tenths

Subtract.

| 1. | 6.8
 −3.4 | 2. | 5.2
 −1.4 | 3. | 7.5
 −3.7 | 4. | 7.7
 −2.9 | 5. | 8.4
 −0.5 |

Find the difference.

6.	0.56	7.	8.43	8.	2.39	9.	3.48
	-0.14		-5.33		-0.05		-1.24

10.	8.86	11.	5.74	12.	2.77	13.	6.44
	-5.32		-2.71		-1.36		-3.24

14.	25.36	15.	39.24	16.	53.36	17.	74.46
	-12.18		-27.41		-15.56		-58.88

18.	34.27	19.	71.62	20.	56.47	21.	90.00
	-25.38		$-\ 8.93$		$-\ 9.99$		-11.11

Line up and find the difference.

22. $0.9 - 0.3$ **23.** $0.83 - 0.71$ **24.** $0.49 - 0.08$

25. $8.34 - 0.15$ **26.** $12.21 - 9.38$ **27.** $10.34 - 7.87$

28. $7.39 - 6.40$ **29.** $8.43 - 6.9$ **30.** $10.00 - 3.73$

Solve.

31. Peter ran a race in 10.6s. Paul ran the race in 9.7s. How much faster did Paul run the race?

32. As a typist, Jeanine averages 63.5 words per minute. Sally averages 42.8 words per minute. How many more words per minute does Jeanine type than Sally?

33. Marge swam the first lap in 2.39 min and a second lap in 2.47 min. How much slower was she in the second lap?

12-7 Rounding Decimals

The 500-yard freestyle swimming race was won in 4.26 min. What is this time to the nearest minute? To the nearest tenth of a minute?

To find the time to the nearest *minute:*

Round 4.26 to the nearest one.

- Circle the digit in the given place.

- Then:

  Increase it by 1 if the digit to the right is *5 or more*.

  or

  Leave it unchanged if the digit to the right is *4 or less*.

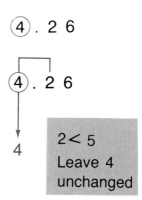

④. 2 6

④. 2 6

4

$2 < 5$
Leave 4
unchanged

- Do *not* write zeros to the right.

4.26 min to the nearest minute is 4 min.

Round 4.26 to the nearest tenth:

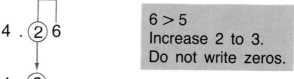

4 . ②6

4 . ③

$6 > 5$
Increase 2 to 3.
Do not write zeros.

Round to the nearest one.

1. 7.3	**2.** 9.2	**3.** 3.9	**4.** 1.5	**5.** 12.8
6. 16.26	**7.** 28.51	**8.** 62.43	**9.** 30.84	**10.** 19.75
11. 4.6	**12.** 15.3	**13.** 25.78	**14.** 41.23	**15.** 20.91
16. 17.52	**17.** 71.18	**18.** 49.62	**19.** 24.03	**20.** 3.95

Round to the nearest tenth.

21. 6.27	**22.** 4.64	**23.** 9.75	**24.** 2.20	**25.** 1.11
26. 31.37	**27.** 25.65	**28.** 85.96	**29.** 24.75	**30.** 38.33
31. 9.47	**32.** 13.53	**33.** 27.13	**34.** 82.75	**35.** 63.08
36. 52.71	**37.** 30.59	**38.** 81.11	**39.** 55.55	**40.** 44.89

Choose the correct answer.

41. Joan needs 23.8 meters of yarn for her art project. The length rounded to the nearest one is:

a. 23.9 m   **b.** 23 m   **c.** 24 m   **d.** 23.8 m

42. Marc's speech on patriotism is 5.23 minutes long. This time rounded to the nearest tenth is:

a. 5.2 min   **b.** 5.3 min   **c.** 5 min   **d.** 5.25 min

43. Maria walks 2.75 km to school each day. This distance rounded to the nearest one is:

a. 2 km   **b.** 3 km   **c.** 2.7 km   **d.** 2.8 km

Complete the table. (The first is done.)

	Event	Winning Times of Field Day Events		
		Time in seconds	Round to Nearest One	Round to Nearest Tenth
44.	500 meter race	48.73	49	48.7
45.	200 meter race	19.36	?	?
46.	100 meter backstroke	83.52	?	?
47.	100 meter freestyle	75.08	?	?
48.	200 meter dash	29.71	?	?
49.	50 meter hurdles	8.45	?	?
50.	30 meter hurdles	6.41	?	?

12-8 Estimating Sums and Differences for Decimals

Ricky scored 7.21 points and Terry scored 2.83 points in a gymnastic meet. About how many points did they score in all?

To find *about* how many points they scored, estimate: 7.21 + 2.83 = _?_

To estimate a decimal sum:

- Find the smaller number.

- Circle the greatest place value of that number that is *not* zero.

- Round each number to that place.

- Add.

Round to ones.	Add the rounded numbers.
7 . 2 1 ⟶ 7	7
②. 8 3 ⟶ 3	+3
	10 Estimated Sum

They scored about 10 points in all.

Study these examples:

Round to tens.

1 7 . 8 ⟶ 2 0
+①3 . 2 ⟶ + 1 0
              3 0 Estimated
                    Sum

Round to ones.

3 5 . 4 ⟶ 3 5
+ ⑧. 9 ⟶ + 9
              4 4 Estimated
                    Sum

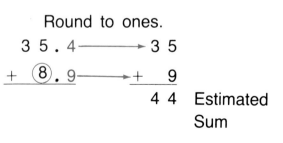

320

Estimate each sum.

1.	5.9 +3.2	**2.**	8.8 +4.1	**3.**	1.3 +7.6	**4.**	6.8 +4.2	**5.**	15.9 +12.8
6.	12.37 − 4.42	**7.**	36.47 +63.71	**8.**	40.7 +33.5	**9.**	19.67 − 2.4	**10.**	37.4 +17.36
11.	21.41 +38.28	**12.**	7.6 +13.7	**13.**	14.81 + 0.29	**14.**	42.5 +46.34	**15.**	79.2 + 8.16

Estimating Differences for Decimals

Estimate: 7.91 − 0.46 = __?__

To estimate a difference for decimals:

- Find the smaller number.

- Circle the greatest place value of that number that is not zero.

- Round each number to that place.

- Subtract.

Round to tenths

$$7 . 9\,1 \longrightarrow 7.9$$
$$\underline{-0 . ④6} \longrightarrow \underline{-0.5}$$
$$7.4$$

Estimated
Difference

Estimate each difference.

16.	9.7 −4.6	**17.**	8.6 −3.4	**18.**	7.1 −2.9	**19.**	5.8 −3.7	**20.**	16.7 −11.3
21.	42.42 −20.31	**22.**	41.8 −27.2	**23.**	39.6 −17.7	**24.**	26.31 − 3.7	**25.**	73.52 − 7.8
26.	11.72 − 2.3	**27.**	25.61 −12.32	**28.**	42.32 −31.1	**29.**	82.24 − 6.28	**30.**	57.8 −16.24

12-9 Problem Solving: Multi-Step Problems

Problem: Adam bought 3 shirts at $7.97 each and a pair of jeans for $26.44. How much change will be returned to Adam from a payment of $55?

1 IMAGINE   Draw and label a picture showing Adam's purchases and payment.

2 NAME

Facts: 3 shirts, $7.97 each shirt
$26.44 jeans
$55 payment

Question: How much is Adam's change?

Total $55

3 THINK   This is a multi-step problem.

Step 1 Multiply to find the cost of the 3 shirts.
$3 \times \$7.97 = \underline{\ ?\ }$
Step 2 Add the cost of the jeans.
$(3 \times \$7.97) + \$26.44 = \underline{\ ?\ }$ Total Cost
Step 3 Subtract to find Adam's change from $55.
$55.00 − Total Cost = Change

4 COMPUTE

Step 1	Step 2	Step 3
$\$7.97$	$\$23.91$	$\$55.00$
$\times \quad 3$	$+\ 26.44$	$-\ 50.35$ Adam's
$\$23.91$	$\$50.35$	$\$\ \ 4.65$ change

5 CHECK   The estimated cost of the 3 shirts and the jeans is about $50.
The estimated change is $5.

So, $4.65 change from $55 seems reasonable.

322

Solve.

1. Mrs. Hammel saves $42.30 each week for
    9 weeks to buy drapes. She buys 5 drapes with
    this money. What is the cost of each drape?

Week 1 $42.30	Week 2 $42.30
Week 3 $42.30	Week 4 $42.30
Week 5 $42.30	Week 6 $42.30
Week 7 $42.30	Week 8 $42.30
	Week 9 $42.30

IMAGINE

Draw a picture of Mrs. Hammel's savings.

NAME

Facts: 9 weeks of saving
             5 drapes bought
    $42.30 saved each week

Question: How much does each
             drape cost?

THINK

There are several steps needed
to solve this problem.
Step 1   9 × $42.30   = Total saved.
Step 2   Total saved ÷ 5 = Cost of each drape

Then → **COMPUTE** — and → **CHECK**

2. A company ordered 100 books. The company
    received 20, 9, and 18 books. How many
    more books must it receive?

3. There is a total of 23,647 ft in three tunnels.
    The Holland Tunnel is 9,250 ft long and the
    Midtown Tunnel is 5,280 ft long. How long is
    the Brooklyn-Battery Tunnel?

4. The Math Team earns 3 points for every question it
    answers correctly. In addition, the team earns an extra
    5 points for every five questions answered correctly. If
    the team answers eight questions correctly, how many
    points will it earn in all?

323

More Practice

Write the value of the underlined digit.

1. 3.<u>1</u>

2. 2.4<u>2</u>

3. 0.<u>9</u>6

4. <u>1</u>.92

5. 59.<u>6</u>

6. <u>8</u>.5

7. 2.2<u>3</u>

8. <u>1</u>5.49

Write as a decimal.

9. five tenths

10. thirty-two hundredths

11. three and four tenths

12. nine and eight hundredths

Compare. Write <, =, or >.

13. 0.03 _?_ 0.7

14. 9.45 _?_ 12.8

15. 0.64 _?_ 0.05

16. 12.8 _?_ 12.80

17. 7.02 _?_ 7

18. 5.06 _?_ 5.6

Add or subtract.

19. 0.6
    +0.2

20. 4.93
    −2.73

21. 23.5
    +13.8

22. 44.5
    − 6.8

**Round each to the nearest one.
Then round each to the nearest tenth.**

23. 12.17

24. 32.74

25. 0.88

Compute.

26. 3.8 + 5.1

27. 8.43 − 6.61

28. 4.69 + 0.04

Solve

29. The weight of one bag is 2.47 lb.
The weight of another bag is 0.73 lb.
Estimate the weight of the two bags.

(See *Still More Practice*, p. 368)

Math Probe

MAGIC SQUARES

In a magic square each row, column, and diagonal has the same sum.

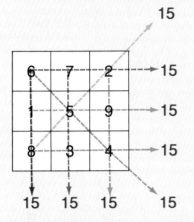

Which of these are magic squares?

1.

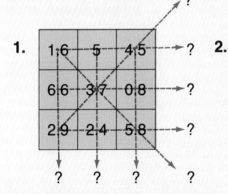

1.6	5	4.5
6.6	3.7	0.8
2.9	2.4	5.8

2.

3.2	3.1	1.7
1.1	2.7	4.2
3.7	2.2	2.1

3.

2.42	8	5.96
9	5.46	1.92
4.96	2.92	8.5

Try some magic yourself!

Find the numbers that will make a magic square.

4.

2.7	3.8	?
5.2	3.6	?
?	3.4	4.5

5.

3.5	7.5	8.5
11.5	?	?
4.5	5.5	?

6.

8.6	7	6.6
5.4	?	?
8.2	7.8	?

Check Your Mastery

Write the value of the underlined digit.

See pp. 306 - 311.

1. 4.6<u>9</u>
2. <u>4</u>7.33
3. <u>2</u>.26
4. 0.1<u>3</u>
5. 6.<u>6</u>1
6. 55.7<u>4</u>

Write as a decimal.

See pp. 306-311.

7. nine tenths
8. thirty-nine hundredths
9. four and six tenths
10. seven and seven hundredths

Compare. Write <, =, or >.

See pp. 312 - 313.

11. 0.8 _?_ 0.4
12. 0.7 _?_ 0.70
13. 0.46 _?_ 0.64
14. 2.43 _?_ 2.39

Write in order from least to greatest.

See pp. 312 - 313.

15. 13.4, 6.5, 13.3, 6.05
16. 2.15, 2.51, 2.05, 2.5

Compute.

See pp. 314 - 317.

17. 0.6 + 0.3
18. 1.4 − 0.2
19. 5.4 + 3.7
20. 4.07 − 2.15

Round to the nearest tenth.

See pp. 318-319.

21. 3.94
22. 17.25
23. 12.53

Solve.

See pp. 318-319.

24. Last year Michele measured 153.8 cm. During the past year she grew 6.8 cm. How tall is she now?

25. Leo ran the race in 63.35 s. Richard ran the race in 3.24 s less than Leo. What was Richard's time?

13

Area and Volume

In this unit you will:

- Recognize and identify plane figures
- Find the areas of plane figures
- Recognize and identify space figures
- Find the volume of a rectangular prism
- Find perimeter, area, and volume using customary units
- Solve problems by finding patterns

Do you remember?

A **line** extends without end in opposite directions.

$\overleftrightarrow{AB}$, line AB

A **line segment** is part of a line with two endpoints.

$\overline{AB}$, line segment AB

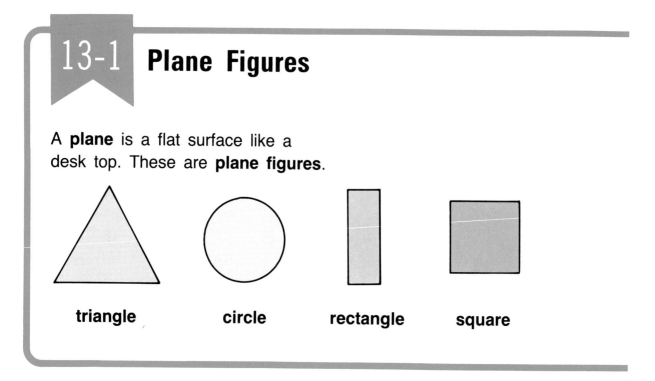

A **plane** is a flat surface like a
desk top. These are **plane figures**.

triangle   circle   rectangle   square

Name each colored shape. Use "triangle," "circle," "rectangle," "square," or "none of these."

1.

2.

3.

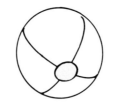

4.

5.

6.

7.

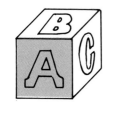

8.

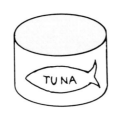

9.

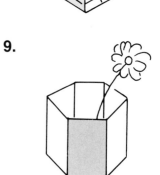

Complete.

	Figure	Number of Sides	Number of Vertices	Number of Angles
10.	rectangle	4	?	?
11.	triangle	?	?	3
12.	circle	?	0	?
13.	square	?	?	?

Choose the correct answer.

14. triangle   a.   b.   c.   d.

15. circle   a.   b.   c.   d.

16. square   a.   b.   c.   d.

17. rectangle   a.   b.   c.   d.

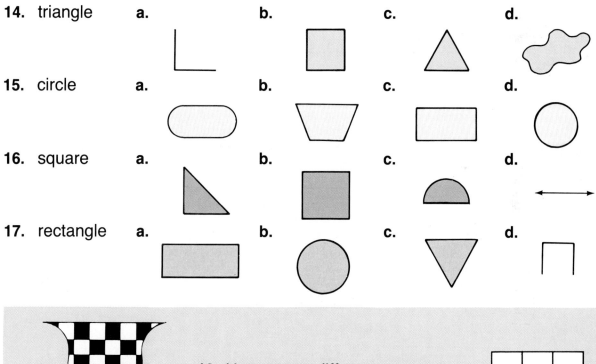

CHALLENGE

18. How many different squares can you find?

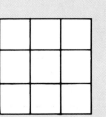

13-2 Area

The **area** of a flat figure is the size of the inside of the figure. The size of the inside of the figure is the number of square units it contains.

Use this square unit to find the area.

1 cm

1 square centimeter

The area is 24 square centimeters.

Another metric square unit to measure area is the **square meter**.

Find the area of each by counting the squares.

1.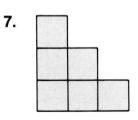

2.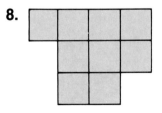

3.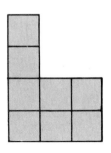

4.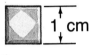

5.

6.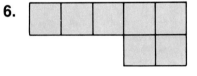

7.

8.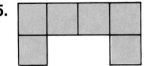

9.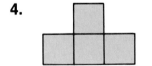

Find each area.

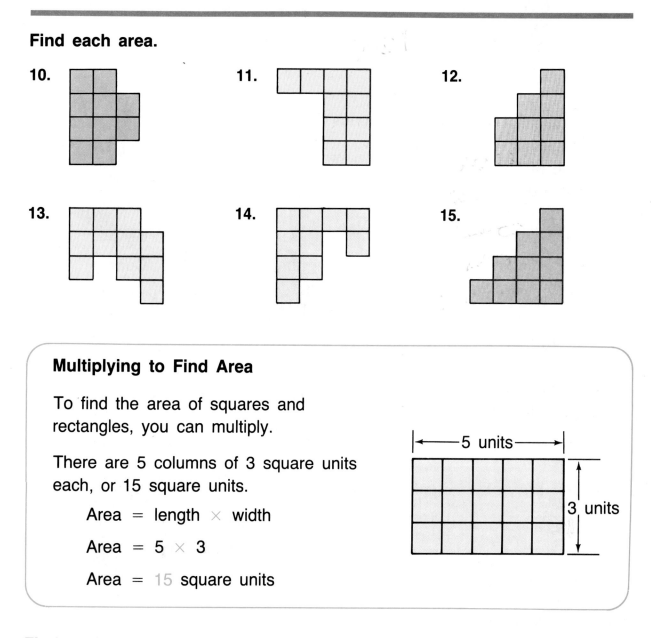

10.

11.

12.

13.

14.

15.

Multiplying to Find Area

To find the area of squares and rectangles, you can multiply.

There are 5 columns of 3 square units each, or 15 square units.

Area = length × width

Area = 5 × 3

Area = 15 square units

Find each area by multiplying.

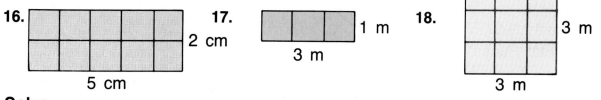

16. 5 cm   2 cm

17. 3 m   1 m

18. 3 m   3 m

Solve.

19. A square garden plot has sides of 9 m. What is its area?

20. A floor has a length of 15 m and a width of 12 m. What is its area?

331

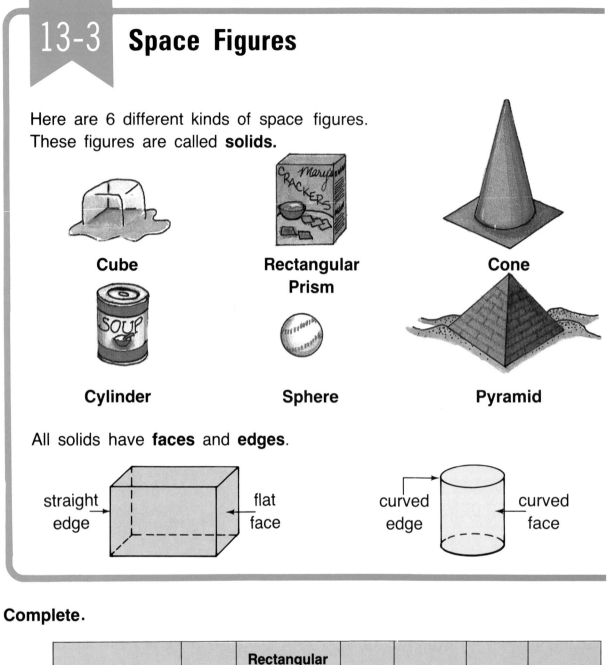

13-3 Space Figures

Here are 6 different kinds of space figures.
These figures are called **solids.**

Cube

Rectangular Prism

Cone

Cylinder

Sphere

Pyramid

All solids have **faces** and **edges**.

straight edge   flat face

curved edge   curved face

Complete.

		Cube	Rectangular Prism	Cone	Cylinder	Sphere	Pyramid
1.	Flat Faces	?	6	?	2	0	?
2.	Straight Edges	12	?	0	0	0	?
3.	Curved Faces	0	?	1	?	1	0
4.	Curved Edges	?	0	?	?	0	0

332

Write the name of the space figure each of these is most like.

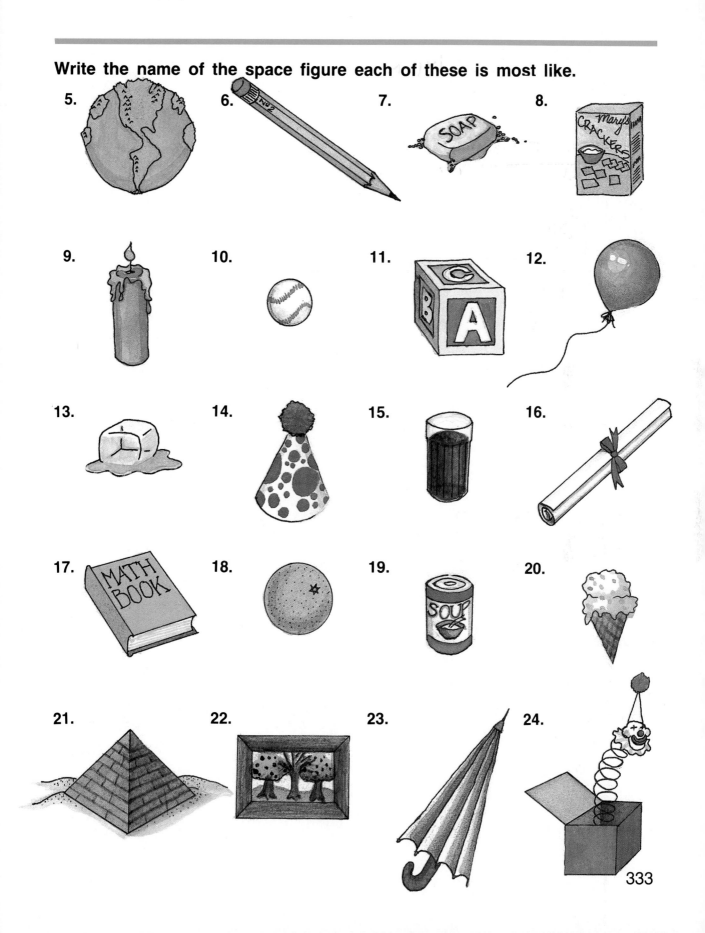

5.

6.

7.

8.

9.

10.

11.

12.

13.

14.

15.

16.

17.

18.

19.

20.

21.

22.

23.

24.

333

Volume

The **volume** or **capacity** of a solid is the size of the inside of the solid. The volume is the number of cubic units it contains.

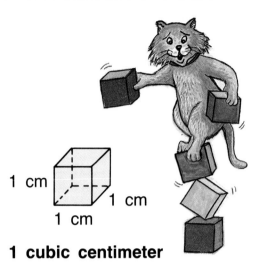

1 cubic centimeter

Use the cubic unit at the right to find the volume of the box below. Count the number of cubic centimeters that are needed to fill it.

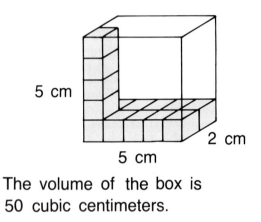

The volume of the box is 50 cubic centimeters.

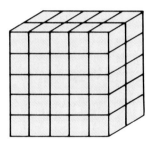

50 cubic centimeters

Find the volume of each by counting the cubes.

1.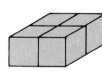

2.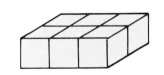

3.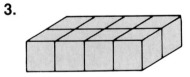

4.

5.

6.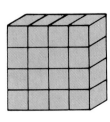

Find each volume.

7.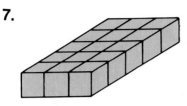

8.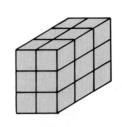

9.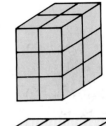

10.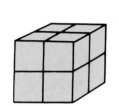

11.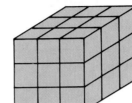

12.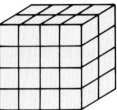

Multiplying to Find Volume

To find the volume of a rectangular prism, you can multiply.

Bottom layer:
$8 \times 2 = 16$ square meters
In the whole prism:
4 layers $\times$ 16 = 64 cubic meters

Volume = 64 cubic meters

height
4 m

length
8 m

width
2 m

Find each volume by multiplying.

13. 3 cm   3 cm   5 cm

14. 2 m   2 m   2 m

15. 3 cm   2 cm   3 cm

Solve.

16. A fish tank is 18 cm long, 12 cm high, and 8 cm wide. How many cubic centimeters of water will it hold?

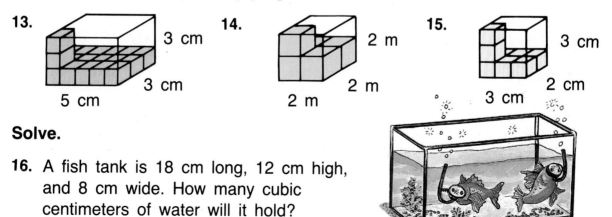

Perimeter, Area, and Volume

Customary units can also be used
to find perimeter, area, and volume.

Some customary units of length used to find
perimeter are the inch, foot, yard, and so on.

Find the perimeter of each.

1.
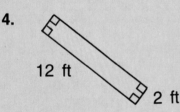
3 in.   3 in.

5 in.

2.
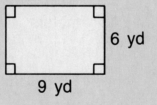
7 in.

7 in.

3.
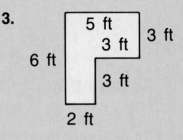
5 ft
3 ft   3 ft
6 ft
3 ft
2 ft

Some customary square units to measure **area**
are the square inch, square foot, and square
yard.

Find the area of each.

4.
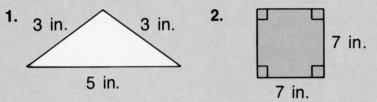
12 ft
2 ft

5.
6 yd
9 yd

6.
8 in.
8 in.

Some customary cubic units to measure
volume are the cubic inch, cubic foot, and
cubic yard.

Find the volume of each.

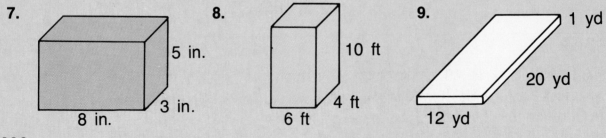

7.
5 in.
3 in.
8 in.

8.
10 ft
4 ft
6 ft

9.
1 yd
20 yd
12 yd

336

Complete the table. Each figure is a rectangle.

	Length	Width	Perimeter	Area
10.	4 ft	10 ft	?	?
11.	5 yd	6 yd	?	?
12.	3 in.	12 in.	?	?
13.	16 ft	29 ft	?	?
14.	8 in.	4 in.	?	?

Complete the table. Each figure is a rectangular prism.

	Length	Width	Height	Volume
15.	9 in.	5 in.	3 in.	?
16.	4 ft	4 ft	2 ft	?
17.	6 yd	3 yd	6 yd	?
18.	6 ft	5 ft	9 ft	?
19.	11 in.	5 in.	6 in.	?

Solve.

20. Mark wants to put a border of wallpaper around a wall 15 ft long and 9 ft wide. Find the length of wallpaper needed by Mark.

21. A tennis court in the shape of a rectangle is 75 yd long and 25 yd wide. What is the area of the tennis court?

22. A tool box is 22 in. long, 8 in. high, and 6 in. wide. What is the volume of this tool box?

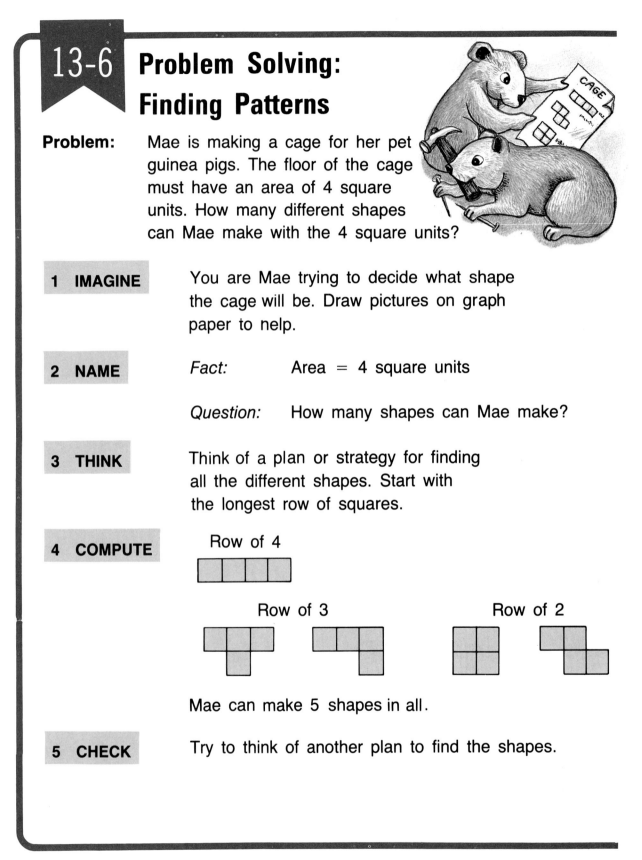

13-6 Problem Solving: Finding Patterns

Problem: Mae is making a cage for her pet guinea pigs. The floor of the cage must have an area of 4 square units. How many different shapes can Mae make with the 4 square units?

1 IMAGINE You are Mae trying to decide what shape the cage will be. Draw pictures on graph paper to nelp.

2 NAME *Fact:* Area = 4 square units

Question: How many shapes can Mae make?

3 THINK Think of a plan or strategy for finding all the different shapes. Start with the longest row of squares.

4 COMPUTE Row of 4

Row of 3   Row of 2

Mae can make 5 shapes in all.

5 CHECK Try to think of another plan to find the shapes.

Find the pattern. Solve the problem.

1. A puzzle is made from squares.
How many squares can you find?

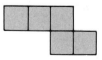

IMAGINE → You buy the puzzle
and try to find the
number of squares.

NAME

Fact: A puzzle made from squares.

Question: How many squares are there?

THINK Think of a plan or strategy for finding all
the squares. Start with the largest square.
Use different colors to outline your square.

Then → **COMPUTE** — and → **CHECK**

2. How many squares can
you find in this puzzle?

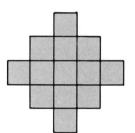

3. How many triangles can
you find in this puzzle?

4. Draw five square shapes so that any two
squares touch along one entire side.
In how many different ways can you
arrange the shapes?

More Practice

What are you finding for each? Write "area," "perimeter," or volume."

1. The capacity of a sandbox

2. The length around your classroom

3. The size of a rug

Name each shaded shape. Write "triangle," "circle," "rectangle," or "square."

4.

5.

6.

7.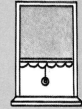

Write the name of the space figure each of these is most like.

8.

9.

10.

11.

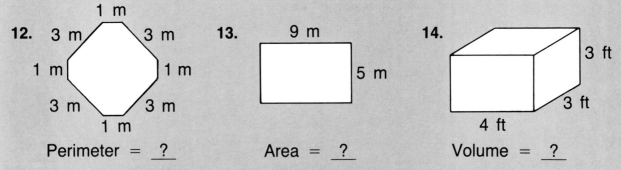

Compute.

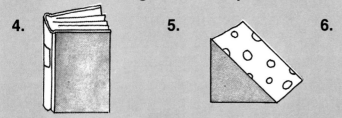

12. Perimeter = ___?___

13. 9 m / 5 m   Area = ___?___

14. 3 ft / 3 ft / 4 ft   Volume = ___?___

Solve.

15. A box of cereal is 12 cm high, 5 cm wide, and 8 cm long. Find the volume. (See *Still More Practice*, p. 369.)

Math Probe

PUZZLE TIME

How many more square units must be added to make these figures rectangles?

1. **2.** **3.** **4.**

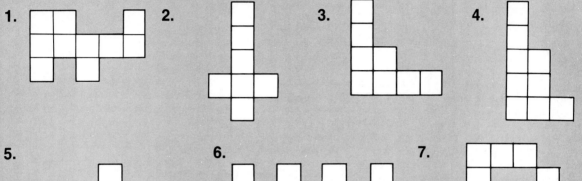

5. **6.** **7.**

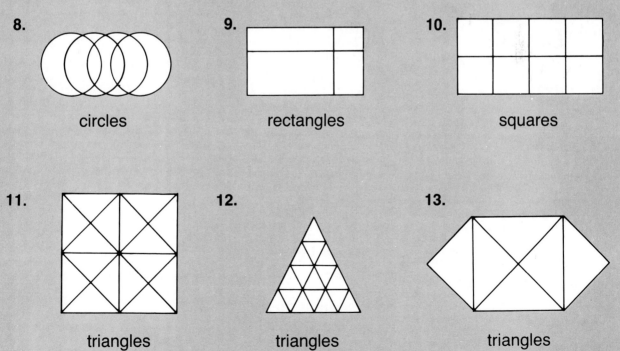

Find the number of:

8. **9.** **10.**

circles   rectangles   squares

11. **12.** **13.**

triangles   triangles   triangles

Check Your Mastery

What are you finding for each? Write "area," "perimeter," or volume."

See pp. 328-337.

1. the total length of new molding around your room

2. the size of tiles for a kitchen floor

3. the capacity of a trunk

Name each shaded shape. Write "triangle," "circle," "rectangle," or "square."

See pp. 328-329.

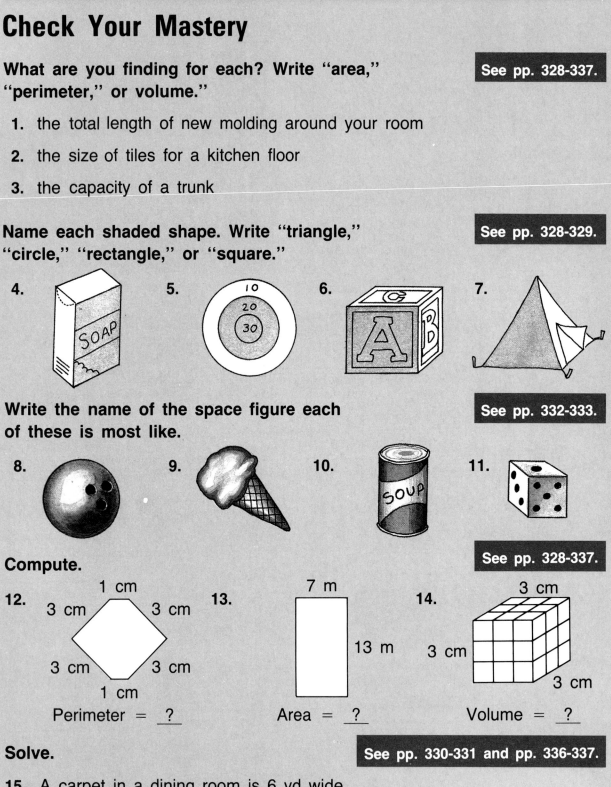

4.

5.

6.

7.

Write the name of the space figure each of these is most like.

See pp. 332-333.

8.

9.

10.

11.

Compute.

See pp. 328-337.

12.
1 cm
3 cm 3 cm
3 cm 3 cm
1 cm
Perimeter = _?_

13.
7 m
13 m
Area = _?_

14.
3 cm
3 cm
3 cm
Volume = _?_

Solve.

See pp. 330-331 and pp. 336-337.

15. A carpet in a dining room is 6 yd wide and 9 yd long. Find the area of the carpet.

342

14

Computers and Research

In this unit you will:

- Learn to use the BASIC commands PRINT and LET
- Learn to draw with LOGO
- Learn how the steps of a flowchart are like a program
- Learn how to prepare a research project

Do you remember?

The three steps in the computing process are: input, compute, output.

The **keyboard** is the most common **input** device.

The **memory** stores the information until it is worked on.

The **monitor** is like a TV screen. It is the most common **output** device.

343

PRINT and LET Commands in a Program

BASIC is a language that computers understand.
Two commands in BASIC are PRINT and LET.

- PRINT is used to compute:

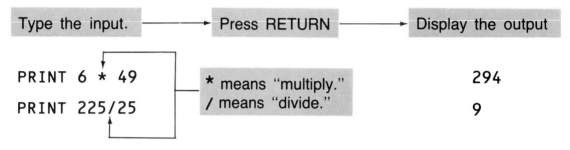

Type the input. ——→	Press RETURN ——→	Display the output
PRINT 6 * 49	* means "multiply."	294
PRINT 225/25	/ means "divide."	9

- LET is used to store numbers:

  LET A = 6

A computer program is one or more numbered commands.
To write a program:

  - Number the commands in order.

  - Type the commands. Press ⟨RETURN⟩ after each.

  - Type RUN. Press ⟨RETURN⟩.

Type. ————————————→	Type RUN. Press RETURN. ——→	Output

10 PRINT 12 + 70 ⟨RETURN⟩	82
20 PRINT 3 * 87 ⟨RETURN⟩	261

10 LET A = 48 ⟨RETURN⟩	
20 LET B = 6 ⟨RETURN⟩	
30 PRINT A + B ⟨RETURN⟩	54

Write the output.

1. 10 PRINT 420/2
   20 PRINT 3 * 87

2. 10 LET A = 50
   20 LET B = 7
   30 PRINT A + B

3. 10 LET A = 40
   20 LET B = 5
   30 PRINT A + B
   40 PRINT A - B
   50 PRINT A * B

4. 10 LET D = 30
   20 LET E = 10
   30 LET F = 15
   40 LET G = D + E + F
   50 PRINT G

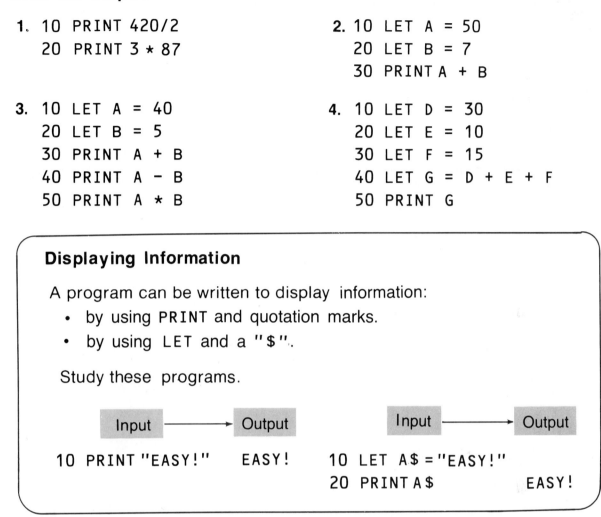

Displaying Information

A program can be written to display information:
- by using PRINT and quotation marks.
- by using LET and a "$".

Study these programs.

| Input | ⟶ | Output | | Input | ⟶ | Output |

10 PRINT "EASY!"   EASY!

10 LET A$ = "EASY!"
20 PRINT A$ EASY!

Enter and RUN each program. Write the output.

5. 10 PRINT "HELLO"
   20 PRINT "8 + 17 = " 8 + 17
   30 PRINT "GOOD-BYE"

6. 10 LET A$ = "RACHEL"
   20 PRINT "MY NAME IS " A$
   30 LET B$ = "BOSTON"
   40 PRINT "I LIVE IN " B$
   50 PRINT "I LOVE TO PLAY"

7. Write and RUN some programs of your own.

8. Type the program in exercise 5. Change the first line number from 10 to 25. How does this change the output?

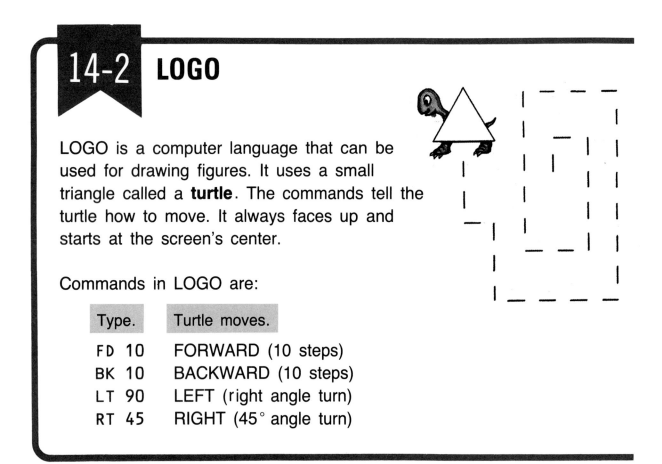

14-2 LOGO

LOGO is a computer language that can be used for drawing figures. It uses a small triangle called a **turtle**. The commands tell the turtle how to move. It always faces up and starts at the screen's center.

Commands in LOGO are:

Type.	Turtle moves.
FD 10	FORWARD (10 steps)
BK 10	BACKWARD (10 steps)
LT 90	LEFT (right angle turn)
RT 45	RIGHT (45° angle turn)

1. Type these commands to draw this triangle:

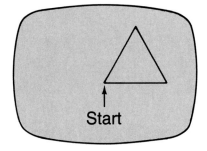

```
RT   30
FD   20
RT   120
FD   20
RT   120
FD   20
```

2. Type these commands to draw this hexagon:

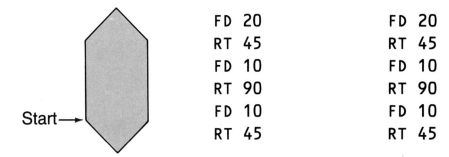

Start →

```
FD  20      FD  20
RT  45      RT  45
FD  10      FD  10
RT  90      RT  90
FD  10      FD  10
RT  45      RT  45
```

3. Finish the commands to draw the house.
(Hint: Use the triangle idea from exercise 1.)

FD 20	RT ___
RT 90	FD ___
FD 20	RT 30
RT 90	FD ___
FD ___	RT ___
RT ___	FD ___
FD ___	

Start→

Additional LOGO Commands

Type	Meaning	Result
PD	PENDOWN	turtle's track shows
PU	PENUP	turtle's track hidden

To draw this figure, type these commands.

Start→

PD	PU	PU
FD 10	FD 10	FD 10
PU	PD	PD
FD 10	FD 10	FD 10
PD	RT 90	
FD 10		
RT 90		

---

4. **Continue the commands above to complete a dashed rectangle.**

5. **Draw the letters E, F, H, and L.**

6. **Draw the house from exercise 3, using PD and PU. Can you add a chimney?**

14-3 Flowcharts

A **flowchart** is used to design a program step-by-step.

Symbols used in flowcharts have special meanings:

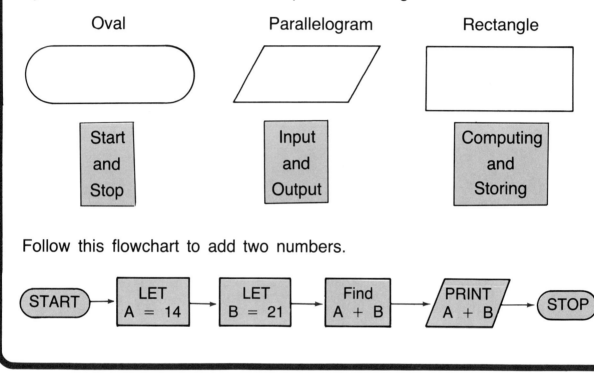

Oval   Parallelogram   Rectangle

Start and Stop   Input and Output   Computing and Storing

Follow this flowchart to add two numbers.

START → LET A = 14 → LET B = 21 → Find A + B → PRINT A + B → STOP

Complete.

1. Study the flowchart above. Finish this program to add 14 and 21. RUN **the program.**

```
10 LET A = _____
20 LET _____ = 21
30 LET C = A + B
40 PRINT _____
```

2. Write a flowchart to subtract 50 from 77.

3. Write a program for exercise 2. RUN **the program.**

Problem Solving: Research Project

These are steps to follow when you do a research report.

1. **Imagine** your teacher has assigned the topic of whales. You start thinking about whales.

2. **Explore** the subject of whales. Your topic on whales could be: mating and raising of young, recognizing whales, how whales communicate, and migration of whales.

3. **Select** one idea to research.

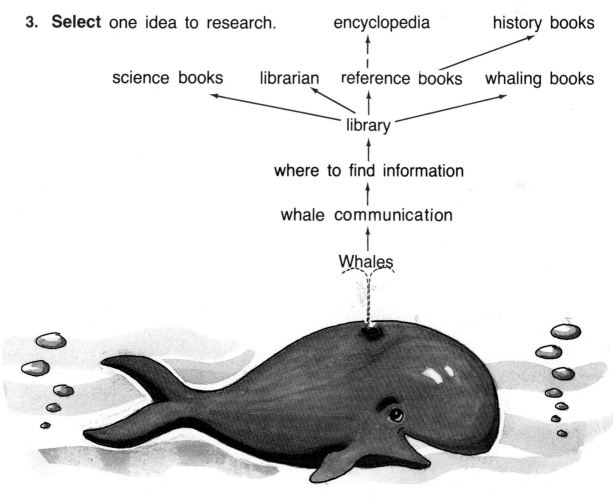

encyclopedia   history books

science books   librarian   reference books   whaling books

library

where to find information

whale communication

Whales

4. **Make a workplan** to organize your
research in an outline. Decide on a title:
Whale Communication.

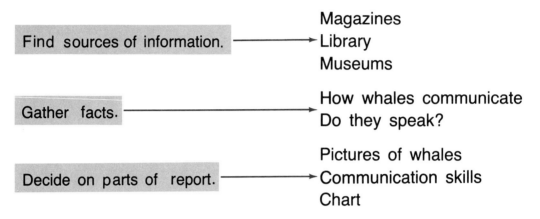

Find sources of information. ⟶ Magazines
Library
Museums

Gather facts. ⟶ How whales communicate
Do they speak?

Decide on parts of report. ⟶ Pictures of whales
Communication skills
Chart

5. **Set up a schedule** of what to do first.
Check off each item as you do it.

Schedule

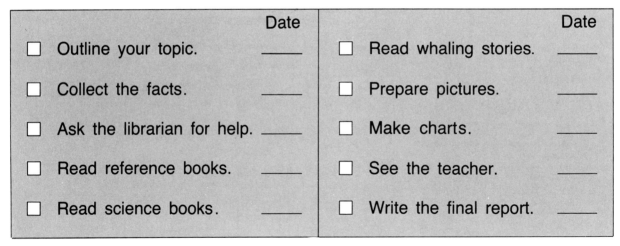

		Date			Date
☐	Outline your topic.	____	☐	Read whaling stories.	____
☐	Collect the facts.	____	☐	Prepare pictures.	____
☐	Ask the librarian for help.	____	☐	Make charts.	____
☐	Read reference books.	____	☐	See the teacher.	____
☐	Read science books.	____	☐	Write the final report.	____

6. **Follow the schedule.** Ask for help when
you need it.

7. **Complete the project.** Collect and
organize information. Finish your work.

8. **Present your project** to the class.

350

Cumulative Test IV

Write the word name for each.

1. 0.3   **2.** 0.14   **3.** 0.06   **4.** 1.7   **5.** 5.92

Write as a decimal.

6. $\frac{7}{10}$ **7.** $\frac{4}{10}$ **8.** $\frac{23}{100}$ **9.** $\frac{9}{100}$ **10.** $\frac{16}{100}$

11. $2\frac{1}{10}$ **12.** $5\frac{8}{10}$ **13.** $21\frac{19}{100}$ **14.** $42\frac{3}{100}$ **15.** $36\frac{9}{10}$

Add or subtract.

16. 0.3 + 0.2   **17.** 0.47 + 0.32   **18.** 3.6 + 5.8   **19.** 0.97 − 0.13   **20.** 0.82 − 0.19

21. 1.7 + 0.1   **22.** 3.5 + 8.6   **23.** 9.6 − 4.2

24. 12.16 + 7.04   **25.** 12.42 − 5.24   **26.** 20.73 − 8.09

Round to the nearest tenth.

27. 0.17   **28.** 0.72   **29.** 3.84   **30.** 9.45   **31.** 12.90

Round to the nearest dollar.

32. $5.49   **33.** $6.04   **34.** $9.54   **35.** $0.98   **36.** $100.79

Compare. Write $<$, $=$, or $>$.

37. 0.29 _?_ 0.91   **38.** 0.8 _?_ 0.80   **39.** 2.7 _?_ 3.2

40. 13.57 _?_ 13.61   **41.** $5.87 _?_ $5.79   **42.** 94.62 _?_ 95.26

Complete.

43. Area is measured in _?_ units.

44. A circle has _?_ sides.

45. The volume of a 3-in. cube is _?_ cubic inches.

46. A line segment has _?_ endpoints.

47. A sphere is a _?_ figure.

48. A quadrilateral is a polygon with _?_ vertices.

Use the chart to answer each question.

Number of Days in a Month						
October	November	December	January	February	March	April
31	30	31	31	28	31	30

49. What is the total number of days for the months of November, December, and March?

50. Find the date that is 30 days after December 23.

51. December 15 is how many days after November 11?

52. How many weeks are there from October 12 to December 14?

53. Which three consecutive months have the least total number of days?

Find the perimeter.

54. sides: 2 cm, 4 cm, 7 cm

55. sides: 3 ft, 4 ft, 5 ft, 7 ft

56. sides: 2.5 m, 6 m, 4.8 m

57. sides: 9 in., 2 in., 9 in., 2 in.

58. sides: 9 m, 9 m, 9 m

59. sides: 12 yd, 12 yd, 12 yd, 12 yd

Find the area of each rectangle.

60. $l = 8$ m, $w = 4$ m

61. $l = 15$ ft, $w = 2$ ft

62. $l = 4$ m, $w = 2$ m

63. $l = 12$ in., $w = 7$ in.

64. $l = 18$ cm, $w = 18$ cm

65. $l = 9$ yd, $w = 6$ yd

Use the bar graph to answer each question.

66. How many laps did Jay swim on Wednesday?

67. How many more laps did he swim on Friday than on Tuesday?

68. Find his average number of laps each day?

69. On what days did he swim the same number of laps?

70. On what day did he swim the least number of laps?

Jay's Swimming Record

Solve.

71. Find the perimeter of a 5-foot square.

72. What is the area of a rectangle with width 8 m and length 9 m?

73. Find the area of a 4-foot square.

74. What is the chance of randomly choosing a nickel from a jar containing 7 nickels and 9 dimes?

75. Pia is 49.5 in. tall and Gino is 48 in. How much taller is Pia than Gino?

More Computer Activities

To be used after Unit 1:

1. Make up an input list and an output list of the following devices. You may need to look some up to list them under input, output, or both:

   keyboard, disk drive, floppy disk, hard disk, cassette tape recorder, cassette, optical mark reader, light pen, video screen, printer, plotter.

2. Write the display for each PRINT statement, then check your answer on a computer.

   a. `PRINT "HAVE A GOOD DAY!"`   **b.** `PRINT "BE HAPPY."`
   c. `PRINT "1990 HERE I COME!"`   **d.** `PRINT "GOOD MORNING!"`

3. Use the PRINT statement to display:

   a. Your name and address   **b.** A classmate's name and birthday

To be used after Unit 2:

Solve the following by using the PRINT statement on your computer.

a. 3621 + 107   **b.** 144 − 114   **c.** 955 − 804
d. 671 − 550   **e.** 8096 − 1104   **f.** 5403 + 506

To be used after Unit 3:

1. Solve the following by using the PRINT statement on your computer.

   a. 9 × 3   **b.** 3 × 6   **c.** 4 × 9   **d.** 8 × 5
   e. 27 ÷ 3   **f.** 15 ÷ 3   **g.** 36 ÷ 6   **h.** 42 ÷ 7

2. Enter this program into your computer and RUN it, then modify it to use with related sentences in multiplication and division.

```
10 LET H = 6              40 PRINT H " + " K " = " H + K
20 LET K = 7              50 PRINT H + K " - " K " = " H
30 PRINT "FACT FAMILIES:"  60 PRINT "THAT'S RIGHT!"
```

To be used after Unit 4:

Estimate each answer. Use the PRINT statement to check your estimate.

a. 762 + 158	**b.** 907 + 326	**c.** 542 + 191
d. 608 − 510	**e.** 897 + 28	**f.** 548 − 173

To be used after Unit 6:

Estimate each answer. Use the PRINT statement to check your estimate.

a. 17 × 164	**b.** 42 × 508	**c.** 76 × 122
d. 65 × 18	**e.** 23 × 54	**f.** 39 × 19

To be used after Unit 7:

Estimate each answer. Use the PRINT statement to check your estimate.

a. 152 ÷ 8	**b.** 76 ÷ 4	**c.** 456 ÷ 3
d. 192 ÷ 6	**e.** 840 ÷ 7	**f.** 93 ÷ 6

To be used after Unit 8:

1. Use the commands: RIGHT 30, FORWARD 100, BACKWARD 100, PENUP, PENDOWN to make the computer draw a pair of parallel lines.

2. Write a program in LOGO to draw a larger triangle around a smaller triangle.

3. Use a PRINT statement on your computer to find the perimeter of:

   a. a rectangle 4 m by 7 m.   **b.** a triangle with sides of 15 m, 12 m, and 9 m.

To be used after Unit 12:

Make up ten addition and ten subtraction exercises with decimals. Use the PRINT statement to solve them.

To be used after Unit 13:

Complete the program. Then RUN it.

1.
```
10 LET S = 3
20 PRINT "THE PERIMETER OF THE SQUARE IS" 4 * S
```

2. Modify the program for Exercise 1 so that the figure is a triangle with sides of 3m, 4m, and 6m.

354

MENTAL MATHEMATICS—By Topic

Set 1—RELATED FACTS: ADDITION AND SUBTRACTION

Give the related subtraction fact.

1. 7 + 3	**2.** 8 + 4	**3.** 3 + 5	**4.** 2 + 9	**5.** 4 + 6	**6.** 8 + 9
7. 6 + 5	**8.** 9 + 3	**9.** 4 + 9	**10.** 8 + 6	**11.** 5 + 3	**12.** 7 + 4
13. 9 + 1	**14.** 6 + 3	**15.** 7 + 5	**16.** 9 + 7	**17.** 5 + 9	**18.** 6 + 7

Give the 4 related addition and subtraction facts.

19. 3, 4, 7	**20.** 5, 4, 9	**21.** 8, 2, 10	**22.** 6, 7, 13	**23.** 4, 6, 10	**24.** 7, 5, 12
25. 9, 6, 15	**26.** 3, 8, 11	**27.** 6, 5, 11	**28.** 8, 3, 11	**29.** 5, 7, 12	**30.** 3, 9, 12
31. 7, 8, 15	**32.** 8, 6, 14	**33.** 9, 5, 14	**34.** 4, 9, 13	**35.** 7, 4, 11	**36.** 9, 8, 17

Set 2—MULTIPLICATION AND DIVISION FACTS

Multiply.

1. 2 ×: 6, 10, 8, 5, 3, 7, 0, 9, 4	**2.** 3 ×: 0, 3, 5, 7, 9, 2, 4, 6, 8
3. 4 ×: 2, 3, 10, 4, 9, 5, 8, 7, 0	**4.** 5 ×: 2, 4, 6, 8, 3, 5, 7, 1, 10
5. 6 ×: 9, 2, 8, 0, 5, 4, 3, 7, 1, 6	**6.** 7 ×: 8, 5, 0, 6, 9, 4, 1, 7, 9, 10
7. 8 ×: 8, 3, 6, 2, 9, 4, 5, 1, 0	**8.** 9 ×: 1, 8, 6, 2, 4, 0, 7, 9, 5

Divide.

1. By 2: 8, 18, 14, 10, 12, 6, 16, 2	**2.** By 3: 9, 15, 21, 27, 6, 12, 18, 3
3. By 4: 36, 4, 8, 32, 16, 28, 20, 24	**4.** By 5: 45, 15, 10, 40, 20, 35, 25, 20
5. By 6: 6, 54, 48, 12, 18, 42, 30, 36	**6.** By 7: 35, 42, 49, 56, 7, 28, 21, 14
7. By 8: 8, 64, 72, 40, 32, 24, 16, 56	**8.** By 9: 18, 81, 9, 27, 36, 45, 54, 72, 63

Set 3—RELATED FACTS: MULTIPLICATION AND DIVISION

Give the related division fact.

1. 3 × 4	**2.** 5 × 7	**3.** 2 × 8	**4.** 7 × 6	**5.** 4 × 9	**6.** 8 × 7
7. 6 × 5	**8.** 4 × 2	**9.** 7 × 3	**10.** 8 × 9	**11.** 5 × 8	**12.** 5 × 9
13. 9 × 2	**14.** 8 × 3	**15.** 6 × 7	**16.** 4 × 5	**17.** 7 × 4	**18.** 3 × 1

Give the 4 related multiplication and division facts.

19. 3, 4, 12	**20.** 4, 5, 20	**21.** 5, 2, 10	**22.** 6, 2, 12	**23.** 7, 5, 35	**24.** 8, 2, 16
25. 9, 2, 18	**26.** 6, 4, 24	**27.** 8, 4, 32	**28.** 9, 5, 45	**29.** 6, 3, 18	**30.** 7, 9, 63
31. 7, 6, 42	**32.** 3, 9, 27	**33.** 6, 8, 48	**34.** 8, 3, 24	**35.** 9, 8, 72	**36.** 6, 9, 54

Set 4—DIVISION WITH REMAINDERS

1. $3\overline{)4}$ $3\overline{)5}$ $3\overline{)7}$ $3\overline{)8}$ $3\overline{)13}$ $3\overline{)14}$ $3\overline{)17}$ $3\overline{)16}$

2. $5\overline{)7}$ $5\overline{)9}$ $5\overline{)12}$ $5\overline{)14}$ $5\overline{)17}$ $5\overline{)19}$ $5\overline{)22}$ $5\overline{)24}$

3. $7\overline{)8}$ $7\overline{)15}$ $7\overline{)16}$ $7\overline{)23}$ $7\overline{)24}$ $7\overline{)31}$ $7\overline{)32}$ $7\overline{)39}$

4. $9\overline{)10}$ $9\overline{)19}$ $9\overline{)20}$ $9\overline{)29}$ $9\overline{)30}$ $9\overline{)39}$ $9\overline{)40}$ $9\overline{)49}$

5. $25 \div 4$ $17 \div 4$ $37 \div 4$ $29 \div 4$
   $18 \div 4$ $38 \div 4$ $30 \div 4$ $34 \div 4$

6. $9 \div 6$ $15 \div 6$ $21 \div 6$ $27 \div 6$
   $10 \div 6$ $16 \div 6$ $22 \div 6$ $28 \div 6$

7. $9 \div 8$ $18 \div 8$ $27 \div 8$ $38 \div 8$
   $10 \div 8$ $20 \div 8$ $30 \div 8$ $36 \div 8$

8. $55 \div 9$ $65 \div 9$ $75 \div 9$ $85 \div 9$
   $57 \div 9$ $67 \div 9$ $73 \div 9$ $77 \div 9$

Set 5—PATTERNS IN MULTIPLICATION

1. 2×1
   2×10
   2×100

2. 3×1
   3×10
   3×100

3. 4×1
   4×10
   4×100

4. 6×1
   6×10
   6×100

5. 9×1
   9×10
   9×100

6. 3×2
   3×20
   3×200

7. 5×2
   5×20
   5×200

8. 6×3
   6×30
   6×300

9. 7×3
   7×30
   7×300

10. 8×3
    8×30
    8×300

11. 2×4
    2×40
    2×400

12. 3×5
    3×50
    3×500

13. 4×6
    4×60
    4×600

14. 5×7
    5×70
    5×700

15. 6×8
    6×80
    6×800

Set 6—PATTERNS IN DIVISION

1. $2\overline{)4}$
   $2\overline{)40}$
   $2\overline{)400}$

2. $3\overline{)6}$
   $3\overline{)60}$
   $3\overline{)600}$

3. $4\overline{)8}$
   $4\overline{)80}$
   $4\overline{)800}$

4. $5\overline{)30}$
   $5\overline{)300}$
   $3\overline{)3000}$

5. $6\overline{)18}$
   $6\overline{)180}$
   $6\overline{)1800}$

6. $2\overline{)12}$
   $2\overline{)120}$
   $2\overline{)1200}$

7. $4\overline{)16}$
   $4\overline{)160}$
   $4\overline{)1600}$

8. $6\overline{)42}$
   $6\overline{)420}$
   $6\overline{)4200}$

9. $7\overline{)35}$
   $7\overline{)350}$
   $7\overline{)3500}$

10. $9\overline{)36}$
    $9\overline{)360}$
    $9\overline{)3600}$

Set 7—USING VOCABULARY OF MATHEMATICS

1. 13 increased by 9 is _?_

2. From 10 take the product of $\frac{1}{6}$ and 54.

3. 32 decreased by 9 is _?_

4. Add 4 to the product of 5 and 7.

5. How much less than 14 is 5?

6. What is 42 decreased by 8?

7. What number must be added to 19 to have the sum equal 21?

8. What fractional part of an hour is 30 minutes?

9. When 72 is divided by 8, what is the quotient?

10. When 35 is divided by 4, what is the remainder?

11. In multiplication, the answer is called the _?_

12. What is the sum of 30 and 50?

13. Divide by 2: 5, 9, 13, 17, 3, 7, 11, 15

14. Divide by 5: 49, 43, 38, 32, 26, 36, 42, 48

356

Still More Practice

Practice 1-1   UNIT 1

Write the standard numeral.

1a. six hundred
seventy-four

b. thirty-four thousand,
five hundred seven

2a. one hundred two
thousand, forty-
four

b. three million,
five hundred fifty
thousand, five

Give the place value of the underlined digit:

3a. 506,823

b. 304,750

4a. 369

b. 14,670

Write the numeral in words.

5a. 26,435

b. 604,572

6. Write the number that has 4 in the
thousands place.
6425   34,560   48,793

7. In the number 280,804, which 8 has
the greater value?

8. The population of a large city is eight hundred
fifty thousand, six hundred twenty-five.
Write that population as a standard numeral.

9. Write in words: 267,451.

10. What is the greatest possible number
you can express with a five-digit numeral?

11. Order from greatest to least.
432, 234, 342, 551, 155, 550

12. In the school cafeteria, Mrs. Brady sold
584 apples on Monday and 548
on Tuesday. On which of the days
did she sell more apples?

13. Owen's test scores for five days were:
75, 86, 80, 95, 92. Write these scores
in order from greatest to least.

14. Tina has 198 stamps in her collection.
Gerald has 1208 stamps in his collection.
Who has more stamps?

15. Write the numeral that expresses 1000
more than 62,780.

Practice 1-2

Compare. Write <, =, or >.

1a. 96 ? 69

b. 809 ? 908

2a. 1476 ? 1764

b. 62,705 ? 62,605

Round to the nearest ten.

3a. 78

b. 43

Round to the nearest hundred.

4a. 436

b. 382

Round to the nearest thousand.

5a. 6789

b. 6289

6. Write the Roman numeral for 150.

7. Tell which has the greater value: DCL or CDL.

8. Which would you rather have: a jar of
786 almonds or a jar of 768 almonds?

9. The distance between two cities is 683 miles.
Round this number to the nearest hundred.

10. Write CDXL as a standard numeral.

11. Write the even number between 606 and 609.

12. Write the next five numbers in the
pattern: 102, 106, 110, ?

13. Order all the odd numbers between 50
and 60 from least to greatest.

14. Write the greatest even number having
two digits.

15. Write in words: 307, 55

Practice 2-1

1a. 7 + 5   **b.** 8 + 9

2a. 13 − 7   **b.** 14 − 5

3a. 9 + _?_ = 15   **b.** _?_ + 6 = 11

Complete.

4a. 7 + 4 = _?_   **b.** 9 + 3 = _?_
   c. _?_ − 4 = 7   **d.** _?_ − 3 = 9

Compare. Write <, =, or >.

5a. 6 + 9 _?_ 8 + 7   **b.** 5 + 8 _?_ 0 + 3

Write the addition and subtraction family for:

6a. (8, 3, 11)   **b.** (7, 8, 15)

7. Therese collected 9 shells on the beach. How many more does she need to make a bracelet of 12 shells?

8. How much less than 14 is 6?

9. What is 7 increased by 4?

10. Liz saved $6, then spent $2. Francine saved $5 but did not spend any of it. Who had more money?

11. Tim and his father caught 14 fish. They caught 6 on Monday, 3 on Tuesday, and the rest on Wednesday. How many fish did they catch on Wednesday?

12. After 3 eggs were taken from a carton, 9 eggs were left. How many eggs were in the carton originally?

13. Which is greater: 4 + 0 or 5 − 0?

14. A class has 17 boys and 13 girls. What is the total number of students in the class? How many more boys are enrolled?

15. David and Mark collect old coins. David has 9 pennies and 4 nickels. Mark has 6 nickels and 5 pennies. Who has more coins?

Practice 2-2

1a.   32
    +45   **b.**   21
             +63

2a.   369
   −145   **b.**   587
            −243

3a.   542
    306
   +151   **b.**   420
             205
           +374

4a. 5868
  −2436   **b.** 6487
            − 205

5a. 1052
    324
  + 13   **b.** 5270
              16
          + 502

6. Write in column form and add:
4203 + 341 + 13.

7. John has 5 pets. Two of them are cats. How many other pets does John have?

8. Find the total number of colored pencils in a box of 24 red, 12 blue, 30 green, and 23 yellow pencils.

9. 250 people came to the school play on the first day, 426 on the second day, and 322 on the third day. How many people came in all?

10. Kerry has three bags of seashells. There are 83, 104, and 112 shells in the bags. How many shells has Kerry collected?

11. Which is greater: 83 + 24 or 67 + 42?

12. How much greater than 427 is 549?

13. There are 36 yards of cotton goods on a bolt. After 24 yards are sold, how many yards of cotton are left?

14. From the sum of 2847 + 5032 subtract 3405.

15. Ruth is reading a book of 178 pages. She has read 67 pages. How many more pages are to be read?

Practice 3-1

1a. 3
  ×4

b. 4
  ×3

2a. 2
  ×4

b. 2
  ×4

3a. 5
  ×3

b. 3
  ×5

4a. 8
  ×4

b. 4
  ×8

5a. 6
  ×5

b. 5
  ×4

6. What is the product of 4 and 7?

7. How much greater is 4 × 3 than 4 × 2?

8. Joel bought 3 boxes of peaches. There were 6 peaches in each box. How many peaches did he buy?

9. The product is 42. One factor is 6. What is the other factor?

10. Peter is 8 years old. His sister is three times his age. How old is Peter's sister?

11. Which is greater: 7 × 1 or 7 × 0?

12. What is the product of seven and zero?

13. What is the difference between 8 × 6 and 5 × 8?

14. Which is less: 8 × 7 or 7 × 9?

15. The product is 54. One factor is 9. What is the other factor?

Practice 3-2

1a. 4 × 2

b. 8 ÷ 2

2a. 7 × 3

b. 21 ÷ 3

3a. 5 × 6

b. 30 ÷ 6

4a. 4 × 0

b. 0 ÷ 4

5a. 6 × 1

b. 6 ÷ 1

6a. 7)28

b. 3)27

Write a related division fact.

7a. 8 × 2 = 16

b. 6 × 3 = 18

Write × or ÷.

8a. 6 _?_ 7 = 42

b. 9 _?_ 3 = 3

Write 4 related facts for each.

9a. (6, 2, 12)

b. (4, 7, 28)

10. 48 tulips were planted in 6 rows. How many tulips were in each row?

11. Twenty packets of raisins were given to 4 students. If they were divided equally, how many packets did each student get?

12. Kathy has 120 stamps. She gave half of the stamps to her sister. How many stamps did she keep?

13. Five shirts cost $35. How much does each shirt cost?

14. Don runs 12 miles in 4 hours. How many miles on the average does he run every hour?

15. One book costs $4. How much do 8 books cost?

Practice 4-1

Rename.

1. 15 = _?_ tens _?_ ones

2. 4 tens 12 ones = 5 tens _?_ ones

3. 654 = _?_ hundreds _?_ tens _?_ ones

4. 3 tens 5 ones = 2 tens _?_ ones

Fill in the blanks.

5. 452 = 4 hundreds _?_ tens 12 ones

Regroup.

6. 3 hundreds 4 tens 6 ones =

2 hundreds _?_ tens 6 ones

7. The librarian bought 345 books for the library. 160 of them are animal stories. How many books are not animal stories?

8. In a box of 224 pencils 148 are new. How many used pencils are in the box?

9. Write in column form and add:
452 + 386 + 47 + 308 + 8

10. There are 220 roses, 175 carnations, and 365 tulips. How many flowers are there in all?

11. Brian collected 86 baseball cards, Colleen had 196 cards, and Tony had 226 cards. Find the total number of cards collected.

12. A teacher has 7 second grade books, 8 third grade books, 4 fourth grade books, and 3 fifth grade books. How many books does the teacher have in all?

13. In a class of 32 students, 27 students completed their homework assignment. How many did not complete the work?

14. A school has 520 students. 43 are absent on a particular day. How many students are present?

15. Judy worked 2 hours on Friday, 3 hours on Saturday, and 4 hours on Sunday. How many hours did she work in the three days?

Practice 4-2

1a. 30 − 19   **b.** 60 − 47

2a. 500 − 347   **b.** 800 − 493

3a. 2386 + 5629   **b.** 6394 + 4337

4. Round $7.98 to the nearest dollar.

5. Round $6.86 + $3.90 to the nearest dollar and add.

6. Round $7.75 − $5.18 to the nearest dollar and subtract.

7. Write in column form and add:
3246 + 1734 + 834.

8. From the sum of 1268 and 3429 subtract 2435.

9. From a box of 5000 envelopes, the secretary took 3450. How many envelopes were left?

10. On a three-day motor trip the White family drove 842 km the first day, 680 km the second day, and 493 km the third day. How far did they travel in all?

11. At the camera shop Ted bought a disc camera for $34.99 and a pocket camera for $10.57. How much did he pay for both?

12. Mr. Carwell bought a $565 TV on sale for $95 less than the regular price. What did he pay for the TV?

13. Add $.94, $1.04, and $.86. Round the sum to the nearest dollar.

14. From Philadelphia the airfare is $49 to Boston and $89 to Chicago. About how much more does it cost to go from Philadelphia to Chicago than to Boston?

15. Add $2.52, $3.05, and $1.63. Subtract the sum from $10.

Practice 5-1   **UNIT 5**

1a. 1 m = __?__ cm   **b.** 300 cm = __?__ m

2a. 2 km = __?__ m   **b.** 4000 m = __?__ km

Compare. Write <, =, or >.

3a. 5 kg __?__ 1000 g   **b.** 50 g __?__ 600 kg

4a. 7 kg __?__ 7000 g   **b.** 871 g __?__ 8 kg

5a. 3 m __?__ 30 cm   **b.** 6000 m __?__ 6 km

6a. 7 cm __?__ 700 m   **b.** 800 m __?__ 8 km

7a. 2 L __?__ 20 mL   **b.** 4 L __?__ 4000 mL

8. Arrange in order from least to greatest:
IL, 15 mL, 115 mL, 15 L

9. Using a Celsius thermometer, tell the degrees at which water boils and freezes.

10. A tree is 4 m tall. What is its height in centimeters?

11. Would the length of a person's thumb be about 5 m or 5 cm?

12. If Andy walked 1 km, then turned around and walked 200 meters back, how much farther did he have to walk to get back to his starting point?

13. Would you make 8 liters or 80 milliliters of iced tea for a picnic?

14. Would you be wearing a coat if it were 10° Celsius?

15. Stacey is ten years old. Would she weigh about 60 g or 30 kg?

Practice 5-2

1a. 10 minutes to 7

b. 15 minutes past 3

2a. 24 in. = __?__ ft   **b.** 4 ft = __?__ in

3a. 4 pt = __?__ c   **b.** 2 c = __?__ pt

4a. 32 oz = __?__ lb   **b.** 3 lb = __?__ oz

5a.   5 ft 4 in.   **b.**   6 yd 2 ft
       − 3 ft 2 in.   + 2 yd 2 ft

6a.   7 ft 9 in.   **b.**   9 yd 1 ft
       − 5 ft 4 in.   + 3 yd 1 ft

Write as money. Use $ and .

7. 3 quarters, 4 dimes, 2 pennies

8. 2 half dollars, 1 quarters, 5 dimes

9. 4 dollars, 1 quarters, 3 nickels

10. Josie weighs 6 lb, 9 oz. Her twin sister, Helen, weighs 5 lb, 5 oz. How much more does Josie weigh than Helen?

11. Mrs. Roger bought a 21 oz bag of potatoes. Mrs. Allen bought a 2 lb bag. Who bought more potatoes?

12. The length of a garden is 24 ft. Give its length in yards.

13. Mary is 51 inches tall. Write her height in feet and inches.

14. Sheri bought 7 yd, 2 ft of cotton fabric, and 3 yds, 2 ft of a polyester fabric. How much fabric did she buy in all?

15. A recipe calls for 2 pints of condensed milk. If Sharon uses a cup to measure the amount of milk needed, how many times will she fill the cup?

Practice 6-1

1a. 44 × 2   **b.** 51 × 6

2a. 123 × 3   **b.** 312 × 4

3a. 56 × 3   **b.** 64 × 5

4a. 162 × 4   **b.** 257 × 7

5a. 525 × 49   **b.** 874 × 26

6a. $7.65 × 2   **b.** $5.89 × 57

Choose the correct product.

7a. 2164 × 7 = 15,144 15,248 15,148

  b. 3625 × 8 = 29,000 28,960 29,806

8a. $6.52 × 7 = $54.64 $65.64 $45.64

  b. $3.84 × 18 = $69.12 $68.32 $68.12

9. There are 12 inches in one foot. How many inches are there in 36 feet?

UNIT 6

10. In a school auditorium there are 72 rows of chairs with 8 chairs in each row. How many chairs are there altogether?

11. For the carnival, Mr. Jones sold balloons of 6 different colors. He sold 144 of each color. What was the total number of balloons sold?

12. There are 4 boxes of pears with 52 pears in each box. How many pears are there in all?

13. Each of 39 children had a box of 64 crayons. How many crayons were there in all?

14. If Pedro sold 45 magazine subscriptions at $7.95 a subscription, how much money did he collect?

15. Carrie bought 3 records at $1.92 each. Julia bought 6 cards at $.85 each. Which girl spent more money?

Practice 6-2

Multiply by 40.

1a. 28   **b.** 73

Multiply by 60.

2a. 700   **b.** 306

3a. 740 × 80   **b.** 820 × 63

4a. $8.00 × 80   **b.** $7.80 × 70

Multiply by 10.

5a. 93   **b.** 1000

Multiply by 100.

6a. 8   **b.** 743

Round the first factor to the nearest ten and multiply.

7a. 87 × 7   **b.** 92 × 8

Round the first factor to the nearest hundred and multiply.

8a. 512 × 6   **b.** 97 × 4

9. On a shelf there are 7 packages. Each contains 500 sheets of paper. Find the total number of sheets.

10. Amy read 4 chapters of a book. If each chapter contained 23 pages, how many pages did she read.

11. If Tony spends $18 a day, how much does he spend in 5 days?

12. An airplane travels at 540 miles an hour. How far does it travel in 7 hours?

13. What is the product of 359 and 26?

14. Find the product of 35 and 53.

15. Mrs. Coyne pays $8 a day to a babysitter. How much does she pay in 25 days?

Practice 7-1

1a. $3\overline{)21}$ **b.** $5\overline{)45}$

2a. $6\overline{)23}$ **b.** $7\overline{)44}$

3a. $48 \div 8$ **b.** $72 \div 9$

4a. $3\overline{)96}$ **b.** $4\overline{)64}$

5a. $5\overline{)78}$ **b.** $7\overline{)86}$

6. Marcie has 35 marbles of 5 different colors. If she has the same number of each color, how many marbles of each color does she have?

7. There are six photos to a page in a photo album. If the album has 96 photos, how many pages are in the album?

8. There are 54 cartons of milk. If 8 cartons are packed in a box, how many boxes are full, and how many cartons are left over?

9. A grove has 91 trees. If they are in rows of 7, how many rows are there?

10. Ellen has 98 inches of ribbon. How many 6-inch pieces can she cut? Will there be any ribbon left over?

11. Sixty apples are to be divided equally among 30 children. How many apples will each child receive?

12. If 3634 is divided by 7, what is the quotient?

13. Susan spent $200.35 on her five-day vacation. On the average, how much did she spend each day?

14. Tony read 168 books in 12 months. On the average, how many books did he read each month?

15. In a fund-raising campaign, 9 students collected $189. On the average, how much did each student collect?

Practice 7-2

1a. $3\overline{)936}$ **b.** $5\overline{)510}$

2a. $8\overline{)648}$ **b.** $9\overline{)387}$

3a. $6\overline{)548}$ **b.** $7\overline{)458}$

4a. $4\overline{)2824}$ **b.** $7\overline{)3565}$

5a. $8\overline{)\$16.96}$ **b.** $6\overline{)\$18.60}$

Estimate the quotient.

6a. $342 \div 6$ **b.** $7214 \div 9$

7. Scott delivered the same number of papers each day. At the end of 5 days he had delivered 235 papers. How many papers did Scott deliver each day?

8. Find the average of 81, 83, 87, 88, and 86.

9. Luke bought 3 loaves of bread for $4.77. What was the cost of one loaf?

10. How many nickels are there in $7.20?

11. Find the average of 82, 73, 25, and 20.

12. What is the average of 104, 205, 35, 45, and 36?

13. Helen worked 3 hours on Sunday, 2 hours on Monday, and 1 hour on Tuesday. On the average, how long did she work each day?

14. A theater has 648 seats in 24 rows. How many seats are in each row?

15. If a farmer divides 1136 peaches equally into 8 baskets, how many peaches will there be in each basket?

Practice 8-1   **UNIT 8**

1. Identify these.
   a.   **b.**   **c.**

   T   S   R   M   N

7. How many angles has a quadrilateral? octagon?

2. What shape is formed when two rays are joined?

8. Find the perimeter.

   6 m
   2 m
   5 m

3. Name this special angle.

   D
   E   F

9. Name the figure to the right.

4. Which lines are parallel?

   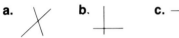

   B   E
   A   F
     C   D

10. Name the diameter and a radius.

   P
   R
   O
   Q

5. Which lines are not perpendicular?

   a.   **b.**   **c.**

11. Find the perimeter.

   3 in.
   3 in.   3 in.
   3 in.

6. How many sides has a triangle? pentagon? hexagon?

12. How many endpoints does a ray have?

13. How many vertices does a pentagon have?

14. How many angles are in a quadrilateral?

15. Find the volume of a cube having an edge of 4 inches.

Practice 8-2

Draw these. Use unlined paper and a ruler.

1. ∠ ABC   2. Ray PQ   3. ∠ E

Name each vertex.

4.
   M
   N
   O

5.
   R
   S   T

6. How does a square differ from a rectangle?

7. Is a rectangle a quadrilateral?

8. How does a hexagon differ from a quadrilateral?

9. How does a triangle differ from a pentagon?

10. Find the perimeter.

   3 in.
   2 in.
   4 in.
   2 in.
   5 in.

11. A person walks once around a rectangular playground 120 yards long and 60 yards wide. How far did the person walk?

12. A hexagon has 6 equal sides. Each is 5 inches long. Find the perimeter.

13. Use a compass to draw a circle. Show the radius.

14. How many feet of fencing are needed to enclose a playground 170 feet long and 90 feet wide?

15. A rectangular picture frame is 12 inches long and 9 inches wide. What is the perimeter?

364

Practice 9-1

Write as a fraction or mixed number.

1a. two sevenths   **b.** three fifths

2a. two and three fourths   **b.** six and one eighth

Write in words.

3a. $\frac{5}{8}$ **b.** $\frac{4}{9}$

4a. $3\frac{2}{5}$ **b.** $7\frac{1}{3}$

Write as an equivalent fraction.

5a. $\frac{1}{2} = \frac{?}{6}$ **b.** $\frac{1}{3} = \frac{?}{9}$

6a. $\frac{2}{4} = \frac{?}{2}$ **b.** $\frac{4}{6} = \frac{?}{3}$

7. A wheel at a carnival is divided into 10 equal parts. Three parts are colored red. Write a fraction to show what part is red.

8. What is $\frac{1}{5} + \frac{2}{5}$? Subtract the sum from 1.

9. An orange has 9 slices. Rose ate 6 slices. Write a fraction to tell what part was eaten.

10. Eight students out of 32 are honor students. What fraction shows how many are honor students?

11. Tammie bought $\frac{2}{3}$ of a yard of blue ribbon and $\frac{2}{3}$ of a yard of pink. How much ribbon did she buy altogether?

12. A recipe called for $\frac{3}{4}$ cup of milk. June added an extra $\frac{1}{6}$ cup of milk. How much milk did she use in all?

13. Write $\frac{4}{8}$ and $\frac{4}{12}$ in simplest form.

14. An empty box weighs $\frac{1}{9}$ of a pound, and $\frac{7}{18}$ of a pound of flour is added. What is the total weight of the box of flour?

15. A quiz had 7 questions. Angela answered 5 correctly. Write a fraction to express what part she answered correctly.

Practice 9-2

Find the GCF.

1a. 4 and 12   **b.** 6 and 10
2a. 9 and 27   **b.** 12 and 16

Arrange in order from greatest to least.

3a. $\frac{2}{5}$ $\frac{4}{5}$ $\frac{3}{5}$ $\frac{1}{5}$ **b.** $\frac{1}{10}$ $\frac{4}{10}$ $\frac{7}{10}$ $\frac{3}{10}$

Compute.

4a. $\frac{4}{4} - \frac{3}{4}$ **b.** $\frac{2}{3} + \frac{1}{3}$

5a. $\frac{3}{8} + \frac{4}{8}$ **b.** $\frac{4}{9} + \frac{2}{9}$

6a. $\frac{5}{6} - \frac{3}{6}$ **b.** $\frac{3}{4} - \frac{2}{4}$

7a. $\frac{3}{3} - \frac{1}{3}$ **b.** $\frac{7}{8} - \frac{5}{8}$

8. In a bouquet of 30 flowers, $\frac{1}{3}$ are red, $\frac{1}{2}$ are yellow, and $\frac{1}{6}$ are pink. How many flowers of each color are in the bouquet?

9. For a school play a teacher needs 20 students from 5 different grades. If an equal number from each grade are selected, how many students are chosen from each grade?

10. Juan and Mary worked together to finish a task. Juan did $\frac{2}{5}$ of the work and Mary did $\frac{3}{5}$. If they earned $50 in all, how much money should each receive?

Practice 10-1

1a. $21\overline{)84}$ **b.** $23\overline{)48}$

2a. $26\overline{)78}$ **b.** $35\overline{)73}$

3a. $40\overline{)360}$ **b.** $30\overline{)277}$

4a. $31\overline{)217}$ **b.** $53\overline{)108}$

5a. $44\overline{)132}$ **b.** $54\overline{)166}$

6. How many dozens are there in 48?

7. Jane wants to arrange a 53-volume encyclopedia in a bookcase. If 22 volumes fit on a shelf, how many shelves will she fill, and how many volumes will be left to start another shelf?

8. Roger's brother worked 30 hours a week at a summer job. He worked a total of 240 hours. How many weeks did he work?

9. If a factory can make 21 toy trains in one hour, how long will it take to make 147 trains?

10. If one box can hold 52 cans, how many boxes are needed for 260 cans?

11. An attendant collected 180 tickets for rides on a roller coaster. If each person needed 6 tickets for a ride, how many people rode the roller coaster?

12. If 682 pieces of fruit are distributed equally among 31 children, how many pieces of fruit will each child receive?

13. 21 boxes are used to pack 1050 bars of soap. If each box contains the same number of bars, how many bars of soap will there be in each box?

14. There are 840 students in a school. If there are 35 students in each classroom, how many classrooms are there?

15. Mr. Barnes painted $\frac{1}{2}$ of a room one day and $\frac{1}{3}$ of it another day. What part of the room was painted in the two days?

Practice 10-2

1a. $27\overline{)972}$ **b.** $29\overline{)958}$

2a. $37\overline{)1665}$ **b.** $49\overline{)2060}$

3a. $13\overline{)819}$ **b.** $15\overline{)1395}$

4a. $6\overline{)\$10.98}$ **b.** $8\overline{)\$472}$

5a. $15\overline{)\$74.55}$ **b.** $29\overline{)\$89.03}$

6. A full carton contains 24 cans of soup. If there is a total of 627 cans of soup, how many full cartons are there, and how many cans are left over?

7. The Royal Paper Company donated 774 packages of paper to 18 schools. If the packages were distributed equally, how many packages did each school receive?

8. Jeff earned $8.25 for working 3 hours. How much did he earn in one hour?

9. Therese bought 8 yards of ribbon for $3.92. How much did one yard cost?

10. Divide 256 into 4 equal parts.

11. Jim saves $195 in 15 weeks. What is his average savings per week?

12. Find the cost of one book if 16 of the same books cost $68.

13. Amy earns $44 in 11 hours. What does she earn in one hour?

14. The dividend is 246. The divisor is 41. What is the quotient?

15. If a ship travels at 29 miles an hour, how many hours will it take to travel 2755 miles?

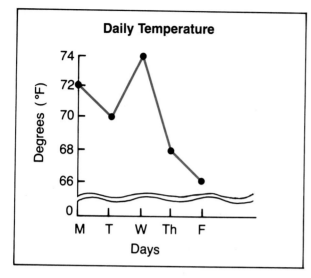

Daily Temperature

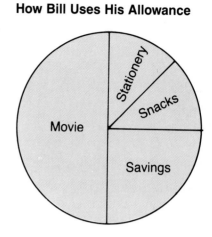

How Bill Uses His Allowance

Use the line graph to answer the following questions.

1. Which day was the warmest?

2. Which day was the coldest?

3. On which day was the temperature 70°?

4. What was the temperature on Wednesday?

5. How many degrees cooler was it on Friday than on Monday?

Use the circle graph to answer the following questions.

1. What part of Bill's allowance was used for a movie?

2. What part was saved?

3. What part was spent on snacks and stationery together?

4. On which two items did Bill spend equal amounts?

5. If Bill received an allowance of $5, how much did he save?

Practice 11-2

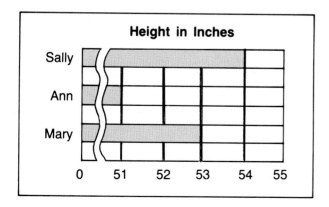

Height in Inches

Use the bar graph at the left to answer the following questions.

1. Which girl is the shortest?

2. How many inches taller is Sally than Mary?

3. Which girl is the tallest?

4. How many more inches must Ann grow to be as tall as Sally?

5. How many inches shorter is Ann than Mary?

367

Practice 12-1 UNIT 12

Write the value of the underlined digit.

1a. 4.<u>2</u>   **b.** 3.5<u>6</u>

2a. <u>9</u>.7   **b.** <u>2</u>.06

Write as a decimal.

3a. four tenths.
 b. nine and five hundredths

Order from least to greatest.

4a. 0.5, 5.0, 5.5   **b.** 6.2, 6.3, 5.9

5. Write $\frac{6}{10}$ as a decimal.

Write as a fraction.

6a. 0.6   **b.** 0.49

7a. seven tenths   **b.** twenty-three hundredths

8. Dirk passes the park on his way to school. The park is 0.2 mile from his house and the school is 0.5 mile from the park. How far is it from Dirk's house to school?

9. Teri has five and three tenths pages of her book left to read. Write the number of pages she has left as a mixed decimal and as a mixed number.

10. Sarah bought 2.5 pounds of apples and 1.4 pounds of bananas. How many pounds of fruit did she buy altogether?

11. Chris is 53.1 inches tall. Mike is 53.9 inches tall. Eddie is 53.4 inches tall. List the boys from tallest to shortest.

12. Susan made 3.5 liters of lemonade and 4 liters of iced tea. How many liters did she make in all?

13. The bus driver drove 52.8 miles one day and 38.5 miles the next day. How many miles did he drive in the two days?

14. One packet of raisins weighs 1.25 pounds, and another weighs 1 pound. What is the total weight of both packets?

15. One bag of berries weighs 1.5 pounds and another weighs 0.9 pound. Which bag weighs more?

Practice 12-2

1a. $0.9 - 0.2$ **b.** $3.7 - 0.5$

2a. $4.5 - 2.8$ **b.** $6.4 - 5.6$

3a. $0.53 - 0.42$ **b.** $0.74 - 0.35$

4a. $0.25 + 0.41$ **b.** $0.38 + 0.15$

5a. $4.36 + 5.12$ **b.** $3.97 + 5.22$

6a. $53.28 + 24.31$ **b.** $35.49 + 2.04$

7. Megan started her art project by drawing two lines. One line was 12.7 cm long and the other was 10.3 cm long. Find the difference in the lengths of the lines.

8. Gary watched the temperature sign on a building change from 76.4° to 75.9°. How much did the temperature fall?

9. Find the difference: 3.45 and 1.23.

10. Paul weighs 56.45 pounds and John weighs 52.92 pounds. How much more than John does Paul weigh?

11. Round to the nearest whole number.
 0.7   2.3   9.8

12. Estimate the sums and differences.

$4.2 \ + \ 1.3$ $6.4 \ - \ 3.4$
$32.4 \ + \ 7.5$ $63.7 \ - \ 5.2$

13. Holly weighs 52.6 pounds. Round her weight to the nearest pound.

14. Ted is 51.2 inches tall and Ralph is 53.6 inches tall. Estimate the difference in their heights.

15. Estimate the sum: $\$8.50 \ + \ \$9.99$.

368

Practice 13-1

UNIT 13

Name the figure.

1a. ▢   **b.** (cube)

2a. △   **b.** (pyramid)

3a. ○   **b.** (sphere)

4a. ▭   **b.** (rectangular prism)

5a. (cylinder)   **b.** (cone)

6. A garden is 30 yd long and 20 yd wide. What is the area?

7. A square card has sides of 4 inches. What is the area?

8. A carpet is 12 ft long and 8 ft wide. What is the area?

9. What is the volume of a container 7 cm long, 5 cm wide, and 4 cm high?

10. A fish tank is 30 cm long, 30 cm wide, and 20 cm high. How many cubic centimeters of water will it hold?

11. A box is 7 inches long, 5 inches wide, and 4 inches high. Find the volume.

12. What is the area of a piece of paper 11 in. long and 8 in. wide?

13. Find the area of a cake pan 10 inches long and 12 inches wide.

14. What is the volume of a box 10 inches long, 18 inches wide, and 2 inches deep?

15. A carton is 12 cm long, 10 cm wide, and 8 cm high. Find the volume.

Practice 13-2

1a. 4 in. + 7 in. + 3 in.   **b.** 2 m + 3 m + 8 m

2a. 6 ft × 7 ft   **b.** 1 cm × 1 cm

3a. 3 yd × 2 yd × 4 yd **b.** 1 km × 1 km × 1 km

4. If you wanted to put a fence around your garden, would you need to know the area, perimeter, or volume of the garden?

5. To know how many liters of water a fish tank holds, would you need to know the area, perimeter, or volume of the tank?

6. Which has the greater area: a square with sides 5 in. long or a rectangle that is 4 in. by 6 in.?

7. Find the area of a rectangle 8 ft long and 4 ft wide.

Complete.

8. A triangle has __?__ angles.

9. A square has __?__ sides.

10. A rectangle has __?__ sides and __?__ angles.

11. The space inside a plane figure is the __?__.

12. Volume tells the space inside of a __?__ figure.

13. The measure around a polygon is called the __?__.

14. Volume is the number of __?__ units that fit inside a solid figure.

15. Square units are used to measure __?__.

369

Brain Builders

Give the place value of the underlined digit.
1a. 6<u>2</u>9   **b.** 8<u>9</u>,372

Which is greater?
2a. 507 or 570   **b.** 3420 or 3240

Order these from least to greatest.
3a. 304, 340, 356, 324
  b. 456, 426, 392, 465

Round to the nearest underlined digit.
4a. 9<u>2</u>   **b.** <u>3</u>87

Compare. Write $<$, $=$, or $>$.
5a. 62 __?__ 26   **b.** 532 __?__ 542

6. Joan has 356 stickers in her collection. Diane has 365. Which of the girls has more stickers?

7. One of the reference books in the library reads, "Vol. XIV." Write this as a standard numeral.

8. Write the five odd numbers that follow 349.

9. Fill in the missing numbers in this pattern.
3, 7, 6, 10, 9, 13, __?__, 16, 15, __?__

10. Mrs. Belle owns 185 acres of land. Mr. Tanner owns seven times that amount. How much land does Mr. Tanner own?

11. Give 4 related facts for 9, 8, 17.

12. A farmer put a dozen eggs into a basket to make 36 eggs in all. How many dozen eggs were there in the basket originally?

13. Round the sum of 350 + 23 + 126 to the nearest hundred.

14. Write all the even numbers between 30 and 50.

15. Peggy's jar contains 578 pennies. Joan's jar contains 586 pennies. Which jar has more pennies?

1a.
$$\begin{array}{r} 3475 \\ 63 \\ +8468 \\ \hline \end{array}$$
b.
$$\begin{array}{r} \$\ 6.95 \\ 15.47 \\ +38.56 \\ \hline \end{array}$$

2a.
$$\begin{array}{r} 4000 \\ -\ \ 96 \\ \hline \end{array}$$
b.
$$\begin{array}{r} 3060 \\ -\ 987 \\ \hline \end{array}$$

3a.
$$\begin{array}{r} 4060 \\ \times\ \ \ 8 \\ \hline \end{array}$$
b.
$$\begin{array}{r} 809 \\ \times\ 76 \\ \hline \end{array}$$

4a. $9\overline{)918}$ **b.** $6\overline{)\$1.20}$

5a. $5\overline{)37}$ **b.** $6\overline{)93}$

6. Write the number: eighty thousand, forty-nine.

7. The Kane family drove a distance of 1800 miles in five days. How many miles did they average per day?

8. If a plane travels 300 miles an hour, how far will it go in 13 hours?

9. Bill had 63 marbles. He gave $\frac{1}{9}$ of them to Chung. How many did Bill have left?

10. At $4 a yard, what is the cost of 8 yards of material?

11. At $309 each, what will a dealer pay for 85 television sets?

12. Julio is buying a sweater for $15.40 and shoes for $22.90. How much change will he receive from $40?

13. How long will it take Traci to read a book of 168 pages if she reads 24 pages each day?

14. If Dan earns $3 each day, how much will he earn in 42 days?

15. Rose paid $2 for a package of stickers. How many packages could she buy for $58?

1a.
```
  365
+ 279
```
b.
```
  4260
+  593
```

2a.
```
  965
− 298
```
b.
```
  800
− 465
```

3a.
```
  37
×  6
```
b.
```
  384
×  52
```

4a. 3)63

b. 4)84

5a. $\frac{1}{6}$ of 48

b. $\frac{1}{9}$ of 36

6. A bookcase has 5 shelves. There are 6 books on each shelf. How many books are in the bookcase?

7. A quart of strawberries was divided equally among 5 children. If there were 40 strawberries in all, how many did each child receive?

8. There are 28 days in February, 31 days in March, and 30 days in April. Find the total number of days in the three months.

9. Hector had 97 baseball cards. He gave 15 of them to his friend. How many cards did he have left?

10. There are 42 desks in a room. If the desks are arranged equally into 6 rows, how many desks are in a row?

11. Amy uses two yards of fabric to make an apron. How much fabric will she need for eight aprons?

12. Twenty-four cards are used for a card game. Each player gets six cards. How many players are there?

13. How much greater is the product of 6 and 7 than the product of 5 and 8?

14. Four out of twenty-seven students are absent. How many are present?

15. Weekend attendance at the local movie house was 335 on Friday, 490 on Saturday, and 436 on Sunday. What was the attendance for all three days?

Write the standard numeral.
1a. one hundred four thousand, three hundred seventy.
b. 100,000 + 20,000 + 300 + 4

2a. 83 + 74 + 36
b. 80 + 24 + 65

3a. 651 − 289
b. 708 − 498

4a. __?__ × 4 = 32
b. 6 × __?__ = 54

5a. 63 ÷ 7
b. 8)48

6. One piece of rope is 40 cm and a second piece measures 5 m. Which piece of rope is longer?

7. Would the water in an aquarium be measured in liters or milliliters?

8. Courtney had 72 cents and spent 19 cents. How much money did she have left?

9. Bob bought a shirt for $6.75 and a cap for $2.98. How much did he spend?

10. There are 144 eggs in 12 cartons. How many eggs are in each carton?

11. Would the height of a room be measured in meters or centimeters?

12. Helen needs a toothbrush for $.62 and soap for $.45. Will $1.00 be enough to pay for those items?

13. 3756 cars crossed a bridge on Saturday, and 2891 crossed on Sunday. How many cars crossed the bridge in the two days?

14. Each of the 36 students in the graduating class will be inviting three family members to the graduation ceremonies. How many family members will be invited in all?

15. Mr. Doyle is traveling 682 km from Pensacola to St. Augustine. If he has already traveled 421 km, how much farther must he travel?

1a.
```
  308
  970
  475
+ 860
```
b.
```
  $2.59
   .09
  4.50
+ 3.84
```

8. What is the weight in grams of a 5-kg bag of flour?

9. A package weighs 756 grams. Is the weight more or less than a kilogram?

2a.
```
  8403
- 5927
```
b.
```
  6000
- 4078
```

10. Books cost $1.65 and $2.25. What is the change from $10.00?

3a.
```
  841
×  42
```
b.
```
  128
× 64
```

11. Light bulbs are packaged 6 to a box. How many bulbs are in 8 boxes?

4a. 23$\overline{)483}$ **b.** 1886 ÷ 23

12. How much less than a kilogram is a box of salt that weighs 340 grams?

5a. 20 mm = __?__ cm   **b.** 3 cm = __?__ mm

13. Name three coins that together have the same value as one quarter.

6. There are 832 students studying karate. If 429 of them are adults, how many are children?

14. A bookcase has 4 shelves. There are 26 books on each shelf. How many books are in the bookcase?

7. What four coins have the same value as one quarter?

15. How many feet are in a spool of cotton that contains 30 yards?

1a.
```
  $4.60
   5.98
+  4.67
```
b.
```
  $23.50
    7.65
+   3.20
```

9. A notepad costs $.79 and a pen costs $.39. What is the cost of six notepads and six pens.

2a.
```
  1873
-  687
```
b.
```
  $9.00
-  2.69
```

10. One third of Jane's birthday cards were from classmates. If Jane received 24 cards, how many were from classmates?

3a. $\frac{1}{2} + \frac{1}{4}$ **b.** $\frac{3}{8} + \frac{1}{4}$

11. If a ship travels 409 miles in one day, how far will it travel in 6 days?

4a. 22$\overline{)647}$ **b.** 31$\overline{)421}$

12. James had $11.23 and spent $8.97. How much did he have left?

5a. 1 yd = __?__ ft   **b.** 12 ft = __?__ yd

13. If a plane goes 1200 miles in 6 hours, what is its speed per hour?

6. Margaret had 18 eggs and used $\frac{2}{3}$ of them for a soufflé. How many eggs did she use?

14. Jack gave the clerk $1.00 to pay for a $.32 item. The clerk then gave him 2 quarters, a dime, a nickel, and 2 cents. How much change did Jack receive? How much — more or less — should he have received?

7. Raymond needs 54 feet of wire. If this wire is sold only by the yard, how many yards should he buy?

8. Myron's spelling marks for the week were 80, 75, 85, 95, 90. What was the difference between his highest and lowest marks?

15. Tricia bought 8 grapefruits at $2. She gave the clerk a ten-dollar bill. How much change did she receive?

Drill and Mental

DRILL

1.

3	2	3	3	3	3
+7	+3	+6	+3	+5	+4

2.

7	10	8	9	6	5
−3	−3	−3	−3	−3	−2

3. 4 × 2   5 × 2   6 × 2   7 × 2

4. 2 × 4   2 × 5   2 × 6   2 × 7

5. 8 ÷ 2   10 ÷ 2   12 ÷ 2   14 ÷ 2

MENTAL

1. Donald is 9 years old. How old will he be 6 years from now?

2. Write 78 as a Roman numeral.

3. Cookies are 8 cents each. How much will Joey pay for 3 cookies?

4. When 7 is divided by 2, what is the quotient? What is the remainder?

5. Change 1 liter to milliliters.

6. When 67 is divided by 9, what is the quotient? What is the remainder?

7. A farmer had 11 cows. He sold 7 of them. How many cows did he have left?

8. Pencils are 8 cents each. How many can Theresa buy for 16 cents?

9. How many nickels can be exchanged for 10 cents?

10. Change 1 yard to feet.

11. 11 birds were in a tree. 3 of them flew away. How many birds were left?

12. Anna picked 8 flowers. Matilda picked 3. How many flowers did they pick in all?

13. What is 4 more than the product of 9 and 7?

14. Change the Roman numeral X to a standard numeral.

15. Change 1 foot to inches.

DRILL

1.

7	5	6	7	7	8
+ 3	+ 6	+ 6	+ 4	+5	+3

2.

12	12	12	12	8	9
− 9	− 8	− 7	− 6	−3	−6

3. 1 × 3   4 × 3   7 × 3   5 × 3

4. 2 × 3   6 × 3   3 × 3   9 × 3

5. 3 ÷ 3   6 ÷ 3   ·12 ÷ 3   15 ÷ 3

MENTAL

1. At 9 cents each, what will 7 pencils cost?

2. There were 12 apples in a basket. The children ate 7 of them. How many apples were left?

3. Frank is 7 years old. His sister is 5 years older than Frank. How old is Frank's sister?

4. Tom paid 15 cents for 3 balloons. How much did each balloon cost?

5. Change the Roman numeral XXX to a standard numeral.

6. Write 45 as a Roman numeral.

7. Change 12 inches to feet.

8. Change 6 feet to yards.

9. 18¢ is divided equally among 3 children. How much will each child receive?

10. Change the Roman numeral XXXVI to a standard numeral.

DRILL

1. 6×4 7×4 8×4 9×4

2. $4\overline{)24}$ $4\overline{)28}$ $4\overline{)32}$ $4\overline{)36}$ $4\overline{)12}$

3. $4\overline{)25}$ $4\overline{)29}$ $4\overline{)33}$ $4\overline{)37}$ $4\overline{)13}$

4. $4\overline{)26}$ $4\overline{)30}$ $4\overline{)34}$ $4\overline{)38}$ $4\overline{)14}$

5. $4\overline{)27}$ $4\overline{)31}$ $4\overline{)35}$ $4\overline{)39}$ $4\overline{)15}$

MENTAL

1. If a cake recipe calls for 8 eggs, and a pudding recipe calls for 4 eggs, how many eggs are needed for both recipes?

2. How much greater than 8 is 14?

3. If the multiplicand is 9, and the multiplier is 4, what is the product?

4. When 36 is divided by 4, what is the quotient?

5. Change 20 to a Roman numeral.

6. Multiply 6 by 4, and add 1.

7. Conrad has 19 marbles in a bag and 5 marbles in his hand. How many marbles does he have in all?

8. How much less than 14 cents is 9 cents?

9. What is the remainder when 15 is divided by 7?

10. Change 30 to a Roman numeral.

11. Rosa had 24 cookies. She gave 7 of them to a friend. How many cookies did she have left?

12. Aunt Sue had 13 yards of cloth. She used 7 yards for curtains. How many yards of cloth were left?

13. 4 nickels = _?_ cents.

14. What is the remainder when 22 is divided by 4?

15. Write 40 as a Roman numeral.

DRILL

1. Add 7 to: 8 18, 28, 38, 45, 58, 68, 78

2. Subtract 8 from: 10, 12, 15, 25, 35, 45

3. Multiply by 3 and then add 4: 4, 8, 0, 9, 5, 6, 7, 3, 2, 1

4. Divide by 4: 24, 16, 36, 28, 32, 8, 12

5. Divide by 4: 25, 17, 37, 29, 33, 9, 13, 21, 26, 18, 38, 30, 34, 10, 14, 22

MENTAL

1. Ramon has 17¢ and Johnny has 8¢. How much money do both boys have?

2. There were 15 roses on a bush and Helen picked 8 of them. How many roses were left on the bush?

3. If 16 doughnuts are shared equally among 4 people, how many doughnuts does each one receive?

4. One engine pulled 7 cars. Another engine pulled 9 cars. How many cars did both engines pull?

5. Write the standard numeral: five thousand, one hundred sixty.

6. Ray has 17 cents. Jack has 9 cents more than Ray. How much money does Jack have?

7. Ned had 63¢ and spent 35¢. How much money does he still have?

8. Find $\frac{1}{5}$ of 20 cents.

9. Find the product of 3 and 20.

10. Which is greater: 2626 or 2662?

11. Each box holds 8 crayons. How many crayons are in 4 boxes?

12. Dan is 36 years old. David is 9 years old. How much older is Dan than David?

13. Paul is 6 years old. Jack is 5 times as old as Paul. How old is Jack?

14. 5 ties cost $30. Each tie costs the same. How much is 1 tie?

15. Which is less: 3575 or 3755?

DRILL

1. 1×6 2×6 3×6 4×6
2. 6×1 6×2 6×3 6×5
3. $6 \div 6$ $12 \div 2$ $18 \div 6$ $24 \div 4$
4. $6 \div 1$ $12 \div 6$ $18 \div 3$ $24 \div 6$
5. Multiply by 6: 1, 2, 3, 4, 5, 6, 7, 8, 9

MENTAL

1. What will 6 shirts cost at $5 each?
2. Dan had 42 ¢. He spent 22 ¢. How much money does he still have?
3. What number must be added to 19 to make the sum of 21?
4. Pedro is 42 inches tall. David is 9 inches taller. How tall is David?
5. Write the standard numeral: forty thousand, two hundred sixty.
6. Change 6 yards to feet.

7. 14 pretzels are shared equally among 6 children. How many pretzels does each child receive? How many are left?
8. Gina is 47 inches tall. Don is 5 inches shorter. How tall is Don?
9. How much less than a foot is 10 inches?
10. Write LX as a standard numeral.
11. Ned bought the newspaper for 20 cents. He gave the clerk a quarter. How much change did he receive?
12. Janet bought 8 six-packs of soda. How many cans of soda did she buy?
13. How many 6-cent stickers can Sue buy with 40 cents? How much money will she have left?
14. Alice has 83 cents. Kay has 9 cents more than Alice. How much money does Kay have?
15. Write XIX as a standard numeral.

DRILL

1. Add 8 to: 5, 15, 45, 25, 35, 55, 66, 76
2. Subtract 5 from: 14, 13, 23, 43, 33, 53
3. Multiply by 7: 2, 4, 5, 7, 9, 1, 0, 3, 6, 8
4. $77 \div 7$ $14 \div 7$ $21 \div 7$ $28 \div 7$
5. $63 \div 7$ $56 \div 7$ $42 \div 7$ $35 \div 7$

MENTAL

1. What does the 3 stand for in the numeral 6324?
2. Change the sum of 1 dime and 1 nickel to cents.
3. Liz divided 35 celery stalks equally among 7 friends. How many did each friend receive?
4. Bob saved 7 cents each day for 7 days. How much did he save?
5. Write the Roman numeral for 80.

6. Change seven nickels to pennies.
7. Change the difference of one quarter and 3 nickels to cents.
8. Nina has 46 cents. Alice has 7 cents less than Nina. How much money does Alice have?
9. How much less than 23 is 14?
10. Change 1 quart to pints.
11. At $.50 a yard, how many yards of ribbon can Ellen buy for $6.00?
12. What number comes between 13,725 and 13,727?
13. What is the difference between $15 and $6?
14. When 53 is divided by 7, what is the quotient? What is the remainder?
15. Change one kilogram to grams.

DRILL

1. Add 8 to: 7, 17, 57, 37, 47, 27, 67, 77

2. Subtract 7 from: 13, 15, 25, 55, 35, 45

3. Multiply by 4: 6, 7, 8, 0, 1, 2, 5, 4, 3

4. Complete: 7, 14, _?_, 28, _?_, _?_, _?_

5. Divide by 7: 61, 62, 58, 57, 60, 59, 31, 36, 39, 38, 37, 40, 41, 29, 34

MENTAL

1. At $.70 a foot, how many feet of wire can Jim buy for $1.40?

2. If Ann saves 8 cents a day, how much will she save in a week?

3. Write XXIV as a standard numeral.

4. Bob's coat cost $37. Ted's coat cost $8 more than Bob's. How much does Ted's coat cost?

5. What is the sum of 9 and 17?

6. Write the standard numeral: twenty thousand, four hundred ten.

7. Tom had 40¢ and spent 5¢. How much did he have left?

8. Velvet costs $8 a yard. How much do 4 yards cost?

9. Grace is 9 years old. Mary is 7 years older than Grace. How old is Mary?

10. Change 1 liter to milliliters.

11. If 65 is divided by 8, what is the quotient? What is the remainder?

12. How much greater than 31 is 38?

13. How much is zero times 18?

14. How much greater is 7×6 than 0×6?

15. What number follows 9999?

DRILL

1. Add 5 to: 9, 19, 38, 59, 29, 49, 68, 39

2. Subtract 9 from: 15, 14, 34, 54, 24, 44

3.
   16 = _?_ × 8   56 = _?_ × 8
   24 = _?_ × 8   64 = _?_ × 8
   32 = _?_ × 8   72 = _?_ × 8
   48 = _?_ × 8   40 = _?_ × 8

4. Divide by 8: 73, 74, 78, 76, 79, 77, 75, 69, 71, 12, 19, 30, 23, 31, 26, 33, 29, 35, 42, 39, 46, 43, 49, 47, 50, 53

5. Multiply by 6 and then add 7: 10, 8, 6, 4, 2, 0, 1, 3, 5, 7, 9

MENTAL

1. If 47 is divided by 8, what is the quotient? What is the remainder?

2. Jose saw 5 planes. The next day he saw 9. How many planes in all did he see?

3. What does zero stand for in the numeral 3064?

4. What number comes after 124,167?

5. At 8 cents each, what will 5 notepads cost?

6. What is 3 more than 9 times 5?

7. Helene is 9 years old. Her father is 4 times older than Helene. How old is Helene's father?

8. Jane spent $.69 for her lunch and $.15 for a snack. How much did Jane spend for both?

9. Change 1 meter to centimeters.

10. Change 1 pound to ounces.

11. What will Ben pay for 8 stickers at 9 cents each?

12. Write the word name for $.09.

13. John's calculator cost $15. Ann's cost $9. Find the difference in the two costs.

14. Change 10 kilometers to meters.

15. Write LXIV as a standard numeral.

DRILL

1. Divide by 9: 27, 81, 18, 72, 54, 45, 9

2. Divide by 9: 29, 11, 46, 20, 38, 40, 31, 15, 48, 33, 14, 49, 19, 42, 44

3. Multiply by 8 and then add 5: 2, 4, 0, 3, 7, 9, 5, 8, 6

4. Multiply by 9 and then add 3 to each product: 2, 3, 7, 5, 0, 1, 10, 6, 4, 9

5. Subtract 9 from: 27, 37, 47, 57, 67, 77, 84, 94, 17, 87

MENTAL

1. Bob read 7 books, and Maria read 4 books. How many books did both children read in all?

2. Donna had 12 pieces of fruit. She gave 2 to each of her friends. How many friends were given fruit?

3. At 6 cents each, what will Sue pay for 9 cookies?

4. When 54 is divided by 9, what is the quotient?

5. Write LXVIII as a standard numeral.

6. When 57 is divided by 9, what is the quotient? What is the remainder?

7. When 47 is divided by 9, what is the quotient? What is the remainder?

8. Jane had 15 pencils and gave away 9 of them. How many did she have left?

9. Use the dollar sign and decimal point to write fourteen dollars and two cents.

10. Henry had 12 marbles. He lost 6 of them in a game. How many marbles did he have left?

DRILL

1. Multiply by 6 and then add 2: 10, 8, 6, 2, 4, 0, 1, 3, 5, 7

2. Divide by 6: 42, 18, 24, 36, 60, 30, 12, 48

3. Divide by 7: 70, 42, 28, 7, 35, 56, 14, 49

4. Find $\frac{1}{6}$ of: 6, 18, 42, 54, 24, 36, 12

5. Find $\frac{1}{7}$ of: 14, 35, 63, 28, 56, 49, 21

MENTAL

1. How much greater than 15 is 22?

2. Round $2.87 to the nearest dollar.

3. Ramon's brother earns $63 a week. He saves $\frac{1}{7}$ of this amount. How much does he save?

4. If 48 muffins are divided equally among 6 children, how many does each child receive?

5. Dan weighs 55 pounds. His father weighs 143 pounds. What is their combined weight?

6. Find $\frac{1}{3}$ of 27¢ and then add 4¢.

7. Write the standard numeral: six thousand, eighty.

8. How many cents are there in the sum of a quarter and a nickel.

9. Write LXXVI as a standard numeral.

10. When 46 is divided by 5, what is the quotient? What is the remainder?

11. Lola is 46 inches tall. Elaine is 8 inches shorter than Lola. What is Elaine's height?

12. Write the standard numeral: thirty-four thousand, two hundred five.

13. Myra pulled out twelve socks from the laundry basket. How many pairs of socks can she make?

14. Pedro had 11 cents. He gave 6 cents to his friend. How much money did he have left?

15. Dad made breakfast for the family and used 8 out of a dozen eggs. How many eggs were left?

GLOSSARY

addend Any one of a set of numbers to be added.

$$3 \leftarrow \text{addend}$$
$$+ \ 4 \leftarrow \text{addend}$$
$$\overline{7} \leftarrow \text{sum}$$

addition (+) An operation on two numbers to find how many or how many or how much in all. (3 + 4 = 7)

angle Two rays with a common endpoint, called the vertex.

vertex

area The number of square units a region contains.

average The sum of a group of addends divided by the number of addends.

bar graph A graph using bars of different lengths to compare information.

BASIC A computer language. Two commands in BASIC are PRINT and LET.

Celsius scale Used to measure temperature in the metric system, in which 0° is the freezing point of water and 100° is the boiling point.

circle A closed figure all of whose points are equal in distance from the center.

closed curve A curve with no beginning or ending and which may or may not cross itself.

common factor A factor that is the same for two or more numbers. 4 is a common factor of 8 and 12.

congruent figures Figures having the same size and shape.

cubic measure A measure of volume.

customary system of measurement The system based on foot, pound, quart, and Fahrenheit scale.

decimal A numeral that includes a decimal point separating the ones place from the tenths place.

degree A unit for measuring temperature.

denominator The bottom number in a fraction. The denominator names the total number of equal parts.

diameter A line segment passing through the center of a circle with both endpoints on the circle.

difference The answer in subtraction.

digit Any one of these symbols: 0, 1, 2, 3, 4, 5, 6, 7, 8, 9.

dividend The number to be divided.

division (÷ or ⟍) An operation on two numbers to find the number of equal groups formed.

$$\text{divisor} \rightarrow 7\overline{)42} \begin{array}{l} \leftarrow \text{quotient} \\ \\ \leftarrow \text{dividend} \end{array}$$

edge A line segment where two faces of a solid figure meet.

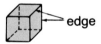

endpoint A point at the end of a line segment or ray.

equivalent fractions Fractions that name the same number.

$\frac{2}{3}$ and $\frac{4}{6}$

estimate To find an answer that is close to the exact answer.

even number A number that ends with digit 0, 2, 4, 6, 8.

expanded form A way to write numbers that shows the place value of each digit. (4000 + 200 + 50 + 7 = 4257)

face A side that makes up a solid figure.

Fahrenheit scale   Used to measure temperature in the customary system on which 212° is the boiling point of water and 32° is the freezing point.

fraction   Part of a region, an object, or a set.

$$\frac{2}{3}, \frac{1}{6}, \text{ and } \frac{5}{4}$$

googol   This is the number 1 followed by a hundred zeros.

gram   The basic unit of weight in the metric system.

graph   A picture used to show information in an organized way. Types of graphs are bar graphs, pictographs, line graphs, and circle graphs.

greater than (>)   A symbol for showing one number is larger than another number. 7>6 Read: 7 is greater than 6.

less than (<)   A symbol for showing one number is smaller than another number. 6<7 Read: 6 is less than 7.

LET   A command in BASIC computer language used to store information.

like fractions   Fractions with the same denominator.

line   A set of points extending indefinitely in opposite directions.

line graph   A graph using a line to show changes.

line segment   A part of a line with two endpoints.

line of symmetry   A line that divides a figure into two congruent parts.

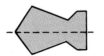

liter   The basic unit of capacity in the metric system.

LOGO   A computer language that can be used for drawing figures.

lowest terms   A fraction is in lowest terms if the numerator and denominator have no common factor.

meter   The basic unit of length in the metric system.

metric system   The system of measurement based on the meter, gram, liter, and Celsius scale.

mixed number   A number having a whole number part and a fraction part.

$$5\frac{1}{3} \text{ and } 7\frac{2}{5}$$

multiple   The product of a given number and any whole number.

multiplication   (×) An operation on two numbers to find the total amount in a number of equal groups. $8 \times 4 = 32$

number line   A line with equally spaced points shown in order.

number pattern   A group of numbers given in a specific order.

number sentence   An equation using numbers.

numeral   A symbol for a number.

numerator   The top number in a fraction. The numerator names the number of parts being considered.

odd number   A number that ends with the digit 1, 3, 5, 7, or 9.

one property   When one factor is 1, the product is always the same as the other factor.

ordinal number   A number indicating order. Example (first, second, third)

parallel lines   Lines in a plane that never meet.

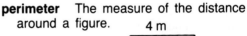

perimeter   The measure of the distance around a figure.

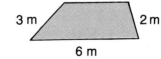

period   A set of three digits separated by a comma. The periods are one, thousands, millions, and so forth. (3,458,012)

perpendicular lines   Lines that meet to form right angles.

pictograph　A graph using a picture to represent a given quantity.

place value　The value of a digit depending upon its position or place in a numeral. In 45, the value of 4 is 4 tens and of 5 is 5 ones.

plane　A flat surface.

point　A location or position, usually named by a capital letter of the alphabet.

polygon　A simple closed figure with sides that are line segments.

prime number　A number that has only two factors—itself and 1. The first five prime numbers are: 2, 3, 5, 7, 11

PRINT　A command in BASIC computer language used to print a message or to compute.

probability　The number that tells the chance of something happening.

product　The result of multiplying two or more factors.

quadrilateral　Any four-sided polygon.

quotient　The answer in division.

radius　A segment from the center of a circle to a point on the circle.

radius

ray　Part of a line with one endpoint.

rectangle　A quadrilateral with four right angles. The opposite sides are parallel and equal in length.

remainder　The number left over when a division is complete.

right angle　An angle formed by perpendicular lines.

Roman numerals　Symbols for numbers used by the Romans (I, V, X, L, C, D, M).

rounding　Writing a number to the nearest ten or hundred, and so on.

simple closed curve　A path which starts at one point and curves back to the original point without crossing itself.

simplest form　A fraction is in its simplest form when the numerator and the denominator have no common factor other than 1.

space figure　A geometric figure, such as a sphere, a cube, a rectangular prism, a pyramid, a cone, and a cylinder.

square　A quadrilateral with 4 right angles and all sides equal in length.

square measure　The measure used to find the area of a region.

standard numeral　The name given to a number as it is written or read. Two hundred thirty five is 235.

subtraction　$(-)$ An operation on two numbers to find how much larger one is than the other.

$$5 \longleftarrow \text{minuend}$$
$$\underline{-\ 3} \longleftarrow \text{subtrahend}$$
$$2 \longleftarrow \text{difference}$$

sum　The answer in addition.

triangle　A polygon with three sides.

unit price　The cost of one item.

unlike fractions　Fractions with different denominators.

volume　The number of cubic units of space a figure contains.

whole number　Any numbers: 0, 1, 2, 3…

zero property of addition　Adding zero to a number does not change the number.

zero property of multiplication　Multiplying a number by zero always gives zero.

Index